UNIVERSITY LIBRARY
UW - STEVENS

W9-BHS-797

Politics in

FRANCE

The Little, Brown Series

in Comparative Politics

Under the Editorship of

GABRIEL A. ALMOND

JAMES S. COLEMAN

LUCIAN W. PYE

A COUNTRY STUDY

Politics in

FRANCE

Fourth Edition

Henry W. Ehrmann

Boston   Toronto
LITTLE, BROWN AND COMPANY

Library of Congress Cataloging in Publication Data

Ehrmann, Henry Walter, 1908–
  Politics in France.

  (The Little, Brown series in comparative
politics. A Country study)
  Includes index.
  1. France — Politics and government — 1958–1982.
2. Representative government and representation —
France. I. Title. II. Series: Little, Brown series
in comparative politics: Country study.
JN2594.2.E5   1982   320.944   82-7235
ISBN 0-316-22289-5   AACR2

Copyright © 1983 by Henry W. Ehrmann

All rights reserved. No part of this book may be reproduced
in any form or by any electronic or mechanical means including
information storage and retrieval systems without permission
in writing from the publisher, except by a reviewer who may
quote brief passages in a review.

Library of Congress Catalog Card No. 82-7235

ISBN 0-316-22289-5

9 8 7 6 5 4 3 2

ALP

Published simultaneously in Canada
by Little, Brown & Company (Canada) Limited

Printed in the United States of America

JN
2594.2
.E5
1983

TO

A.G.   B.G.   F.G.

S.H.   G.L.   M.M.

R.R.   J.T.

all of Paris

AND TO

G.Z.

of Berlin

336094

330091

Foreword

The first edition of Ehrmann's *Politics in France* appeared in the immediate aftermath of the "events" of May 1968. The quick subsidence of this populistic explosion seemed to portend a conservative restoration, but a deeper, more complex, and progressive set of changes had been set in motion or accelerated. The second edition, in 1971, appeared at a time when the survival of the Fifth Republic without de Gaulle, its inventor, seemed assured; and under Pompidou, as well as Giscard who followed him, France continued to make steady progress in economic and social modernization.

The third edition, in 1976, appeared at a time when the polarized, fragmented French party system was being supplanted by right and left coalitions, each one dominated by their moderate partners. And the fourth edition appears soon after the election of a Socialist president, a Socialist majority in the National Assembly, and the formation of a government including Communist ministers for the first time since 1947. In this substantially rewritten and updated version of *Politics in France,* Ehrmann explains and interprets these dramatic political changes and brings to bear on these and other aspects of French politics and society the newest findings of American, European, and French research.

Gabriel A. Almond
James S. Coleman
Lucian W. Pye

Preface
to the Fourth Edition

When publisher and author agreed that the time had come to prepare a new edition of this book, the French presidential elections were several months away. French and foreign experts believed, almost without exception, that the reelection of Giscard d'Estaing was assured. True, the record of the incumbent administration was far from brilliant. Stagflation had made France one of the worst performers among the Western nations. Seven years in office had tarnished the luster of the president-candidate. But the opposition was in disarray. The rift between socialists and communists was deepening. There seemed to be no valid alternative to the conservative rule under which Frenchmen had lived for almost a quarter of a century.

But even in the absence of a political turnover a revision of the book was called for. Because of the country's ever more complete integration into the world economy, the drastic changes in the international environment have recently affected France far more than under the administrations of de Gaulle and Pompidou. The modernization, whose manifold aspects have been recorded in all of the previous editions, has continued to transform French society at a more rapid rate than many observers had foreseen. An entire generation has come of age, and of voting age, which has never experienced another environment and other institutions than those of the Fifth Republic. Over the last years, and especially on the occasion of the twentieth anniversary of that Republic, a number of searching inquiries, French as well as British and American, have applied all the techniques of modern social science to collect evidence on and to evaluate the significance of the changes that have occurred. On the pages that follow the findings of many of these inquiries have been summarized. The American student is apt to notice that of late much attention has been paid to the role which women play in the French polity.

When my wife and I left for France in the spring of 1981 in search of additional documentation, we assumed that poll-watching, in which we had indulged so frequently since the advent of the Gaullist republic, would hold little interest since nothing new would emerge in the campaign or result from the election. The French voter decided otherwise. Now every chapter of the book had to be rewritten even more thoroughly than previously planned. A surprise event, such as the victory of the French Left, always illuminates the history of the recent, and sometimes of the not so recent, past. The new political actors had to be presented, the onrushing reforms to be explained, even when their outlines are not yet entirely clear. The lack of distance makes any prognostication precarious even though the concluding chapter shows that the temptation to engage in it is not easy to resist. Henry Kissinger has reported on a conversation with Mao in which he asked what the Chinese leader thought of the French revolution of 1789. Mao answered that "it was too early to tell." Even those of us who do not take the exceedingly "long view" of classical marxism will wish to be careful not to rush to judgment. The account given here includes events up to mid-winter 1982, a time when the major reforms on the socialist agenda have been enacted and when it can be expected that a period of consolidation is to follow. But it might be years before it will be possible to evaluate the long-range effects, either intended or unforeseen, of the "Mitterrand experiment."

After fairly extensive consultations with the publisher, colleagues, and students, I have decided not to change the style or the character of a book which has always tried to address a varied audience. Undergraduate students without a previous knowledge of French politics have described the book as challenging but not forbiddingly difficult, especially when supplemented by classroom discussions which can offer more comparisons with American experiences than space here permits. Throughout I have tried to live up to Albert Einstein's cordial advice: "Make everything as simple as possible. But not more so!" To explain a complicated society, such as France, by over-simplifying matters will not do. The advanced and graduate students will discover in the comprehensive footnotes ample suggestions for research or additional information. In the past, discussions presented in the book have found their way into the French press and into scholarly colloquia. The author can only hope that the new edition will enjoy similar notice.

As previously, a number of French friends and colleagues, many of them "participant observers" of the political process, have given indispensable help by answering my questions, by drawing on their own experiences to confirm or correct my impressions, by directing me to out-of-the-way materials or to their own writings, or by helping with bibliography. When I mention here Martine Anziani, François Bloch-Lainé, Jean-Luc Bodiguel, Bernard Cazes, Bernard Ducamin, Daniel Gaxie, François Goguel, Pierre Grémion, Bernard Gournay, Alain Lancelot, Michel and Pierre Laroque, Georges Lavau, Marcel Merle, Edgard Pisani and Jean-Louis Quermonne, I wish of course to express my sincere thanks to them. But I also want to emphasize that books like the present one derive whatever value they might have not alone from printed sources and questionnaire-structured interviews, but from human contacts.

In the United States, Gabriel Almond, Eric Nordlinger, and my friend Peter Gourevitch have read the manuscript with care and made valuable suggestions. During our talk-walks in and around Hanover, extending now over many years, my friend Roger Masters, himself a connoisseur of *all* things French, has often asked the right and important questions. The staff of the French Consulate General in Boston was extremely helpful in providing official information. A Dartmouth student of the class of 1982, Alex Blumrosen, served as my research assistant during several summer months. His excellent command of French, his understanding of what makes and unmakes a text-book, his careful attention to exasperating details, and his good-humored patience kept me going.

To incorporate innumerable changes into the tearsheets of

the previous edition, to prune the old text with care and to keep the new one legible presented difficulties which Deborah Hodges, star secretary and computer wizard, overcame elegantly. At the University of California at San Diego Bobbie Sutera typed further revisions and additions in record time. The intelligent assistance of Patricia Carter of the Dartmouth Library and that of Anita Schiller at the Library of the UCSD proved that even in periods of budgetary stress scholarship need not suffer.

Will Ethridge, political science editor of the College Division at Little, Brown and Company, and his able staff combined professional skill with extraordinary speed to rush the book through the various stages of production so as to put before the reader an up-to-date picture of *la France immuable et changeante,* immutable and changing France.

March 21, 1982   H.W.E.
La Jolla, California

Preface
to the First Edition

The Frenchman Montesquieu once remarked that those nations are happy whose annals of history are boring to read. To the extent that this is true, France is of course an "unhappy" country — for her history has been fascinating and turbulent, not boring. No wonder that the political systems under which she has lived have invited unending and frequently passionate comments by Frenchmen and foreign observers alike.

Such an abiding interest is caused in part by high expectations — expectations which the present leader of the French Republic is not the first to have voiced. Because the country has been the beacon of Western enlightenment, the performance of its political system is measured by exacting standards. There are puzzling inconsistencies in the political and social life of every nation. Those of France have frequently aroused irritation; explanations that have been offered are stubbornly contradictory because they fasten on different aspects of the country's internal contradictions. Does the turbulence of political life hide a pattern of basically undisturbed fundamental values? Or is, in a rapidly changing environment, an all too persistent adherence to basic values responsible for political explosions?

When discussing "Some Characteristics of Historians in Democratic Times," [1] Alexis de Tocqueville suggests that the

[1] Alexis de Tocqueville, *Democracy in America* (New York: Vintage Books, 1954), Vol. II, pp. 90–93.

lot of historians writing in an aristocratic age was an easy one. They were content simply to detach from the mass of general events "the particular influence of one man or of a few men." Anyone trying to explain the present French regime cannot quite fail to comment upon the "influence of one man." Yet present-day political science fits well, as it must, the characteristics which Tocqueville attributes to the historians of democratic times. We seek, as he puts it, to "assign general causes" to a mass of incidents and are "given to connect incidents together so as to deduce a system from them." Instead of attempting to discern the influence of individuals we prefer "talking about the characteristics of race, the physical conformation of the country, or the genius of civilization" — now conveniently summarized under the heading of "political culture."

Just because France shares with other democracies many political institutions which have worked adequately elsewhere but have failed her, a discussion of the country's political culture as a major variable determining political behavior has always appeared to be particularly relevant. It also provides the main theme of this book. To avoid the stereotypes which a discussion of this kind easily invites, the functional approach suggested in the writings of Gabriel Almond and common to this series in comparative politics has proved particularly, and to this author almost surprisingly, helpful. The categories here employed seem to clarify where choice and where circumstances have shaped the structures of the French political system and how they have determined the functioning of these structures. By sorting out what is unique and what is common to societies of similar development, our classifications should serve the purposes of comparison.

All comparative studies suffer from the limitations imposed by the paucity of strictly comparable data. I do not share the optimism of those who believe that the growing number of comparative statistical studies of national politics are sufficient to test general propositions. Where I have used such data I have regarded them as suggestive illustrations, not as evidence. Until quite recently most French statistics were notoriously unreliable and were, for that reason alone, unlikely to mirror reality better than subjective judgments. I have regarded polling and survey data, also, as suggestive illustrations. French techniques in this field have been refined greatly and their results, too, provide interesting comments. But they "prove" little and, as some French political scientists have shown, to me convincingly, even less than in some other countries.[2]

This study is one of an old country undergoing rapid development. My footnotes should show how much I have profited from the literature on political development — some of which appears in this series. Circumstances have not permitted me to investigate in necessary detail the impact which the international environment has had on French domestic politics. It is obvious that the political development of a country such as France has been drastically affected by her frequent exposure to large-scale wars and more recently to the tensions caused by the cold war.

Yet however heavy the heritage of past events, whether generated within the national borders or outside, present-day France is not just a prisoner of its past. The "silent revolution" described on many pages of this book as taking place in many fields would not be possible if a nation's values were foreordained and unalterable. The limits and constraints conditioning the ongoing development must be clearly understood if France is to hold, as she has so often in the past, pertinent lessons for general and democratic political theory. But again Tocqueville reminds his disciples not to get embroiled too far in "doctrines of necessity" and, instead, to "acknowledge the strength and independence of men united in society." For, as he concludes, "the great object in our time is to raise the faculties of men, not to complete their prostration."

The research for and the writing of this book were substantially aided by Dartmouth College. Its generous leave policy, grants awarded by its Committee on Research, and altogether an atmosphere in which research and teaching are equally recognized made this study possible. But the book also owes much to my earlier musings and wanderings supported by the Social Science Research Council, the Rockefeller Foundation, and the Ford Foundation.

[2] See Association Française de Science Politique, *Les Sondages et la Science Politique* (Paris: Mimeographed, 1966).

My colleagues and friends to whom this book is dedicated have contributed more than they might wish to acknowledge when they see the results of their counsel. Whether they have read, with great attention to ideas and details, parts of the manuscript, whether they have answered precisely my manifold inquiries or engaged with me, over many years, in lengthy discussions of French politics, their knowledge and understanding were indispensable. In the United States, Gabriel Almond, Lewis Edinger, and Richard Rose have commented helpfully and with acumen on parts of the manuscript. My colleague and friend at Dartmouth, Professor Howard Bliss, has gone with great care over the entire manuscript. His thoughtful suggestions have resulted in many improvements of content and style. To be edited by as competent a staff as that of Little, Brown and Company is an intellectual joy. The efficiency of the staff of Baker Library at Dartmouth and especially of its Order Department should prove attractive to any scholar.

One of my students, Mr. Roger Witten of the Dartmouth Class of 1968, proved his mettle as an untiring research assistant. Mrs. Louise Spiess can only be described as a paragon among secretaries. The reader is bound to profit from Mrs. Joan Erdman's skill as a judicious indexer.

My wife Claire made no suggestions whatsoever, nor did she proofread. She did not even read. Ever since we met more than thirty years ago in Paris — to be sure in the midst of acute political crisis — we have talked, lived, and breathed French politics, with a frown or a smile, in France and from afar. This book will teach her nothing. But all through the writing process she fulfilled her usual and indispensable function. She never ceased insisting that there are broader horizons and more urgent problems in the world at large than a work-centered author will admit. For this my undivided thanks go to her.

March, 1968   H.W.E.

Table of Contents

Illustrations and Tables

Politics in

FRANCE

ENGLAND

North Sea

NETH.

English Channel

Calais

Lille
NORD

BELGIUM

Rhine R.

GERMANY

LUX.

Le Havre

HAUTE
Seine R.

PICARDIE

NORMANDIE
BASSE

Paris
RÉGION
PARISIENNE

CHAMPAGNE

LORRAINE
Nancy

ALSACE

Stras-
bourg

BRÊTAGNE

PAYS DE
LA LOIRE
Loire R.

CENTRE

BOURGOGNE

FRANCHE-
COMTÉ

Nantes

SWITZ.

POITOU-
CHARENTE

LIMOUSIN

Vichy

Clermont-
Ferrand
AUVERGNE

Lyon

RHONE-ALPES

St. Étienne

Rhone R.

Bay of Biscay

Bordeaux
Garonne R.

ITALY

AQUITAINE

MIDI-PYRENÉES
Toulouse

LANGUEDOC

PROVENCE-
CÔTE D'AZUR

Nice

Marseilles

Corsica

Mediterranean Sea

S P A I N

FRANCE
(Regional Organization)

CHAPTER I

Origins and History
of the System

A NATION OF PATRIOTS — DIVIDED

As one of the oldest nation-states of Europe, France has been free of many of the tensions characteristic of countries which have found their national unity and identity only in more recent times. Many of her borders are not determined by natural barriers as are those of the British Isles. Yet, except for some relatively minor though hotly contested frontier areas, France's territorial limits were determined far earlier than those of other Continental countries. Brought together over centuries by accidents of history rather than by facts of geography or of ethnic origin, Frenchmen have developed a strong sense of national identification. Theirs is an adult "civilization," a term which to them is more meaningful than "culture" or *Kultur*. It not only denotes a long-term achievement but also encourages missionary zeal to spread its values.

Geographically the country is at once Atlantic, Continental, and Mediterranean, and hence occupies a unique place in Europe. Ethnically, no such thing as a French race exists. "We are a race of half-breeds," a French historian has written; but he added wistfully: "Mongrels are often more intelligent than

1

purebred dogs." [1] Which of their gifts and deficiencies the French owe to the Latins, the Celts, or the Germanic tribes is far less significant than the fact that in a nation fashioned by common historical experience, existing diversities have been encompassed by a strong national unity. Neither substantial regional differences, nor the survival of different languages (not just dialects) were as divisive as they have been for all of France's neighbors, including Switzerland. Yet Frenchmen often refer to the place of their origin or of residence as *"mon pays"* (my country), one of many indications that in modern France a variety of minicultures has survived. [2] Only in recent times has a newly awakened regional nationalism entered the political arena in novel ways which will be discussed in Chapter IX.

The French monarchy played an outstanding role in national integration. It also gave to French national feeling some of its distinguishing characteristics. Unlike other European monarchs, the French kings claimed and received, for close to a thousand years, sacerdotal and religious dignity. Such status has marked not only French Catholicism but all concepts of authority. [3] A French monk described the first crusade as *Gesta Dei per Francos:* the Franks were presented as the chosen instruments of God. There are other nations that from time to time have claimed to be pacesetters for the rest of the world. But among Frenchmen a belief in the universal value of their own civilization has remained strong whatever the setbacks of their national destiny. In his campaign literature for a second term the incumbent President Valéry Giscard d'Estaing wrote, somewhat extravagantly, about "the profound biology of the

[1] Charles Seignobos, as quoted in André Siegfried, "Approaches to an Understanding of Modern France" in *Modern France: Problems of the Third and Fourth Republics,* ed. Edward M. Earle (Princeton: Princeton University Press, 1951), p. 4. In some respects Siegfried's article contains still valid generalizations about the political culture of the country.

[2] Hervé Le Bras and Emmanuel Todd, *L'invention de la France. Atlas anthropologique et politique* (Paris: Livre de Poche, 1981), emphasizes throughout and with fascinating examples the existence of many Frances which neither a centralized administration nor the emergence of an industrial society has reduced to uniformity.

[3] Ernst Robert Curtius, *The Civilization of France* (New York: Vintage Books, 1962), pp. 72 ff.

[French] people, forever different from all others and, if it surmounts remaining dangers, destined to be an elite for the world." [4]

Claims that attribute general significance to a national civilization have been common to the political Right and Left. The very term "nationalism" in its pejorative sense was coined to reproach the Jacobins for their all too burning desire to export ideals at the point of French bayonets. In 1793, at the height of the Terror, "patriotism" described the resolve not only to defend the soil of *la patrie,* but also to cultivate civic and republican virtues and to share with other nations the blessings of the Revolution. The Paris Commune of 1871, hailed by Karl Marx as the harbinger of a worldwide class struggle, was in fact an act of defiance addressed to the "Prussian" Bismarck as well as to the bourgeois government at Versailles.[5] The language and thought of communist and socialist resistance movements during the Second World War showed the same amalgam of patriotism and democratic values.

Even an insistence on the nation's greatness, its *grandeur,* is not the monopoly of any particular political orientation, for it is raised in the name of a civilization rather than in defense of martial ventures. Jules Michelet, influential historian of the Revolution, wrote sweepingly that the concept of French national grandeur belonged to a tradition which was common to the National Convention of 1792 and to St. Louis, the most illustrious of the Capetian kings.

More recently, the opening sentences of General de Gaulle's memoirs have given to such a mythology of the nation an expression that already has become classical.

> All my life I have thought of France in a certain way. This is inspired by sentiment as much as by reason. The emotional side of me tends to imagine France like the princess in the fairy stories or the Madonna in the frescoes, as dedicated to an ex-

---

[4] Valéry Giscard d'Estaing, *L'État de la France* (Paris: Fayard, 1981), p. 8.

[5] For a convincing argument demonstrating the erroneousness of Marx's interpretation, see Theodore Zeldin, *France 1848–1945,* vol. 1 (Oxford: Clarendon Press, 1973), pp. 735–45.

alted and exceptional destiny. . . . In short, to my mind, France cannot be France without *grandeur*.[6]

In 1981 the socialist candidate for the presidency, François Mitterrand, concluded the televised debate with his opponent in strikingly similar terms: "The grandeur of France, her self-confidence. France is something strong which must be respected. It is [part of] French history and I shall inherit it." However deep the roots of a common national mythology, Frenchmen are divided by conflicting views as to which political system is most appropriate to attain the goal of greatness. If every Frenchman loves France, this does not preclude his poorly concealed contempt for the Frenchmen outside of his own immediate or political family. When the momentary destiny of the country appears mediocre, he is inclined to impute this to the faults of his fellow citizen, while the genius of the land remains unimpaired in his eyes.

Wherever historical events have created deep divisions, mutual distrust is frequent and agreement on fundamentals tenuous. It was natural enough that the Revolution of the eighteenth century opened long drawn-out controversies between monarchists and republicans. But it also shook and split, on the most sensitive level, the conscience of elites and common people. The Revolution amounted not merely to a collective desertion from the Catholic church, but to such a violent break with Christianity as, prior to the Bolshevik seizure of power, no other European nation had experienced. From then on France became the champion of emancipated reason and yet remained a refuge for Catholic faith. The sharp political discontinuities, the revolutions and counterrevolutions of the nineteenth and twentieth centuries, were at least in part a consequence of the rift between believers and nonbelievers.

The more vividly the conflicts of the past are remembered, the more heavily they weigh on the behavior of political actors and onlookers. Edmund Burke spoke of society as "a partnership . . . between those who are living, those who are dead and those who are to be born." French society frequently ap-

---

6 Charles de Gaulle, *War Memoirs, I: The Call to Honour* (New York: Simon and Schuster, 1955), p. 3.

pears overcommitted to the experiences of past generations. A habit of historical thinking can prove a bond, but also — as the American Civil War shows — a hindrance to consensus. Frenchmen are so fascinated by their own, admittedly exciting, history that the feuds of the past are constantly superimposed on the conflicts of the present. The passionate use of historical memories, resulting in seemingly inflexible commands and warnings, narrows the scope of authoritative and private decision-making. The old country that is France is, again in de Gaulle's words, "weighed down by history." [7]

The very nature of political conflicts is in part determined by the style that defines them. "Politics are ideas," a modern French writer has claimed.[8] Hence, at least at a certain level, the style of politics has remained as ideological as it became in the age of the Enlightenment when the Old Regime, in order to compensate for the servile condition to which it had confined the educated classes, left them free to voice their views on many topics. Philosophy, religion, ethics, and even politics could be discussed provided the discussion remained on a general and abstract plane. At about the same time, the bourgeoisie was compelled to abandon those local administrative functions which it had exercised previously. Hence its political initiation, sophisticated though it was, was derived entirely from men of letters and philosophers. "Thus alongside the traditional and confused, not to say chaotic, social system of the day there was gradually built up in [these Frenchmen's] mind[s] an imaginary ideal society in which all was simple, uniform, coherent, equitable, and rational in the full sense of the term." [9]

Since then the urge to discuss a wide range of problems, even the most trivial ones, in broad philosophical terms has hardly diminished; nor has the endless search to find a solution to the problems of the day in a system, a doctrine, or a faith. "Politics is not everything," Emmanuel Mounier, spokesman

---

[7] Charles de Gaulle, *War Memoirs, III: The Salvation* (New York: Simon and Schuster, 1960), p. 330.

[8] Albert Thibaudet, *Les Idées politiques en France* (Paris: Stock, 1932).

[9] Alexis de Tocqueville, *The Old Régime and the French Revolution* (New York: Doubleday Anchor Books, 1955), pp. 64, 146.

for young Catholic intellectuals between the wars, has written, "but politics is in everything."

Symbols and rituals perpetuate the political style. Today, two rural communities which fought on opposite sides in the French Revolution pay homage to different heroes nearly two centuries later. In the eyes of an American observer who knows them both, they have no real quarrel with each other. Yet inherited symbols have kept them apart so that their political and religious habits have remained disparate.[10] In a small town of Brittany a French sociologist has described a "red" and a "white" community (largely but not entirely identical with the political Left and Right). Their conceptions not just of politics but of the world, of God, of science, of progress are so different that there does not even exist a *de facto* community extending to the entire town. The "whites" will not be seen in a café named "Rights of Men" or work on the fishing boat called "Love of Humanity." [11]

Formal symbols to which all Frenchmen respond are not entirely lacking but rare. The "Marseillaise" is now accepted as the national anthem in spite of its somewhat bloodthirsty revolutionary text. But it is customarily played at a different speed in political gatherings of the Right and of the Left. The armed forces parade as a symbol of national unity on public holidays and state occasions. But after having reviewed the troops on the day of his inauguration the first socialist president of the Fifth Republic went to the catacombs of the Panthéon, a building dedicated since the French Revolution to the nation's great men, and deposited flowers on the tombs of three heroes of the French Left: the socialist leader Jean Jaurès, the leader of the anti-Nazi resistance movement, and a Lincolnesque figure of the nineteenth century who had set the French blacks free and granted them citizenship.

Abiding faiths create deep hatreds. Ever since the Jacobins denounced their opponents as "enemies of the people," such

---

10 Laurence Wylie, "Social Change at the Grass Roots," in Stanley Hoffmann et al., *In Search of France* (Cambridge: Harvard University Press, 1963), p. 230.

11 Edgar Morin, *Plodémet: Report from a French Village* (New York: Random House, 1970), pp. 39, 43, and *passim*.

accusations have belonged to the arsenal of French political polemics (long before they entered the terminology of modern totalitarianism). In every democratic country, a scandalous mistrial such as that of Captain Dreyfus with its backdrop of intrigue, motivated by anti-Semitism and caste spirit, would have provoked indignation and possibly prolonged unrest. What was characteristically French was the fact that at the turn of the century *L'Affaire* became a violent conflict over values among the country's elites. Both sides went to fanatical extremes; guilt or innocence of Dreyfus was not a question of evidence but of unshakable dogma.[12] The legacy bequeathed by the upheaval and its aftermath was the confinement of the officer corps and a majority of the practicing Catholics for many decades to a political ghetto, in which they lived apart from the mainstream of national life.

For all its drama, the Dreyfus affair was only one, if characteristic, episode in the political history of a nation united by almost universal admiration for a common historical experience yet divided by conflicting interpretations of its meaning.

TENSIONS BETWEEN REPRESENTATIVE
AND PLEBISCITARIAN TRADITIONS

Although the controversies between monarchists and republicans have continued well into our century, their effect on the various political systems that have emerged in rapid succession since the Revolution has been less significant than the opposition between the temptations of two other patterns of government. One is indentifiable with the representative tradition of democracy, the other with a plebiscitarian. (For the dates of the political regimes that succeeded each other and of the constitutions they engendered, see the Chronology of Events on pp. 325–355.)

In the early days of the Revolution, mere lip service was paid to Rousseau's concept postulating the direct participation of the citizenry in the political process. The system then estab-

---

[12] Zeldin, *France 1848–1945*, pp. 679 ff., offers an interesting and partially new interpretation of the Dreyfus Affair. Among others the case demonstrated to what extent the French legal system loads the odds against the accused.

lished was based on a belief, shared by most of the middle-class
deputies to the National Assembly, that the intentions of the
sovereign people could be expressed validly only through its
elected representatives; that legislative as well as constituent
power should be exclusively in their hands. A few years later,
the constitution of 1793 rejected such views, and denouncing
"representative despotism," it tried to organize the general will
by annual elections and referendums. But before this constitution could come into existence it was superseded by revolutionary rule which climaxed in Napoleon's rise to power.[13] His
rule set the pattern for a system which was as hostile to the
representative ideas of the first National Assembly, of the
American Constitution, and of the parliamentary monarchies
of Europe, as it was to the absolute monarchy of the Old Regime. It was more than a device of political cleverness that for
several years French coins bore the double inscription: "French
Republic — Napoleon Emperor." Bonaparte claimed to continue the Revolution rather than to abrogate it.

Hence France, just freed from its old shackles, experienced
within the short span of a decade two novel and different forms
of authority. They were to form the opposite poles between
which French political life has moved ever since, even if some
of the sixteen constitutions under which Frenchmen have lived
since the Revolution have aimed at combining elements of
both traditions. With each change of regime the tradition
which was temporarily eclipsed lived on as a strong undercur-
rent creating perpetual internal tensions.

Since Napoleon Bonaparte was the first to develop the pattern of a political system which claimed that its rule was sanctioned by the voice of the sovereign people, practices of direct
democracy in France are easily identified with bonapartism.
Shorn of all accidentals, the theory and practices of the two
Napoleons scorned intermediaries in state and society which
might stand between the unorganized masses and the popularly

13 The historical background of the two traditions is traced in greater
detail by Henry W. Ehrmann, "Direct Democracy in France," *American
Political Science Review* 57, no. 4 (1963): 883 ff. Cf. also Stanley Hoffmann,
"Paradoxes of the French Political Community," in Hoffmann et al., *In
Search of France*, p. 14.

acclaimed head of the executive. There was in their system room neither for a totalitarian party nor for voluntary associations. Accordingly, the role of the legislative branch was reduced; the political life of the nation was carefully circumscribed and potentially extinguished. Any infringement of constitutional and other laws by the ruler could be given legitimacy by popular approval. The Napoleonic plebiscites combined the threat of social chaos which would follow the demise of the providential leader with the flattery of the people by giving them the opportunity of choosing their master directly — or of perpetuating his rule. The temper of the regime was decidedly antilibertarian: Napoleonic codes and legislation strengthened authority: that of the head of the family, of the employer, of the administrative official.[14]

What distinguishes French bonapartism from other forms of caesarism is the allegiance it paid to certain Jacobin traditions of the Revolution. At all times, Napoleon's appeals to the masses over the heads of the traditional notables had egalitarian undertones. The Napoleonic legend, on which Napoleon's nephew Louis Bonaparte would draw in his campaign for a popularly elected republican presidency, was distinctly tinged with egalitarian socialism — or at least with its terminology. The constitution of the Second Empire (as would that of the Fifth Republic) explicitly referred to the "principles of 1789" and boasted of having given the constituent power back to the people.

With the demise of Napoleon III, the opposite, representative tradition established itself firmly and exercised its sway with only short interruptions until 1958 when turmoil in Algeria returned General de Gaulle to power. But during every crisis of the Third and Fourth Republics, the critics of the existing system liked to argue in terms established by bonapartism. All political parties were condemned as hampering the expression of a general will — assumed to be unequivocal on all major political decisions. Parliament was likened to a

14 For the plebiscitarian ideology of bonapartism cf. Robert Michels, *Political Parties* (New York: Collier Books, 1962), pp. 212–19; and the excellent recent treatment of René Rémond, *La Vie politique en France*, Tome I (Paris: Colin, 1965), pp. 221–47 and Tome II (1969), pp. 131–69.

broken mirror misrepresenting the true interests of the electorate. Popular sovereignty should be reestablished by giving the voters constitutional power and the right to vote in referendums. The executive should be enabled to rule efficiently above and despite political and social divisions. Constitutional amendments aiming at restricting parliamentary prerogatives in favor of a direct appeal to the electorate were from time to time proposed by conservative deputies or senators. Antiparliamentary feelings, both vague and vehement, were at times quite widespread and frequently associated with longings for a strong-arm rule. The tenacity of this mood even during the height of the representative regime tended to drive the defenders of the existing regime to exaggerations of their own.

To the authentic spokesmen of the representative tradition the elected deputy, "entrenched, fortified and undefeatable in his constituency like the feudal lord of old in his castle," [15] was superbly qualified for the defense of constituency interests and for the control of an ever-suspected executive. He could be counted upon to decide for himself, without directives from an extraparliamentary body — even a political party — how best to resist authority. Any direct appeal to the people was viewed as a manifestation of "supreme decadence." In fact, historical experiences had instilled in deputies and senators such fear of executive leadership and of the popular acclaim it might seek, that they frowned upon any address by a political leader which was not made either from the tribune of parliament or within the narrow confines of his small constituency.

It will be explained in Chapter VIII why until recently republican France has never developed a modern party system of the kind which, in other democracies, has accomplished the necessary transformation of parliament "from the representa-

---

[15] Alain, *Éléments de la doctrine radicale* (Paris: Gallimard, 1925), p. 42. The (unfortunately untranslated) writings of the curious philosopher-journalist Alain are indispensable for an understanding of the French version of the representative system and of the period during which it flowered, i.e., the first thirty years of the present century. For a recent evaluation of Alain's significance, see Roy Pierce, *Contemporary French Political Thought* (London: Oxford University Press), pp. 4–10.

tive corporation which it was into a plebiscitary expedient." [16]
In the absence of such a system, the tensions created by the
oligarchic deformations of the representative traditions and the
caesaristic temptations of plebiscitarian regimes were never
resolved.

TENSIONS BETWEEN BUREAUCRATIC TRADITIONS
AND INDIVIDUALISM

To both distrust government and expect much from it is a
widespread ambivalence of modern times, which might well
betray some unresolved inner conflict about the interaction of
government and society.[17] In most countries this ambivalence
is a consequence of the rise of the modern service-state which
is unavoidably burdened with ever new tasks. But in France
such feelings can again be traced to centuries-old traditions.
A recent government report which was to formulate proposals
for a thorough-going administrative decentralization traced
"our inclination to appeal always to a higher authority" to the
days when Saint-Louis sat under an oak tree and settled all
conflicts large and small that Frenchmen brought to him.[18] The
Old Regime, and especially the long reign of Louis XIV, gave
the country a rigidly centralized administration, recruited and
operated according to functional criteria. Its activities reached
deep into many phases of economic and social life. It proved
so pervasive that it "deprived Frenchmen of the possibility and
even the desire to come to each other's aid. When the Revolution started it would have been impossible to find . . . even
ten men used to acting in concert and defending their interests
without appealing to the central power for aid." [19] What shel-
tered the individual from constant interference by governmen-

---

[16] Gerhard Leibholz, "The Nature and Various Forms of Democracy,"
Social Research 7 (1938): 99.

[17] Cf. Felix Frankfurter, *The Public and Its Government* (New Haven:
Yale University Press, 1930), pp. 3–4.

[18] Commission de développement des responsabilités locales, *Vivre ensemble* (Paris: Documentation Française, 1976), p. 22. This comprehensive
report on desirable reforms (431 pages!) was never acted on. For details see
Chapter IX.

[19] Tocqueville, *The Old Régime*, p. 206.

tal authorities was, in an age of underdeveloped communications, the relative remoteness of the central government which had not abolished the existing patchwork of local privileges and traditions of lax enforcement.

The Jacobins and Napoleon took over the techniques and, frequently, the men that the monarchy had bequeathed to them and used them for their political ends. The egalitarian temper of sans-culottism, bent as it was on uprooting privileges, soon became hostile to hopes for a federal structure of government alive during the early days of the Revolution. The demand for equality was to be satisfied by the greatest possible uniformity of rules, over which an ever stronger, better qualified, and more centralized administration was to watch. The more significant the central power became, the more tenacious grew the fight for its control. Because the stakes were high, political forces not only denied the wisdom of their opponents, which is normal, but contested the very legitimacy of their power or of their claim to power.

French society is not altogether hierarchical and centralized; there is much that is pluralistic and varied in the special traits of various regions and in the behavior of individuals and groups. But over the centuries a centralized administration has molded society according to its own needs and in accordance with its highly developed procedures until an all-but-complete congruence between the many communities and the centralized state apparatus has emerged.[20]

The French citizen's fear and distrust of authority and his simultaneous need for strong authority feed on both his individualism and his passion for equality. In France social mobility has remained steady if limited; a preindustrial mentality shared by the peasantry and the bourgeoisie has long persisted (for details see Chapters II and III). Such a country produces a self-reliant individual who is convinced that he owes to himself (and perhaps to his immediate family) what he is and what he may become. In his eyes the obstacles in his way are created by the outside world: "they" who operate beyond the circle of

[20] See Michel Crozier in Crozier et al., *Où va l'administration française?* (Paris: Éditions d'Organisation, 1974), p. 221.

the family, the family firm, the village. Most of the time, however, "they" are identified with the government.

A stock of memories reaching possibly all the way from the eighteenth century through the most recent wars is used to justify a state of mind which is one of latent, even if seldom actual, insubordination. If the government is nefarious, it must be controlled and is not looked upon as a possible source of reform. The authentic republican tradition is again exemplified by Alain's "radical doctrine": the government deserves distrust without revolt, and obedience without commitment. A strong government is considered reactionary because it is strong, even if it pretends to follow a politically progressive course of action.

Since the citizen feels that no one but himself can be entrusted with the defense of his interests, he is inclined to shun constructive cooperation and to distrust his neighbor almost as much as the authorities. He fears that the discipline involved in any cooperation might put social constraints on him. Where he participates in public life, he hopes to weaken authority rather than to encourage change, even when change is overdue.

At times this commitment to individualism is tainted with outright anarchistic tendencies. Yet, inasmuch as it is wedded to a sharp sense of equality, it is quite able to accommodate itself to bureaucratic rule. Once more Tocqueville bore testimony when he wrote: "Frenchmen want equality in liberty and when they cannot get it they still want it in slavery." And General de Gaulle added in his memoirs: "The desire for privilege and the taste for equality, [have been the] dominant and contradictory passions of Frenchmen of all times." [21]

On the lower level of administration, the government may act through incompetent civil servants whom the citizens are wont to criticize as unjust masters. Another French philosopher, Charles Péguy, has spoken sarcastically of that one true division between Frenchmen, more marked than all class division — the one between those who wait in front of an official's

[21] Both quoted here from Jean Charlot, "Les Élites politiques en France de la IIIe à la Ve République," *Archives Européennes de Sociologie* 14 (1973): 78.

window and those who sit behind it. But however despised the government and its officials, the abstract entity that is the state is indispensable since for all its oppressive ever-presence it safeguards the uniformity of rulings which guarantee equality of treatment.

The solutions which the state imposes from above permit the citizen to escape responsibility for resolving conflicts and to avoid face-to-face relationships with either his peers or his superiors.[22] This in turn gives to the administration enough leeway to stand firm amid the vagaries of the political system. Its rulings may meet with the derision and bitterness of the citizenry; they will still be condoned as guaranteeing egalitarian standards. This explains the often noted paradox that traditionally France, the country of weak governments, appears as a strong state until an acute crisis reveals the feebleness of state *and* government. For this, the dramatic events of May 1968 offered the most recent evidence.

Individualism and administrative centralization are therefore complementary rather than contradictory and able to mitigate their mutual effects. The pattern of authority they create is neither liberal nor totalitarian, but has been characterized as the coexistence of *limited* authoritarianism and *potential* insurrection against authority.[23]

CONSEQUENCES FOR THE POLITICAL SYSTEM

Even though in fact the Revolution of 1789 did not effect as complete a break with the past as is commonly believed, it has conditioned the general outlook on crisis and compromise, on continuity and change. Sudden rather than gradual mutation, dramatic conflicts couched in the language of opposing and mutually exclusive, radical ideologies — these are the experiences that excite Frenchmen at historical moments when their

---

[22] All the writings of Michel Crozier have emphasized the basic avoidance of face-to-face relationships in French society. They are summarized and expanded in his study, *The Bureaucratic Phenomenon* (Chicago: The University of Chicago Press, 1964), esp. pp. 220 ff. For more detailed treatment see esp. Chapters III and VI in this book.

[23] Hoffmann et al., *In Search of France*, p. 8.

minds are particularly malleable. Even at the end of the nineteenth century, history itself appeared to an illustrious French historian, Ernest Renan, as a "kind of civil war." In fact, what is to the outsider permanent instability is a fairly regular alternation between violent crises and more or less prolonged periods of routine. Dramatization also means personalization of history. Hence such terms as bonapartism, boulangism, pétainism, and gaullism are frequently referred to in French political discourse; they have no equivalent in the history of other democracies which remember their great (or notorious) men by other means than by identifying their names with subsequent political and social movements.

It is perhaps noteworthy that in France there is an abundance of political biographies of the figures of exalted times, but hardly any of the great parliamentary leaders, to say nothing of administrators or judges. To contend that Frenchmen, whether illustrious or humble, "love" crisis may be invidious. But they have become accustomed to think that no thoroughgoing change can ever be brought about except through a major upheaval. Since the great Revolution, every adult Frenchman has experienced — usually more than once in his lifetime — occasions of political excitement followed by disappointment. This leads periodically to moral exhaustion and almost permanent and widespread skepticism regarding any possibility of change. The aphorism that "The more things change, the more they stay the same" may be quite worn, but it still expresses general feelings.

In addition to what has been discussed so far, wars and other pressures from the international environment have constantly sharpened crises. Before the Revolution, the very development of the French nation and state was closely related to the dynastic conflicts of Europe. Since then many of the political upheavals and constitutional breaks were caused by, or at least connected with, wars in which the country became embroiled. Whether they originated within the country or were brought about by international conflicts, each of the frequent national emergencies has resulted in a constitutional crisis. Each time, the social and political forces emerging temporarily triumphant codified their norms and philosophy, usually in a comprehensive document. Because of frequent changes, constitutions have never played the role of fundamental charters, nor have they laid down generally accepted rules for the political game. Their conflicting norms have been satisfactory only to one segment of public opinion, and they were hotly contested by the others. This in turn has invited a lack of respect for fundamental norms which appeared to be forever in flux. With the one exception of the Third Republic (1875–1940), none of the sixteen constitutions which the country has given itself between 1791 and 1958 have been in force longer than eighteen years. That the Third Republic enjoyed unaccustomed longevity was in part due to the fact that its text was so summary and little more than a guide to proper procedure; hence the regime came close to living under an unwritten constitution.[24]

The highly ideological and historically oriented language of politics has deepened the chasm between actual and declared policies. To wrap the political discontent of the day in metaphysics, to give to the tritest discussion the dignity of philosophy, has not furthered the French contribution to political theory, in spite of some brilliant thinkers.

The prevailing style of debate has encouraged a proclivity for false conflicts, and for play-acting by public figures. To the degree that behavior of the political actors and of the electorate corresponded to past alignments, it was unsuited to the solution of actual conflicts. On the other hand, whenever it became finally unavoidable to solve pressing problems and to accommodate conflicting interests by compromise, agreements were reached without any reference to fundamentals. This increased the contempt not only for politicians but for the political way of life itself as seemingly betraying the principles by which men ought to live. Middle-of-the-road politics were considered an eternal "swamp" which muddied every forthright action. As far as possible, the political system was put outside the rational and emotional loyalty of the citizens, which strengthened their nonparticipatory disposition. "Turbulence on the one side," a French sociologist concluded on the eve of the Fifth Republic, "and a nearly unbelievable tolerance of the provisional and

24 See Zeldin, *France 1848–1945*, p. 372.

the confused on the other, are evidence that the French do not take social situations seriously." [25]

The high sensitivity of the public at moments of crises and its withdrawal into apathy during periods of unexciting routine are again only different aspects of the same phenomenon. France is not the only country where one has observed in recent times the pulling back of the public from the political game and its exclusive devotion to private life. But the alienation of the French citizen has been particularly acute because there was no modern party system to mediate between the public and its government and because of the seeming insensitivity of parliament and the administration to currents of public opinion.

That Frenchmen are people difficult to govern is a commonplace voiced in over-quoted statements by Caesar, Tocqueville, and, most recently, by the first prime minister of the Fifth Republic, Michel Debré. The chapters that follow will show which are the traditional attitudes that have persevered, and where there has been change. Subsequent chapters will examine whether the institutions under which France has lived since 1958 prove adequate to the transformations of French society and to the changes in the attitudes of Frenchmen.

De Gaulle once confided to one of his ministers: "I have not founded a new republic. I merely gave the republic foundations which it had never had before. . . . What I have tried to do is to achieve a synthesis between the monarchy and the republic." [26] Will history vindicate his claims?

[25] François Bourricaud, "France," in *The Institutions of Advanced Societies*, ed. Arnold M. Rose (Minneapolis: University of Minnesota Press, 1958), p. 520.

[26] Alain Peyrefitte, *The Trouble with France* (New York: Knopf, 1981), p. 48. This extensive commentary by a Gaullist insider is quite valuable, though the author's judgments are at times very personal.

CHAPTER II

The Economic and Social Setting

FOR AN EIGHTY-YEAR PERIOD, from the last decades of the nineteenth century until the early 1950s, France was regarded as a perennially retarded developer. Her economic growth was the slowest of all developed countries (about 1.1 percent annually). But the economic vitality manifest during much of the Fourth Republic and consolidated since then has put France into the ranks of the highly industrialized countries of Western Europe. An enthusiastic, though not uncritical, French economist has spoken about the period from 1946 to 1975 as the "thirty glorious" years.[1]

In terms of per capita gross national product, France ranks with the wealthiest nations of the world: in 1980 it occupied the eighth place among the countries belonging to the Organization for Economic Cooperation and Development (OECD). Its per capita GNP was 17 percent higher than the average of the member countries. Only in France has the GNP doubled between 1960 and 1978 (in constant values). Until the energy crisis and an economic recession befell France as well as other countries of Western Europe, the annual growth rates of the gross national product have been steady and between 1965 and 1973 reached between 5 and 6 percent per year, an increase sur-

[1] See Jean Fourastié, *Les Trente Glorieuses: La révolution invisible de 1946 à 1975* (Paris: Fayard, 1979). The book offers a wealth of data and wise reflections.

passed only by Japan. Even after the economic recession had hit, the GNP continued to expand at a rate which no other industrial nation was able to achieve at that time. Since then, it is true, growth has at times been reduced to zero and stood at 1.7 percent in 1980. But other industrial nations of the West did not fare better and some of them worse. During a single five-year period (1969–1974) industrial production rose by 37 percent. Equally satisfactory and steady has been the annual increase in productivity: about 7.5 percent annually between 1968 and 1973. Because of some widely held views about Germany's record for efficiency it is worth noting that in manufacturing industries the output per work-hour has increased faster in France than in Germany. Moreover, for many years, France has also been the country with the longest average working week among all industrialized nations.[2]

What should not be forgotten is that in part such growth was a catching up on past retardation. Hence statistically economic growth profited from a low starting point, and progress, though more than respectable, did not reach the proportion of an "economic miracle." [3]

DEMOGRAPHY, URBANIZATION, AND MOBILITY

Economists and demographers will continue to argue about the respective significance of population trends and economic growth at various stages of economic development. For France there is no doubt that the slow growth of her population since

[2] These and most of the following statistical data are from Statistical Office of the European Communities, *Basic Statistics of the Community*, (Luxembourg: Office for Official Publications, n.d.); and *Annuaire Statistique de la France. Resultats de 1979* (Paris, 1980).

[3] This point is made in what I consider one of the most careful studies of French economic development, A. Cotta, "La Croissance de l'économie française, 1945–1965," *Analyse et Prévision* 2, nos. 1–2 (1966): 519–60, at p. 533. The same author has updated his earlier discussion in *La France et l'impératif mondial* (Paris: Presses Universitaires de France — abbreviated hereafter PUF — 1978). His findings have been criticized in one of the most succinct and yet fairly complete surveys of the French economy to appear in English. Bela Balassa, "The French Economy under the Fifth Republic, 1958–1978," in *The Fifth Republic at Twenty*, eds. William Andrews and Stanley Hoffmann (Albany: State University of New York Press, 1981), pp. 204–26.

FIGURE I. *Age Structure of the French Population*

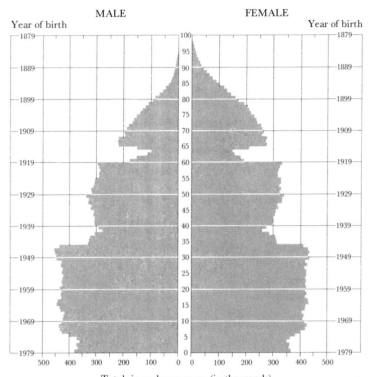

Totals in each age group (in thousands)

	Percentage of Population		
Date	*Young (0–19 years)*	*Adults (20–64 years)*	*Old (65 years and over)*
January 1, 1946	29.5	59.4	11.1
January 1, 1965	34.0	54.0	12.0
January 1, 1972	32.7	54.3	13.0
January 1, 1979	30.7	55.3	14.0

Source: Statistics — *Annuaire Statistique de la France, 1980* (Paris: Institut National de la Statistique et des Etudes Economiques, 1981). Chart — Gérard Vincent, *Les Français 1976–1979* (Paris: Masson, 1980), p. 129. Used by permission.

1850, a declining birthrate, and a net reproduction rate below the level of replacement had not only an adverse economic but, even worse, a disastrous psychological effect. Widely publicized pictures of the age pyramid show quite dramatically the direct and indirect effects of the two World Wars (see Figure 1). Until recently, conversations about the future of France turned frequently to the consequences of this tragic loss for the country's vitality, labor force, and leadership. During the interwar period, the population grew at a rate less than half that of Germany, becoming almost stagnant with the depression. The continuation of interwar trends would have meant a population of 39 million by 1960 and 36.9 million by 1970. Instead, the population reached the 50 million mark in 1968 (at about the same time the United States population rose to 200 million) and amounted to 53.4 million in 1978. Within the age pyramid, the proportion of those under twenty years of age is expanding so fast that France today is one of the "youngest" nations of Europe. Before the war there were only 5 million in the dynamic fifteen to twenty-four years age group; thirty years later, in 1968, their number had increased to almost 8 million.

Part of this upswing is undoubtedly due to a systematic policy of material inducements, such as family allowances and other devices. Since 1932, with unusual consistency every successive regime enacted measures favorable to population growth. There is, however, ample evidence to show that the drastic upward swing in the size of families is due principally to a change in attitudes toward procreation. Demographic malthusianism had been particularly widespread among the bourgeoisie and the peasants. To them too numerous a progeny meant the dividing up of land, of business property, and of inheritance. By limiting the possibilities for a better education, it might destroy class status or upward mobility. Worse yet, it might upset the carefully preserved equilibrium of society at large.

The seemingly curious fact that the birthrate was shooting up during the bitter years of military defeat and occupation is most likely due to generalized feelings of absolute insecurity which destroyed traditional concerns. Also since the war former restraints have been overcome and a new view of family life prevails, which seems to indicate a "more trustful and future-oriented view of the human condition." [4] Economic conditions alone cannot be responsible for this development since during the most prosperous years of the sixties and early seventies the French fertility rate — live births per couple — again dropped. Yet the situation in France was still more favorable than in other Western European nations. Moreover, it has once more improved rather substantially during the last years.[5] Quite remarkable is the fact that the periodic up- and downward trends have never altered the substantial differences in fertility (and mortality) rates between various regions, certainly another indication of cultural diversity.[6]

As a nation France remains lowest in population density among the nine Common Market countries. In the "garden that is France" (and French children are commonly taught to think of their country in this way) there live only 269 persons per square mile, as compared with 639 in West Germany, and 836 in Holland. If France had the same population density as other major European powers, there should be more than 125 million Frenchmen.

Only by leaving its gates open for immigration can the country provide the necessary manpower for certain branches of the economy: one-third of the workers in the building industry and highway construction are foreigners. It is estimated that more than 4 million foreigners live in France, which amounts to 7.5 percent of the total population; an additional 1.5 million are foreign-born. A higher than average percentage of both foreigners and foreign-borns are employed and their fertility rate is considerably higher than that of native-born Frenchmen. Assimilation of those from Southern Europe is generally easy, but the concentration of workers from North Africa (a total of more than 1 million) in certain regions and cities has provoked occasionally dangerous tensions and, especially among French

[4] Michel Crozier et al., *Où va l'administration française?* (Paris: Éditions d'Organisation, 1974), p. 307; and Charles P. Kindleberger, "The Postwar Resurgence of the French Economy," in Stanley Hoffmann et al., *In Search of France* (Cambridge: Harvard University Press, 1963), pp. 131–35.

[5] For the demographic situation, see Fourastié, *Trente Glorieuses*, pp. 51–73.

[6] See Hervé Le Bras and Emmanuel Todd, *L'Invention de la France: Atlas anthropologique et politique* (Paris: Livre de Poche, 1981), pp. 84 ff.

workers and their families, a bitter xenophobia and a racism which occasionally explode into violence.[7] Nonetheless the situation has never reached the level of seriousness that has developed in Great Britain. Indeed when at the approach of the 1981 elections some communist city administrators sought to exploit prevailing feelings by taking brutal measures against foreign slum dwellers, election results seem to indicate that they alienated their own voters. In the 1970s the government introduced increasingly stringent legislation to stop the influx of foreign labor and to control illegal immigration which, in France as elsewhere, has added to the misery of the slums.

Apart from the population increase itself, the most remarkable demographic development since the war has been the mobility of the growing population. Geographical and occupational mobility have supported each other and both have been an important stimulus to modernization. Unavoidably they also have generated certain problems. Many developments which other Western societies have been undergoing since the end of the last century have taken place in France only since the last war.

The geographical mobility of individuals has reached proportions that, while far smaller than those found in the United States, are quite novel for France: at present 20 percent live in a region different from that in which they were born; 15 percent have moved from another community within the last five years; and 15 percent expect not to stay for the rest of their lives in their present place of residence. Today only one-fourth of the people living in a particularly dynamic city, such as Grenoble, were born there. While before the war only one-fourth of Frenchmen died in a department other than that of their birth, this was true of 35 percent in 1975.

Urbanization has drastically altered the distribution of the population, even though it has not deprived the country of some of its traditional characteristics. If one draws the dividing line between urban and rural population at 50,000 (as French national statistics do), then the urban population has

---

[7] See Gérard Adam et al., *L'Ouvrier français en 1970: enquête nationale auprès de 1116 ouvriers d'industrie* (Paris: Armand Colin, 1970), p. 92.

risen during the thirty post-war years from 53 percent to 72 percent of the total, and the rural population has corresponding-ly declined from 47 to 28 percent. But it can be argued that in the specific French context only towns of less than 15,000 population have a predominantly rural character. If one ac-cepts this, then the rural population has decreased since the war only from 44 to 42 percent of the total. With an almost stable figure of about 22 million "rurals," one cannot really speak about an abandonment of the French countryside or of a "French desert," as it is sometimes put.[8] Moreover, as in other countries, motorization, mass media, and modern merchandis-ing have narrowed the gap between the life style of the urban and rural populations. Only the very small villages of less than 1,000 (in some regions, of less than 2,000) are being deserted, especially by the young. The number of people living from agricultural pursuits has indeed diminished drastically (see be-low). But those who have left the farms have often not left the countryside and did not become citydwellers. Moreover, the growth of big and middle-sized cities has brought many people still living in rural communities into professional and social contact with urban life and preoccupations.

The massive urbanization that has taken place has therefore drawn population mostly from the demographic upturn and from immigration. Almost one-half of the total population lives now in what French census figures regard as "big cities," namely urban areas with more than 100,000 inhabitants. Before the war there were only sixteen such areas; now they number forty-nine. Fourteen cities now number more than 300,000 in population, which makes France similar to such highly urban-ized nations as West Germany and Great Britain. In the span of seven years (1968 to 1975) the population of the twenty-one largest cities has increased by more than 25 percent.

In some respects population shifts and a corresponding re-distribution of national wealth have accented rather than miti-gated traditional differences. The increase in population has

[8] See the observations of one of the foremost students of rural France: Henri Mendras, "Une figure de la France," in *La sagesse et le désordre. France 1980,* ed. Henri Mendras (Paris: Gallimard, 1980), p. 19

profited only one-third of the country; more than two-thirds of the ninety-six departments into which the country is divided now have a lower population than in 1950. Discrepancies between the capital city and the rest of the country continue to be enormous. As early as the seventeenth and eighteenth centuries, royal edicts tried to put a stop to the growth of Paris; present-day attempts are similarly unsuccessful. In 1975, 9.9 million people, i.e., close to one-fifth of the entire French nation and more than one-fourth of its total urban population, lived in the metropolitan region of Paris, even though mostly as suburbanites. This creates, as in other metropolitan areas of the world, staggering problems on every level. But in a country with centuries-old traditions of administrative, economic, and cultural centralization, it has also produced a dramatic gap in human and material resources between Paris and the rest of the country. "It is above all the capital city which shapes the culture of nations," Montesquieu wrote in the eighteenth century. "It is Paris which shapes Frenchmen." The Paris region accounts for more than one-fourth of total industrial production; only two other regions, one in the North, the other in the Rhône Valley, contribute 10 percent each to the national industrial product. This explains why the per capita income of individuals in the Paris region is about 60 percent higher than the national average; the regions that rank next in wealth are barely reaching that average. The difference between them and the capital is about twice as great as that between them and the poorest region of France. Vigorous economic growth and the progressive development of other urban centers have alleviated the situation somewhat. It is no longer quite true, as it has been for a long time, that ambitious professional men and women feel slighted if they do not succeed in "mounting" (*monter*) toward the capital. Culturally, life in the provinces has become more rewarding, which is a necessity if efforts toward decentralization are to succeed (see Chapter IX).

Another economic division of the country, dating back at least to the Second Empire, also continues to exist. So far, efforts to overcome it have proven hardly more fruitful than the attempts to halt the population influx into the Paris region. While industry has spread into new regions, especially into the

MAP 1. *Distribution of Employment in France*

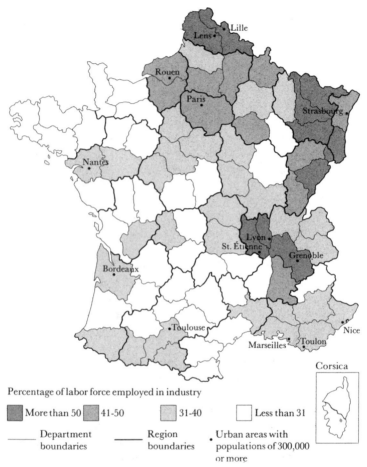

Percentage of labor force employed in industry

More than 50   41-50   31-40   Less than 31

Department
boundaries

Region
boundaries

Urban areas with
populations of 300,000
or more

Corsica

Source: Adapted from *Atlas Historique de la France Contemporaine, 1800–
1965* (Paris: Colin, 1966), pp. 38, 47.

Southeast of the country, France west of a line that runs from Le Havre to Grenoble and thence to Marseilles is, compared with the rest of the country, quite underdeveloped. The western part of the country comprises 56 percent of its territory and only 37 percent of its total population. But 80 percent of the country's industrial production and 76 percent of industrial employment are located east of the line. (See map 1.) In the East where farming is intensive, only 15 percent are employed in agriculture. Sixty-five percent or two-thirds of the entire agricultural population live in the West. Growing differences and tensions, breaking occasionally into open revolts, arise between the rapidly developing regions northeast of the Le Havre–Marseilles line and the regions which are losing population and are lagging in investment, productivity, and, with some notable exceptions, industrial development. The demands of the dynamic and the static parts of the country are sometimes in conflict, and governmental intervention has not always been able to reconcile them without slowing down overall growth.

In the country as a whole drastic changes in the structure of the labor force were one of the consequences of increased mobility. They have made France more like other industrialized countries. In 1976 the labor force amounted to about 21.8 million or 40.8 percent of the total population. During the single decade 1970–1980 an additional 2.3 million entered the labor market, a far larger and faster increase than in other countries.

On the eve of the last war 37 percent were employed in agriculture; the figure is now down to 9 percent and still declining (this compares to 6.5 percent in West Germany and 3.7 in the United States). Industry now employs 36 percent as against 30 percent before the war. Employment in the tertiary sector has risen from 33 to 53.8 percent, still below corresponding figures for the United States and Great Britain. However in France this sector, usually considered as an indicator of modernity in a "post-industrial" society, comprises more stagnant and archaic branches of trade and commerce than in other countries.

Occupational distribution has changed drastically also and, as we shall see (in Chapter VIII), with some striking political consequences. During twenty-one years (1954 to 1975) the percentage of owners of industrial and commercial firms, while still quite high in comparison with other countries, declined by 4 points; that of managers, the high civil service, and the professions rose from 2.9 to 7.8 percent. What the French call *cadres* (middle management, technicians, civil servants, etc.) increased from 9.5 to 14.2 percent. White-collar employees, a category which includes the lowest paid salaried men and women, rose from 10.8 to 17.5 percent. The percentage of workers has risen little (from 33.8 to 35.5 percent) because modern industry has become less labor intensive.

All of these data reveal the great transformations which French society has undergone during the last quarter of a century. In the words of one author commenting on them: "Another society is born. . . ." [9] But figures alone do not give a vivid and precise image of the changes as they have affected public and private life. They must now be described.

"FRANCE WITHOUT PEASANTS"? [10]

Even those who rightly refused to explain the unimpressive performance of the French economy in the past by single facts agreed that the survival of the marginal family farm played an important role in the economic backwardness of the country. "The peasant destroyed the feudal regime [at the time of the Revolution]," it has been said, "but he consolidated the agrarian structure of France." [11] When, toward the end of the last century, the multicrop, nonintensive production methods of the small family farm had become obsolete, the French peasants were not driven off the land as was the case in Great

[9] Gérard Vincent, *Les Français 1945–1975* (Paris: Masson, 1977), p. 277. In this and his subsequent *Les Français 1976–1979* (Paris: Masson, 1980) the author presents and comments on the results of official statistics with great acuity. Both books are invaluable for those in search of an original chronology of events and data on the country's social structure.

[10] This is the suggestive title of a useful if now slightly dated book which discusses the agricultural situation, past and present, with a great amount of data — Michel Gervais, Claude Servolin, and Jean Weil, *Une France sans paysans* (Paris: Seuil, 1965).

[11] Georges Lefèbvre, "La Révolution française et les paysans," *Études sur la révolution française* (Paris: PUF, 1954), p. 256. The long delayed and slow integration of the peasants into the national community is admirably analyzed by Eugen Weber, *Peasants into Frenchmen* (Stanford: Stanford University Press, 1976).

Britain. The republican government and its minister of agriculture, Jules Méline, came to their aid with massive measures of protectionism. Behind sheltering tariff walls French farmers (as well as small businessmen) were able to cling to established routines.[12] In a sense, France never repealed its Corn Laws. A web of protective regulations, including exorbitant tariffs and other privileges, isolated the rural sector of the economy from the mainstream of national life. At different periods protectionism took on different forms. But the mentality which originated in the Méline era has not everywhere run its course.

By comparison with other highly developed industrial countries, the agricultural sector of France remains economically important. Cultivated acreage amounts to about half of that of the nine Common Market countries combined and it furnishes 30 percent of the total agricultural production of the member nations. To the domestic economy it contributes about 6.3 percent of the gross domestic product (as against 2.9 percent in the United States). But between 1954 and 1979 alone 3.2 million people — farmers, family members, or agricultural workers — left farm employment. Between 1929 and 1975 the number of farming units has decreased from 3.9 million to 1.5 million; in a mere twenty years (1955–1975) more than 1 million farms have disappeared, and for the years 1963 to 1985 the decline in the number of farms is projected to exceed 40 percent.[13] Yet the total cultivated area has not diminished significantly. With an increase in productivity higher than in the rest of the economy, agricultural production has progressed constantly and has doubled between 1959 and 1975.

Neither concentration nor modernization have altered the fact that the average net income of the drastically reduced agricultural population is just about half that of the rest of the nation. Because specialization and productivity progress at

[12] For background and details of this politically all-important legislation, see Gordon Wright, *France in Modern Times* (Chicago: Rand McNally, 1960), pp. 346 ff.

[13] These and other data in this section are provided by an excellent symposium, Yves Tavernier, ed., *L'Univers politique des paysans dans la France contemporaine* (Paris: Colin, 1972), pp. 12 ff.; and by Jean Baumier, *Les Paysans de l'an 2000* (Paris: Plon, 1979).

very different rates in different regions, such averages distort
reality even more than usual. In 1972 regional disparities of
agricultural incomes were greater in France than in all other
European countries and were still increasing. The differences
between the richest and the poorest departments, between the
large efficient producer and the marginal farmer, were one to
ten.[14] About one-third of the farmers derive less income from
their work on the farm than the legal minimum salary of wage
earners.

A decisive problem remains size. If fifty acres are generally
considered a minimum for Western European farms, then not
less than 925,000 among the 1.2 million operating units in
France are marginal and generally too small to be economically
viable. It is expected that over the next decade the elimination
of the marginal farms will at least in part result from the fact
that today this particular group of farmers is overaged and that
their sons are unwilling to stay on the family farm. The smaller
the farm the higher the percentage of sons and daughters leaving agriculture. This process, however, is long, humanly painful, and economically wasteful. Recent legislation has eased it
somewhat by providing grants to farmers willing to retire early
and by including them in the social security system. But the
social mobility of the young who leave is usually mediocre:
they are likely to join the ranks of the lowest paid categories
of wage earners in city or countryside.

In the early post-war years and with greater energy under
the first governments of the Fifth Republic, new ways have
been tried to make the agricultural sector less dependent on
public support. A "silent revolution" was to change outlook
and mentalities. The rural interest groups have brought to
some key posts men that represented the younger generation
and the poor regions of mixed agriculture. Together with a
number of influential civil servants, and backed, at least at
times, by the government, the younger peasant leaders drafted
legislation which sought a new solution to the old problems of

[14] See John T. S. Keeler, "The Corporatist Dynamic of Agricultural
Modernization in the Fifth Republic," in *Fifth Republic,* Andrews and
Hoffmann, p. 277; and Jean Baumier, *Les Paysans,* p. 152.

ensuring income parity between the farmers and other sectors of the economy. The joint exploitation of adjoining family farms and the cooperative processing and marketing of products were encouraged. The consolidation of marginal holdings, the improvement of a particularly inadequate technical education, and further mechanization and experimentation were used as avenues for long-range reforms. Underlying such reforms was a "vision of a modernized agricultural structure, composed of farms that are neither the tiny, inefficient units predominant in the past nor the giant agro-business concerns found in the United States, but rather a compromise between those two extremes: medium-sized family farms which are socially and humanly viable." [15]

But if hopes had been fairly high in the early 1960s, they have been dissipated since. Traditional individualism has won out in many instances and has prevented more cooperative forms of farming from spreading. Rural cooperatives of various kinds, while never as widespread as in some other European countries, have at all times been quite strong in certain regions of France. In others they have run afoul of a deep-seated disinclination to engage in common ventures beyond the nuclear family.[16] Many of the technologically backward farmers, especially in Brittany, in some other western areas, and in the center of France have been unable or unwilling either to modernize or to abandon their holdings. Hence the marginal farms which do not provide sufficient income to their owners or tenants continue to survive. The hoped-for increase in medium-sized farms has been relatively modest and no further increase is expected for the period 1980 to 1985. Improved productivity has mostly benefitted the large farms whose share in acreage and total production has risen substantially. Many of their operators are reported to be among the wealthiest of Frenchmen.

[15] Keeler, in *Fifth Republic,* Andrews and Hoffmann, p. 275.
[16] The achievements of rural cooperatives are described by Baumier, *Les Paysans,* pp. 96 ff. Edgar Morin, *Plodémet: Report from a French Village* (New York: Random House, 1971), pp. 173 ff., dramatizes their difficulties in a village in which they have never taken root. The chapter in Morin's book dealing with the farming population is significantly entitled "The Wretched of the Earth."

Agriculture as a whole has generally done well by the Common Market. The community's price structure, stubbornly defended in Brussels by every French Minister of Agriculture, is a burden for the European consumer but a boon for the most efficient of the French producers, many of whom have turned to specialization. Smaller farms are faring less well, if not badly. Recent government reports describe a new category of the "rural poor": farmers who have incurred debt in order to modernize and specialize but have gone bankrupt in the process. Southern farmers are dreading the competition from Spain, Portugal, and Greece after these countries are admitted to the community. The double-digit inflation of recent years has curtailed agricultural revenue by driving up production costs. Hence it appears that ever fewer farmers share in the benefits derived from increased production and rising exports.

Discontent explodes into violence in many parts of rural France. A confusing array of agricultural interest groups expresses the widely divergent wishes of their constituents. The contradictory goals and the tactics of these groups will be discussed in Chapter VII. Pressures coming from many sides exact from every government, conservative as well as socialist, ever higher subsidies or other forms of assistance. Between 1960 and 1976 the budget of the Ministry of Agriculture increased by 900 percent. Presently it represents 13.5 percent of the total budget[17] and is said to siphon the entire revenue derived from personal income taxes.

THE ENTREPRENEURIAL SYSTEM
AND THE PUBLIC SECTOR

"Each country develops a political economy suited to its temperament, to its traditions and to the exigencies of the moment." [18] The transformation of the French economy has not left behind all of the traditional structures of its entrepreneurial system nor has it altered some of the mentalities incident to those structures. The complement of the family farm is the

[17] Keeler, in *Fifth Republic*, Andrews and Hoffmann, p. 279.

[18] Jean-François Poncet, Foreign Minister in the Giscard administration, quoted here from Christian Stoffaes, *La Grande menace industrielle* (Paris: Calmann-Lévy, 1978), p. 157.

French family firm. More than half of the 662,000 industrial enterprises belong to individuals; another third are classified as *entreprises artisanales* (craftsmen). Close to 80 percent of the 590,000 commercial firms do not employ a single salaried employer, only 17 percent of them employ more than fifty. In industry, 86 percent of the firms have fewer than ten workers and are therefore hardly to be classified as "industrial." Over 45 percent of all wage earners in industry are employed in firms of less than 50 employees, less than a third in firms employing between 50 and 500. While in France 73 percent of the labor force works in firms employing less than 500, the corresponding figures are 61 percent in West Germany and 58 percent in the U.S.A.

Less than 900 of all industrial and commercial firms have more than 1,000 employees on their payrolls. Quite unusual for an advanced "managerial" economy is the fact that more than half of the top 200 industrial concerns are still family controlled, even if most of them are managed by outsiders.[19] Whether and in which situations family control imposes itself on the decision-making process in these large firms and reproduces traditional entrepreneurial behavior is a subject of controversy.

Size, dispersion, and concentration are not the only factors that determine the efficiency of an economy. Past discussions have emphasized the obstacles which the mentality of the patrimonial employer, his extreme individualism, and his concern for secretiveness and stability have put in the way of economic development. On the whole, and brilliant exceptions notwithstanding, the performance of the family firm has been found mediocre both in terms of technical innovation and of support given to economic growth. Many patrimonial employers voiced openly their distrust of engineers and engineers' mentality. Many commercial firms engaged in something approaching guerrilla warfare, directed both against the wholesaler and the

---

[19] See, with many significant details on the French business structure, the books by François Morin, *La Structure financière du capitalisme français* (Paris: Calmann-Lévy, 1974), and, especially significant in view of the forthcoming nationalizations, *La Banque et les groupes industriels à l'heure des nationalisations* (Paris: Calmann-Lévy, 1978).

state, so that "the shopkeeper was doubly the *small* man." [20] Fears of glutting the market were stronger than willingness to expand. Vigorous competition was considered inadvisable since bankruptcies might upset the social status of other bourgeois families. Méline's policy of protecting agriculture by high tariffs was designed to slow down industrialization and consequently offered little incentive or support for modernizing industry. The outcome was that the country was saddled with many of the problems of industrialism without fully enjoying its material benefits.

Until recently, society did not fully honor success in business ventures; it regarded failure as justification for the relatively low esteem in which the business community was held. Much of this was due to a belief, not uncommon in Catholic and Latin cultures, that moneymaking lacked nobility. Hence the most talented sons of the bourgeoisie sought careers in the professions or in the civil service. Only as a last resort might they turn to running the family enterprise.[21] As late as 1977 Catholic businessmen of various income levels expressed opinions which showed them to value security higher than profits.[22]

Since prerevolutionary times, entrepreneurial timidity was partly compensated for by the role which the French state played in technological innovation and economic development. The royal *fermiers*, Colbert's mercantilism, and the way in which Napoleon III's entourage interpreted the doctrines of Saint-Simon created traditions in which government was considered the motor, not a parasite, of the national economy. In Max Weber's terms, a "politically oriented capitalism" emerged and was accepted with the same ambivalence that char-

[20] Theodore Zeldin, *France 1848–1945*, vol. 1, p. 109.

[21] See Cotta, "La Croissance de l'économie française," p. 534. The abundant literature, mostly American, on this subject has recently been ably summarized and criticized by Crozier, *Où va l'administration?*, pp. 272 ff.

[22] Jacques Capdevielle et al., *France de gauche, vote à droite* (Paris: Presses de la Fondation Nationale des Sciences Politiques — abbreviated hereafter PFNSP — 1981), p. 200. The conservatism and low degree of technical sophistication of a majority of employers in firms with less than 500 employees is illustrated by an opinion poll reported by Suzanne Berger, "Lame Ducks and National Champions: Industrial Policy in the Fifth Republic," in *Fifth Republic*, Andrews and Hoffmann, p. 309.

acterizes French attitudes toward authority in general: protection and promotion by the state were at the same time expected and dreaded. The tradition-bound employer who owned his business and was producing or distributing for a local or at best regional market, felt harmed, not benefited, by governmental intervention and regulation. On the other hand, the managers of modern and larger enterprises have long accepted the positive role of government, notwithstanding certain flamboyant pronouncements to the contrary.

The modernization of the French economy, initiated under the Fourth and accelerated under the Fifth Republic, would hardly have been possible without a "striking . . . national conversion to growth." [23] Much of the conversion was promoted by incentives coming from outside the business community. The funds available from the Marshall Plan, the investment policies of the French Modernization Plans (see below), and the stipulations of the Treaty of Rome establishing the Common Market channelled the willingness to modernize and to restructure. During the years of de Gaulle's presidency the expansion of basic and heavy industries was given priority because of de Gaulle's concern with the country's "rank" in the world. Pompidou and his governments sought to promote industrialization on a broad front and, as it now appears, sometimes indiscriminately. What the efforts under both administrations had in common and what continued, with some important modifications, under the similarly conservative administration of Giscard d'Estaing, was the involvement of the state in this process. A modern version of "Colbertism" was able to use existing if renovated institutions such as the public and private banking system and state enterprises of various kinds. In the words of the spokesman of a leading private bank: "The state is everywhere, nothing is possible without the state." [24]

[23] Stanley Hoffmann, "Conclusion: The Impact of the Fifth Republic on France," in *Fifth Republic*, Andrews and Hoffmann, p. 451.

[24] Quoted by John Zysman, "The Interventionist Temptation: Financial Structure and Political Purpose," in ibid., p. 256; ironically enough the very same bank and its spokesman here quoted entered into violent conflict with the socialist government when "the state" proceeded to nationalize it in 1981.

To give but one example: In a country whose total energy production covers less than one-fourth of its needs and which must import practically all of its oil, state control of energy policies and especially of nuclear energies was bound to become almost complete. But where the state regulates, finances, and supports so much of business, errors cannot be attributed to the caprices of the market or the short-sightedness of private management; they become political errors and liabilities of the government.

Incongruities of official economic policies have often been noted. They betrayed time and again an ambivalence between a desire for efficiency and traditional protectionism. To further rapid industrialization the government promoted, by tax and other privileges, the sometimes ill-advised merger of large concerns. But the government also sponsored legislation prohibiting, in the interest of small and high-priced stores, the further extension of supermarket and discount houses.[25] A new professional tax introduced in the seventies favored small business over more efficient producers. While the number of small firms has diminished somewhat, their rate of extinction has never equalled that of the small farms.

For some years the government's industrial policy engaged in what was called sectorial development, the assistance to some technologically promising "champions." Pitfalls were not always avoided: the failures in the computer field, the overextension of the steel industry which had to be salvaged by the state, the commercially disastrous supersonic *Concorde.* However, with the onset of the recession and the shrinking of the conservative majority in national and local elections, the Giscard administration changed course. Assistance was shifted to the "lame ducks," traditional industries no longer competitive in the world market but labor intensive and hopefully furnishing a temporary shield against rising unemployment. The downgrading of systematic state intervention in the economy which the government undertook did not exclude capitulation

[25] The legislative history of the so-called Royer Law (Royer was a one-time minister under Pompidou) offers a case study of conflicting tendencies in both the Pompidou and the Giscard administrations; see Pierre Birnbaum, *Les Sommets de l'état* (Paris: Seuil, 1977), pp. 127–34.

to multiple pressures which clamored for rescue operations.[26]

On the eve of the Fifth Republic the French economy was already characterized as being "less capitalistic and more socialistic than the economies of other European nations." [27] Though essentially true, such a diagnosis needs elaboration and refinement before its political implications can be understood.

Government-operated business enterprises have existed in France since before the Revolution in widely diversified fields — fields that in other countries of Western Europe are under private ownership. For centuries France has illustrated the proposition that the relationship of public to private enterprise in a society is a function more of a country's cultural heritage than of its level of development. Contingencies of politics and of leadership rather than the degree of modernity determine the way in which public regulation of enterprise is exercised.

The strongest impulses for a wider public sector arose during the period of the Popular Front (1936–1937) and after the Liberation (1944–1945). In its preamble the constitution of the Fourth Republic (1946) had proclaimed: "Any property and undertaking, which possesses or acquires the character of a public service or of a monopoly must come under collective ownership." Since the preamble of the earlier constitution has become valid law of the present republic (see Chapter X), the provision quoted here became the legal foundation for the nationalizations of the 1980s.

Since the end of the war the government has owned and operated all or part of the following: railroading; almost all energy production (mining, electricity, nuclear energy) and much of telecommunication (radio and television); most air and maritime transport; most of the aeronautic industry; 85 percent of bank deposits; 40 percent of insurance premiums;

---

[26] The closely argued book by Stoffaes, *La Grande menace industrielle,* presents a searching critique of recent economic policies. Further details are discussed in the articles by Hoffmann and Berger quoted above.

[27] Raymond Aron, *France, Steadfast and Changing* (Cambridge: Harvard University Press, 1960), p. 62.

one-third of the automobile industry; one-third of the housing industry — in addition to the old state monopolies of post, telephone, telegraph, tobacco and match manufacture, and sundry less important activities. Public concerns accounted for about 11 percent of the gross national product; their investments represented more than one-third of the gross capital formation of all enterprises. Fifteen percent of the total active population, or 27 percent of all salary and wage earners (agricultural labor not included), were paid directly by the state either as civil servants or on a contractual basis. Their income came close to one-third of the total sum of wages and salaries. These data, however, are only indicative. The most complete and up-to-date description of the public sector insisted that "it is difficult if not impossible to determine exactly the economic and social weight of France's public enterprises." [28]

It is also impossible to generalize on the ways in which the public sector is run. There exist substantial differences in legal structure, control, and management personnel among the various enterprises. After difficult beginnings during the immediate postwar period, political influence in the newly nationalized industries all but vanished. In terms of productivity and modernization, the record of the nationalized firms was far more favorable than in Great Britain. Massive investments helped to make many nationalized concerns pacesetters for an entire industry or branch of industry, and governmental banking institutions, some of them created in Napoleon's time, were playing an important role in the otherwise still limited financial market.

Most important is the fact that the public sector was thoroughly integrated with the economy as a whole. Private business, especially corporate management, has abandoned its initial hostility and clearly settled for cooperation with its colleagues in public enterprises. In the most optimistic view (not shared by all) the assimilation of the two groups whose professional background is often identical (see Chapter VI) has reduced both bourgeois and bureaucratic traditions and furthered the

[28] François Chevallier, *Les Entreprises Publiques en France* (Paris: Documentation Française, 1979), p. 28.

emergence of a new managerial spirit in both the private and the public sectors.[29]

The general public had become rather indifferent to the question as to whether the public sector should be extended by further nationalizations. But the nationalizations became once more a political issue when in 1972 the parties of the Left included in a "Common Program of Government" (to be discussed in Chapter VIII) a lengthy list of industries, banks, and insurance companies to be transferred to public ownership in order to "break the domination by big capital and to inaugurate a new economic and social policy." The program spelled out detailed provisions about equitable compensation to be paid to former owners and about the future management of the public sector.

Five years later the unity among the partners to the Common Program broke, presumedly over the question of whether the list of nationalizations was to be lengthened, a communist request to which the socialists refused to accede. During his 1981 campaign for the presidency François Mitterrand introduced into his program a shortened but still substantial list of firms to be taken over by the public hand. It included all banks and a number of industrial groups described as "basic." This, he now declared, was necessary to increase efficiency, to ensure economic growth, and to guarantee social justice.

When the socialist Prime Minister Pierre Mauroy addressed for the first time the parliament elected in the wake of Mitterrand's accession to the presidency, he announced immediate legislation nationalizing all banks still in private hands and the industries designated in the socialist program, "not one more, not one less." "We want to insure," he concluded, "that the nationalizations enable the state to control the key industries on which a dynamic investment and employment policy depends." [30]

After five months of technical controversies within the gov-

[29] Interesting controversies concerning the impact of this assimilation on the managerial mentality are reported by Pierre Birnbaum et al., *La Classe dirigeante française* (Paris: PUF, 1978), p. 80.
[30] For an English translation of the full text of the important speech of July 8, 1981, see French Embassy, Press and Information Service.

ernment and passionate debates in parliament where partisans and opponents faced each other with crusading fervor, the majority parties accepted comprehensive legislation which restructures French industry and banking in line with the electoral promises. For one side nationalizations acquired the characteristics of a liberating myth; for the other they represented an assault on the very institution of private property.

Through its nationalization of all but a few small family banks, and of two important financial holding companies, the state will control about 96 percent of all deposits. (But it should be noted that since the end of the war private banks never held more than about 15 percent of total deposits.) The five large-scale industrial groups that are passing into public hands are leaders (not all of them prosperous) in such fields as machine tools, chemistry (including pharmaceutical products), glass, metals, and electrical power. The shares of the companies are transformed into public bonds offered as compensation to the former shareholders. In addition the government obtains majority control of two important armament firms and several ailing steel companies. About one million wage earners move from the private to the public sector. The latter will now represent 17 percent of the gross national product as compared with a previous 11 percent, at least quantitatively not a major change.

The government intends to leave a great degree of autonomy to the nationalized firms and banks and to provide for their insulation from too tight a political control. Their directors will be nominated by the government but are promised all necessary freedom of action; several of them transfer from the private to the public sector without changing positions. In order to justify its optimism concerning the future prosperity and independence of the newly nationalized firms, the government points to the technical and commercial success of such previous nationalizations as the Renault works, the railroads, and others. Instead of a bureaucratic organization, novel structures inviting the participation in decision making by the workers and other employees are to be tried out. However, in the opinion of some trade unionists devoted to more radical concepts of *co-gestion* (see Chapters VII and VIII) the legislation has not gone far enough in that direction.

The government is well aware of the risks it takes when it forces rather hastily structural changes on an economy pressed by inflation and unemployment. It answers its critics by insisting that these very changes are needed for a reversal of the conjuncture and for improved competitiveness of French industry. The new president of the Republic has often pointed to the Swedish experience where in his interpretation some of the bold social reforms have finally come to naught because economic command posts were left in private hands.

As was to be expected the opposition parties contested the legislation before the Constitutional Council which is empowered to annul laws found to be in contradiction with the constitution. The Council, however, did not (see Chapter X) invalidate the nationalizations as such, but found the compensation awarded to the former shareholders insufficient and technically faulty. In order to meet such objections it was necessary to increase compensation, which was expected to amount to about five billion dollars, by at least 30 percent, in the eyes of a reform committed government not too high a price for avoiding a constitutional conflict.

WHICH PLANNING FOR WHAT?

In the aftermath of World War II, which had deprived the country of much of its economic substance, General de Gaulle, then president of the provisional government of the Fourth Republic, entrusted to Jean Monnet, a former businessman, the task of preparing a modernization plan, now called the Plan of Economic and Social Development. Since its beginning the Planning Office, officially called the General Commissariate of the Equipment Plan and of Productivity, has elaborated a series of four-, and lately of five-year plans: from an era of shortages and rigid regulation, through alternating periods of inflation and deflationary stagnation, amid prosperity and renewed recession, the numerous governments in the two republics have allowed the commissariate to carry on.

The preparation of each plan has been a long and elaborate

affair.[31] The most original phase of the planning process has consisted in submitting the proposals formulated by the small staff of the commissariate to planning commissions and working parties made up of members of the planning staff, other civil servants, and representatives of the interests concerned. Every plan has called on between 2,000 and 3,000 people to participate in these deliberations. There never was a commitment to a definite ideology of either compulsory planning or of economic liberalism. A long-time observer of postwar European economics has characterized the activities of the commissariate and its collaboration with business leaders as a "conspiracy in the public interest" and has described French planning "as a device that mobilized a number of instruments of public enterprise and pressure which had been lying around for some time, and pointed them all in the same direction." [32]

Its most obvious and intended limitations resulted from the fact that the French plan has never been compulsory, but only "indicative." The objectives, laid down in the plan, whether they be growth rates, investment policies, or modernization projects, were merely an indication of what was deemed desirable and, maybe, possible. The agreements reached were not an enforceable contract; nor did the government issue orders on the basis of the agreements.

At different periods the successive plans had different effects, which fact, by itself, prevents any overall evaluation of the planning experience. In retrospect, it appears that the earliest years were the most successful. The commission was laying

[31] The most complete discussion in English of all aspects of French planning is Stephen S. Cohen, *Modern Capitalist Planning: The French Model* (Berkeley, California: University of California Press, 1977). The author has updated his findings (and added new criticism of the process) in his "Twenty Years of the Gaullist Economy," in *Fifth Republic*, Andrews and Hoffmann, pp. 244–47. For an excellent comparative treatment of economic planning in Western democracies, including France, see *Planning, Politics and Public Policy*, eds. Jack Hayward and Michael Watson (Cambridge: Cambridge University Press, 1975).

[32] Andrew Shonfield, *Modern Capitalism: The Changing Balance of Public and Private Power* (New York: Oxford University Press, 1965), pp. 85, 130. The remarks that follow owe much to conversations with M. Bernard Cazes, head of the Long-Term Studies Division of the Planning Commissariate.

down industrial policies and was convinced, as Colbert was three centuries earlier, that the state knew best what industrialists should produce and what consumers should buy. When the market economy, both domestic and international, began to function more freely, an "insufficient attention to uncertainty" became the chronic disease of the French, as it is of any planners. Additional difficulties arose from the desire, and indeed the necessity, to include in the planning process objectives of social policy, less easy to define in quantitative terms but quite easily defeated by the restrictions that market developments might put on available resources. One of the planning commissioners called the projections of the commissariate a means of "putting mathematics at the service of democracy" because they permitted the economic actors, as well as parliament, to which the plans were submitted, to make their decisions by choosing between distinguishable alternatives. But the length of the planning period — five years — and the uncertainties of a world economy in recession prevented realistic estimates of such basic data as growth rates. Under the pressure of events politicians were anxious to preserve as much freedom to maneuver as possible, while the planners sought adherence to a definite course.

Already under Pompidou the prestige of the commissariate had declined. Many labor representatives felt slighted and withdrew from the planning committees; industry manifested more than unusual unwillingness to abide by the directives of the plan; the government returned to earlier practices of negotiating directly with organized groups rather than through the planning mechanism.

As Finance Minister under his two predecessors, Valéry Giscard d'Estaing had been known for being out of sympathy with the purposes and methods of planning. In his opinion the economic planners were creating social tensions by raising expectations and at the very least amounted to an unwarranted interference with executive prerogatives. Early in his presidency Giscard set up a Central Planning Council which he presided over and which was to "organize the future development of the economy." But it failed in its endeavor to coordinate industrial, monetary, and budgetary policies. The work of the commissariate became quite marginal to actual decision making and even without the elections of 1981 the VIIIth Plan, which was to cover the years 1981–1985, would hardly have seen the light of day.

With socialists in power the planning enterprise was once more given central importance. The government established a Ministry for the Plan and Regional Development, while previously the commissariate had been attached to the office of the Prime Minister. The new Minister, Michel Rocard, has for years played a leading role in the Socialist Party. Trained for a position in the high bureaucracy and well versed in modern economics, his writings and political activities have accredited him as a social-democratic reformer rather than as a doctrinaire.

An Interim Plan, covering the first two years of the new administration, was drawn up and speedily accepted by parliament. It is concerned with the most pressing problems such as the reduction of unemployment and creating the conditions for renewed economic growth. But its underlying and clearly expressed philosophy as well as the reorganization of the new ministry indicate a new departure. The planning office is also actively engaged in preparing the next five-year plan (1984–1988) whose termination coincides with the end of the Mitterrand presidency.

It is not astonishing that the new plan has the ambition to restore to comprehensive planning the prestige and the — intermittent — success of earlier days. It espouses the principles developed by Jean Monnet, the "founding father" of the plan in post-war France: it rejects autarky and wants the French economy to be responsive to international competition and especially to exchanges with the countries of the European Community. It refuses compulsion and direct interference with the private sector of the economy: informed cooperation between the economic and social partners, public and private, will be the vehicle of short- and long-term planning under the auspices of the government. Lessons of the past will have to be learned, the new plan asserts. An annual review procedure which will involve parliament should bring planning objectives in line with unforeseen developments on the national and international levels.

Admittedly, planning will face new challenges; but the planners also hope for more effective leverage. The new nationalizations of important industries and of the entire banking sector will make the directives contained in the plans more plausible and lend them additional importance for the guidance of the economy as a whole. The drastic decentralization inaugurated by the socialist government (see Chapter IX) gives the twenty-two regions into which the country is divided foremost responsibility for economic and social planning in their respective areas. To coordinate their, hopefully, unfettered initiatives with the objectives of the national plan will require new institutional arrangements and procedures which are presumably facilitated by putting national planning and regional development into the same ministry.

The tasks which planning thus assumes appear quite formidable. A governmental report describing them regards "lyrical illusions" on the one hand and "demobilizing pessimism" on the other as the two dangers to be avoided.

SHOALS AND ACHIEVEMENTS
OF THE WELFARE ECONOMY

France is not the only Western country with a mediocre record for spreading the benefits of the postwar boom and of prosperity among all of its citizens. But in a nation whose urge for equality has been particularly pronounced, protest against inequities has often taken violent forms, and social tensions have hampered the development of the country's economic and industrial potentialities. In 1978 shortly after an election had once more sent a conservative majority to parliament, 78 percent of the respondents in a public opinion poll were in favor of "suppressing the privileges of quite a few Frenchmen so as to reduce social inequalities between people." [33] In order to claim for France a foremost rank in the concert of nations, General de Gaulle had emphasized the steady growth of the economy and seemingly ignored perennial obstructions and

[33] Capdevielle, *France de gauche,* p. 25. At that time only a minority were in favor of such reform proposals of the left as nationalizations and drastic tax reforms.

tensions. In private conversations de Gaulle himself recognized the shortcomings of such policies. "This egalitarian country," he said to one of his ministers, "is one in which the inequalities are greatest. And the category which fares worst at the common table, are the workers." [34] Statistics uphold such impressions and comparative statistics, for all their uncertainties, leave little doubt that, both in terms of income and of wealth, discrepancies between the rich and the poor are greater than in other countries of equal development.

Forty-seven percent of all income goes to the 20 percent on the top of the income pyramid, but only 4 percent to the 20 percent at the bottom. The earnings of the top 10 percent are 21 times higher than those of the bottom 10 percent. This gap is much wider than in West Germany, Sweden, and the United States.[35] There have been improvements in the situation during the last decade, mostly because of a rise in the lowest and some flattening out of the highest incomes. Between 1970 and 1980 the difference between the earnings of the household of an agricultural worker and that of a member of the liberal professions has narrowed by about 10 points on both ends. During the same period the elderly have profited from new assistance programs. The government was correct when it claimed that during the Giscard administration real wages had risen, and at a faster rate than in the United States and Germany, but it must not be forgotten that they were substantially lower at the

[34] See Edgard Pisani, *Le Général indivis* (Paris: Albin Michel, 1974), p. 81. The author, several times minister during General de Gaulle's administration, later joined the Socialist Party and now represents France at the Common Market headquarters.

[35] The literature on this point is vast and controversial. The best documented, if highly technical, study is by Malcolm Sawyer, "Income Distribution in OECD Countries," in *OECD Economic Outlook; Occasional Studies* (July 1976). The French government has disputed its data, but they are to be found, with unimportant variations, in many official government publications. Many of the latter are cited in *Rapport de la Commission des Inégalités Sociales* (Paris: Documentation Française, 1975), and in *Rapport Français presenté à la Commission des Communautés Européennes, La Pauvreté et la Lutte contre la Pauvreté* (Paris: Fondation pour la Recherche Sociale, 1980). A skeptical view of the entire discussion is taken by a Professor of Economics, Alain Wolfelsperger, "Regard sceptique sur la mesure des inégalités de revenu en France," *Commentaire* 3, no. 10 (Summer 1980): 254–59.

start. Of the original Common Market partners France remains the country which assigns the smallest share of national income to wage earners and ranks highest in undistributed income of corporations. In the 1970s an official of the Giscard administration calculated that (in a population of 53 million) there were 11.2 million underprivileged poor and without a drastic change in policies they will still number 9.3 million in 1985.[36]

Since large incomes permit the accumulation of wealth, the concentration of wealth is even more conspicuous than the steepness of the income pyramid. It is estimated that the richest 10 percent control between 35 and 50 percent of all wealth; the poorest 10 percent own not more than 5 percent.[37] Because of the notorious unreliability of tax declarations, these figures probably underestimate existing inequalities.

"Nothing tells us more about the political condition of a country than its tax system," François Mitterrand noted years before his election, and after commenting on the defects of the existing system, he concluded that fiscal reform would be a top priority for a government of the Left.[38] Before him both Pompidou and Giscard d'Estaing had lamented publicly that in France income taxes had become, as Giscard put it, "a factor of fiscal iniquity rather than of social justice." [39]

In spite of some assertions to the contrary, it is not true that the French economy as a whole is burdened with higher taxes than other countries of similar development. What is special about France is the distribution of its taxes. Even though in the modernizing economy of the Fifth Republic the number of income tax declarations has increased and direct taxes represent a larger part of total revenue than previously, the share of indirect taxes remains far higher than in other industrialized countries.

As is well known, indirect taxes not only drive up prices but

[36] Lionel Stoléru, *Vaincre la pauvreté dans les pays riches* (Paris: Flammarion, 1974), pp. 52, 114.

[37] Data on the distribution of wealth are to be found in André Babeau and Dominique Strauss-Kahn, *La richesse des Français* (Paris: PUF, 1977), and in the studies mentioned in fn. 35.

[38] François Mitterrand, *La paille et le grain* (Paris: Flammarion, 1975).

[39] Quoted here from Maurice Parodi, *L'économie et la société française de 1945–1970* (Paris: Colin, 1971), p. 326.

also weigh most heavily on the poor. The foremost reasons for
such prevalence of indirect taxation are the widespread and
time-honored practices of tax evasion. Since Tocqueville's
classical description of the devious ways by which the French
peasant, under the Old Regime, evaded the "arbitrary, not to
say ferocious, methods of taxation," [40] the legacy of a peasant
mentality has been blamed for the low tax morale of Frenchmen. The survival of many small units in industry and agriculture which everywhere, not only in France, are able to conceal
part of their earnings, magnifies the problem of evasion. French
sources have estimated that fraud is practiced by more than
one-third of those with taxable incomes, among them admittedly many members of the professions. Because of a lack
of personnel, tax audits are rare and perfunctory. If outright
tax evasions cost the public treasury at least 15 percent of
revenue, loopholes, exceptions, and exemptions leave at least
56 percent of business and 77 percent of agricultural income
untaxed. A timid inheritance tax yields little even from large
estates. Net wealth is taxed in most European countries, but
not in France. The corporate and personal income taxes are
far less progressive than elsewhere.[41] The fate of a government-
sponsored bill to introduce a capital gains tax during the Giscard administration offered a case study of the difficulties that
stand in the way of tax reform. Countless amendments moved
by deputies of the governmental majority deprived the law of
its intended effects. Its discussion in the National Assembly revealed a bitter conflict of interests and the brittleness of the
governing coalition.[42] Treasury officials and other civil servants

[40] Alexis de Tocqueville, *The Old Régime and the French Revolution*
(New York: Doubleday Anchor Books, 1955), p. 127.

[41] A well-documented and exceedingly sharp criticism of the existing
tax system is provided by a socialist economist, Pierre Uri, *Changer l'impôt
(pour changer la France)* (Paris: Editions Ramsay, 1981). See also, Christian
de Brie and Pierre Charpentier, *L'Inégalité par l'impôt* (Paris: Seuil, 1973).

[42] The events and issues at stake are well documented in a book by a
former minister, Françoise Giroud, *La Comédie du Pouvoir* (Paris: Fayard,
1977), pp. 204–11, and by Uri, *Changer l'impôt*, pp. 97–125. "Without a
profound reform of the tax system, no equitableness can be obtained," Uri
concludes, "no decentralisation can be effective" (p. 47). About the relationship between the fiscal system and projects of administrative decentralization, see Chapter IX.

have frequently formulated proposals for comprehensive tax reform. But so far they have never been translated into legislation. Whatever new tax legislation has been introduced has usually complicated the system and rarely increased its equity.

Where France has been most effective is in the field of social transfers. They have risen from 16 percent of the GNP in 1960 to 27.3 percent in 1980, which puts France behind Holland and Sweden but ahead of Western Germany and most other European democracies. A comprehensive social security system, established in its present form after the war but extended since then, and a variety of programs assisting such groups as the aged, large families, the handicapped, and others disburse substantial benefits. When unemployment benefits, the cost of job training programs, and housing subsidies are added, total costs are as high as the entire public budget, but they are largely borne by employers and employees. Whether they represent too heavy a burden on production costs and are hence responsible for the high price level and diminished competitiveness continues to be the subject of bitter controversies.[43] When industry attempts to ease the burden through the replacement of labor by capital, it creates new unemployment. Undoubtedly the existing social transfers are a response to the economic inequalities that have been described; they reflect the search for security in a society which has only a limited confidence in the distributive capacities of the free market.

Policies of cautious liberalization, initiated by Giscard's Prime Minister Raymond Barre, included the lifting of the last price controls that had survived for three decades. The policies were a calculated risk which the government took — and lost. In spite of strenuous and multiple efforts, the government was unsuccessful in controlling inflation: in 1980 the consumer price index was rising by an annual rate of 13.6 percent, a much faster increase than in neighboring countries.

At the time of the 1981 elections unemployment had reached the highest level since the war: 1.8 million (as against 425,000

[43] For conflicting opinions on the economic effect of social transfers, see Stoffaes, *La Grande Menace*, p. 260, and Parodi, *L'économie*, pp. 324–34. On the deficits of the social security system, see Vincent, *Les Français 1976–1979*, pp. 179–83.

at the beginning of Giscard's presidency); official calculations predicted a further increase of more than 900,000 over the next five years. A problem, common to many Western countries, was aggravated in France by the previously mentioned rapid increase in the labor force. Forty-six percent of the unemployed are younger than twenty-five. Among those employed temporarily or part time, 55 percent come from the same age group. In the total employable population, those between sixteen and twenty-one amount to 8 percent; but they are making up 28 percent of the unemployed. In part the employment picture reflected the collapse of private investments: an average annual increase of 7.6 percent was reduced during the years of the Giscard presidency to an average of 1.1 percent.[44] This record proved a handicap which the incumbent was unable to overcome when he ran for reelection in 1981.

The socialist government proceeded immediately to inaugurate policies designed to attend to the most pressing social needs. The minimum wage, allowances for families and the handicapped, and old-age pensions were raised, sickness benefits improved. In order to help ailing branches of the economy which needed pump-priming, subsidies and credit were granted at preferential rates of interest. Students leaving school were assisted in their search for employment. Tens of thousands of new jobs were created in the public sector, both national and local, and many more will be added. The age of (voluntary) retirement has been lowered to sixty years; the legal workweek shortened from forty to thirty-nine hours, one among the many measures that need implementation by employers and trade unions. The goal announced by the government is the thirty-five-hour week.[45]

[44] For complete data on the structure of unemployment, see Vincent, *Les Français 1976–1979*, pp. 172–78, and the report of the *Commission chargée par le Premier Ministre d'établir le bilan de la situation de la France*. I have also used other data in this and subsequent chapters from the foregoing report to be published by the government. The Commission's President was kind enough to make the report available to me before its publication.

[45] For a good overall view of governmental policies during the first months of the new administration see Vincent Wright, "The Change in France," *Government and Opposition* 16, no. 4 (Autumn 1981): 414–31.

The impact of these policies on the public budget is considerable: expenses in 1982 are expected to be 23 percent higher than in 1981. This will result in a budgetary deficit of at least 20 billion dollars, twice that of 1981 and three times that of 1980. The deficit which is now expected amounts to 2.8 percent of the gross national product, a figure which is not higher than that in the Federal Republic of Germany.

A socialist government in search of new resources for its ambitious reform program will turn to fiscal measures apt to relieve social inequality. A new tax on wealth has been introduced but care has been taken not to frighten the middle classes into a panic which, in the past, has often had a contraproductive effect on public revenues. The government remains convinced that a thorough overhauling of the entire tax system, a redistribution of direct and indirect taxes, and more effective measures against fraud and evasion will be necessary to bring tax receipts to a more satisfactory level.

The government also knows that the stopgap measures which it has introduced and which have generally been popular will be insufficient to master the problems of inflation and unemployment. Almost unavoidably both the rate of inflation and the number of unemployed have risen during the first months of the new administration, even though less steeply than under its predecessor's.

A reversal of the situation can only be expected, the government asserts, from the long-term effects of the structural reforms to which it is pledged and which it has inaugurated, such as the nationalizations, the planning of industrial revival in certain key fields, the administrative decentralization, the reintegration of the young into the labor market, and others. (For a fuller discussion of these objectives see Chapter XI.)

CHAPTER III

Political Socialization

POLITICAL SOCIALIZATION AND POLITICAL CULTURE

This volume, like others in the Comparative Politics Country Studies Series, attempts to explain the significance of the political attitudes and political behavior of its citizens for a country's politics. Such an emphasis does not exclude an analysis of governmental institutions, nor that of the political infrastructure — formed mainly by interest groups and parties. Yet, we assume that the way people act within the political system is of foremost importance both for the functioning of the system and for an adequate explanation of how it functions.

Like all human beings, Frenchmen of all ages play many roles, some of them relevant to the political system. Which roles they play and how they perform depends on a variety of objective factors, as well as on their values, beliefs, and emotions. Many social scientists, dissatisfied with a narrow and legalistic interpretation of politics, have studied the basic values existing in a society to explain political behavior and through it the political system. These studies, however, have sometimes led to erroneous generalizations[1] or to high-level abstractions with little explanatory force.

[1] Cf. the trenchant remarks by the French author François Goguel, in Stanley Hoffmann et al., *In Search of France* (Cambridge: Harvard University Press, 1963), pp. 374 ff., commenting on such generalizations by two American social scientists, appearing in the same volume.

To understand the particularities of the political realm, we need not be concerned with all the ideas that swirl around in a society, nor with all the patterns that mold the individual and determine his conduct. What matters is the individual's political socialization, a learning process that proceeds in part by observing and experiencing authority. But authority patterns, the ways in which orders are given and how people look at those giving them orders, exist not only in the political life of a society. They are observed and experienced first and, at least in a democracy, foremost in the family and other primary groups, in the church and the schools, on the job and in associations. An active role in family life or participation in social activities often provides training for roles assumed in political life, just as the exclusion from meaningful participation in other spheres of life may result in political passivity. The subsequent sections of this chapter will therefore deal with various social settings.

Like any other learning process political socialization passes on from one generation to the next a "mixture of attitudes developed in a mixture of historical periods."[2] Centuries ago Montesquieu spoke of the composite of values, emotions, and beliefs as "the general spirit, the morals of a nation." More recently several authors have defined this composite as political culture. They have acknowledged that the notion of political culture — and of political culture change — has been a theme of reflection on politics since antiquity.[3]

The relationship between political culture, political socialization, and the political institutions of a given system is never unidirectional; none of these variables can be said to shape the

[2] Sidney Verba, "Comparative Political Culture," in *Political Culture and Political Development,* eds. Lucien W. Pye and Sidney Verba (Princeton: Princeton University Press, 1965), pp. 512 ff.

[3] See, e.g., with a wealth of references, Gabriel Almond, "The Intellectual History of the Civic Culture Concept," in *The Civic Culture Revisited,* eds. G. Almond and Sidney Verba (Boston: Little, Brown, 1980), pp. 1–36. Almond developed his concept of political culture first in "Comparative Political Systems," *Journal of Politics* 18 (August 1956): 391–409, and expanded it in G. Almond and S. Verba, *The Civic Culture: Political Attitudes and Democracy in Five Nations* (Princeton: Princeton University Press, 1963). But see also, with some variations, Samuel H. Beer, *Patterns of Government* (New York: Random House, 1973), esp. pp. 23 ff.

others without themselves also being affected. There is constant interaction between a country's political culture and its citizens' political socialization.

Attitudes toward authority, shaped by direct or transmitted experiences, will leave an imprint, and possibly a lasting one, on a nation's political culture. The political orientations of individuals are themselves influenced by the total culture of the communities in which people live. The modern nation-state is the foremost of these communities; yet the manifold cells making up a nation, such as localities, classes, generations, and minorities (and indeed a majority in most societies: women) have their own political culture, often called subcultures, which may be in accord with or in opposition to *the* political culture of a country. The way a Frenchman looks at political events, especially at the decisions of his own government, has much to do with the attitudes he has observed and learned in the social and in the political realm. Conversely, the capabilities of the political system, whether it can act forcefully or must temporize and maneuver, often depend on the behavior of the citizens. Their actual or presumed reactions to specific events or general policies may condition the content and style of political decision and thereby structure governmental institutions.

An understanding of the limitations which an inherited political culture imposes on political development is of particular importance in studying an old country such as France. More than a century ago Tocqueville spoke of his compatriots as "a people so unalterable in its *primary instincts* that it is recognizable in its portraits drawn 2,000 or 3,000 years ago. . . ."[4] Political institutions, even if they are seemingly created anew, are shaped by the political culture.

The Frenchmen, who after the Second World War gave a new constitutional framework to the Fourth Republic, had the mandate to establish a regime totally different from that which led the country to the disaster of 1940. Most of them honestly

[4] Alexis de Tocqueville, *The Old Régime and the French Revolution* (New York: Doubleday Anchor Books, 1955), pp. 210–11. Emphasis supplied: what Tocqueville called "primary instincts" appears to overlap the two present-day terms, "socialization" and "political culture."

believed that this was what they were doing. Yet, in spite of past experiences and of great differences in the *texts* of the constitutional laws, it soon turned out that the Fourth Republic was unable to avoid the pitfalls of the Third. The attitudes and beliefs not only of the political actors inside and outside parliament but also of the French citizens as voters, as members of interest groups, etc., frustrated the intended change. These and similar episodes in the history of France do not justify that form of determinism which is inclined to argue that cultural traditions are so confining that a country cannot avoid repeating forever its fortunes, good or bad.[5]

Tocqueville himself ascribed unforeseen changes in the country's destiny to the changeability of the "moods [and] . . . tastes" of Frenchmen. Today, the contrast between politics in the Fourth and Fifth Republics shows that constitutional texts, i.e., new institutions, are not necessarily devoid of political effect. The experiences accumulated since the war and the acute crisis precipitated by the fighting in Algeria had opened the way for seemingly fundamental changes in attitudes. Where these changes have altered the traditional political culture and where they have not will be discussed throughout this study.

If one sets out to construct a model of basic values which will presumably explain the major manifestations of political life, one should guard against giving undue weight to the attitudes of one group of society.[6] It is therefore necessary to investigate as concretely as possible the socialization process of various categories of citizens and of leaders alike. Only by looking subsequently at the political process, as it unfolds at a particular historical moment, will it be possible to determine what values and beliefs (or, to draw once more on Tocqueville, what

[5] For some excellent remarks emphasizing the importance of cultural factors in French developments and yet rejecting any form of determinism, see Stanley Hoffmann, "Conclusion: The Impact of the Fifth Republic on France," in *The Fifth Republic at Twenty,* eds. William Andrews and Stanley Hoffmann (Albany: State University of New York Press, 1981), p. 482.

[6] To have done this has been one of the criticisms, in some respects well taken, in others unwarranted, against Almond and Verba's *Five Nations* study. The rich literature to this point is now critically and ably reviewed in *The Civic Culture Revisited,* one of the most interesting recent works in the field of comparative politics.

"sentiments" and what "principles") have been and continue to be dominant.

RELIGIOUS AND ANTIRELIGIOUS TRADITIONS

France is at once a Catholic country — 83 percent of the children born in 1968 were baptized into the Catholic faith (92 percent in 1958) — and a country which the church itself considers as "dechristianized." Until well into the present century, the mutual hostility between believers and nonbelievers was one of the main features of the political culture. Since the Revolution, it has divided society and political life at all levels.

In 1789, very few people started with the idea of making war on religion. But a series of historical accidents achieved an early split between the Revolution and the church. The forces of counterrevolution based their legitimacy on a religious faith for which unquestionable authority and ecclesiastic discipline were more central than in some other countries, while the double revolt against king and church gave to the democratic creed a rationalist basis whose purest French expression was voltairianism. (It has been said of Voltaire that only a Catholic country could produce him.) Just as for Catholic Frenchmen the Revolution was the work not just of erring or evil men but of Satan, antireligious beliefs took the form of a militant faith. The Jacobin-inspired cult of reason was indeed a "cult," which lives on in spirit though no longer in form. This explains why the secularized state and its institutions have never been given sacral dignity: there is no reference to God in any of the republican constitutions, no prayer at official functions, no "In God we trust" on the coins, no religious oath for officeholders. Such practices, quite common in many countries that respect the separation of church and state, would have been sacrilegious to *both* camps in France.

With the establishment of the Third Republic in 1870, the gulf between the political cultures of Catholicism and anti-clericalism reopened and deepened further. After a few years the errors of its enemies permitted militant anticlericalism to take over the republic.

Parliament rescinded the centuries-old concordat with the Vatican, expelled most Catholic orders, and severed all ties between church and state, so that "the moral unity of the country could be reestablished." There was a time when the hostility between Catholicism and anticlericalism almost broke out into generalized violence. In those rural regions where Catholic observance had already become an expression of habit rather than of genuine faith, dechristianization spread when the new legislation deprived the church of all official prestige.[7] From the rostrum of parliament Viviani, premier at the outbreak of the First World War, boasted that his generation had extinguished forever in the minds of the oppressed classes all hopes for salvation by divine providence.

The intransigence of the republican regime was matched by that of the Pope, who excommunicated every deputy who had voted the separation laws. Faithful Catholics were driven into a political ghetto. Regular attendance at mass by army officers became a hindrance to promotion. A feeling of being besieged from outside the walls of their faith was given expression in many Catholic publications of the period. The faithful saw no other way than the overthrow of the existing political regime to overcome their isolation.

The Catholic subsystem existing within the republic drew its strength from a well-developed network of private education and associations (see later in this chapter and in Chapter VII). The mass pilgrimages to cathedrals or shrines were not ordinary church services but rites of communion: the sermon-speeches held at such occasions stressed the distinctiveness of those assembled and denounced the sins of those outside the community of faith.

The opposition between the political Right and Left was frequently determined by attitudes toward the Catholic church. In rural regions where religious practice continued to be lively and where the advice of the local clergy counted on election day, conservative candidates carried the vote. But even governments of the center usually did not invite the support of conservative deputies whose anticlerical lineage was dubious. For a total of sixty years (1879 to 1939), with rare exceptions, no

[7] Gordon Wright, *France in Modern Times* (Chicago: Rand McNally, 1960), p. 332.

practicing Catholic obtained cabinet rank in any of the numerous ministries. The political isolation of the Catholics can be
compared to that of the communists between 1947 and 1981.
The existence of such political ghettos of whatever kind necessarily narrows the basis of representation.

The situation changed during the interwar period and especially after Catholics and agnostics found themselves side by
side, and sometimes joined together, in the resistance movement of the Second World War. Divisions remain, but there is
"no longer the Homeric struggle in which two civilizations
concentrated all their strength. . . . Christianity and secular-
ization are no longer the nuclei of two worlds, but two competing principles within a single world." [8]

The space of the Catholic "world" is shrinking, though not
dramatically.[9] In 1977, 81 percent of a representative national
sample described themselves as "Catholic" compared to 86.5 in
1974. But only 17 percent of them attended Sunday Mass regularly, a decline of 4 percent in three years. The number of
occasional church-goers declined at the same rate, and half of
the Catholic population no longer attends church at all. The
number of people describing themselves as "without religion"
rose from 10 to 16 percent of the total population (25 percent
among those younger than forty). These average figures conceal
enormous regional differences: in one rural and poor department in the center of France regular attendance was down to
6 percent of the Catholic population, but it was as high as 68
percent in one of the Alsatian departments of the East. Com-

[8] Edgar Morin, *Plodémet: Report from a French Village* (New York:
Random House, 1970), pp. 189, 205.

[9] The data which follow are taken from a variety of sources usually
based on public opinion polls. Occasional divergencies are due to uncertainties in defining categories. See François A. Isambert, "Le sociologue, le
prêtre et le fidèle," in *La Sagesse et le désordre. France 1980*, ed. Henri
Mendras (Paris: Gallimard, 1980), pp. 225–45; Jacques Capdevielle et al.,
France de gauche vote à droite (Paris: PFNSP, 1981), pp. 43–45 and 157–
59; Christel Peyrefitte, "Religion et politique," in SOFRES, *L'Opinion
française en 1977* (Paris: PFNSP, 1978), pp. 117–21; Hervé le Bras and
Emmanuel Todd, *L'Invention de la France; Atlas anthropologique et
politique* (Paris: Livre de Poche, 1981), pp. 430–31; and A. Coutrot and
F. Dreyfus, *Les Forces religieuses dans la société française* (Paris: Colin,
1965).

parisons between departments of similar structure and located in the same region seem to indicate that historical rather than socioeconomic factors determine the degree of dechristianization. Yet on a national scale church attendance by the farming population is 20 to 30 percent higher than the average; fewer farmers than the average describe themselves as "without religion." But in most regions wealthier farmers attend church services more regularly than the owners or tenants of marginal farms, sharecroppers, or agricultural workers.

Another generalization that seems to hold is that where social hierarchies have remained strong, religious practices are more firmly rooted: this is true in the border regions of the North, where family life is close, and in the West, where nobility and clergy have long been a determining factor in village life.[10]

According to a detailed study of a village community situated in a region of about average religious practices and considered in many respects typical, Mass, religious weddings, and funerals have little religious significance. Those who do attend these rites are there mostly from habit and for social reasons. They look upon the priest as they look upon the mayor: each fulfills different public functions. Religious faith is regarded as something beyond the reach of the uninitiated: it is the clergy's business.[11] Confessions have declined almost everywhere. Another problem for the church arises from increasing difficulties in recruiting priests: in 1965 there was one priest for 1,188 inhabitants; ten years later one for 1,460. There are indications that many young clergymen experience what has been described as an identity crisis.

In the Middle Ages, Christianity was propagated from the

[10] Edward R. Tannenbaum, *The New France* (Chicago: The University of Chicago Press, 1961), p. 41, and his entire chapter on Catholic practices, significantly entitled "Children of the Past." For a broader (and excellent) study of Catholicism in various rural regions, see Gabriel Le Bras, *L'Église et le village* (Paris: Flammarion, 1976).

[11] Lucien Bernot and René Blancard, *Nouville, un village français* (Paris: Institut d'Ethnologie, 1953), pp. 239, 299. A more recent study, based on extensive interviewing and rich in insights, if occasionally confusing, is Guy Michelat and Michel Simon, *Classe, réligion et comportement politique* (Paris: PFNSP, 1977).

urban agglomeration. Now the large cities and the lines of
communication between them seem to contribute most to dechristianization. From a survey of young people, it appears
that the attitudes in city and country will continue to differ:
59 percent of those living in large urban centers believe that
for their generation religion is less important than for their
parents; only 42 percent of those living in communities of less
than 2,000 population think so. For the cities, regional variations remain important: in Strasbourg there are more than 33
percent practicing Catholics; in the Mediterranean harbor of
Marseilles less than 11 percent go to church with any regularity.

Most telling are the differences among the social classes in
big cities. In the Paris region, which the clergy has long considered as "mission territory" because of low church attendance, 19 percent of the managerial group but only 1.7 percent
of workers go to Mass. In less dechristianized cities such as
Lille, 3 percent of the unskilled, 8 percent of the skilled workers, but 60 percent of the professional group are church-goers.
On a national level, almost half of all Frenchmen who have
severed church ties belong to the working class: 58 percent of
Catholic workers never attend church; 15 percent of the general working class population describe themselves as "without
religion"; the figures for white-collar employees are about the
same. The estrangement between the working class and the
church, which occurred in France as in other countries of Continental Europe during the early stages of industrialization,
contributed to the class consciousness of the workers. It made a
majority of them into followers of radical rather than conservative parties. The legacy of this estrangement remains a central
fact of French religious, cultural, and to a considerable extent,
political life.[12]

The urban bourgeoisie continues to be traditionally divided:
at various historical periods, especially the nineteenth cen-

[12] For a careful inquiry into the relationship between the church and
working class, see Gérard Adam and Marc Maurice, "L'Église catholique
et le monde ouvrier," in Société Française de Sociologie, *Tendances et
volontés de la société française* (Paris: SEDEIS, 1966), pp. 285–321 and the
study by Michelat and Simon quoted in the preceding footnote.

tury, contradictory experiences have deposited here a layer of devout Catholicism, there an unrepentant voltairianism. Sometimes the divisions run within the same family. But by and large, church services in the urban centers are mostly attended by the upper and middle classes, with a predominance of women and young girls.

The difference between the religious attitudes of men and women is more pronounced in France than in other countries of similar development. A far higher proportion of men describing themselves as Catholics have severed all church ties: 55 percent as against 45 percent among women; a far greater number of women attend church with regularity: 21 percent as against 13 percent among men. Among those who find the church an institution that deserves "outright criticism," 64 percent are men and only 36 percent women. Only 47 percent of the men, but 62 percent of the women who believe that the church still has considerable political influence in France approve of this situation. Such differences, even though to a varying degree, are common to all classes, including the working class, all regions, to the rural as well as to the urban milieu. According to a recent inquiry they can in part be explained by the fact that girls, even those from working-class families, attend parochial schools in a far greater number than boys.[13]

When young Frenchmen were asked to list the values they cherished most and whose loss they would most regret, there were no significant differences between the first three preferences of religious youth and of nonreligious youth. Both groups listed health, money, and love, though not quite in the same order. For those who attended church regularly, religious faith occupied fourth place, while it appeared at the bottom of everybody else's list. On many problems the current thinking of the faithful and of the faithless coincides rather than diverges. Two-thirds of the students in Catholic schools approve of divorce "in certain cases," as against three-quarters of students in public institutions. However, in their answers

[13] See Janine Mossuz-Lavau and Mariette Sineau, *Les Femmes françaises en 1978. Insertion sociale. Insertion politique* (Paris: Microfiche, Centre de Documentation Sciences Humaines du CRNS, 1980), pp. 151–62.

to questions of a more definite political significance, children attending state schools and Catholic schools in Grenoble revealed different attitudes. The greatest difference, one of 25 percentage points, came on the statement that the revolution of 1789 was "good": 66 percent of the public schoolchildren, but only 41 percent of the parochial schoolchildren, agreed. The symbolic importance of divisive historical events remains strong.[14]

There are indications that the separation of church and state is losing the rigidities which have so far characterized the secular character of a republican regime in France. While the constitution of the Fifth Republic was being written, a public opinion poll asked whether the electorate would be in favor of inserting into its preamble a reference to "God the Creator and the Father of all mankind": 37 percent approved, 33 percent disapproved, 22 percent declared themselves to be indifferent to the question. (No such reference was included in the actual text of the constitution, which simply affirms that the Republic is *laïque* or secular.) In a poll, conducted during the presidential election campaign of 1969, 38 percent preferred a churchgoing president of the Republic, only 10 percent frowned on one, while 43 percent were indifferent.

There are no longer any walls built around the religiously devout: he is no longer barred from careers; he may be different but he is no longer estranged from the world that lies beyond his own community of faith. The changes that have occurred are a consequence both of shifts in the general environment and of mutations in French Catholicism. Traditions of a nonauthoritarian, democratic, and socially conscious Catholicism have been revised. They had been quite lively during the middle of the nineteenth century but had dried up during the Second Empire and the struggles with the anticlerical republic.

After the Second World War the diverse Catholic movements and the church hierarchies changed outlook and meth-

---

[14] Charles Roig and F. Billon-Grand, *La Socialisation politique des enfants* (Paris: Armand Colin, 1968), p. 115.

ods of action. In a pluralistic society, Catholic organizations, publications, and teachings became themselves pluralistic and gave expression to a wider range of social and political choices. A new style and better defined role assigned to lay members enabled Catholic action groups to become more effective as innovators in a variety of fields.

In the organizations of farmers, workers, and employers and among intellectuals, in certain administrative bureaus (such as that of the modernization plan), there now exists a novel (and entirely informal) fraternity of those who have been active in the various branches of the Catholic youth movements. It is estimated that more than 3,000 (of a total of 36,400) mayors of local communities have such a background. The use that the church, church-affiliated educational institutions, and the multiple Catholic organizations make of the mass media shows little of the sectarianism of earlier days.[15]

After the war, the experience of the worker-priests holding Mass in factories and slum dwellings was the most widely noted and most dramatic sign of a novel orientation. Yet upon orders of the Vatican this form of missionary work had to be abandoned, at least temporarily, when it turned out that when placed in a working-class milieu many of the priests admitted that they were overwhelmed by the justifications of communist ideology.

Modernization of church ceremonies and an intellectualization of the clergy, especially in urban settings, have provoked a fundamentalist reaction whose strength seems to wax and wane, but which the Vatican has not been able or is not willing to dominate completely.

In discussions about the political orientation of practicing Catholics, much attention has been paid to the fact that the Socialist party and organizations, which place themselves to the left of the Communist party, have attracted a relatively large number of faithful young Catholics of all origins.

[15] See Coutrot and Dreyfus, *Les Forces religieuses,* pp. 292–305, and William Bosworth, *Catholicism and Crisis in Modern France* (Princeton: Princeton University Press, 1962), esp. Chapters IV–VII.

However interesting these developments might be, on a national scale it remains as true as it has been in the past that religious orientation is an outstanding factor in determining political alignments. (Of course religious orientation and socioeconomic status may, and often will, combine to determine party choice.) Faithful Catholics continued to vote for candidates and parties of the Right. In the 1981 presidential elections François Mitterrand, the candidate of the Left, obtained 52 percent of the popular vote. But among regular churchgoers he attracted only 20 percent and 40 percent among those attending church occasionally. He drew his support from 61 percent of the Catholics no longer going to church and from 88 percent of voters classified as "without religion." These results are identical to those obtained by the Right and the Left in preceding elections won by the conservative-gaullist majority in 1974 and 1978, except that 4 or 5 percent of the occasional church-goers had changed allegiance between 1974 and 1978. Whether and how much the decline in church attendance during the years between the two presidential elections has benefited the Left is difficult to ascertain.

Freemasonry in France, as in other Latin countries, has shunned the religious and political conservatism and deism of Anglo-Saxon Masonry. During the formative years of the Third Republic, the agnosticism of the Masons turned into fervid anticlericalism. Since Masons occupied leading positions in many organizations, both public and private, they exercised, at least until 1914, a greater influence on the minds of republican Frenchmen than their number (probably never more than 50,000) would suggest. When the hostility between practicing Catholics and agnostics lost its acuity, the Freemasons abandoned their political and cultural militancy and refrained from taking sides in political contests. Yet a broad congruence of liberal and undogmatic views had long encouraged overlapping membership between the Socialist Party and the Grand Orient, today the most representative of the Masonic lodges. Several ministers in the Mitterand government are Masons; many more are to be found among socialist members of parliament and the political appointees in the administration. It is, however, unlikely that this will affect in any way the policies of the new government.[16]

French Jews (since the recent exodus from North Africa numbering about 650,000, the largest Jewish community in Europe outside of the Soviet Union) are politically so integrated that they do not need to be discussed as a separate element of the political culture. This seemed to have changed when General de Gaulle's hostile criticism of Israel created for the first time a "Jewish vote" and one opposed to the governmental majority of the Fifth Republic. Under de Gaulle's successors the phenomenon has subsided. Sporadic antiSemitic acts of vandalism are committed, as elsewhere in Western Europe, by people on the political fringe. In France they evoke bitter memories of the Dreyfus Affair and of the policies of the Vichy regime during the war.

By contrast to the attitude of the Jewish population, the Protestants (800,000 or 1.6 percent of the total population) have, at least until recently, lived somewhat apart — a heavy concentration in Alsace, in the Paris region, and in some regions of the center and of the southeast of France has been characteristic of this small religious minority. About two-thirds of its members belong to the upper bourgeoisie; business, banking, the civil service, journalism, and the professions are heavily represented. Socially, and even economically, a clannishness and a rather deliberate style of life mark the Protestant milieu. Politically, they voted until recently much further to the left than others in the social milieu to which they belonged or the regions in which they resided. They identified themselves with the advanced opinions of republicanism, not because of an explicit political influence of their churches which has been minimal, but because of the corresponding identification of Catholicism with the political Right and antirepublican movements. If the Protestants were

[16] For an interview with the leader of the Grand Orient after the 1981 election, see *Le Monde*, August 13, 1981. For general studies of modern Freemasonry in France, see Paul Naudon, *La Franc-maçonnerie* (Paris: PUF, 1979) and Josette Gennaoui, "La Franc-maçonnerie aujourd'hui," *Projet* 107 (July–August 1976): 831–41.

faithful, even though culturally different, republicans, the republic did not confine them to a ghetto: on the contrary, the number of Protestants in high public positions was and remains very large in proportion to their number in the country.

The new alignments which the recent mutations of French Catholicism have made possible have had a corresponding impact on the beliefs and attitudes of Protestants. Since the Liberation it can no longer be said that Protestants vote "Left" with any consistency. Their electoral behavior, like their activities in cultural and economic associations, is now determined by factors other than religious affiliation. They too, and for the first time in almost 300 years, have been fully integrated into the mainstream of French political culture.

FAMILY

For Frenchmen who viewed their neighbors and their fellow citizens with distrust and the institutions around them with considerable cynicism, the family group was a safe haven. Balzac's novels, among others, illustrate how the immediate family (parents-children) was embedded in the larger extended family, how both supported each other and might be ruthless in ensuring family well-being. To the outsider, French or foreign, the Frenchman was always sociable, especially when met on neutral ground, such as restaurants and other people's salons, for the purposes of stimulating conversation. But otherwise distance was maintained and intimacy rarely granted: people had a tendency to barricade themselves in their homes as if they were fortresses.[17] Concern for stability, safe income, property, and continuity (including rational calculations as to matrimony and conception) were the characteristics common to bourgeois and peasant families: the urban and rural proletariat were excluded from this pattern which was sanctioned by legislation and highly valued as a generalized standard.

The belief that the family must remain the foremost training ground for acculturation was matched by a resolve of all

[17] André Siegfried, *France: A Study in Nationality* (New Haven: Yale University Press, 1930), pp. 12–13. The respects in which Siegfried's "classic" is now outdated will be discussed in the text.

competent family members — parents, older siblings, and others — to contribute to the training of the child. Close supervision, incessant correction, threatened and applied sanctions (though usually little physical punishment), and a rather authoritarian style were characteristic of family life. "No use discussing," "as long as you live in this house, you won't . . .," etc., were accepted parental formulae. But the great difference from authoritarian family life elsewhere, e.g., in Germany, was that in general little more than outwardly conforming behavior was required. The child and adolescent were free to withdraw emotionally and intellectually into their own thoughts and build, if they were so inclined, their own value system.[18] The fear of face-to-face authority relationships which characterizes the French administrative and political style was prevalent in many families before it was reproduced and strengthened by the educational system.

Since the war, and particularly during the last twenty or thirty years, the life of the French family, the role of its members, and its relationship to outsiders have all undergone fundamental changes. What did not change is a broad consensus on the importance of the family. Not only conservatives but 87 percent of socialist and 83 percent of communist voters agreed with a statement that "to maintain the family as it has always existed is one of the most important things for our society."[19] This acknowledges at least implicitly the continuing and important role of the family in the socialization process.

There is more justification now than in the past to draw a picture of "the" French family. Not that class distinctions have vanished (see below). But a greater similarity of life styles, family "togetherness" (however silent it may be in front of a TV set), and, most importantly, altered views on the exercise of authority within the nuclear family have modified cultural

[18] These processes within a family of the upper bourgeoisie are masterfully described in Roger Martin du Gard's great novel *The Thibaults* (New York: The Viking Press, 1939).

[19] See SOFRES, *L'Opinion . . . 1977*, pp. 64–65. More critical of the traditional family are the young between eighteen and thirty-four, the ecologists and extreme Leftists, groups that generally overlap. For an excellent study on today's family life, see Sabine Chalvon-Demersay, "Aimée ou haie: la famille" (a significant title!), in *La Sagesse*, Mendras, pp. 247–69.

traits. Previous differences between regions, between the traditionally more egalitarian family relations in the North of France and a more authoritarian pattern in the South, seem to have disappeared.[20]

Patriarchy was always mitigated by the fact that in France both lines of kinship — the father's and the mother's — were considered important for the nuclear family and its protection. Yet legislative changes modified only gradually the legal incapacities of married women which the Napoleonic code had spelled out. Not until 1970 would a law proclaim the absolute equality of the two parents in the exercise of parental authority and for the moral and material management of the family. Opinion polls reveal that from year to year a larger majority of respondents approve of the cooperation of both parents, especially in financial matters, and in all questions concerning the education of the children.[21] Women have been described as the "secret agents of modernity" in the countryside. They insist on labor-saving devices for house and farm. By bringing the men out of the taverns into more attractive homes, they fight alcoholism, which is rampant in many parts of the country.[22]

The idealized image of the "woman at home," an image which inhibited the political socialization of women, has been discredited by the continuous increase of married "women at work." During the 1960s the number of women in the labor force has risen by about one million and amounted in 1975 to over 38 percent of the total. The percentage of married women either employed or seeking employment has increased even faster: from 52 percent of all working women in 1966 to 62 percent in 1973.[23]

[20] See Le Bras and Todd, *Invention,* pp. 56, 86. This statement is all the more credible, as it comes from authors who emphasize the continuing cultural diversity of different regions.

[21] SOFRES, *L'Opinion . . . 1977,* pp. 194–95.

[22] See Morin, *Plodémet,* pp. 41–45, remarking on the noisy revolution of the teenagers and the silent one of women. On the role of women in the present-day family, see Odile Benoit-Builbot et al., "Domination et révolte des femmes au travail," in *La Sagesse,* Mendras, esp. pp. 120–23. The entire article is most informative about problems of the working women.

[23] See Benoit-Builbot, in *La Sagesse,* Mendras, p. 116, and Gérard Vincent, *Les Français 1945–1975* (Paris: Masson, 1977), p. 279.

The employment of a greater number of married women has had an impact on the effectiveness of the family as a vehicle of socialization. There is strong evidence that working women differ from those who are not gainfully employed in regard to moral concepts, religious practice, political interest, electoral participation, party alignment, etc. In their general orientations those employed are far closer to the milieu, the class, or the age group to which they belong and, frequently, to their husbands than to women that are not employed.[24] So far there are no data available to determine whether children from households with two working parents differ in their attitudes from others in some basic attitudes such as political trust, etc.

In a dynamic society, family members, including employed mothers and children, bring into the family circle the results of their varied experiences, instead of merely receiving and passing on traditions. Leisure time activities, especially travel by parents and children, have influenced the style of family living and often the relationship of the family with the world outside. The search by the family group for equilibrium and balance is, of course, not abandoned. But to enable the family to continue its role as one of the molders of individual motivations, a fresh equilibrium is sought to take into account the new forces pressing from the outside. André Siegfried's characterization of the French family as fundamentally "antisocial," stated some forty years ago, is no longer a valid generalization.

Adolescents of both sexes (in the sixteen to eighteen age group) usually take a more liberal view than their parents on questions concerning morality, religious beliefs, women's emancipation, public order, military service, and the like. However, the differences between the generations are not enormous and vary on most questions only between 12 and 26 percentage points. The differences become more pronounced in regard to specific political problems such as atomic armament, nationalizations, and strikes. But only a small minority of the young

[24] This is the amply documented thesis of Mossuz-Lavau and Sineau, *Les Femmes françaises.* The authors also found that women who were no longer working but had been employed previously were likely to express opinions closer to those of working than of nonworking women.

respondents are in favor of revolutionary change. For the others "essentials" should not be changed even if bold reforms are desired.[25]

Parents transmit to their children broad ideological preferences and, frequently, identification with a social class: 67 percent of the adolescents who identify with the Left come from similarly oriented families; 53 percent of those on the Right come from families that vote conservative. But allegiance to specific parties is seldom demanded or given. The reluctance of a majority of parents to reveal for whom they have voted or even to talk politics in front of their children is held responsible for a relatively low rate of interest in politics among adolescents. This is particularly true of working-class families, except of those where the parents are political activists. Adolescents, and even more so younger children, have traditionally rejected politics as an impersonal universe from which they are excluded. Of late such attitudes seem to have been less pronounced on the Left than on the Right.

CLASS

The existence of class stratification in a society and the intensity of feelings about it result in different attitudes toward authority and in a different style of exercising it. Frenchmen, like Englishmen, remain conscious of living in a society that is divided into classes. But since in France equality is valued more highly than in England, deference toward the upper classes — at least until recently an important element of the British political culture — is far less developed, and indeed a resentful antagonism is widespread. The number of

---

[25] The most important studies on the political socialization of the young are Annick Percheron et al., *Les 10–16 ans et la politique* (Paris: PFNSP, 1978); the same author's "Se faire entendre: morale quotidienne et attitude politique des jeunes," in *La Sagesse*, Mendras, pp. 129–65, and her *L'Univers politique des enfants* (Paris: Colin, 1974). These publications, besides reporting on original investigations, give an exhaustive account of other studies on the socialization of youth. See also, Janine Mossuz-Lavau, *Les Jeunes et la gauche* (Paris: PFNSP, 1979). For a more recent report on a sharply critical mood and renascent political activism among the young, see Nicolas Beau and Edwy Plenel, "Jeunesses de l'Après-10 Mai," *Le Monde*, December 11, 1981.

those who are conscious of belonging to a class remains high, the solidarity within the same group intense. In 1977, 68 percent of respondents in a public opinion poll (73 percent of the men) felt that they belonged to a class; 26 percent denied it. While such feelings were most intense among farmers and workers (74 percent), the most privileged groups in the population were not far behind with 68 percent; only the identification of small businessmen and middle management were less acute (57 percent).[26] While adolescents belonging to different classes frequently share opinions on major problems, 59 percent of the eighteen to twenty-four group also think of themselves as members of a social class. When all respondents who had acknowledged the existence of class stratification were asked to identify with a given class, their answers (see Table I) gave evidence of widespread feelings of class identification in all social categories and all political parties.

When shortly after the elections of 1978 (won by the conservatives) another poll asked whether the respondents had the "impression" of living in a society "characterized by what is called class struggle," 26 percent replied that this was indeed their impression, another 42 percent that this was "rather" what they thought. That the percentage of these affirmative answers was highest among communist voters and not much lower among socialists might be expected. But close to 60 percent of conservative voters also shared such feelings.[27]

In the Third Republic both houses of parliament, made up of the defenders of small business and the family farms, delayed social legislation for so long that the much decried reforms of the Popular Front in 1936 did little more than catch up with developments in other industrialized countries. Protectionism, slow economic growth, and the resulting difficulties in obtaining credit were not propitious for the social promotion of workers. Nor were they apt to instill in the worker an esteem for the functioning of the capitalist system.[28]

---

[26] SOFRES, *L'Opinion . . . 1977*, p. 107.

[27] Capdevielle, *France de gauche*, p. 251.

[28] See Val Lorwin, "Reflections on the History of the French and American Labor Movement," *Journal of Economic History* 17, no. 1 (1957): 25–44.

TABLE I. *Class Feelings in French Society*

The question, "To which class do you belong?" elicited the following self-classifications (listed by percentages):*

	Bourgeoisie	Middle class	Working class	Paysannerie (agricultural)	Other
Total	5	34	40	13	8
Sex					
Men	3	29	45	16	7
Women	7	40	36	9	8
Age					
18–24	9	29	40	11	11
25–34	6	38	36	9	11
35–49	3	28	46	15	8
50–64	3	38	41	13	2
65 and over	5	36	38	13	8
Occupation of Head of Family					
Farmers and agricultural workers	—	12	8	70	10
Shopkeepers and craftsmen	4	52	23	2	20
Executives, industrialists, professionals, businessmen	23	59	9	—	9
Middle management, technicians, and middle-range civil servants	9	61	25	—	5
White-collar workers	1	46	44	1	8
Workers	—	19	76	—	—

TABLE I (continued)

Political Preference	Bourgeoisie	Middle class	Working class	Paysannerie (agricultural)	Other
Communist Party	—	11	82	1	6
Socialist Party	4	35	47	6	8
Conservative parties	10	43	20	19	8

* All respondents had already indicated that they felt they belonged to a social class.

Source: SOFRES, L'Opinion Française en 1977 (Paris: PFNSP, 1978), p. 108. Used by permission.

As a reaction, the industrial working class, numerically weak by comparison with other countries, developed in the midst of bourgeois society a counterfaith appropriately called *ouvriérisme:* workers should never entrust their defense to members of the bourgeoisie, not even to those who in parliament mouthed the cause of socialism; to send workers into parliament was acting the part of a mother who sold her daughters into a house of prostitution. Deprived of expectations of individual social promotion, the proletariat was reduced to harboring apocalyptic dreams of collective emancipation. At the end of the last century, the ugly working-class suburbs of Paris and the elegant *beaux quartiers* of the capital had become symbols of two hostile civilizations facing each other.[29]

The sense of belonging and being loyal to a class has long been matched by a generalized lack of communication between the classes. Sensibility to social precedence, rather than deference, and a spontaneously produced particularism of collective behavior led to far greater differences in the style of living than the disparity in financial means would have warranted. Eating places, cafés, weddings, dances, and funerals cater even today to different classes and have different rites. They are manifestations of separateness, rarely of common folklore.

The deep fissure between bourgeoisie and working class has molded the social history of the country for more than a century. Such problems as church-state relations have invited temporary political alignments between parts of the middle classes and the proletariat. Nonetheless the struggle between the classes was the more permanent fact and has resulted in antagonistic values and beliefs, i.e., a divided political culture with different symbols, flags, and holidays. The legislation and policies of the Third Republic evoked rather than compensated for the memories of the working-class massacre in

[29] The isolation of the working class during that period is described in Maurice Halbwachs, *La Classe ouvrière et les niveaux de vie* (Paris: Alcan, 1913). For more recent views on the question of a separate working-class culture, see René Kaës, *Images de la culture chez les ouvriers français* (Paris: Éditions Cujas, 1968).

1848 and especially of the bloody and revengeful suppression of the Paris *Commune* in 1871.

The opinion polls we have quoted indicate that the recent economic and social transformations, massive though they are, have so far failed to eradicate subjective feelings about class differences and class antagonism. Are they justified by the existing structure of society? The degree of upward mobility — the facility of moving from one class to another — has always been an important criterion for the rigidity of class stratification. For the individual Frenchman it has long been true that, partly because of the prevalent egalitarian ideology, classes had the function not only of serving as barriers but also of leveling.[30] Once an individual has overcome the obstacles that barred his access to a higher class, his humble origin will be forgiven and forgotten. He usually found that he had obtained more than mere legal equality. The peer group not only exercised pressure to obtain a degree of outward conformity, it also granted protection by insisting that its members, new or old, be accorded that *considération* (esteem) which creates the desired barriers against lower classes. Although this particular pattern of stratification was initiated by the elite group of a bourgeois society, it shaped relations between other social classes and categories.

If in the past social ascension has been possible for the talented individual, did social mobility become more general now that the structure of France has come to resemble in many respects that of its neighbors?[31] If one regroups, as newer studies have done, the categories long familiar in French sociology (and used in Table I) into the elite, the middle classes, and the "popular classes" (the latter comprising workers and farmers), one finds a certain fluidity between the middle

---

[30] The problem is described in these terms and with interesting though partially dated details by Edmond Goblot, *La Barrière et le niveau, étude sociologique de la bourgeoisie française moderne* (Paris: Alcan, 1925), see esp. pp. 4, 6, 16. For recent inquiries see Alain Girard, *La réussite sociale en France: ses caractères, ses lois, ses effets* (Paris: PUF, 1961) and Claude Durand, "Mobilité sociale et conscience de classe," in *Le Partage des bénéfices*, ed. Darras (Paris: Éditions de Minuit, 1966), esp. pp. 275–93.

[31] See Hoffmann, "Conclusion," in *The Fifth Republic,* Andrews and Hoffmann, p. 451.

classes and the elite and between the popular and the middle classes. There is little transition from the lowest to the highest group; social promotions usually proceed from the higher ranks of one category to the lower ranks of the next higher and stop there.[32] (Why hopes that an expansion of educational opportunities would accelerate mobility have so far been disappointed will be discussed below.)

Until now neither the somewhat greater fluidity between classes nor the substantial changes in life style made possible by the consumer society have eradicated the feelings and the practices of separateness. To the question of whether class-bound subcultures do in fact survive, one of the foremost students of class stratification has replied: "Decidely — yes!" [33]

Other observers have pointed out that it is necessary (and in France probably more so than in other modern industrial societies) to distinguish between the spheres of consumption and of production.[34] As a consumer, the worker has ceased to live apart or in a class ghetto; once he leaves the factory he may no longer regard himself as a worker. But as a producer, the fundamental characteristics which have always distinguished the working class from other social strata have remained unchanged, or at any rate are perceived as unchanged: hierarchism, inequality, and an authoritarian style are resented as before.

Separateness is not only experienced by the working class. For the middle classes the life style of the upper bourgeoisie might occasionally be the subject of envy; it is not imitated. The elite is conscious of living in its own gilded ghetto and knows that it lacks sufficient contact with outsiders. Intermarriage between members of different classes remains relatively rare.

[32] On one of these studies and its result, see Gérard Vincent, *Les Français 1945–1975,* pp. 287–89.

[33] Jacques Lautman, "Où sont les classes d'antan?" in *La Sagesse,* Mendras, p. 96. His entire essay (pp. 81–99) is important for the problems discussed here. See also the masterly study by Pierre Bourdieu, *La Distinction. Critique sociale du jugement* (Paris: Editions Minuit, 1979).

[34] Serge Mallet, *La nouvelle classe ouvrière* (Paris: Seuil, 1963), pp. 9, 31, and 32; André Andrieux and Jean Lignon, *L'Ouvrier d'aujourd'hui* (Paris: Rivière, 1960), p. 189 and passim. For a comparative discussion see also T. B. Bottomore, *Classes in Modern Society* (New York: Pantheon, 1966).

Yet Frenchmen are confident that the future will be different. At the time (1977) when 68 percent described themselves as members of a social class, 60 percent thought that "little by little manual workers and white-collar employees will integrate with other groups in something like a large middle class." Workers believed in such a development almost to the same extent as others, though members of the upper middle classes were most sanguine about the lessening of class divisions.[35] Could it all be a matter of time?

ASSOCIATIONS

Many observers, the great nineteenth-century French sociologist Durkheim among them, have deplored France's lack of secondary groups organized for some common purpose standing between the state and the individual and able "to drag them [the citizens] into the general current of social life." [36] A bias against authority might have encouraged association if the egalitarian thrust and the competition between individuals did not cast suspicion on those who recommended that efforts be combined. The ambivalence toward participation in group life was not merely negativistic apathy, but due to a lack of belief in the value of cooperation.

During the first years of the Gaullist republic, concentration on rebuilding and legitimizing the institutions of the state did harm to all intermediary organizations. Frenchmen turned their backs on parties, trade unions, and associations as well.[37] When politics became more normal and economic activity rewarding, the situation changed to the extent that one now speaks about an "association explosion." Figures are deceptive and not a meaningful way to assess the social significance of the movement. One high official in the Giscard administration, which was generally given to praising the virtues of "associative

35 SOFRES, *L'Opinion . . . 1977,* p. 110.

36 Emile Durkheim, *The Division of Labor in Society* (New York: Macmillan, 1933, originally published in 1893), p. 28. Characteristically enough the "bourgeois" professor ignored the rather numerous singing, drinking, and theatrical societies which catered to the artisans and highly skilled workers of an only half-industrialized society.

37 See François Dupuy and Jean-Claude Thoenig, "Le Marchandage régulateur," in *La Sagesse,* Mendras, pp. 352–53.

democracy," stated that every other Frenchman belonged to an association; others have spoken about 300,000 to 500,000 existing organizations and of 35,000 new ones entering the field every year. A 1977 opinion poll gives a more sober picure: 61 percent of the men and 43 percent of the women in a representative panel belonged to at least one association. These figures do not account for likely multiple memberships but reveal that, as in other countries, the urban upper middle class are most involved in associational life (76 percent as against 49 percent of workers).[38]

There are uncertainties about the role of associations, old and new, in the socialization process of individuals. To which extent do they determine activities and emotions of the citizens? Some observers seem to confirm that membership in French organizations involves less actual participation than in American or British organizations and hence has less impact on social and political attitudes.[39] But generalizations are difficult because of the wide range of activities in which associations engage and because of the different membership which they attract. There are also regional variations, as for instance between two cities of comparable size such as Lille and Grenoble, where an entirely different style of associational life has developed. Some would consider a statement by one of the foremost French observers of organizational life as too sweeping and too optimistic: "What characterizes all these organizations is the need to make contact between category and category, between spiritual family and spiritual family, the horror of a priori formulas and systems, the passion for reform and the ideology of participation." [40] Whether associations will be able

[38] See the debate presided over by the then Undersecretary for Social Action, René Lenoir, "La Participation des citoyens à la vie sociale," *Projet* 107 (July–August 1976): 757–99; Olivier Duhamel, *La Gauche et la Ve République* (Paris: PUF, 1980), p. 121; and SOFRES, *L'Opinion . . . 1977*, pp. 172–73.

[39] See Eric Nordlinger, "Democratic Stability and Instability: The French Case," *World Politics* 18, no. 1 (1965): 127–57.

[40] Michel Crozier, "The Cultural Revolution: Notes on the Changes in the Intellectual Climate of France," in *The New Europe,* ed. Stephen R. Graubard (Boston: Houghton Mifflin, 1964), p. 624.

to fulfill this "passion" and this "ideology" will obviously determine their success or failure in concrete situations and in the long run as well.

In a highly centralized state such as France, the role of a mediator between the public authorities and the citizens is more than elsewhere thrust on associations. The more independent the mediator, the greater his chances for success. This would require that on the one hand association activities are self-sustaining, and on the other that they are given free rein to assume functions which public authorities cannot or do not perform in satisfactory fashion. On both grounds French associative life encounters special difficulties. Long accustomed to arrangements by which the paternalistic state attends to community needs, the membership is little inclined to provide financial support for association activities. The idea of making contributions tax-exempt has been rejected almost universally, since it is feared that in a country of low tax morale the likely outcome would be more tax evasion. Hence the associations must turn for help to fiscal or parafiscal sources and thereby possibly lose their independence. Where associations wish to play a role in the desirable decentralization of administrative activities, they often meet with the resistance not only of the state bureaucracy but also of local authorities; the latter might be all the more unwilling to relinquish functions traditionally assigned to them, since their powers and privileges are altogether too limited (see Chapter IV).[41]

A fairly recent experience might serve as an example. As a reaction against the virtual exclusion of citizens from participation in municipal affairs, the *Groupes d'Action Municipale* (GAM) had been formed in about one hundred cities and towns. They are both citizens' associations and civic pressure groups trying to steer free of party affiliations. Their information campaigns extend to the communities surrounding a city; they organize hearings before the municipal councils even where this means overcoming resistance; they are engaging in

[41] See the observations by Stanley Hoffmann, "Conclusion," in *The Fifth Republic*, Andrews and Hoffmann, p. 476.

cultural activities and have been quite successful in overcoming civic apathy.[42] In Grenoble the lists which the GAM presented won municipal elections twice. But in Grenoble and elsewhere the established parties and local officials have since taken over not only the ideas but also some of the personnel of the associations. Whether or not such institutionalization improved the quality of local government, it deprived the GAM of its initial purpose of serving as a vehicle for citizen participation and socialization.

Some critics regret that the present plethora of associations results often in a dispersion of efforts and a loss of prestige. Where the associations try to emulate, as they sometimes do, the existing cooperative movement, they often inherit a bureaucratic apparatus. The needed balance between public regulation and spontaneous activity by the association is not always found.

Yet the gains outweigh the observed shortcomings.[43] Many now regard associations as necessary and normal elements of modern society rather than as "movements" or standard bearers of a cause. If such attitudes were to be accepted widely, associational life might furnish a far more important contribution than heretofore to the learning process of elites and of common men.

EDUCATION

Education is the foremost process by which a community preserves and transmits its values and purposes. At a dramatic moment of its history, France was ruled by a man who recognized the central significance of education for the perpetuation of his values. Well into the second half of the twentieth century, the French educational system has remained an imposing

[42] For a full account of the GAM experience, see Peter A. Gourevitch, *Paris and the Provinces; The Politics of Local Government Reform in France* (Berkeley: University of California Press, 1980), pp. 165–73.

[43] For a penetrating discussion of the shoals and opportunities of the associative movement, see François Bloch-Lainé, "Pour le progrès des associations," *Pour* 74 (December 1980): 1–71. The author, one of the most respected high civil servants in postwar France, is now the president of the Association for the Development of Associations.

historical monument — in the unmistakable style of the First Empire.

The edifice that Napoleon I erected integrated education at all levels, from primary school to postgraduate professional training, both public and private, into one centralized and strictly structured corporation: *the* imperial university. Its function was to teach the "national doctrine." "My main purpose," Napoleon was reported to have said, "is to have a means of controlling political and moral opinion." According to him, the teachers were to have the Jesuit mentality, but that of secularized Jesuits free from Rome and devoted solely to defending the public interest. A "grand master" presided over the entire institution; he ensured the uniformity of programs at the various levels and the conformism of students and teachers at all levels. The development of secondary education and the training of its teachers became a particular and personal concern of Napoleon. The lycées and collèges, selecting their pupils at an early age, were invaluable in recruiting the elites for a regime unwilling to rely solely on privilege or birth. Both an egalitarian temper and the need to develop rapidly a nontraditional loyalty shaped the structure and the program of these training grounds for the future servants of civil and military society. Enforced by strict military discipline, enlivened only by vulgar patriotism, an otherwise deliberately abstract instruction used Latin, rhetoric, logic, and mathematics as vehicles for molding what was called the "cultivated" mind.[44]

Succeeding regimes have loosened disciplines; the outwardly military style has disappeared; the tides of clerical and anticlerical influence have advanced and receded. But whether imperial, royal, or republican, all regimes discovered that the machinery created by Napoleon was an admirably convenient

---

[44] For the description of the napoleonic origins of the system and of its later development see Hippolyte Taine, *Les Origines de la France contemporaine: le régime moderne*, vol. II (Paris: Hachette, 1894), pp. 153 ff. The legislation which determined the actual organization of the universities dates only from the end of the nineteenth century. See Antoine Prost, *L'Enseignement en France, 1800–1967* (Paris: Armand Colin, 1968), pp. 235 ff.

and coherent instrument for dispensing both changing and permanent values of French civilization. Hence the centralized imperial university has never been dismantled. The "grand master" is nowadays the minister of national education. Through government-appointed rectors he commands the twenty-three academies into which the country is divided for purposes of educational administration. An army of more than 800,000 is on his ministry's payroll, more than 80 percent of them teachers, all the way from those employed by nursery schools to professors in institutions of advanced higher learning.

Habits of centralization and devotion to a special kind of egalitarian ideology feed on each other and mark many teachers of all ranks in the public education system. The curriculum and teaching methods, the criteria for the selection and the advancement of pupils and teachers, the content of examinations, and the perpetual changes of all of the foregoing continue to be centrally imposed, usually by the ministry in Paris. It may no longer be true as it once was that the minister can determine merely by looking at his watch which verse of Vergil is being translated in all third-year Latin classes of the realm. But in the Fifth Republic, to give a present-day example, the songs used to recruit voice teachers in all public schools are still designated annually by ministerial ordinance. Such centralization leaves little room for administrative, cultural, or pedagogic initiative at any level. Local authorities, educational associations, parent-teacher organizations, and especially the powerful teachers unions are active as legitimate interest groups. But until recently they left the discussion and determination of educational policies to the administrative hierarchy.

The practice of making the individual's advancement at every step dependent on an appropriate examination is not peculiar to France. "An examination," Karl Marx had thundered, "is nothing else but the bureaucratic baptism of knowledge, the official recognition of the transfiguration of profane into sacred knowledge." In France the particularly widespread cult of competitive examinations draws its strength from an obsessive and quite unrealistic belief that everybody is equal before an examination. In one important respect there is little difference between the certificate of studies delivered at the county seat to the fourteen-year-old upon leaving school (this certificate has now been phased out), the *baccalauréat* sanctioning secondary studies, the senselessly specialized *agrégation* needed for a professorship, or the various *concours* by which the elite of the nation is selected: success or failure in the examination shake not only the candidate and his family but the entire milieu to which he belongs. The walls of many cathedrals are hung with votive tablets imploring or thanking the Virgin Mary for assistance in examinations. French society is strewn with individuals to which failure or a lower than expected rank have inflicted irreparable psychological damage. Some rigidities of earlier times may have been overcome, but a voluntarily centralized and anonymous system still offers little opportunity to judge candidates by any other performance than their oral or written answers in an examination and the jury's appreciation of them.

On the other hand, there is no mechanism to ensure or control a continuing high performance once the prize is won. This may result in increased bureaucratic rigidity and, in the educational system, intellectual sclerosis. Moreover, the seemingly egalitarian process of selection frequently hides outright corporatist practices, such as the long-practiced, though now officially abandoned, co-optation of university professors by secret faculty ballot.

Altogether it would be wrong to assume that the educational system is tyrannical because it is so vastly different from the schools and universities that train for the "civic culture" in England and the United States. Beginning with Napoleon's times, the centralization of authority in a far-removed national government has often resulted in a wholesome weakening of controls and in a lessening of community pressures which because of their closeness might have become offensive. Since the demise of the Empire, there has developed within the framework of uniform rules considerable freedom of expression in the classrooms and lecture halls. Such freedom was backed early by generous tenure rules which satisfied both libertarian and egalitarian conventions. Education as an effective weapon for emancipation and social betterment has been more than an official ideology — farmers' and workers' families regard the instruction of their children (and a better instruction than they had) as an important weapon for fighting "them," which includes the authorities organizing the instruction. In the past, the moving of rural youth into the ranks of elementary school teachers has been of great importance for a two-step social promotion.

The French child and adolescent is trained primarily in those arts of living which profit the critical and civilized individual who is an island unto himself. France is the country with the highest nursery school enrollment in the world, and many of these schools are excellent. But even a first-grader might be compelled to "repeat" his first year in school, because already at that level the system is out to test the pupil's capacity to absorb the knowledge imparted to him rather than to train him how to acquire knowledge. A vivid and sometimes quite ruthless competitiveness isolates the child from his fellow students. The generally authoritarian stance of his instructors is not conducive to warmth in the teacher-pupil relationship, and the mutual fear of the face-to-face relationship determines the climate of many classrooms. Rote learning rather than insight into the learning process, a minimum of oral discussion and hence passivity on the part of the students, in the secondary schools, at least, an almost undiminished emphasis on rhetoric and logical presentation, are still widely accepted pedagogic methods.

Neither French parents nor French teachers seem to be inclined to worry whether or not the atmosphere in the classrooms and some of the pedagogical methods used have a traumatic effect on children.[45] In 1978 a representative panel was

45 There exists no more accurate picture of the typical French classroom than the one provided by the rightly celebrated film *Les 400 coups*. For a more learned portrayal see William R. Schonfeld, *Youth and Authority in France: A Study of Secondary Schools* (Beverly Hills: Sage, 1971). For a vivid comparative treatment see Laurence Wylie, "Youth in France and the U.S.," in *Youth: Change and Challenge*, ed. Erik Erikson (New York: Basic Books, 1963), pp. 243–60. Also excellent is the chapter devoted to "Children" in Theodore Zeldin, *France 1848–1945*, vol. I (Oxford: Clarendon Press, 1973), pp. 315–42.

asked to decide between two propositions: whether schools should communicate "most of all a sense of discipline and of work" or whether they should develop in children "open and critical faculties." Sixty percent of the respondents preferred the first, only 35 percent the second alternative. Voters of the Left took a more liberal attitude than those of the Right, but even 54 percent of socialist voters rated discipline higher than creativity. In another recent poll 67 percent expressed opposition to any decentralization of the school system and of the curriculum.[46] The very strong, socialist-oriented National Teachers Union and its membership of over half a million are known for preferring the status quo.

A French social psychologist has described the causes and consequences of these educational and intellectual traditions in revealing terms:

> [The Frenchman's] love of clarity results simultaneously from a certain laziness which turns him away from a deeper search and complications; from a desire never to be fooled and from the example set by an elite group which has been trained for two millennia by the exercises of composition and by dialectics. The love for order is in the classical tradition: the Romans have imparted it to the Gauls, the lasting influence of the rhetors, the Justinian and Aristotelian renaissance, humanism, the Jesuit program, and later the [Napoleonic] University have reinforced ancient traditions. The qualities of the French mind are a precious gift for the entire world. . . . The risk is that taken altogether, a certain superficiality neglecting the shadowy zones of thought simplifies decisions excessively or complicates them by an excess of abstract logic. It sometimes resolves a difficulty with an elegant sally.[47]

The role of the schools in that particular form of socialization which trains either directly or indirectly for citizenship has varied over time. In the early days of the Third Republic,

[46] See Capdevielle, *France de gauche*, p. 254, and SOFRES, *L'Opinion . . . 1977*, pp. 171, 175.

[47] Gabriel Le Bras, "Psychologie de la France," *Revue de psychologie des peuples* (1952), quoted here from Michel Beaujour and Jacques Ehrmann, *La France contemporaine* (New York: Macmillan, 1965), p. 70.

and especially during its period of virulent anticlericalism, the government had no difficulty in relying on the teacher for the propagation of the rationalistic, positivistic faith. In all classrooms, but particularly in those of the countryside, such teaching was also imbued with an emotional patriotism that drew its strength from anti-German feelings, and from the belief that France remained the epitome of civilized humanity. The revered history textbooks of the period were almost disarmingly ethnocentric. For many a young Frenchman they provided an early introduction to the dichotomy of an abstract, ideal *patrie* and a frequently despised government, of a country in whose defense one was willing to die but whose political institutions were considered badly suited to daily life. After the horrors of the First World War the teachers in the public schools turned from patriotism to internationalism and pacifism. An entire generation, especially of rural youth, bore the impact of such convictions imparted to them.

In the classical curriculum of the secondary schools, citizenship training has always been as alien as any empirical social science. History instruction usually combines stress on humanistic values with resigned determinism. "Civic instruction," as prescribed by ministerial directives, has generally been turned into a farce. Most decisive, however, is the fact that the human climate and the educational atmosphere are isolating and therefore in essence anticivic.

In the early seventies a European-wide inquiry pointed to the social consequences of the prevailing system:

> . . . by and large, all students, however different their backgrounds or needs, have been measured on a single scale of talent and achievement. Since this scale of talent and achievement has reflected the perspective and life style of one particular class, the paradoxical consequence, in practice of the pursuit of legal equality, has been the perpetuation of class differences and inequalities.[48]

[48] Organization for Economic Co-operation and Development, *Reviews of National Policies for Education: France* (Paris: OECD, 1971), p. 23. The "particular class" in question is of course the bourgeoisie or, in American terms, the upper middle class.

In terms of numbers the increase in students at the secondary level and in higher education has been phenomenal. The secondary schools, which at the beginning of the century trained 200,000 and only 700,000 as late as 1945, now provide instruction for close to 5 million. Between 1958 and 1977 the number of students in higher education rose from 170,000 to 850,000. After the compulsory school age had been raised to 16 years, 55 percent of adolescents between 15 and 18 years of age were in school in 1977, a much larger proportion than in Great Britain and West Germany, though still substantially smaller than in the United States. It was hoped and expected that broadening access to education would increase social mobility and further the democratization of society. Whether so far this goal has been achieved is controversial.

Recent educational reforms have acknowledged that style and teaching methods of the traditional secondary school, the lycée, put even the most gifted children who came from other than the bourgeois milieu at a disadvantage. The dropout rate of children from modest backgrounds, talented enough to be admitted to the lycée, was many times that of upper middle class children.[49] Now the secondary schools more resemble the American high school, and the transition from a technical to a college preparatory curriculum is facilitated. Yet the class stratification within the schools and between the more or less prestigious secondary schools is by no means abolished. It might, however, be too early to assess the full impact of the reforms.

Table II illustrates the continuing disparities in the class composition of the student body. Actually there has been over the last years a steady if slow increase of university students from working-class and farmers' families. On the other hand in some of the *grandes écoles* (to be discussed later in this chapter), schools that are strategically important for the training of the country's political and administrative elites, the students

[49] See Raymond Poignant, *L'Enseignement dans les pays du marché commun* (Paris: Institut Pédagogique National, 1965), p. 105. For an excellent and many-sided inquiry into attitudes of secondary school students, see Gérard Vincent, *Le Peuple Lycéen: enquête sur les élèves de l'enseignement secondaire* (Paris: Gallimard, 1974).

TABLE II. Social Origins of Students (in percentages)

	Farmers	Agricultural workers	Employers in trade and industry	Shopkeepers and craftsmen	Professions, management, and high civil service	Lower civil service and middle management	White-collar workers	Manual workers	Service personnel	Diverse other categories
Social origin of students enrolled in Universities	5.1	0.4	10.4	—	30.3	15.5	8.5	11.3	0.8	17.7
Social origin of students at the ENA (see p. 164) (1970–1975)	3.6	—	6.8	5.9	48.5	19.7	9.7	5.6	—	—
% in the total labor force (1978)	7.6	1.7	1.1	6.7	7.0	12.7	19.2	37.7	5.7	0.5

Sources: Universities — Gérard Vincent, Les Français, 1945–1975 (Paris: Masson, 1977). ENA — Gérard Vincent, Les Français, 1976–1979 (Paris: Masson, 1980). Total Labor Force — Daniel Gaxie, "Les Logiques du recrutement politique," RFSP 30, no. 1 (February 1980): 25. Used by permission.

are now more exclusively of bourgeois origin than they were during the immediate postwar years.[50]

Even for the universities the statistics do not reveal the difficulties that continue to hinder social promotion. Because of the principle of open admission, every holder of the *baccalauréat* (now close to one-fourth of the age group) can theoretically gain entrance to a university. But there is, as in some American state universities, a rather ruthless elimination at the end of the first year and sometimes later. Here again students of lower class background fare worse. A survey of academic disciplines reveals that the number of students from such backgrounds is disproportionately great in fields whose diplomas have the lowest value in the professional market and where unemployment is greatest.[51] Other inquiries show that in the same field not "all diplomas are equal": a higher social background might further professional advancement more than performance in final examination.[52] Of course this is not only true in France, but in France such an outcome runs against widely held expectations about the equalizing effects of education. The reformers are finding out that to change a society more might be needed than merely to change the educational system.

The most ambitious attempt ever made to reform a university system at one stroke was made during the last year of de Gaulle's presidency in the wake of the "events" of 1968, as the student rebellion of that year and the ensuing mass strikes

[50] The important question of the social composition of the French student population has been discussed at length in the writings by Pierre Bourdieu. See especially his "L'École conservatrice: les inégalités devant l'école et devant la culture," *Revue Française de Sociologie* 7, no. 3 (1966): 325–47; also Pierre Bourdieu and Jean-Claude Passeron, *Les Héritiers: les étudiants et la culture* (Paris: Éditions de Minuit, 1964), most valuable are the tables on pp. 126–79; and, with yet more recent data showing relatively little change, P. Bourdieu and J.-C. Passeron, *La Reproduction: éléments pour une théorie du système d'enseignement* (Paris: Éditions de Minuit, 1970). These writings have been criticized for arguing from too short a time span.

[51] See Vincent, *Les Français 1976–1979* (Paris: Masson, 1980), p. 149; Stanley Hoffmann, "Conclusion," in *The Fifth Republic*, Andrews and Hoffmann, p. 470.

[52] See Pierre Birnbaum et al., *La Classe dirigeante française* (Paris: PUF, 1978), p. 116.

are still referred to. (For a fuller discussion of this episode, see Chapter VII.)

In the midst of turmoil President de Gaulle had attributed the crisis of the university to the inability of those in charge "to adapt themselves to the modern necessities of the nation"; he pledged that the system of higher education would be "reconstructed not according to centuries-old habits, but in line with the actual needs of the country's development."

Backed by the president, the minister of national education, Edgar Faure, elaborated over opposition from many quarters and in record time a comprehensive reform law. Not a single member of parliament dared oppose it, although it was well known that the forthrightness of the reform ran counter to the preferences of many members of the Gaullist majority — not a good omen for the success of the reform.[53]

The new law, laying down broad principles rather than detailed regulations, was intended to create an autonomous university system and thereby to undo the Napoleonic structure. France now has a total of 73 universities (13 of which are located in the Paris region) and about 700 *Unités d'Enseignement et de Recherche (UER)*. The latter correspond roughly to the academic departments in an American university and have replaced the sometimes monstrously large *Facultés* which had been criticized as an administrative impediment both to closer student-faculty relations and to interdisciplinary exchanges. At the university as well as at the level of the UER, councils, composed of elected faculty, student, and staff representatives, were to control all educational matters and to report to the president of the university, a newly created institution. The president himself is elected by the University Council and, although in need of ministerial confirmation, was to have broad discretionary powers in his relations with the Ministry of Education.

The reform legislation hoped to inaugurate the autonomy of each university, the participation of teachers, students, and

[53] For a good summary of the complicated law, see *Année Politique 1968* (Paris: PUF, 1969), pp. 367 ff. The author of the law has furnished an interesting explanation of its motivation, in Edgar Faure, "Loi d'orientation: les idées derrière les textes," *Preuves* (3e Trimestre 1970): 92–99.

staff in the running of the university, and the collaboration between academic disciplines. Almost from the beginning many of those on whom a successful reform depended were determined to frustrate it. The professorial staff had its "emigrés and legitimists" who were fundamentally opposed to the new order.[54] Students boycotted the elections to the university councils: the radicals denounced them as a sham and a fraud; the majority abstained from voting at an ever-increasing rate out of indifference for a flawed experiment in participatory democracy.

Administrative autonomy remained fragmentary as long as the ministry held the financial purse strings. A widespread malaise led in 1976 to another student strike, which was a reason, or a pretext, for the newly created Ministry of Higher Education to withdraw from the universities most of whatever autonomy still existed. During the last years of the Giscard administration governmental interference not only with university administration but also with educational policies and examinations was described as more excessive than ever. Students no longer resisted the trend toward uniform requirements because in an economic recession the equal valuation of all university degrees had become all-important to them.

From all that has been said, it should not be concluded that nothing has changed in the lecture halls and seminar rooms. New methods were tried before 1968 and continue to be practiced. Reform proposals informed by past experiences and by the failure of the Faure law are being put forward by prestigious professors who, however, do not conceal their present despair.[55] The socialist Minister of Education, appointed in 1981, has abolished the special Ministry for the Universities so as to demonstrate his preference for a unified system of education at all levels. How the newly proclaimed goals of autonomy for the universities will be achieved remains to be seen. In the

[54] See René Rémond, *La Règle et le consentement* (Paris: Fayard, 1978), pp. 41, 422–62. This book by one of the most reform-minded professors and one-time president of the University of Nanterre (Paris) is at once an eyewitness report and a profound reflection on recent developments.

[55] See Association Universitaire pour l'Entente et la Liberté, *Pour que l'Université ne meure . . .* (Paris: Le Centurion, 1977), and Marcel Merle (one of the coauthors of the above book), "L'Université en liberté surveillée," *La Croix* (January 15–16, 1980).

terms of a report published by the French Council of State: "Between the napoleonic centralization and the Anglo-Saxon autonomy, the university has not yet chosen. It moves away from the former because it considers it obsolete . . . but it does so without having the courage to undertake the adventure of the latter." [56]

The so-called *grandes écoles,* one sector of higher education, have escaped much of the criticism directed against the universities; at any rate they have not been subjected to large-scale reforms. These schools exist in various regions of France, but the most prestigious are all located in the Paris area. At a time when universities have seen their enrollment multiply (in the case of Paris by a factor of fourteen), the grandes écoles have hardly increased the number of their students (a total of about 67,000), who are admitted upon strict entrance examinations; the rate of admissions varies between 9 and 19 percent of applicants. The teacher-student ratio is about 1 to 10, while there are still hundreds in some university lecture halls. For more than a century the best of the grandes écoles have been the training ground of highly specialized elites. The schools prepare for many careers, among others for those in engineering of various kinds, in business management, and in the top ranks of the civil service. Their recruitment of students and of teaching staffs as well as their teaching methods are different from those of the universities. This reflects on the outlook and even on the temperament of many of their graduates. A great number of the graduates of the leading engineering school, the so-called "X," are the sons of alumni of the school. In 1971, 56 percent of its students came from families of professionals, executive managers, or top administrators; 15 percent were the sons of businessmen; 1 percent had working-class fathers. Where university students often face unemployment upon graduation, all graduates of the grandes écoles are immediately placed and often assume positions of great responsibility. That there is little cross-fertilization between the universities, including their

[56] François Gazier and Jacques Robert (the latter one-time president of the University Paris I), "L'Autonomie des Universités," *Conseil d'État, études et documents* 31 (1979–1980): 69. This report offers indispensable source material, both legal and political, on the crisis.

science faculties, and the grandes écoles is an often heard complaint.[57] Yet with the decline in the quality of a university education, which serves a far larger group of students than previously, the grandes écoles appear more indispensable than ever. The Common Program on which the socialist and communist parties agreed in 1972 insisted that these elitist institutions should be integrated with the university system. In his campaign for the presidency in 1981 Mitterrand no longer included this demand in his proposals for educational reforms. The outstanding role which these schools play in the recruitment and training of the country's administrative elites will be discussed in Chapter VI.

With the election of a socialist president of the Republic and of a parliament with a socialist majority, the discussions about the future of the private schools have once more moved into the foreground. Almost all private schools are parochial Catholic schools. Their total student body of close to 2 million children comprises about 16 percent of the total school population, but almost one-fourth of all students in college-preparatory classes attend private schools (the role of Catholic universities is insignificant).

As could be expected from what has been said earlier about the well-defined regionalization of religious practice and of dechristianization, Catholic schools are very unevenly distributed throughout the country. The number of girls enrolled in parochial schools has traditionally been far higher than that of boys. Even in dechristianized working-class families it has not been unusual to entrust the girls' schooling to the nuns while sending the boys, as a matter of course and of principle, to the public schools.

In an opinion poll of 1977 almost two-thirds of the respondents considered the existence of Catholic schools a "very" or "rather important" factor for the functioning of democracy.

---

[57] For a particularly sharp criticism of the grandes écoles, and of the mentality they produce, see Michel Crozier, *The Stalled Society* (New York: Viking Press, 1973), p. 156. A useful discussion of the relationship between universities and grandes écoles is to be found in François Bourricaud, "L'Avenir de l'institution universitaire en France," *Commentaire* II (Autumn 1980): 494–95.

Somewhat astonishing was the fact that 40 percent of the communist and 42 percent of the socialist voters also thought so.[58] If, therefore, the existence of such schools is no longer at stake, as was still the case at the beginning of the century, the question of their status remains open. In the post-war years the allocation of public funds to the parochial institutions which the Catholic community was unwilling to rescue from financial starvation was still discussed in ideological terms. Reopening old wounds, the fight over subsidies, transmitted to parliament by the feuding organized interests, was one of the reasons for governmental instability under the Fourth Republic. In the Fifth Republic, presidential authority was needed to accredit a compromise solution which might not have displeased Napoleon: to receive financial assistance including teachers' salaries and pensions, parochial schools must accept some administrative control by the state and conform to government-set standards. During Pompidou's presidency the fear of antagonizing conservative Catholic voters led to the prolongation of what had originally been envisaged as a temporary solution: rising state subsidies to the Catholic schools continued, but the gradual integration of the parochial school system into state education was postponed indefinitely.[59]

During the 1981 campaign the socialist candidates promised their voters that a socialist government would move farther along on the way to integration or, as it is called, to the nationalization of the private schools. This would presumably not deny the parochial schools the freedom to teach what they wanted, as long as standards are met. The schools would also have the right to select their staff according to their cultural preferences. But the teachers at schools which still wish to receive subsidies would have to become civil servants, rather than remain private employees. What differences this will make compared to the present status is unclear. It appears that the

[58] SOFRES, *L'Opinion . . . 1977*, p. 292.

[59] See Jack Hayward, *The One and Indivisible French Republic* (London: Weidenfeld & Nicolson), pp. 194 ff, and a report on subsequent legislation in Gérard Vincent, *Les Français, 1976–1979*, pp. 149–50. For valuable reflections on the problem of private schools in the general context of French politics, see René Rémond, "Consensus et querelle d'école," *Pouvoirs* 5 (1978): 113–17.

Minister of Education is under contradictory pressures coming from the teachers' unions and from different segments of his party, which is as divided on educational questions as it is on others. The entire problem gains in importance because there is a growing tendency, at least among upper middle-class parents, to send children to private rather than public schools. Catholic authorities note with some concern that the reasons for such preference are often not questions of faith but the search for a better quality of education and for stricter discipline at a time when the mass influx into public schools dilutes the quality of public education.[60] For the socialists this raises the question of whether they should provide state subsidies for schools which become more exclusively schools for the children of the upper bourgeoisie.

CONCLUSION: SOCIALIZATION AND CONSENSUS

Until fairly recently the question has often been asked why a nation whose history has frequently been an inspiration to free peoples everywhere and which is made up of self-reliant, rational, and mature individuals has been unable to establish a stable democracy. The answer to this question may be found in the fact that the values which the individual Frenchman has learned to accept as normal and which many of them cherish have often been in conflict with the needs of a political system combining freedom and authority.

Tensions between the desire to assert the "uniqueness" of the individual and long-time experiences with a centralized bureaucratic control of society have produced ambiguous attitudes toward authority. These attitudes request that strict rulings treat everybody and everything alike in order to minimize possibilities for capricious discretion and discrimination. Since one suspects that the "others" — the authorities or the peers — will flout these rules in the interest of privilege, not willing obedience but only a minimum of commitment, of outward compliance with community rules, can be expected. Hence, again in the words of Michel Crozier, "the disproportion between the authority which seems to us indispensable to gov-

[60] See Vincent, *Français 1976–1979*, pp. 150–51.

ern a human group and the authority that we can accept as members of a group." [61]

The distrust of others as a threat to individual self-fulfill- ment demands the distrust of, indeed wherever possible rebel- lion against, conventions and beliefs established by others. As another French sociologist has remarked: whereas many Ameri- cans believe that self-fulfillment consists in adjustment to a society whose basic values are not challenged, Frenchmen think that man is himself only when he rebels.[62] "I revolt, therefore we are," Albert Camus has written to dramatize the univer- sality of protest. Since much protest is raised in the name of principle, since it is seen as a phase in the struggle against the forces of evil, it is usually highly moralistic.

The insistence on authoritatively enforced rules and the simultaneous distrust of established authority and of the peer group have produced a political culture that expects little from cooperation or a broad-based participation in decision-making. The individual is self-confident enough not to expect strength from cooperation with others. Face-to-face relationships, with- out which no cooperative form of action is possible, are avoided as a possible source of friction. Intransigent insistence on one's own position is regarded as more promising to conflict solution than bargaining. Typically enough, French dictionary defini- tions of the equivalent of bargaining and of compromise are all slightly pejorative. Only the arbiter who forces the conflict- ing parties to accept his verdict for a binding *compromis* earns prestige. It is obvious that such reservations against direct negotiations are likely to perpetuate the estrangement between groups and classes.

The overall result of such mental attitudes has frequently been *incivisme,* that lack of solidarity and of civic sense which many Frenchmen deplore even while they are practicing it. When it resulted in a stalemate which stalled overdue changes, the nation was likely to turn to an authoritarian pacifier to

[61] "La France, terre de commandement," *Esprit* 25, no. 12 (December 1957): 779–97.

[62] Raymond Aron, as quoted by Stanley Hoffmann, "Protest in Modern France," in *The Revolution in World Politics,* ed. M. A. Kaplan (New York: John Wiley, 1962), pp. 69 ff.

solve the crisis. To accredit the solution which he imposes, he will frequently resort to a heroic style which in such a situation appears far more acceptable than the humdrum of laborious bargaining.

In spite of superficial similarities, this setting is not identical with the one in which a people try to be saved from themselves by a totalitarian rule which they are unable to control. Since the confidence which Frenchmen have in themselves as individuals is not impaired, they do not see the need for totalitarian manipulation of their minds. They still distrust their government as well as their neighbors and want to voice their distrust. The freedom left for such criticism and the unwillingness to enforce conformity distinguish the authoritarian from the totalitarian regime. The Fifth Republic under de Gaulle was as little totalitarian as the liberal phase of the Second Empire to which it has been sometimes compared. But, when in 1968, to the greatest surprise of all, and in the midst of prosperity, students, workers, and many others defied not only the government but most established authorities, it became evident that also the Gaullist regime had been unable to get to the roots of the citizens' perennial ambivalence toward authority.

During the ensuing years acute observers have testified to the emergence of a broad consensus whose manifestations should lay to rest the old "myth" of a divided country, fighting forever the battles of the past in a harsh doctrinaire style and resisting the learning process suggested by a modern democratic society. Extensive public opinion data are mustered to demonstrate that a nonsectarian national pride has taken hold; that the existing governmental system is given preference over others; that the basic tenets of foreign and military policy, practiced since the establishment of the Fifth Republic, meet with wide agreement; that good citizenship, evidenced by regular voting and by informing oneself about public affairs, is highly valued. The range of continuing differences and of political partisanship is described as being not greater than in any pluralist system.[63]

---

[63] So with many details, Alain Duhamel, "Le Consensus Français," in SOFRES, *L'Opinion . . . 1977*, pp. 87–115. Jean Ranger, "Les Comporte-

Can such consensus as exists be taken as evidence that attitudes toward authority in the polity and in society at large
have undergone a fundamental transformation and that a
deeply rooted value system has been altered? It has been
pointed out that for all their usefulness public opinion polls
are of dubious value when one wishes to use their data for
testing changes in fundamental orientations. One does not
need to impute to the polls any intended manipulation to acknowledge that they necessarily limit the range of responses
and tend to provoke rational answers without revealing hidden
emotions.[64]

Consensus is never and nowhere spontaneous but rather the
outcome of a complicated socialization process. The foremost
student of traditional French attitudes, Michel Crozier, has
evaluated more cautiously than others the changes that have
occurred:

> During the fifties Frenchmen still subscribed to order and au-
> thority as (dominant) values to be counterbalanced only by a
> strong desire for independence and by the wish to isolate oneself
> systematically from others. At present the values of order and
> authority are on the decline. The need for expression and for
> personal development and the dislike of imposed authority are
> today the prominent values. Certainly the desire for indepen-
> dence remains central. But it no longer requires self-imposed
> isolation. These are different and almost mutually contradictory

---

ments politiques," in Jean-Luc Parodi et al., *La Politique* (Paris: Hachette,
1971), pp. 72–73, believes that many of the attitudes presented as an indication of "consensus" are rather the earmarks of a politically passive citizenry in Western democracies. A comparative study also based on survey
material puts certain regions of France among the lowest of European
regions as regards "satisfaction with life as a whole"; this would be indicative of low rather than high consensus. See Ronald Inglehart, *The Silent
Revolution: Changing Values and Political Styles among Western Publics*
(Princeton: Princeton University Press, 1977), pp. 160–61.

[64] See Patrick Champagne, "Sondages d'opinion et consensus politique,"
Pouvoirs 5 (1978): 93–102. This very critical article is marxist-oriented. But
writing in a similar sense is Robert E. Lane, "The Politics of Consensus
in an Age of Affluence," *American Political Science Review* LIX (1965):
877: "The difficulties of showing change through survey data are substantial." The entire issue of *Pouvoirs* 5 (1978) discusses the notion of "consensus" in the French setting.

sensibilities which must seek accommodation with the old and still weighty constraints. There has been a shock (*ébranlement*), but as yet no important change.[65]

The "old and weighty constraints" with which accommodation must be sought result above all from the ever-presence of the centralized state. "The state is everywhere" is not only true for bankers (see above), but also for farmers, school children and students, for local authorities and private associations, employers and workers. Even after the dislike for face-to-face relationship has been overcome, the state-imposed solution of conflicts is still preferred to one by mutual agreement. But the hegemony of the state is also resented, and sudden revolts, feeding on such resentment, remain possible.

[65] "La Crise des régulations traditionelles," in *La Sagesse,* Mendras, pp. 375–76.

CHAPTER IV

Political Participation

IN A DEMOCRATIC SOCIETY the citizen's participation in the process by which political decisions are made influences both his political socialization and his political recruitment. When he takes part, directly or indirectly, in the selection of candidates for political office, when he votes in local or national elections, he experiences at first hand manifestations of the political system to which he belongs and he thereby undergoes further socialization. By getting involved in this kind of elementary political activity, the citizen also performs a political role and is therefore recruited into the system.

Hence socialization (discussed in the preceding chapter), political participation discussed in this chapter, and the recruitment into active decision-making positions (to be treated in Chapter VI) are tied together by the role which the citizen might play in any or all of these processes.

THE CITIZEN IN LOCAL POLITICS

The concept of "grass roots democracy" is not peculiar to Anglo-American political systems. The notion that a viable democracy must have a solid grounding in democratic institutions at the local level is widespread and generally realistic, even though not always free of illusions about the soundness of the community spirit. "The strength of free nations is rooted in their local governments," Tocqueville has written.

In France, as elsewhere, politics at the local level play a multiple role in the socialization of the citizen. They continue the process of civic education which home and school have begun. They offer possibilities for political participation beyond but including casting a ballot for local officials. They are a vantage point from which the political process can be watched at first hand and without some of the distortions which the observation of distant national politics entails. In many countries, and France among them, the local scene also provides the training ground for the political activist, for those who seek and find fulfillment in local government as well as for those who move on to a wider stage. All of these functions are interconnected. Whether and how effectively local politics can discharge them depends on the place of local government in the institutional framework of the total political system, and on the political culture surrounding both.

A marked characteristic of the French system, centralized though it is, is the great number of local government units.[1] Even after recent consolidations there are 36,393 communes (the basic area of local administration), or about as many as in the original five Common Market countries and Great Britain together. For comparison: there are fewer than 35,000 local school boards in the United States! Almost 35,000 French communes have less than 2,000 inhabitants and of these 22,500 have less than 500. This administrative structure is inherited from the Revolution and Napoleon, and in part goes back to the parishes of the Old Regime. It has survived stubbornly the economic and social transformations which an erstwhile agricultural country has undergone since then. It was deliberately frozen into its present form during the early years of the Third Republic by a legislation that wanted, above all, to provide for stability. In merely quantitative terms, it offers unrivaled opportunities for political socialization and participation. Since every commune is administered by a municipal council elected by universal suffrage and composed of between nine and thirty-

[1] For an excellent and detailed description of local government in its traditional setting, see Brian Chapman, *Introduction to French Local Government* (London: Allen and Unwin, 1953). For an account reporting on the present status and recent changes, see *Local Government in Britain and France: Problems and Prospects,* eds. Jacques Lagroye and Vincent Wright (London: Allen and Unwin, 1979).

seven members,[2] there are almost half a million municipal councillors in France — the equivalent of 1.8 percent of the electorate. At election time at least twice as many candidates are seeking a seat on the councils, and recently 26 percent of respondents in a public opinion poll expressed their willingness to run in municipal elections; from this one could conclude that eight million Frenchmen are interested in municipal office. The extreme fragmentation of local government is illustrated by the fact that three-fifths (300,000) of the municipal councillors serve communities of less than 500 population with a total of six million people; the twelve million living in cities of more than 100,000 are represented by only 1,500 councillors.

The communes are combined into ninety-six departments, an upper-tier unit of local government, created during the Revolution from a desire to give France a uniform and rational structure that would eliminate the dangers of a centrifugal pull by the old provinces.[3] The 3,000 seats on the elective bodies presiding over the department, the *Conseil Général,* opens additional avenues for elective office and, more particularly, for the local notables of the countryside. Until recently rural interests were strongly, indeed predominantly represented in the general councils: often three-fourths of their members were mayors of small communes. In the sixties and seventies urbanization and professionalization had an impact on the composition of the councils: members of the professions, civil servants, and *cadres* (higher and middle management) are now holding more than half of the seats. The composition of the councils has always been significant also because they serve, together with representatives of the municipal councils, as electoral colleges for the upper house of parliament (see Chapter X and Figure II). The success of the local government reform which the socialist administration has announced will, in large part, depend on the competence of the members of the general councils which are to assume a far more important role than previously. (For details see Chapter IX.)

---

2 Only the city councils of Paris, Marseilles, and Lyons are larger.

3 The socialist government has announced that the two Corsican departments will be given a special status outside the departmental setup.

FIGURE II. *The Structure and Levels of French Government (as of 1981)* *

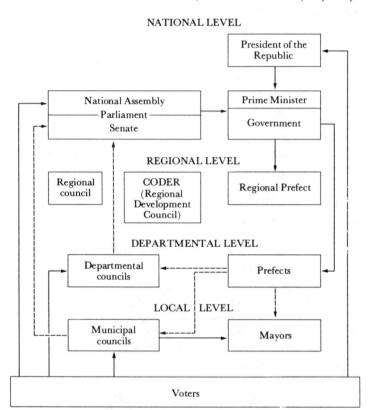

NATIONAL LEVEL

President of the Republic

National Assembly — Parliament — Senate

Prime Minister Government

REGIONAL LEVEL

Regional council

CODER (Regional Development Council)

Regional Prefect

DEPARTMENTAL LEVEL

Departmental councils

Prefects

LOCAL LEVEL

Municipal councils

Mayors

Voters

⟶ Direct election (and censuring) or nomination

- - -▶ Indirect election or "tutelage"

* For pending changes on the regional and departmental level see Chapter IX.

The formal equality bestowed on the local government units recognizes no legal difference between a metropolis and a mountain hamlet, between a department of over 1½ million or one of 71,000 inhabitants. As could be expected, discrepancies have increased considerably since 1789. Yet if there was artificiality when the structure was created, its very age has lent legitimacy to the established units. For citizens' identification, departments and communes have become natural, because traditional, entities of local government upon which to center political attention.[4]

Another characteristic of French local government differs sharply from American and British practice; it also affects fundamentally the roles of all of the main actors on the local political scene. Because of governmental centralization, municipal government possesses no constitutional autonomy beyond the right of existence. All the powers exercised by the local government units are granted by the national government. Such decentralization as is practiced means merely that local officials have the legal right to exercise "their" powers. What these powers actually consist of is determined by the central government.[5] And the manner in which such centrally decreed decentralization is made operational is of great importance. Bureaucratic and representative institutions function side by side; every individual operating on the level of either the department or the commune acts in a dual capacity. Whether they are elected by the citizens, as are the mayors of the communes, or appointed by the minister of interior in Paris as are the administrative heads (the prefects) of the ninety-six departments, their every act is both that of a local government official and that of an agent of the national government. (Whenever the mayor acts in an official capacity, such as marrying the couples appearing before him, he dons the tricolor sash, symbolizing state authority.)

The instrumentality tying together bureaucratic and representative institutions is the "tutelage" (*tutelle*), in principle, and largely also in practice, quite different from the hierarchi-

[4] The problem of citizens' attachment to the department as both an "affirmation and negation of the state" is discussed with great insight by Pierre Grémion, *Le Pouvoir périphérique: Bureaucrates et notables dans les systèmes politiques français* (Paris: Seuil, 1976). The author also reviews the vast sociological literature on French local government. For a study of the past membership of the general councils, see Marie-Helène Marchand, *Les Conseillers Généraux en France dupis 1945* (Paris: Colin, 1970).

[5] See Mark Kesselman, *The Ambiguous Consensus: A Study of Local Government in France* (New York: Knopf, 1967), pp. 171 ff. This work is largely based on excellent direct observations; its material, however, is mostly drawn from small villages and towns. Therefore not all of the author's findings apply to local government authorities in larger municipalities.

cal supervision within a governmental administration. Political tutelage is exercised in two directions: control over the personnel of the decentralized authorities and control over their decisions. As in all democratic regimes the elected local authorities are chosen by the electorate without the intervention of the state; yet under certain conditions they can be dismissed, and, more importantly, their decisions can be annulled as illegal by the prefects to whom they must be submitted for approval.

The level of local taxation is determined by the local councils; but for fear of incompetence and dishonesty local taxes are collected by the central government which permits, among other things, the complete audit of local finances by the national administration. In the total budget of local finances, block grants by the national government are of increasing importance, especially for all long-range investments. A commune that wants to float a loan will in general turn to one of the institutions controlled by the state, since, except for the very large cities, the market for municipal bonds is extremely limited. Even more restricting is the fact that local government authorities are not even expected to finance expenditures of certain local operations. The budgets of all French local government units amount to 19 percent of total public expenditures; in West Germany, the corresponding figure is 25 to 30 percent. Neither education (except for the buildings and for janitorial help) nor the police forces (except for the *garde champêtre*) are financed out of the local budget. This means that local government authorities have little control over these services.

There have been frequent complaints about the prevailing system of finances which has been criticized as obsolete and inimical to economic growth and modernization.[6] A slight modification of the tax structure was the only local government reform which the Giscard administration was able to achieve; its more general projects came to naught.

[6] For a recent critique of the present system of local taxation and for suggestions for reform, see Pierre Uri, *Changer l'impôt (pour changer la France)* (Paris: Ramsay, 1981), pp. 179, 198.

For the smaller communities the existing setup does not regularly result in a slow and impersonal process. For here the partner of the local authorities is not some ministerial bureau in Paris but the prefect, and even more frequently the subprefect, presiding over one of the 317 *arrondissements* into which the 96 departments are divided. It is quite true that in rural regions most initiatives for change come from the prefects, and that all initiatives starting from below become effective only with prefectural approval. But this does not condemn the mayor to passivity. It means rather that the mayor and his staff are expected to bargain incessantly with the authorities of the state for such approval.

The tone of prefectural directives may often be harshly authoritarian, and publicly the mayor will seldom cease complaining about the lack of understanding shown by the representatives of the state; but more often than not relations between local authorities and their partners representing the central government are quite close and cordial. Prefect (or subprefect) and mayor need each other for the successful performance of their tasks. In Paris the worth of a prefect is evaluated according to his ability to preserve public order, and to mediate effectively the conflicting demands of groups and individuals. A modern prefect must use his contacts to persuade, influence, and manipulate, rather than cajole, command, or coerce those who have the capacity to obstruct him in his activities.[7] Here the mayor will prove indispensable. The tutelage authorities value him, and in many cases the members of the departmental councils as well, as a link between the myriad of human problems within every commune and the remote power of the state. As an elected official the mayor provides the democratic legitimation for the initiatives and decisions originating with the central authority and transmitted by its delegate, the

[7] See Jean-Pierre Worms, "Le Préfet et ses notables," *Sociologie du Travail* 8, no. 3 (1966): 249–75; and Jack Hayward, *The One and Indivisible French Republic* (London: Weidenfeld & Nicolson, 1973), p. 24 for an excellent analysis of the role of the modern prefect; see also Sidney Tarrow, "Local Constraints on Regional Reform: A Comparison of Italy and France," *Comparative Politics* 6, no. 1 (1974): 20 ff. for a convincing picture of what the article calls "the integration of the French mayors into the administrative system as a whole."

prefect. As in any relationship based on permanent interaction and on cross-functioning controls, it is not always clear who controls whom in the tutelage system.[8] It is quite understandable that, according to a recent inquiry, 67 percent of local government officials in small communities had high praise for the role played by the prefect. (The feelings of elected officials in urban areas are radically different: only 4 percent see any usefulness in the prefects' role.)[9]

In public opinion polls the mayor or the persons to whom he delegates functions, such as an assistant and especially the town clerk, are usually singled out as the "most important" or the "most useful figure around here," outranking deputies to the national parliament and civil servants. "The mayor remains for Frenchmen an essential element of collective social identification and of political credibility." [10] Interviews have revealed that at least the more energetic mayors think of themselves as aggressive entrepreneurs rather than as bureaucratic technicians or elected notables. In general the other members of the municipal council, although they have elected the mayor from their own midst, are quite content with an at least outwardly rather passive role of leisured notables who regard their election as reward for social status and economic success. For all the informality of local government proceedings, the mayor, even one of humble social status, resembles a local potentate in the midst of his council of elders and vassals. The latters' interests and values are by no means ignored but are taken into account by the mayor.

[8] See Kesselman, *The Ambiguous Consensus,* pp. 66 ff., and pp. 38–52 for an excellent composite "portrait of a mayor." In a carefully documented article, the same author concluded: "The closeness of the relationship [between the mayor and the prefect] stems from a host of common goals and interests. Each wants the kind of legitimacy that the other has the power to grant. . . ." See "Over-Institutionalization and Political Constraint: The Case of France," *Comparative Politics* 3, no. 1 (1970): 32.

[9] See Michel Crozier and Jean-Claude Thoenig, "La Régulation des systèmes organisés complexes: la cas du système de décision politico-administratif local en France," *Revue Française de Sociologie* 16, no. 1 (1975): 17, 21.

[10] François Dupuy and Jean-Claude Thoenig, "Le Marchandage régulateur," in *La Sagesse et le désordre, France 1980,* ed. Henri Mendras (Paris: Gallimard, 1980), p. 353.

This explains why conservative methods, or an acknowledged conservative, are successful even in those communes which otherwise feel and vote to the left. It also explains why, barring a scandal, an incumbent mayor gets reelected as long as he wishes to serve. In a recent municipal election (1977) 84 percent of all incumbents who stood for reelection were in fact reelected. One of the best-known political figures of the Third and Fourth Republics, Edouard Herriot, was mayor of Lyons for forty-five years. There are municipalities where the office of the mayor has remained in the same family for many generations.

Bonds of sympathy between the elected local authorities and their constituents are quite strong. Fifty-eight percent of respondents in a national poll (and 72 percent of socialist voters) are in favor of giving additional powers to the mayors and their municipal councils, which rank highest in popularity among the various local government authorities. The confidence that exists is enhanced by the fact that municipal administration is the natural symbol for a community of local interests which are forever considered threatened by the central government — and frequently also by a neighboring town. The commune thus becomes a bastion manned by the mayor and his "team." Because of the narrow limits within which it must move, the achievements of local government often fall short of expectations. The central government will regularly be blamed for this, and in the next national election the citizen might react by casting a vote of protest against the government. Hence the interest of the citizenry in the affairs of local government, their parochial commitment, can sometimes be disturbing for the stability of the system as a whole. "There exists," French observers have noted, "a local society far richer and more lively than Parisians generally imagine. If its capacity to innovate has been extremely weak, its capacity to resist changes remains extremely strong." [11]

After what has been said, it is not surprising that legislation

11 Pierre Grémion and Jean-Pierre Worms, "La Concertation régionale, innovation ou tradition?" in Institut d'Études Politiques de Grenoble, *Aménagement du territoire et développement régional*, vol. I (Paris: Waltz & Puget, 1968), p. 59.

which wished to encourage the merging of small communities met with almost complete failure. The intended reform hoped to give more vigor to local government by consolidating areas and resources. By their negative response the mayors and other local notables demonstrated their "capacity to resist change." But the state bureaucracy also was unwilling to force such changes on its collaborators in local government. Neither side seemed to have been in sympathy with legislation disrespectful of the "cult of the small." In spite of the incentives offered by the law, the number of existing local authorities was cut by less than 4 percent; little over 7 percent of the total population was affected. (A comparable law in Great Britain led to a decrease from 1,500 to 400 local government units; in West Germany merger legislation has been similarly successful.) By now reformers on both the Left and the Right might still argue for administrative decentralization, but they no longer advocate mergers of existing local governments. Modernization should be achieved by other means.[12]

If one wishes to judge citizens' interest in municipal affairs in terms of their participation in local elections, one encounters great differences between large and small communities. In the latter the vote is as heavy as in national elections, in large cities it is usually light.[13]

Since local government is regarded above all as a dispenser of effective administration and as the focus of communal solidarity, a nonpartisan stance has been fairly widespread both in elections and in the behavior of the elected. The political labels which the candidates wear are quite meaningless. Sometimes the opposing candidates represent mere local factions. Often, lists "For the Defense of Local Interests" are considered more attractive than party lists. They resemble frequently the

[12] See the report on local government reform signed by a prominent Gaullist (Olivier Guichard), Commission de Développement des Responsabilités Locales, *Vivre ensemble* (Paris: Documentation Française, 1976), p. 20, and François Mitterrand, the present socialist President of the Republic, *La Paille et le grain* (Paris: Flammarion, 1975), who criticizes all mergers as "brutalizing history, geography and sensitive bonds" (p. 58).

[13] See also, for some interesting comparative material, Sidney Tarrow, *Between Center and Periphery: Grassroots Politicians in Italy and France* (New Haven: Yale University Press, 1977), pp. 215–16.

"balanced ticket" of an American municipality: representatives of various economic interests and social groups, local notables, sometimes representatives of minority groups are all given a place. In most of the very small communes (with a population of less than 1,000) there is usually only a single list and no opposition. But also elsewhere an incumbent mayor who stands for reelection used to enjoy an almost complete freedom from the institutional restraints which well-organized political parties might place on the selection of candidates and on electoral programs.

By and large not only the elected representatives but also the tutelage authorities take the nonpartisan character of local government at its face value. This explains in part the success of communist-administered communes flourishing under regimes which have for more than twenty years pushed communism to the outer reaches of the political system. If communist mayors complain more frequently that the prefects suspend their decisions and interfere with their projects, this merely indicates that their administrations are trying to break out somewhat more boldly from the narrow confines of French local government.

The price that has to be paid for nonpartisan harmony on the municipal level is, at least in the small rural communities, frequently quite high. A constantly renewed effort not to destroy the consensus often discourages dynamic action and indicates more interest in stability than in progress. Political activity and problem solving are not carried to the marketplace where opposition would have to be faced and where bargaining would have to take place in public. Instead, success and failure depend on personal relations, many of which are hierarchically ordained. Given the fact that willing incumbents can recover their office in election after election and that vivid partisanship is altogether frowned upon, one must conclude that true choice is limited. Even where participation in elections is fairly high, under the circumstances described here, this is not necessarily an indication of an active interest of the citizens in their local affairs.[14]

[14] This is the conclusion reached in an article by Pierre Grémion, "Réforme régionale et démocratie locale," *Projet*, no. 44 (1970): 411–29.

Once the elections are over, the citizenry in many communes pay scant attention to the activities of their local representatives. The meetings of the city council are hardly ever attended by the public. Nothing of importance seems to happen there since most mayors prefer to make decisions and take action behind closed doors. In the larger cities the mayor will require carte blanche from his colleagues on the city council in order to conduct difficult negotiations with the central authorities. There the personalization of the mayor's office becomes even more pronounced. If citizens feel aggrieved they will assemble to protest in front of the buildings housing the prefect or subprefect rather than lay their case before the city council. In fact, local government is "representative" government in the strict sense, which does not permit the electorate to interfere in any way with its work. The rules set by the council are accepted as rulings coming from above, i.e., from the conjunction of the two strong executives: the mayor and the prefect. Such a system is hardly suited to teach citizens the art of solving problems together.

In the local elections of 1977 even many of the smaller communities abandoned the nonpartisan stance. The gain in electoral sympathies by the Left in a series of national and cantonal elections and the bipolarization of party alignments (see Chapter VIII) also gave a more partisan character to elections in towns and villages. Whether this is a passing phenomenon or an indication of more dynamic local politics cannot yet be determined. In a national poll in 1977 not less than 80 percent of the respondents believed that the forthcoming municipal elections were of "great" or "rather great importance" for the country as a whole. The larger the city, the greater was the percentage of those who believed that their vote for the municipal council was "political." In cities over 100,000 they outnumbered the "traditionalists" six to one.[15]

The impact which differences in the political orientation of city government might have on the actual conduct of municipal affairs in larger communities is illustrated by a recent study of two cities of comparable size located in the same region, one

[15] SOFRES, *L'Opinion Française en 1977* (Paris: PFNSP, 1978), p. 36.

under a conservative, the other under a progressive mayor. The study revealed so many outstanding differences in methods, programs, and results of municipal management, that in conclusion the author spoke about "the myth of centralization." [16]

This might be an exaggeration, but in the larger cities, especially in those that are growing rapidly, the traditional system has indeed become meaningless. The equilibrium between local and state power has been destroyed.[17] (The attempts to replace this balance by departmental and regional reforms will be discussed in Chapter IX.) Neither the departmental nor the regional prefects can offer the cities what they need. Their mayors, many of them also influential members of parliament, negotiate directly with the administrative bureaus in Paris, the staffs of the cabinet ministers, and, when needed, with the collaborators of the president of the Republic. These mayors have therefore become kingpins not only of the local but also of the national political system. Their professional association is considered to be one of the most powerful of French interest groups. On the other hand, it is also true that whenever the political situation permits it, cabinet ministers use their own party connections to intervene actively in municipal politics.

This situation has not produced uniformity. The number of municipalities in control of the opposition parties after more than two decades of conservative rule attested to that. But everywhere the involvement of citizens in local affairs remains mediocre as long as drastic reforms have not brought about an effective decentralization (see Chapter IX).[18]

16 See Jerome E. Milch, "Influence as Power: French Local Government Reconsidered," *British Journal of Political Science* 14, no. 2 (1974): 139–61.

17 For an analysis of the system's malfunctioning in larger cities, see L. J. Sharpe, "French Local Government and Society," in *Local Government,* Lagroye and Wright, esp. pp. 77–78, 89–92; and Pierre Grémion, "L'Administration des villes et l'administration des champs," *Projet* 77 (1973): 770–84.

18 For a very critical account of past attempts at reforming local government, see Jean Dumas and Pierre Sadrou, "Le Processus de la réforme communale en France," *Revue française d'administration publique* 17 (January–March 1981): 98–129. For the failure of the reforms encouraged and then abandoned by President Pompidou, see the testimony by the principal Minister concerned, Alain Peyrefitte, *The Trouble with France* (New York: Knopf, 1981), esp. 280 ff.

VOTING IN PARLIAMENTARY ELECTIONS

Writing in 1910, Alain, philosopher-preceptor of classical French republicanism, stated that election day had only one significance: the citizen designated the deputy best suited to resist the ever-encroaching power of the central government. Parliament was not there to launch reforms which in the end would only result in more infringements upon the rights of the individual. Its mandate was rather to submit to the authorities, like the States-General on the eve of the French Revolution, the citizens' complaints against unending arbitrariness.[19]

As in most of his writings, when giving such advice Alain did not prescribe novel attitudes but admonished his fellow Frenchmen not to forget old, established traditions (see Chapter I). All through the Third and Fourth Republics, with the exception of a short interlude between 1945 and 1947 when a modern party system seemed to be in the making, the French voter looked upon his representative in parliament as his personal "ambassador" in Paris. By his vote he entrusted him with the defense of constituency interests, caring little as to how a coherent national policy could emerge when the cleavages of society were faithfully reproduced in parliament. France remained the classical example of an atomistic representative system, conceived for another age. In this sense, a deputy who harassed every government until he could finally destroy it by a vote of censure was carrying out the assignment which his constituents had given him.

In other Western parliamentary systems, the emergence of structured and disciplined parties has modified (in the age of mass democracy) the earlier system of representation. Binding instructions from party or parliamentary groups leave to the representatives little room for independent decisions based on constituency considerations, but determine instead the course of action for government or opposition. In the United States,

[19] Alain, *Politique* (Paris: PUF, 1952), pp. 2, 7. For Adolphe Thiers, the shrewd "father" of the Third Republic, general elections would provide symbolic support for the authority structure but exclude the electorate from any significant impact on policy making; see Robert J. Mundt, in *Crisis, Choice, and Change: Historical Studies of Political Development*, eds. Gabriel Almond et al. (Boston: Little, Brown, 1973).

where the parties do not wield such power, not the congressional but the presidential elections give to the electorate a voice in deciding who should govern and who should be replaced at the helm of the government. In republican France, neither disciplined parties nor popular elections of the executive allowed that involvement of the electorate which has elsewhere given strength and legitimacy to representative institutions.

In the words of an astute and close observer of French parliamentarianism speaking about the situation in the Third and Fourth Republics:

> They [the French voters] were not consulted on concrete problems, as might have been the case if elections had been able to establish a clear sanction for durable and coherent government administration and a choice between specific programs. They were not even consulted on the way the Parliamentary "game" was played between elections. . . . The weakness of the political parties and their narrow oligarchical organization was such that it was impossible to assume that they represented the opinion of most Frenchmen.[20]

This explains the longstanding ambivalence of the French voter toward the parliamentary system. As the guardians of constituency interests, deputies and senators still commanded respect. Either as an individual or as the member of an interest group, the voter would lay his grievances before "his" deputy either in writing or during the deputy's frequent tours of his constituency. But when the deputies engaged in what de Gaulle used to call the "games, poisons and delights" of the system, when they made and unmade governments, seemingly and in fact without any regard for the "popular verdict" of the preceding elections, popular contempt engulfed both the representatives and the system. The electorate felt that it was "absent," kept away from meaningful participation and outside the centers where policy alternatives were decided. Such feel-

---

[20] François Goguel, in Stanley Hoffmann et al., *In Search of France* (Cambridge, Mass.: Harvard University Press, 1963), p. 396. At the time of his writing the author was secretary general of the French Senate.

ings were at the root of a basic antiparliamentary bias on the part of many regular voters.

During the post-war years popular attitudes toward the proper functions of parliamentary elections remained as ambivalent as they had always been. In 1944, shortly after the Liberation, 72 percent of the voters were of the opinion that votes should be cast on the basis of programs put forward by the political parties: only 16 percent said that they would vote "for a man." In January 1958, just before General de Gaulle reentered the political scene, only 27 percent of the voters (overwhelmingly Communists) wished to decide on the basis of sympathies for a party; for 52 percent the "man" would determine their vote.[21]

After the fall of the Fourth Republic, the insistence of the new leadership that the old parties were unrepresentative was widely accepted by the citizens whenever an electoral contest pitted the traditional parties against the new regime. In the opinion of the voters this did not mean that a democratic system could do without parties: only 26 percent thought so in 1962 and 20 percent in 1965, after the Fifth Republic had been in power for seven years.[22] In 1977 voters were yet more definite in their expressions of attachment to free elections and a multiparty system: a suppression of the right to vote was considered as a "grave" measure by 92 percent; 81 percent were convinced that in elections "every vote counts"; 51 percent declared their willingness to participate in protest activities, such as mass demonstrations or strikes, if a government wanted to introduce a one-party system (however, voters of the Left were far more inclined to take to the street in such an eventuality than others).[23]

It has often been argued, by Frenchmen and foreigners alike, that the electoral systems as practiced in France have been responsible for the weakness of the party system, for cabinet instability, and thereby ultimately for the voters' ambivalence toward parliamentary elections and representative institutions.

[21] See *Sondages* 20, no. 3 (1958): 56–57.

[22] Ibid., 28, no. 1 (1966): 37 and for an overall evaluation of political parties in public life, ibid. 31, nos. 1, 2 (1969): 32.

[23] SOFRES, *L'Opinion . . . 1977,* pp. 224, 226.

It is true that since direct and general manhood suffrage was introduced in 1848, French men have never voted under the system practiced in both the United States and Great Britain. In these two countries single-member constituencies in which the leading candidate is elected, whether or not he has won an absolute majority, have apparently been an important factor for the emergence of a two-party system. Could one not have expected the same development in France, if a similar voting system had been adopted in time?

Ever since parliamentary institutions were introduced in France, the electoral system "has been treated as a weapon in the struggle between different political camps and between different political forces for the control of State and society." [24] Since the establishment of the Third Republic in 1871, about a dozen different electoral laws governing national elections have been adopted and tried. The mode of local elections has also frequently been tampered with. Obviously, such constant modifications have not lent to any system that legitimacy which comes from permanence. Instead these modifications have fostered the voters' cynicism and their feeling of being used for the ends of a "political class" over which they had no control.

Nonetheless, the proposition that a single-ballot, simple-majority system as practiced in Great Britain and the United States would have bestowed greater stability on French politics is untenable. If such a solution has not been adopted by now it is largely due to the fact that the two camps which must be formed to make such a system work never had sufficient cohesion. The divisions that have existed within the Right and the Left were not created by the electoral systems. Rather, the electoral systems that were tried appeared unavoidable because of existing divisions. In order to reduce the vote of the people to a simple alternative, their representatives should have been able to reduce their differences to simpler terms — until recently such a simplification has never appeared to be within reach. [25]

---

[24] See Peter Campbell, *French Electoral Systems* (Hamdon, England: Archon Books, 1965), p. 17.

[25] See Raymond Aron, "Électeurs, partis et élus," *Revue Française de Science Politique* (abbreviated hereafter *RFSP*) 5, no. 2 (1955): 252.

The two major electoral systems that have governed all parliamentary elections, albeit with innumerable variations, have mirrored rather faithfully a divided body politic. During the Fourth Republic proportional representation was practiced, a system which in the Scandinavian countries and now, in slightly modified form, in the Federal Republic of Germany has not prevented strong parties and stable government coalitions. In France it was soon in need of modification because if the extremist parties on the Right and the Left had been represented in accordance with their electoral strength, no government whatsoever would have been possible. In the Third Republic most elections were held under a system in which runoff elections were necessary unless one of the candidates obtained an absolute majority of the votes cast. Because of the multiplicity of groups and factions few seats were won in the first ballot. Since in the second ballot a plurality of votes was sufficient to win, the less successful candidates withdrew in favor of their competitors, which gave to the earlier ballot some of the characteristics of an American primary election. But the coalition of factions or parties which obtained between the two ballots in order to reach agreement on the most promising candidate never persisted for long in parliament: fundamental divisions reappeared.

If under the present regime greater stability has prevailed, this must be attributed to other factors than the method by which the deputies to the National Assembly are elected. For in essence it is the same system, slightly modified, which was in force during the most troubled years of the Third Republic, and which had been discarded after the war because its small constituencies had been likened to "stagnant pools" and because it encouraged murky deals between the two ballots.[26] When in 1958 General de Gaulle designated this system as his personal preference, to the surprise of many of his closest collaborators, he did so in the tradition of all electoral reformers

[26] The main difference between the prewar and the present system consists in the rule that only candidates who in the first ballot obtained at least 12.5 percent of the votes can run in the second ballot. This has narrowed the field somewhat but not much. Previously, a candidate who had proved to be that low in voters' appeal was inclined to give up voluntarily.

in France: he wished to promote short-range goals, in this instance to prevent the strong expression of any one current of opinion in parliament, which he preferred to keep divided in order to reserve to himself the role of arbitrator. As has happened before, the outcome was quite different from what had been expected, for politics are shaped by factors other than the electoral system. That the system which was adopted does not provide for the equal representation of the voters is not surprising, for no system outside of proportional representation guarantees that. There are electoral districts with less than 50,000 voters, and others with almost three times that many, each electing a single deputy. It is also true that the final number of seats obtained by the various parties seldom corresponds to the number of votes cast for them. But to simplify representation at the price of sacrificing political nuances is the purpose of all majority systems, the American as well as the French.

In both the Third and the Fourth Republics general disenchantment with parliamentary institutions never prevented a high turnout at national elections. Since the consolidation of republican institutions in 1885 (and with the one exception of the somewhat abnormal post-World War I election of 1919), electoral participation never fell to less than 71 percent of registered voters.[27] In most elections participation was much higher; in the last election of the Third Republic (1936) it rose to 84 percent and, twenty years later, in the last election of the Fourth Republic it was almost as high. Altogether, the frustrating results of most elections notwithstanding, the political mobilization of the citizenry by the election process remained

[27] It must be noted — and this is true for all figures on electoral participation throughout this book — that French statistics calculate electoral participation on the basis of registered voters, while American statistics take as a basis the total number of people of voting age. It is generally assumed that about 5 to 6 percent of French citizens entitled to vote are not registered. This percentage must therefore be added to the published figures when one wishes to estimate the true rate of abstention and to compare it with the American record. For an interesting comparison of electoral participation in the United States and France, see William R. Schonfeld and Marie-France Toinet, "Les Abstentionnistes ont-ils toujours tort? La Participation électorale en France et aux États-Unis," *Revue Française de Science Politique* (*RFSP*), 25, no. 4 (August 1975): 645–76.

strong all through the lives of the now-defunct republics. Constituency interests and an individualized appeal to the voters kept tension and hence interest high.

Women's suffrage was established only after the Second World War and, beginning with the elections of 1946, women's vote became a new factor in electoral (and political) participation.[28] In the absence of official statistics separating the voters by gender, uncertainties are great. Opinion polls are unreliable because in a society which regards voting as a moral duty, respondents might wish to conceal failure to vote. In the early years of the Fourth Republic a study concluded that 24 percent of registered women voters did not vote (as against 17 percent of men in the same election). In the Fifth Republic the foremost student of electoral participation concluded that about two-thirds of the nonvoters were women. An analysis of elections in a single district and another one of voter registration generally seem to indicate that the gap between the sexes is narrowing though not closing. This also shows in answers regarding the degree of interest in politics. The same general factors which determine electoral participation (see below) are of increasing importance also for the women's vote.

Voting participation in the parliamentary elections of the Fifth Republic appears to have undergone a significant change and at any rate fluctuated more than before. Such fluctuations as have occurred need to be explained. Since the establishment of the Fifth Republic in 1958 Frenchmen have been called to the voting booths more frequently than ever before. In addition to four presidential elections and six referendums (both to be discussed below), there have been six parliamentary elections,

[28] For estimates of electoral participation by women during the early postwar years, see Mattei Dogan and Jacques Narbonne, *Les Françaises face à la politique* (Paris: Colin, 1955), esp. pp. 85–87. For more recent findings, see Alain Lancelot, *La Participation des Français à la vie politique* (Paris: PUF, 1971), esp. pp. 44–45; Monica Charlot, "Women in Politics in France," in *The French National Assembly Elections of 1978,* ed. Howard Penniman (Washington, D.C.: American Enterprise Institute, 1980), pp. 171–80; and Janine Mossuz-Lavau and Mariette Sineau, *Les Femmes françaises en 1978: Insertion sociale, Insertion politique* (Paris: Microfiche du CNSR, 1980), pp. 15–18. For the most thorough discussion of the "inequal politisation of the sexes," see Daniel Gaxie, *Le Cens caché* (Paris: Seuil, 1978), pp. 122–36.

one for the European parliament, and eight local government
elections. In three of the parliamentary elections participation
in the first ballot was low by French standards: 77 percent in
1958, 69 percent in 1962, and 70 percent of registered voters
in 1981. However, the first two of these elections took place
within weeks of a national referendum of great importance, the
third after a presidential election which had broken the conservative hold on the presidency for the first time. Hence for
many voters, whether of the Right or of the Left, the elections
were merely an act of confirmation of what they had already
done and elicited less interest. Special circumstances which provide additional explanations for the relatively low turnout in
1981 will be discussed below (Chapter VIII). In other parliamentary elections the rate of abstention remained low and its
pattern regular.[29]

As in other countries, social class, age, and education were
and remain important factors in determining the degree of
electoral participation: the least educated, the lowest income
groups, and the youngest and the oldest age groups voted less.

What makes for the higher rate of abstention among the
younger voters, generally believed to be about twice as high as
that of the older age groups, is difficult to decide. Does the
socialization into the citizen's voting role take a certain time
beyond the date at which he or she reaches the legal voting
age? Are the preoccupations of the young with private concerns
so paramount that they pay as yet little attention to their voting obligations? Or have parliamentary elections lost some of
their significance for the politically more conscious youth? In
1974 the voting age was lowered, as it has been in other countries, to eighteen years, which added about 2.5 million new
voters to the rolls.

More pronounced than in other countries has been the difference involving behavior between rural and urban constituencies. Quite generally, voting has been heavier in the country-

[29] This pattern is investigated through a wealth of materials and in-
genious extrapolation for the period from 1876 to 1967 by Alain Lancelot,
L'Abstentionnisme électoral en France (Paris: Armand Colin, 1968). The
preface by René Rémond (pp. ix–xiv) advances hypotheses which lend
themselves to comparative investigations.

side (averaging 86 percent of the registered voters) than in the cities to the point of offsetting other determinants, such as education and income. This is generally attributed to the greater personal intensity experienced by the rural voter during the campaign and afterward in his relation with his deputy. During an electoral campaign, the smaller the district the more fascinating become the personal confrontations of the candidates, their mutual accusations in the election literature, and the equally vehement discussions among their followers. Local antagonisms usually have the effect of mobilizing voter interest.

Regional differences continue to exist. In some departments, especially in the north, electoral participation is consistently higher than in others. But sometimes this is compensated for by other expressions of political participation, such as attendance at electoral meetings and reading of election materials; elsewhere political discussions might be more prevalent.

In the parliamentary elections held in the Fifth Republic the style of the campaigns and the citizens' reactions to them strike one as a somewhat baroque mixture of the old and the new. Campaigning and political propaganda have acquired a national dimension which they often lacked in the past. Modern communications and an apparent simplification of issues have brought this about. The national and regional press, radio and television, and uniform tracts and posters for the entire nation, the latter only slightly altered to fit local needs, put candidates and issues before the voter. The professionalization of campaigning has made rapid progress: the use of public opinion polls and of public relations experts, and the systematic observation of electioneering in other countries have become widespread. As long as the conservative majority was in power, the campaign of its candidates was orchestrated more and more by the government, either directly by the minister of interior or by the personal staffs of either the prime minister or the president of the Republic. This results in stereotyped electoral pronouncements which also characterize the campaigns of communist candidates.

Nonetheless local electioneering has not lost its individuality. The two-ballot system with small constituencies encourages a multiplicity and variety of candidacies and ensures thereby a considerable amount of decentralization and parochialism. In spite of a simplification of the party system, the number of candidates for each of the 491 available seats in the National Assembly remains large, even though it dropped from 4,208 in 1978 to 2,720 (or almost six candidates for each seat) in the 1981 elections. If one likens the first ballot to primaries, then primary fights in the Fifth Republic are at least as vivid as in the United States.

Even though attendance at electoral meetings is no longer large, except for those of a few star performers, candidates cannot afford to neglect them. It is true that rather than addressing themselves to individual voters, they now seek out local notables, foremost among them the mayors, which is additional evidence of the political vitality of local government. Candidates grant interviews to interest group representatives in their districts and see to it that such talks are publicized.

On the second ballot usually only two candidates are facing each other. Tension, however, remains high and might bring more voters to the polls in the second than in the first ballot. In the parliamentary election of 1981 abstention dropped from 30 to 25 percent between the first and second ballot.

There is no doubt that interest and participation in presidential elections is higher than in parliamentary contests. But the fascination with other forms of voting has obviously not deprived parliamentary elections of their function in the socialization of the citizens. The two forms of elections exist side by side, each with a different appeal and with a correspondingly different style, not unlike congressional and presidential elections in the United States.

VOTING IN PLEBISCITARIAN CONTESTS: REFERENDUMS AND PRESIDENTIAL ELECTIONS

During the seventy years of the Third Republic, proposals for the direct appeal to the electorate were weapons in the arsenal of antirepublican and bonapartist critics of the regime (see Chapter I). It came therefore as a surprise when shortly after the Liberation of the country, in a climate of democratic frenzy, General de Gaulle proposed to consult the electorate on the problem of the new constitution.

However, the political atmosphere in which the three referendums were held in 1945 and 1946 seemed to clear them of plebiscitarian or bonapartist suspicions. Only later did General de Gaulle interpret the first ballot which Frenchmen were invited to cast after the war as a mark of confidence in his person and as a condemnation of "party omnipotence." [30] In the midst of the material harshness of the post-Liberation period, 80 percent of the voters cast their ballots in the first two direct consultations of the electorate since the declining days of the Second Empire. Massive abstentions in the third referendum, when only a minority of registered voters adopted the constitution of the Fourth Republic, were not due to a lack of interest. Rather, conflicting pressures resulted in hesitations to cast either a negative or an affirmative vote.

The constitution of the Fifth Republic, as enacted in 1958, was fairly modest in its departures from a classical representative regime. It is true that the constitution itself was submitted to the electorate for approval. But the direct appeal to the voters which it permitted under carefully circumscribed conditions (articles 11 and 89 of the constitution) was hedged by parliamentary controls. The government gave official assurances that the referendum would never be used by the executive as a means of arousing popular opinion against the elected assemblies. Moreover, parliament remained the sole, directly elected trustee of the sovereign nation. The popular election of the president of the Republic was explicitly rejected as being "too political" in favor of his designation by an electoral college of some 80,000 local government officials.

In fact, the attraction which the referendum held for General de Gaulle, the introduction of direct popular suffrage for presidential elections, and the attitude of the electorate toward such novel modes of consulting the voters, permitted the thorough transformation of political institutions.

Since 1793 the French electorate has been convened seventeen times to vote in a national referendum. It has been said correctly that all but the two consultations in 1946, when sub-

[30] Charles de Gaulle, *War Memoirs, III: The Salvation* (New York: Simon and Schuster, 1960), p. 270.

sequent drafts of a constitutional text were submitted to the voters, have in fact been not referendums but plebiscites.[31] A referendum (such as practiced in the American states and in Switzerland) is a device, handled with more or less political felicity, but always inviting the voters to decide between equally available solutions. By contrast, a plebiscite usually requests the voters to endorse an already established policy from which the return to the status quo ante either is impossible or can be obtained only at a seemingly exorbitant price. At the very least, a providential leader (such as the two Bonapartes or General de Gaulle) demands an act of faith from the electorate by declaring that he could not continue at the helm without a massive vote of confidence. He thus raises the specter of political or social chaos as the alternative to his continued rule. In the eighteenth century, Jean-Jacques Rousseau assigned to the leader the task of formulating correctly the few questions which were to be put before the people in such a way that the general will would "see things as they are [and] sometimes as they ought to appear to it." With the approach of mass democracy, the nineteenth-century Swiss historian Jacob Burckhardt had stated that the "future belongs to the masses and to the men that can explain things simply to them." Since in fact political problems have become immensely more intricate rather than simpler, this means that issues may be simplified to the point of distortion. Moreover, by wrapping several propositions into one, the plebiscite not only maximizes chances for approval but also usually ties the sanction of an irretrievable past to the acceptance of dimly specified future policies.[32]

On some or all of these grounds the five referendums initiated by General de Gaulle qualify as plebiscites. (For the results, see Table III.) In 1958, a vote against the new constitution might in fact have brought the country back to the civil

[31] See Gilbert Bortoli, *Sociologie du référendum dans la France moderne* (Paris: Librarie Générale de Droit et Jurisprudence, 1965), pp. 2 ff. On p. 9, there is a useful table of all referendums held in France between 1793 and 1962.

[32] For the difference between a true referendum and a plebiscite, see Otto Kirchheimer, "France from the Fourth to the Fifth Republic," *Social Research* 26, no. 4 (1958): 403.

TABLE III. French Referendums (R), 1958–1972, and Second Ballot of Presidential Elections (E), 1965, 1969, 1974, and 1981 (Voting in Metropolitan France)

Date	Registered voters (in millions)	Abstentions (in millions)	Abstentions % of registered voters	"Yes" votes and votes for the winning candidate % of registered voters	"Yes" votes and votes for the winning candidate % of votes cast	"No" votes and votes for the losing candidate % of registered voters	"No" votes and votes for the losing candidate % of votes cast
9/28/58 (R)	26.62	4.01	15.1	66.4	79.2	17.4	20.7
1/8/61 (R)	27.18	6.39	23.5	55.9	75.3	18.4	24.7
4/8/62 (R)	26.99	6.59	24.4	64.9	90.7	6.6	9.3
10/28/62 (R)	27.58	6.28	22.7	46.4	61.7	28.8	38.2
12/19/65 (E)	28.22	4.36	15.4	44.8	54.5	37.4	45.5
4/18/69 (R)	28.66	5.56	19.4	36.7	46.7	41.6	53.2
6/15/69 (E)	28.75	8.90	30.9	37.2	57.5	27.4	42.4
4/23/72 (R)	29.07	11.48	39.5	36.1	67.7	17.2	32.3
5/19/74 (E)	29.80	3.60	12.1	43.9	50.7	42.8	49.3
5/10/81 (E)	35.5	4.81	13.6	43.8	52.2	40.1	47.8

125

war which it had narrowly escaped a few months earlier. Forty percent of the general electorate declared they had reached their decision on the constitutional project on the basis of its intrinsic values, 41 percent because of the personality of General de Gaulle.[33] The two following referendums prepared or endorsed in highly ambiguous terms the peace settlement of the unending Algerian war, isolating successfully the diehards who by their rebellion threatened both order and prosperity. Only six months after the second referendum on peace in Algeria the president asked the electorate to endorse once more a personal policy decision by direct vote: a constitutional amendment (article 7) introducing the direct popular election of the president of the Republic. In October 1962 all of the non-Gaullist parties objected to the constitutional novelty of electing the president by direct suffrage; they also had no difficulty in denouncing as illegal the form in which the amendment was submitted: the amendment procedure of the constitution (article 89) permitted a call for a referendum only after the concordant vote of the two houses of parliament, which the government had neither sought nor obtained.

This explains why the new referendum aroused more resistance than the previous consultations: the majority of those casting an affirmative vote declined to 46 percent of the registered voters; the proposition was approved by only 62 percent of the votes cast as against 91 percent in favor of the preceding referendum. For General de Gaulle these results were extremely painful: less than half of the electorate had stood by him this time, a slim margin for a leader seeking popular confirmation of his rule.[34]

De Gaulle's preference for the referendum as an instrument of direct democracy was shared by a sizable segment of public opinion. In 1962 and again in 1969, only a few weeks before a

[33] See *Sondages* 22, no. 4 (1960): 44.

[34] Presumably he considered resigning already at that time, but decided to carry on in order to pursue his foreign and atomic power policies. See J.-R. Tournoux, *La Tragédie du Général* (Paris: Plon, 1967), p. 439, like all writings by this author, a highly interesting though probably not always reliable account. For de Gaulle's own version of the events, see the last volume of his memoirs, *Memoirs of Hope: Renewal and Endeavour* (New York: Simon and Schuster, 1971), pp. 312 ff.

majority of "no" votes in another referendum was to bring about General de Gaulle's resignation, 51 percent of respondents in a public opinion poll favored the direct consultation of the electorate.[35]

When in May 1968, the country was shaken by one of the most violent crises in its history, it was quite natural for General de Gaulle to seek a way out by promising another referendum. While there was fighting in the streets of the capital, while all over France factories and public buildings were occupied by workers and students in revolt, the president of the Republic explained in a televised speech that he "needed, indeed needed, once more an expression from the people to tell him what they wanted." A referendum would be submitted to the electorate spelling out what the "renovation" would amount to in all the domains where dissatisfaction with past policies of his regime had led to rebellion. "Of course," he concluded, in the case of a negative vote, he would have to relinquish his office.

The appeal fell flat. With participatory democracy being acted out throughout the country, de Gaulle's version of direct democracy proclaimed from the Élysée Palace had lost its attractiveness. "Imagination and eloquence had changed sides." [36] Shortly afterwards, General de Gaulle announced that the government was abandoning the plans for a referendum and instead was dissolving the National Assembly and calling for new elections, hence using article 12 rather than article 11 of the constitution. This turned out to be a masterful tactical stroke. Instead of crystallizing opposition against a referendum to which de Gaulle had once more and willfully given all the characteristics of a plebiscite, the regime forced the major political forces to muster their strength in a traditional electoral contest. Circumstances, it is true, were bound to give to the elections the significance of a plebiscite. By promising law

[35] *Sondages* 31, no. 3 (1969): 7. This opinion was now shared by followers of the opposition parties.

[36] Jean Lacouture, *De Gaulle*, 2d ed. (Paris: Seuil, 1969), p. 10. This small essay remains the best and most judicious biography of de Gaulle. The English translation (New York: New American Library, 1966) is that of the first edition (1965) with only a few additions.

and order and brandishing the threat of "totalitarian communism," [37] the Gaullist party and its allies, rather than the president himself, won their greatest electoral victory yet.

But for General de Gaulle the outcome was unsatisfactory. To him, parliamentary elections confirmed only indirectly and temporarily what he liked to call his own "profound legitimacy." In his assumed role of a "revolutionary" [38] he was concerned that a conservative parliament would want to forget the lessons of May. It was therefore incumbent upon him to lead the way to fundamental reforms, playing once more the "legislator" of Rousseau's *Social Contract* and soliciting an expression of the general will through another referendum.

After considerable hesitation, General de Gaulle decided that two questions that had preoccupied him for some time were best suited to overcome the conservatism of structures and habits: the reform of the upper house of parliament, the Senate, and a strengthening of the administrative structure of the twenty-one regions into which the country had been divided for some time (for a discussion of the substance of these proposals, see Chapters X and IX, respectively).

Differing from the rather monumental law enacted by the referendum of 1962 on the election of the president, the sixty-nine articles of the new proposal, covering fourteen closely printed pages never aroused strong popular interest. Since he wished to see his position sanctioned not just by a referendum but by a plebiscite, de Gaulle once more declared explicitly midway during the campaign, that he would resign if there were no majority of "yes" votes. Public opinion polls showed

[37] A historical injustice if there ever was one. The French Communist Party had done its utmost to distance itself from the events which it had neither foreseen nor been able to control. For details, see Richard Johnson, *The French Communist Party versus the Students: Revolutionary Politics in May–June 1968* (New Haven: Yale University Press, 1972).

[38] "I am not at all embarrassed to be the kind of revolutionary which I have been so frequently," he declared in a radio interview; see *Année Politique 1968* (Paris: PUF, 1969), p. 384. For an excellent interpretation of General de Gaulle's initiatives between the events of May and the referendum of 1969, see Alain Lancelot, "Comment ont voté les Français le 27 avril et les 1er et 15 juin 1969," *Projet* 38 (1969): esp. 929, and J. E. S. Hayward, "Presidential Suicide by Plebiscite: de Gaulle's Exit, April 1969," *Parliamentary Affairs* 22 (1969): 289–319.

that this announcement met with widespread disapproval and that, instead of mobilizing support for the referendum, it hastened the voters' disaffection. If de Gaulle's appeal was as plebiscitarian as it had been previously, the situation no longer was. There was no immediate emergency on the horizon. The voters as well as their representatives in parliament were quite willing to forget the shock of the previous year while the referendum wished to remind them of the unfinished business which the events of 1968 had left.

There was also, for the first time in the history of the Fifth Republic, an alternative other than assumed chaos to General de Gaulle's rule: Georges Pompidou, former prime minister under de Gaulle, had made it known, well before the referendum campaign, that he was a candidate in case of a presidential vacancy. Hence, General de Gaulle's threat of resignation did not conjure previous anxieties. Nothing in the constitution compelled General de Gaulle to resign in the aftermath of an unsuccessful referendum. It was only the highly personal concept he held of his role that led him to resign.[39]

When, after the retirement of General de Gaulle, his former prime minister Georges Pompidou acceded to the presidency, he expressed, at least by implication, little taste for wielding the weapon of a referendum. It had driven his predecessor from office and had acquired from the start plebiscitarian connotations which did not suit Pompidou's style of governance. Hence his announcement in the spring of 1972 that he was seeking approval by referendum for the treaty opening the Common Market to Great Britain and other countries caused surprise but little enthusiasm. Undoubtedly Pompidou's decision was motivated primarily by considerations of domestic politics. At the approach of parliamentary elections he wanted to consolidate the majority and weaken the opposition by driving a wedge between the Socialists and Communists, who were bitterly divided on the question of European unity. That the

---

[39] A passionate defense of General de Gaulle's step was offered in an interview by the staunchest Rousseauan among his advisers, the late Professor René Capitant, at one time his Minister of Justice; see *Der Spiegel,* May 26, 1959: "The people is sovereign. It wanted de Gaulle's departure [sic]; he has accepted the verdict. He could not do otherwise."

"yes" would outnumber the "no" was enough of a foregone conclusion to deprive the campaign of plebiscitarian drama. What had not been expected was the record number of abstentions which amounted to almost 40 percent, to which most of the 7 percent of invalid ballots must be added. Hence the affirmative vote, while enough to give force of law to the text submitted for approval, amounted to a bare 36 percent of the registered voters.

Giscard d'Estaing drew the consequences of past experience. There was no referendum during the seven years of his presidency. In his campaign for the presidency François Mitterrand included in his program a proposal for "enlarging the possibilities for calling a referendum." When he illustrated what he had in mind, he spoke about referendums on nuclear energy policies, atomic weapons development, administrative decentralization, and the like. An earlier opinion poll (1977) had indicated that on this point the candidate was in agreement with the thinking of a majority of the electorate: three-fourths of the respondents had been in favor of "direct democracy" when such questions as the building of additional nuclear power stations were at stake. In his first press conference Mitterrand returned to the question by stating that he would like to see more referendums *"à la Suisse,"* as he put it, but that this would call for an important constitutional amendment which had to be postponed because of the urgency of the government's legislative program.[40] His mention of the Swiss practice was clearly designed to distinguish future consultations of the electorate from the plebiscites practiced by de Gaulle.

Whatever the future use of the referendum, at present the presidential elections by direct popular suffrage are for French voters the most important expressions of the "general will." Such a way of electing the head of state had been suspect to true French republicans since Napoleon III had risen to imperial power through a popular majority in presidential elections. In both the Third and the Fourth Republics, the presi-

[40] For the 1977 opinion poll, see SOFRES, *L'Opinion . . . 1977,* pp. 230, 232; for Mitterrand's press conference, see *Le Monde,* September 26, 1981.

dent was, therefore, elected by the two houses of parliament, convening as one body for the occasion.

Ever since the presidential elections of 1965 (the first popular elections for the presidency since 1849) it had become evident that the French voters derived great satisfaction from knowing that, unlike in past parliamentary elections, national and not parochial alignments were at stake and that they were invited to pronounce themselves effectively on such issues. The traditional and at one time deeply rooted attitude that the only useful vote was a vote against the government no longer made sense when almost everybody knew that the task at hand was to elect the head of an executive endowed constitutionally with strong powers, for a normal term of seven years. It has been said quite correctly that the constitutional position of the president and the extent of his powers have been at stake not only in the presidential elections of the Fifth Republic, but in all of its electoral contests and referendums.[41] To refuse a plebiscitarian appeal or to defeat a parliamentary majority supporting the policies of the president would necessarily have immediate repercussions for the exercise of presidential powers. This meant that presidential elections have become the central event of political life around which other consultations of the electorate turn like satellites. The voters have understood this well and have repeatedly expressed their approval of a popularly elected presidency as an institution that has proven its worth. Accordingly electoral participation in presidential elections has been unusually high (see Table III). The one exception, the second ballot of the Pompidou election in 1969, when abstentions reached 31 percent, was not due to indifference but to a directive issued to its followers by the Communist party which for political reasons wanted to prevent the election of Pompidou's opponent. If there were slightly more abstentions in 1981 than seven years earlier, this was again not due to a lack of interest but to conflicting pressures, appearing this time more on the Right than on the Left (see Chapter VIII).

---

[41] See François Goguel, "Culture politique et comportement électoral," in *La Sagesse,* Mendras, p. 300. The entire article is valuable for the problems discussed here.

The nomination procedures for presidential candidates reflect General de Gaulle's dislike for giving any role to political parties. Even after some slightly more stringent requirements were introduced in 1976, it is still not difficult to put a candidate on the first ballot. He or she must secure 500 signatures by people holding electoral office (at whatever local or national level) and residing in at least thirty different departments; not more than one-tenth of the signatures should come from the same department. Once a candidate has fulfilled these requirements, he or she is granted free time on radio and television and, provided the candidate obtains at least 5 percent of the vote, sizable contributions to campaign expenses out of public funds. Such an arrangement explains why some previously unknown, and often fanciful, candidates emerge, only to disappear again after the first ballot. (A second ballot becomes necessary, as it has been so far in all presidential contests, when no candidate has obtained 50 percent of the votes cast.) In the 1974 elections the "also-rans" in the first ballot included, among others, two Trotskyites, two European federalists, an environmentalist, a royalist, and a palladin of small businessmen who was also a vociferous antiabortionist; in 1981 there was again one Trotskyite (the same one), an environmentalist (a different one), one candidate from a left-wing socialist splinter party, one radical-socialist (a small party which is neither radical nor socialist), and two candidates who represented different shades of dissident factions of Gaullism — all of them happy to put their cause and case before an otherwise unavailable audience. In addition, in 1981 there was a total of fifty-four other would-be candidates from many political camps who had not been able to meet the legal requirements for a candidacy. But so far all *serious* candidates have been backed by a party or by a coalition of parties, the provisions of the law notwithstanding. The French understood soon what the citizens of the United States had learned during the seedtime of their republic: it is impossible to mount a national political campaign without the support of a political party.

This, however, has not meant that the most prominent candidates, unless they are communists, owe their political ascent to a party or are recognized leaders of a well-structured party, as is the case for the heads of state and of the executives in most European democracies. To say nothing of de Gaulle, who was contemptuous of all parties, including his own, neither Pompidou nor Giscard d'Estaing could be regarded as "party men." The former was never a member of the Gaullist party; Giscard's party was fairly insignificant at the time of his election. Only Mitterrand ran for the presidency in 1974 and won it in 1981 as the leader of the Socialist party. But when he had stood for election for the first time in 1965 against General de Gaulle, he started out without any organization and imposed himself from the outside as the candidate of existing parties. For him, as well as for his predecessors in office, notoriety from past achievements, personality, and a set of favorable circumstances counted for far more than organization.[42]

It is therefore not surprising that candidates drew their campaign staff mostly from a circle of personal friends or past associates rather than from parties, and this was true even when Mitterrand was the candidate of the Socialist Party. This, of course, parallels closely American practices. But since party preferences determine the choice of most voters an analysis of the changing alignments in the recent presidential elections and of their outcome must await the discussion of political party developments, in Chapter VIII. (See Table IV for results in the first ballot of the 1981 elections.)

If all the presidential campaigns have fascinated French voters and foreign observers, this is not only due to the novelty of a nationwide competition in a country accustomed to small constituencies and parochial contests. Style and content of campaign oratory have generally been of rather high quality even if some of the most critical issues are usually dealt with in generalities or in merely personal terms. Since the campaigns are short and concentrated, radio, television, and newspapers are able to grant candidates, commentators, and forecasters considerable time and space. The televised duels between Giscard and Mitterrand in 1974 and 1981, patterned after the presi-

---

[42] See Hugues Portelli, "La présidentialisation des partis français," *Pouvoirs* 14 (1980): 97–106. Most of this issue of this excellent journal is devoted to the question: *élire un président*.

Table IV. *First Ballot of Presidential Elections 1981*

	In millions	*% of votes cast*
Giscard d'Estaing	8.2	28.3
Union for French Democracy (UDF)		
Mitterrand	7.5	25.8
Socialist Party (PS)		
Chirac	5.2	17.9
Rally for the Republic (RPR)		
Marchais	4.5	15.3
Communist Party (PC)		
Lalonde	1.1	3.9
Environmentalist		
Laguiller	0.7	2.3
Trotskyite		
Crépeau	0.6	2.2
Radical-Socialist		
Debré	0.5	1.6
Indep. Gaullist		
Garaud	0.4	1.3
Indep. Gaullist		
Bouchardeau	0.3	1.1
Indep. Socialist		

dential debates in the United States, but much longer and of far higher quality, were viewed each time by a majority of the voters. Whether and how much they changed the voters' minds has been debated hotly but inconclusively.[43]

In addition to the use of the mass media, there were also im-

[43] The best general accounts of the 1974 campaign are to be found in *L'Élection présidentielle de mai 1974* (Paris: Dossiers et Documents du Monde, 1974), and in *France at the Polls: The Presidential Election of 1974*, ed. Howard Penniman (Washington, D.C.: American Enterprise Institute, 1975). The companion pieces for the 1981 elections are *L'Élection présidentielle, 26 avril–10 mai 1981* (Paris: Dossiers et Documents du Monde, 1981). The complete text of the televised debate is printed on pp. 119–32. There will undoubtedly also be a volume on the 1981 election published by the American Enterprise Institute. Of a different nature, but highly interesting, is the account given by François Mitterrand of the 1974 campaign which ended in his (narrow) defeat: see his *La Paille et le grain* (Paris: Flammarion, 1978), esp. the description of the televised debate, pp. 288–300.

pressive mass meetings held throughout the country. Campaign literature, issued by hastily improvised headquarters, was abundant; much of it gave evidence that position papers had been prepared long before the start of the election. The campaign of 1981 which was to end in as complete a turnover of political leadership and personnel as the country had known since the end of the war was, on the whole, singularly unexciting. Both the incumbent and the challenger felt that the voters were going seriously about serious business and that they expected not less from the candidates. As in the preceding presidential elections the involvement of citizens in a novel electoral process opened a new dimension for political participation and thereby left its mark on the socialization of both citizens and elites.

CHAPTER V

Mass Media

THE FLOW OF COMMUNICATIONS

If one wants to explain the role of the mass media in France one must try to find out: "Who Says What, in Which Channel, to Whom, with What Effect," [1] a paradigm that points to many important political problems.

Families and classrooms, playing fields and meeting halls, interest groups and parties are all providing channels of information and communication. The mass media of modern society "do not simply displace or supersede other channels; rather, they link existing networks while giving rise to a host of dependent nets which service, disseminate, and frequently transform their product." [2] In a country such as France, the effectiveness of the communications process as used by the mass media is often determined by the way in which Frenchmen appraise the integrity of this process, whether they believe that it serves or disturbs the functioning of the political system.

In many of the political crises of the past, the French press played a dramatic role. During major campaigns, and great scandals or *affaires,* newspapers politicized the elites and mo-

---

[1] Harold Lasswell, quoted here from Richard R. Fagen, *Politics and Communication* (Boston: Little, Brown, 1966), pp. 4, 5.
[2] Ibid., p. 45.

bilized the masses. They were used, and often subsidized, by the antagonists. In the absence of strong political parties and of sufficient revenue from advertising, business firms, tycoons, and governments (both French and foreign) habitually backed major newspapers. The widespread and largely justified belief that much of the press was run by "hidden forces" seriously impaired its function as a channel of political communication.

When during the Second World War the resistance movement developed blueprints for the future, quite naturally much attention was given to the future status of press and radio. A nationalized enterprise was to allocate printing presses and other resources to all existing political forces; the sources of information were to be kept clean and lean. For as the spokesmen for the resistance movement declared solemnly: "The press is free only when it depends neither on the government nor on the moneyed powers, but solely on the consciences of journalists and readers."

The realities of postwar politics soon did away with such aspirations. Today, the press operates under the same conditions as it does in other Western democracies, except that for the daily press revenue from advertising remains comparatively low. Most newspapers and magazines are owned by business enterprises, many of them conglomerates that extend into fields other than periodical publications. In becoming more like newspapers elsewhere in the West, the French press has departed in many respects from its prewar structure and approach. Most important among such departures are the fusion of many newspapers and the deemphasis of their open political commitment.

In spite of a growth in population, the circulation of daily newspapers in France declined between 1946 and 1977 from 15.1 to 11.4 million a day; of these 3.1 million are published in Paris. The decline in readership, a common phenomenon in most Western democracies, is due, among other factors, to the competition from other media, such as television and radio. It is accompanied by a decline in the number of newspapers. In 1977 Paris had only eleven dailies as against twenty-eight in 1946 and sixty before the First World War. Outside the capital, their number has decreased in the years since the last war from

138 *Mass Media*

175 to 71.[3] According to public opinion polls, 75 percent of Frenchmen are regular readers of the daily press; 12 percent admit that they never look at it. In a representative sample of eighteen- to twenty-two-year-olds, the corresponding figures are 45 percent and 21 percent. Among the farming population nonreaders make up 22 percent, and in the least developed regions 39 percent of the total adults.

The most striking difference from prewar days is the emaciation of the party press. The Communist *Humanité,* the national newspaper of a party which had 5.8 million voters in the 1978 elections, had at that time a circulation of approximately 150,000 copies, as against close to one million copies for the two Communist dailies after the Liberation. In 1981 the circulation had dropped according to rumors to about 80,000 copies. Only the far less politically and more culturally oriented Sunday edition of the *Humanité* still sells better. The Socialist party had to abandon altogether its once highly respected daily which for many years had been subsidized by other European socialist parties. The victory of the French socialists in the 1981 presidential and parliamentary elections is not likely to lead to the resurrection of a party-owned daily; the periodicals which the party publishes are mostly designed to reach its active militants. The Gaullist party, which between 1962 and 1981 attracted a larger percentage of votes than any other French party in history, has not had any newspaper since 1974; it now merely publishes a daily handout so that its editorials can be quoted on radio and television. But the two fore-

[3] For a lengthy and interesting account of the general newspaper situation at the beginning of the 1970s, see "Le Journal et ses lecteurs," *Esprit* 400 (1971): 193–402. Very informative also are the discussions by François Goguel and Alfred Grosser, *La Politique en France,* 8th ed. (Paris: Colin, 1980), pp. 162–69. In English the best reports, covering all media, are Alfred Grosser, "The Role of the Press, Radio, and Television in French Political Life," in *France at the Polls: The Presidential Election of 1974,* ed. Howard Penniman (Washington, D.C.: The American Enterprise Institute, 1975), pp. 207–26; and Roland Cayrol, "The Mass Media and the Electoral Campaign," in *The French National Assembly Elections of 1978,* ed. Howard Penniman (Washington, D.C.: The American Enterprise Institute, 1980), pp. 144–70. Strictly factual, but very complete, is the account of the press in *The Europa Yearbook 1981: A World Survey* (London: Europa Publications, 1981), pp. 644–54.

most nonpartisan Paris newspapers which shun an editorial opinion on many issues, the *Parisien Libéré* and *France-Soir*, skyrocketed at one time to a total of 2.1 million copies, or almost 45 percent of all papers published in the capital. In the 1970s their circulation too dropped to about one-third of the earlier figure; they are hard hit by the economic recession and the diminished revenue from advertising. The same difficulties might soon beset other papers, and the indirect subsidy which all newspapers receive from the government in the form of special postal rates and reduced rates for newsprint might not be sufficient to ward off the insolvency of many of them.

Since the appeal of the two most successful Parisian dailies is directed to the general reading public, they try to reflect as faithfully as possible the social composition of the adult population at large. Half of the readers of the *Parisian Libéré* are workers and therefore presumably, at least until recently, communist voters. But they do not seem to be disturbed about the bias their daily paper showed when it expressed sympathy for the rebellious generals in Algeria and when it indulges now in crude xenophobia, directed especially against foreign workers. Two other Parisian papers, *Le Figaro* and *L'Aurore* (with 325,000 and 290,000 copies respectively, but whose circulation is declining) have a more definite orientation: the first appeals to an upper-class, the second to a lower-class conservatism. But they too shun all party affiliations and might both endorse different candidates, at least for the first ballot of elections. Other Paris newspapers also appeal, by their presentation and style, to one social class or group over others. But their audience is differentiated according to socioeconomic status rather than to political opinion.

Two Parisian dailies occupy a special place as communication media: *La Croix* (circulation 120,000 copies, half of which are going to subscribers outside of Paris) and *Le Monde* (about 500,000). The former, issued by an important Catholic publishing house which also circulates about twenty other periodicals with a much wider reader appeal than the daily, was founded to combat the institutions of the Third Republic with all the violence it could muster. Today its columns give limited space to religious information as such. Not committed to any party and open to divergent opinions, it seeks nonetheless to develop a coherent stand on major political and social issues and to represent and possibly develop a dominant trend in modern French Catholicism.

The influence of *Le Monde,* which is owned by its staff, is far wider than its circulation although it may be declining; it is estimated that it is read by about one and a half million people. It recruits readers in many political camps and provides food for daily reflection, a basis for discussions, and a working tool for intellectuals, professionals, students, and especially the political and economic elite. Its editorial and reportorial staff are of unusually high quality; the covering of such events as political elections is unequaled by any American paper. Its editorial policy has been as critical of the Fifth Republic as it was of the defunct Fourth. During the presidency of Giscard d'Estaing its antigovernmental bias became so strident that many readers discounted its objectivity in reporting; nonetheless, they continued to read it. In the 1981 election campaigns its sympathies were with the opposition, and since the latter's victory at the polls, the paper has, at least for a time, muted its criticism of governmental policies. Its foreign correspondents are outstanding, if generally critical of both the United States and the Soviet Union. Its *Tribune Libre* solicits widely divergent opinions but only from well-known writers or from spokesmen for political or social movements.

Unlike their British counterparts major regional newspapers in France have stood the competition from the capital quite well. They have lost fewer readers than the Parisian dailies and provide some counterbalance to the centralization of political and administrative life.[4] Their continuing vigor attests to the strength of cultural life in the provinces. (Other evidence is the *maisons de culture,* attractive and lively centers of artistic and cultural life in a number of cities.) There are seventeen provincial newspapers which have a circulation of more than 150,000 copies. One of them, *Ouest-France* (almost 700,000 copies), is now, in terms of circulation, the most important

---

[4] Jack Hayward, *The One and Indivisible French Republic* (London: Weidenfeld & Nicolson, 1973), p. 143.

daily in the country; its national and international reporting have left narrow provincialism behind. Other dailies hold a quasi-monopoly in their respective regions; after having absorbed many of the strictly local newspapers, they are issuing separate local editions. They too are no longer mainstays of political parties, as many regional papers had been before the war. But many of their publisher-owners, who are frequently also their editors, are public figures carrying considerable weight in the political and cultural life of the region. If they have definite political opinions, these might be expressed here and there, without, however, endangering the generalized appeal their newspapers wish to preserve.

There are no reliable data as to the proportion of readers that turn to their dailies in search of political information. Twenty-one percent of all readers, 37 percent of women, and 45 percent of the farmers admit that they never pay attention to political news in the dailies, although in some isolated regions farmers read more newspapers than the average.[5] At the approach of the 1981 presidential elections only 39 percent of the respondents in a public opinion poll believed that the daily press would influence their choice, against 46 percent who attributed such a role to television. This, however, was not uniformly so: 53 percent of professional people, upper management and high civil servants, and 58 percent of those who were classified as "passionately interested in politics" considered the dailies their most important source of information.[6]

Some of the needs for political controversy and partisan information are filled by a number of weeklies. Their audience has increased considerably of late and they function as an important channel of communication for information not otherwise available, even though their information is not always reliable. The three major news weeklies, publishing between

[5] See Philip E. Converse and Georges Dupeux, "Politicization of the Electorate in France and the United States," *The Public Opinion Quarterly* 26, no. 1 (1962): 6. Their comparative data, which indicate a much greater political interest on the part of the American newspaper reader, are noteworthy but not quite convincing.

[6] Thierry Pfister, "Les Media vont-ils faire les élections?" *Le Nouvel Observateur* 848 (9–15 February 1981): 14.

250,000 and 500,000 copies, all have rather distinct political profiles: *Le Nouvel Observateur* has socialist sympathies, but is independent of the socialist party; *Le Point* is conservative but not narrowly so; the oldest, *L'Express,* has always been slightly left of center until the British press magnate who acquired it took it off that course in a row which created a scandal in the publishing field. The long-established satirical weekly *Le Canard Enchaîné* (printing 350,000 copies) is devoted to investigative journalism and publishing so much political inside information that its offices were discovered to be bugged, presumably by the government which wished to discover the journal's confidential sources — a mini-Watergate affair.

The concentration of ownership and of control of newspapers and all periodical publications in ever fewer hands is progressing also in France (though not yet to the same degree as in the United States, Great Britain, and West Germany). Publishing "empires" are built by takeovers; newcomers with political ambitions have entered the field. The concentration also extends to book publishing. One firm, Hachette, controls about one-fifth of all book publishing, including textbooks and paperbacks; it owns newspapers and important periodicals and is the central distributor for many newspapers in the country.

So far this development has not limited freedom of expression nor has it led to drab uniformity. The French equivalent of muckraking has talented practitioners. Nonconforming thought is not silenced, though it might have difficulties in reaching the mass media. During major electoral campaigns the partiality of many of the large-circulation newspapers and of media appears at times overwhelming, but experience has shown that it does not necessarily decide the outcome.[7]

Complaints that French governments are parsimonious with information and keep the media and the public in the dark about important developments antedated the Fifth Republic.

[7] F. D. Roosevelt won two landslide victories in spite of an overwhelmingly hostile press. François Mitterrand, in *La paille et le grain* (Paris: Flammarion, 1978), lists on three pages (pp. 291–93) the information media that supported his opponent in 1974. Seven years later the situation had not changed, yet — he won.

In the first years of de Gaulle's presidency the situation worsened considerably. The flow of information from the centers of decision making to the printed media was thinned, its substance altered. As a result, the level of political information declined. "Finally one wonders," an outstanding journalist wrote, "whether . . . one does not hear anything because nobody says anything, whether one does not know anything because nothing happens, or whether the regime is able to mask everything, to mute everybody." [8]

During his presidency, General de Gaulle used each of his carefully timed and staged biannual press conferences as an important occasion to spell out his world views and to communicate major decisions ranging over a broad field. The content and form of such communications were determined unilaterally, since questions addressed to the chief of state were either predetermined or arranged in such a way that the answers amounted to resumed speech making by the president. Under de Gaulle's successors presidential press conferences have been less formalized without ever approaching the give-and-take of White House conferences. In his initial press conferences Mitterrand ranged, with the same mastery as de Gaulle, over broad fields and, like him, determined unilaterally which topics he wanted to treat and which were to be passed over.

Each new government has stressed the need for a more informed citizenry and promised to do its best to make information available. But as late as 1980 a keen observer complained that the official taste for secrecy had not abated and seemed endemic to a political culture in which people were at once fascinated and repelled by the state.[9] The socialist government has promised relief. When it became clear that, contrary to expectations, it would not change nuclear policies and that it

---

[8] Pierre Viansson-Ponté (leading political columnist of *Le Monde*), "Vingt ans d'information politique (1946–1966)," *La Nef* 22, no. 27 (1966): 50. The entire issue of this magazine was devoted to a discussion of political information in the sixties.

[9] See Jacques Delors's remarks in a debate, "La France est-elle sous-informée?" *Revue parlementaire et politique* 82, no. 884 (March–April 1980): pp. 466 ff. The author has since become Minister of Finance.

would resume the building of power stations, the government's spokesman explained that there would be a change nonetheless — from now on the public concerned would be informed about and involved in new projects.[10]

The modern mass media such as radio and television were particularly appropriate to the style of the regime during its Gaullist phase. De Gaulle did not create the mass media channels which he used to widen and continue the bases of his charismatic relationship with the masses. But popularity of television became so great and the techniques employed by the government in handling the new medium so highly developed that the regime was sometimes spoken of as a "telecracy." Those who described the Fifth Republic as "de Gaulle plus television" wished to point to the institutional shapelessness which prevailed during much of General de Gaulle's rule.

Most characteristic were de Gaulle's appeals to the nation (in general's uniform rather than in a double-breasted suit) when mutinous settlers or officers threatened the republic from Algeria. On these occasions, the hero, merely by confirming his presence, invited the citizens to share with him not only the experience of exciting events but also the responsibility of resolving the crisis. In fact, twice rebellions collapsed shortly after almost the entire population watched a television appearance by de Gaulle. The effective use of modern communications made the rebels realize that the national community was intact, and this proved far more decisive than the post hoc utilization of presidential emergency powers. On the other hand, each time when for whatever reason de Gaulle's performance on the "little screen" was unsatisfactory — such as during the elections of 1965, the May 1968 events, or during the last of his referendum campaigns — public attitudes toward the regime were directly affected.

Almost all households possess a radio. About 14 million TV sets now reach about 88 percent of the population; the "average" viewer daily spends two hours and fifty minutes in front of the TV set. There has been, especially over the last years, a steady increase in "current affairs" programs. In normal times

10 See *Le Monde,* October 1, 1981.

— i.e., with no elections on the horizon — such programs occupy 36 percent of the total output of all TV chains. In the villages, television has frequently and drastically transformed leisure time habits and social life. It has often been said in the past that for Frenchmen politics was a "spectator sport": they felt uninvolved in the games played by the politicians. As TV viewers they are still spectators. But to watch their representatives, members of the government, party and group leaders at close range has involved the public (as well as the political actors appearing on the TV screen) in unprecedented ways. By becoming more familiar, even if often trivial, politics and politicians are less suspect.[11]

GOVERNMENTAL CONTROL OF INFORMATION

Since the war telecommunications have been a public monopoly. Until the socialist government introduced changes in 1981, all broadcasting and television stations which originated programs on French territory were owned by the state and operated by personnel whom the state appointed and remunerated. However, the legal pattern, common to most Western European countries, was less decisive for the role of radio and television in the communications process than the government's conception of its stewardship in the operation of the media. For the unstable cabinets of the Fourth Republic, not less than for the forceful presidents of the Fifth, telecommunications were the "voice of France" and that "voice" was identified with the government in power.[12]

To conceive of the mass media as a public service, which was to be put at the disposal of all political forces, remained a difficult concept for a political community in which government and opposition contested each other's legitimacy. Before 1958 each majority, however ephemeral, claimed to speak in the name of all and therefore saw no virtue in permitting dissonant voices to be heard over the publicly owned air waves. Such

[11] See Henri Mendras, "Une figure de la France," in *La Sagesse et le désordre: France 1980*, ed. Henri Mendras (Paris: Gallimard, 1980), p. 46.
[12] See Goguel and Grosser, *La Politique,* p. 157. On pp. 156–61 the authors provide an excellent survey of the past and present history of the public media.

practices rapidly created a body of precedents which every government used when it wished to interfere with the presentation of political and, often, of general information.

In the government's opinion no fundamental difference existed between operating the media and any other administrative activity. The minister of information would ensure, often by daily conferences, that the news was presented in accordance with governmental wishes. One of de Gaulle's ministers explained that at a time when the press was overwhelmingly critical of official policy, it was natural for the public media to be partisan in order to provide a "balance." The habit of French journalism of mixing news reporting and editorial comment facilitated biased accounts.

For many years "listening to the news" meant for most French listening to the private radio stations whose broadcasts from neighboring nations cover all of France. They are far more respected than the so-called pirate stations in Great Britain. Since they are financed largely by advertising and address a broad clientele, they resemble in style and quality the better news broadcasts in the United States. Although by now the government exercises some financial control over these stations, they still leave more room for initiative and controversial comment than the government-operated networks.

But there has never been any alternative to public television. For almost two decades controversies about a more satisfactory organization of the media have been at the center of public discussions. "The regulation of broadcasting and television," a deputy belonging to the governmental majority has written, "becomes more important than the articles of the constitution."

Over the years there have been frequent changes in organization and in personnel. More liberal policies alternated with a tightening of the reins. The Pompidou administration controlled the media most of the time, "with an iron fist." [13] The history of the ORTF, the Office of Radio Broadcasting and

---

[13] See Françoise Giroud, *La Comédie du pouvoir* (Paris: Fayard, 1977), pp. 198–200. The author was a journalist during the Pompidou years and, for a time, a cabinet member under Giscard. Her, however biased, report on experiences with the media under both administrations is therefore particularly valuable.

Television, illustrated vividly some of the more disquieting aspects of the Fifth Republic under de Gaulle and Pompidou: arbitrariness in the exercise of power and intellectual confusion combined with administrative rigidity.[14]

One of the first laws accepted by parliament after the election of Giscard d'Estaing to the presidency dissolved the unwieldy ORTF, which by that time employed some 12,000 people, and turned the various networks, TV chains, and other services into six autonomous government corporations. The new organizational structure appeared to give more freedom to the managers of the corporations, usually ranking civil servants. Yet the dismissal of one of the directors before the end of his contract impaired the belief in a true autonomy of the chains. Members of parliament sitting on the executive committees of the corporations were recruited exclusively from the majority parties.[15]

Nonetheless, the independence of the staffs increased perceptibly, quality improved, and the public gained greater confidence in the reliability of information. Not that control was entirely lifted, but its style changed. There was no longer day-by-day interference, even if programs were controversial. But the ministerial and presidential staffs let it be known which approach or which commentator was judged to be "too negativistic." Invitations to outsiders were sometimes extended, only to be withdrawn without explanation. If it had been hoped that different networks would offer a varied fare, it turned out that there was hardly any difference between the various chains. The regional relays did little to provide a measure of at least cultural autonomy. Quite typical was a remark by Giscard's Prime Minister, Raymond Barre; he rejected the

14 Hayward, *The One and Indivisible French Republic*, pp. 143 ff., provides a good summary account of that history. For an excellent collection of documents and readings see Georges Dupuis and Jean Raux, *L'O.R.T.F.* (Paris: Armand Colin, 1970).

15 For well-informed critical views on developments during the Giscard administration, see Olivier Duhamel, *La Gauche et la Ve République* (Paris: PUF, 1980), esp. pp. 96–102; and F. de Tarle, "France," in *Television: Political Life in Six European Countries*, ed. Anthony Smith (New York and London: Macmillan, 1979), pp. 59–68. The book analyzes the situation in several Western democracies and permits useful comparisons.

very idea of local radio stations because they were apt to become "destructive cells of anarchy." In 1979 the report of a parliamentary inquiry concluded that, in spite of improvements, the public media were still wanting in true independence, and that they failed to live up to the requirements of a democratic information policy.

Here too the socialist government has promised thorough reforms, but it is quite conscious that such reforms have been promised by each incoming administration. There has been, as was to be expected, once more an important turnover in personnel, although president and prime minister had promised that "no heads would roll." At least during the first months of the new era, the government made less use of the public media than its predecessors.

The Mitterrand government has announced that a new law to be submitted to parliament in 1982 would eliminate governmental control of the media and that a true decentralization of information services would be forthcoming. As a first and quite important step the government introduced legislation authorizing private radio stations to operate in France, but insisted that their radius should not exceed thirty kilometers and that they should not live on advertising revenues so as not to become dependent on "moneyed power," presumed to be hostile to the socialist government.[16]

It is quite evident from past experience that the changes that are needed and desired call for a change in habits and mentality, always more difficult to bring about than a well-intentioned piece of legislation.

[16] See Prime Minister Mauroy's speech to the National Assembly on July 8, 1981. For a well-informed article on the reform plans, see Richard Eder, "Socialists Loosen the Knots that Bind French TV," *New York Times*, October 30, 1981. For details on the legal status and the likely future of the private radio stations see Annick Cojean, "Le statut des radios libres," *Le Monde*, December 24, 1981.

CHAPTER VI

Recruitment and Style
of Decision Makers

THE "POLITICAL CLASS"

A study seeking to explain the facts of political life must determine not only who the leading actors on the political scene are, how they got there, and where they came from, but also how they wield their power. Therefore, an analysis of their own socialization and recruitment, of their background, and of their style of action is needed. Besides the decision-makers' origin many other factors, particularly the milieu in which the politicians act and interact, explain their particular style.

How to reconcile the existence of a political elite, comprising both those who live for politics and those who live off politics,[1] with the original assumptions underlying a democratic polity is a universal problem. Many modern critics of representative regimes, especially Mosca, Pareto, and Michels, have questioned the realism of democratic theory by pointing to the existence of a "power elite" holding a near-monopoly of decision making. In their writings they both scorn and praise the "political class," usually in the same moralizing tone in

[1] The distinction is made by Max Weber in "Politics as a Vocation," in *Essays in Sociology* (New York: Oxford University Press, 1958), p. 84.

which Jean-Jacques Rousseau denounced the dangers inherent in all political representation. Because of their polemic use of the term, the designation of the political decision makers in a democratic society as a "political class," has generally become the earmark of an antidemocratic bias.

However, in modern France not only the "elitist" enemies of the representative regime speak of a "political class" when they wish to criticize those who in their opinion have succeeded in "confiscating the theoretical sovereignty of the people as expressed in universal suffrage." [2] Before the First World War, Robert de Jouvenel in a still widely quoted statement referred to a few thousand political decision makers who use their monopoly of political power not to control each other, which they are supposed to do, but to further each other's ends.[3] Besides the 700 to 800 members of both houses of parliament, the holders of the more significant elective offices in municipalities or the departments, party leaders at various levels, and perhaps some journalists of national renown were counted among the political class — which altogether totaled at any one time not more than 15,000 or 20,000 persons. All of them, whether already elected to parliament, whether actual or potential candidates for national office, gravitated toward the halls of the lower or the upper house, the Chamber of Deputies, now called the National Assembly, or the Senate.

During the Third and Fourth Republics weakly organized parties, voting habits, and electoral laws combined to cut the deputies loose from any expression of political will on the part of the electorate. Isolated in their legislative chambers ("the house without windows," a scornful comment on the perhaps symbolic architecture of the parliamentary building), the deputies exercised a seemingly limitless power. Their

[2] For a typical statement, see François Goguel, in Stanley Hoffmann et al., *In Search of France* (Cambridge: Harvard University Press, 1963), p. 395. The term is also widely used by intellectual spokesmen for the political Left, such as Professor Duverger, and by liberal newspapers and periodicals, such as *Le Monde* and *Esprit*.

[3] Robert de Jouvenel, *La République des camarades* (Paris: Grasset, 1914), p. 262. For an excellent, more recent description of the French parliamentary system and its mores, see Roger Priouret, *La République des députés* (Paris: Grasset, 1959).

ritualistic style has been criticized from within no less than from the outside. Decades before General de Gaulle denounced it, the socialist leader Léon Blum, shortly before he himself became a deputy, spoke about the depressing, shut-in atmosphere of parliament and linked it to the monotonous quarrels of married couples. "If only we had in France political parties," he sighed, "and if these parties had an organization and a doctrine!" And he concluded (as early as 1917!) that the understandable reactions of the electorate toward the mores of parliament were rapidly becoming a "public danger." [4]

In the closed circuit to which it was confined, the incessant struggle for political power in parliament was actually little more than a reshuffling of cards by professional politicians "who maintained their dominance by placating the particularist interests of more influential constituents." [5]

The style in which this game was played — the rules according to which the roles were distributed — was sometimes criticized as overly dogmatic and ideological, sometimes as recklessly opportunistic. In fact it was both. Without clear mandates from either the electorate or political parties, relying on continuing mass apathy but with the traditional mission of rebelling against authority, decisions were postponed by the endless debates on matters of principle rather than bargaining realities The professed egalitarianism resulted in a passion for anonymity and made it difficult to build a stable leadership. As a matter of fact, anonymity or at least restraint in behavior was demanded from the successful member of parliament. Time and again outstanding men were resented by the public as well as by their peers. At least the appearance of mediocrity was the preferred style. Yet there developed here another dichotomy between an egalitarian style and reality. Those likely to qualify for a Cabinet post, especially those who had already been members of a government, formed a group quite distinct from the ordinary deputies or senators.

Before the First World War, the esoteric games played by

[4] "Lettres sur la réforme gouvernementale," *Revue de Paris* 6 (December 1, 1917): 453–54.

[5] Theodore Zeldin, *France: 1848–1945*, vol. 1 (Oxford: Clarendon Press, 1973), p. 570.

the representatives were not considered incongruous by the outside world, since politics itself was believed to be a game and not a condition shaping men's lives. Constantly shifting majorities gave most deputies the impression that they were simultaneously in power and in opposition. But when the crisis of the thirties changed this, the behavior of its representatives became meaningless and irritating to the French nation outside the restricted circle of an all but autonomous political class.

The constitution of 1958 shifted power away from parliament and deprived it of many of its previously important functions (for details, see Chapter X). This, however, did not alter the status of the elected representatives, deputies, and senators as a key group in the political system. They retained their importance, among other reasons, because many who aspire to positions in the political executive still seek a parliamentary seat as a stepping stone to ministerial power. But even though the political class remains anchored in parliament, the transfer of functions from parliament to the executive has nevertheless changed its makeup and style. The result has been that mixture of traditional and novel features which is characteristic of the Fifth Republic.

As before, the normal career of the French deputy (and senator as well) begins in elective offices on the local or departmental level. Because of their structural weakness, most political parties do not provide a sufficiently large and solid base for the recruitment of aspirants to a parliamentary seat. Hence a career in local government serves as the selection process, and the local implantation of deputies and senators is far stronger than in Great Britain or Germany. If in fact local government does not always provide a suitable training ground, it serves nevertheless as jumping-off point for the politically ambitious. To be taken seriously in Paris, a politician must have the credentials of local success. Traditionally the combining of the functions of a deputy or senator with those of a mayor, of a member of a departmental council, or of both, has been one of the goals of a political career.

If anything, this tradition has been reinforced in the Fifth Republic. In all of the recent legislatures the number of deputies who were concurrently mayors or members of any of the councils of local government varied between 63 and 80 percent. In the upper house, the Senate, 93 percent were also local government officials.[6] Among the 182 deputies elected for the first time in 1981, 140 were local officials. Since many of them occupied several offices simultaneously — a frequent practice made possible by the existence of various levels of French local government — these freshmen deputies held a total of 233 posts at the time of their election to parliament. Most of them were socialists. In their long years of local office they had accumulated considerable political and administrative experience, even though, on the national level, their party had been in opposition for more than twenty years.

Undoubtedly, such interlacing of national and local elective office has a stabilizing influence on both levels. Flash political movements whose activists had no local ties have usually lost momentum after a short time, and municipal affairs are not seriously disrupted by sudden upheavals.

But so close a relationship is also unsettling. Deputies and senators who know that their constituents will judge them on the basis of their successful defense of local interests will frequently spend much of their time and energy obtaining satisfaction for local concerns rather than discharging their broader national responsibilities. The situation is particularly harassing for the deputy-mayors of large cities. As "ambassador" of his commune in Paris, the deputy calls on the national executive (cabinet or administration) for the solution of local problems, and this intensifies further the centralization of decision making.[7] In European countries with a strong party system, the national parties are apt to arbitrate between centrifugal forces and national policy goals. Lacking such support, the member of parliament who is also a local officeholder must do

---

[6] For data on the local implantation of members of parliament in the Fifth Republic, see Roland Cayrol, Jean-Luc Parodi, and Colette Ysmal, *Le Député français* (Paris: Colin, 1973), pp. 115 ff., and Jean-Louis Quermonne, *Le Gouvernement de la France sous la Ve République* (Paris: Dalloz, 1980), p. 535, and the literature quoted by him.

[7] See, on this problem, Pierre Grémion, *Le Pouvoir périphérique* (Paris: Seuil, 1976), pp. 340–41.

this by and for himself, and in trying to do so, he might have to rely on the municipalities for resources which the parties lack (staff, building, money, and even programs). Those who wish to see political participation widened and competence extended beyond the fairly narrow confines of the present political class have additional reason to regret the accumulation of national and local power in one hand.[8]

The role of the political parties in nominating candidates for parliament is not altogether insignificant.[9] Especially for the Socialist and Communist candidates previous party activity is a condition of endorsement, although even for them local notoriety is a strong recommendation. For the National Assembly elected in 1968 Table V indicates the first political activities of a representative sample of deputies. It shows a considerable difference from party to party. But once elected, deputies become a more homogeneous group than one might assume from their first and varied contacts with politics.

If there is a political class, an inherited political career is very rare. It is true that Giscard d'Estaing belongs to this exceptional species of a "political family." But generally speaking there are increasingly fewer families for which elective office is a tradition as it is still in Great Britain. The chronological age of the deputies reflects, as is to be expected, the breaks that occur when one regime succeeds the other. In 1936, after the last elections of the Third Republic, 120 deputies were younger than forty, and 250 older than fifty. In the first parliament of de Gaulle's Republic, the under-forty outnumbered the over-fifty. But the average age of the deputies, although lower than in the last elections of the Fourth Re-

[8] The report, Commission de développement des responsabilités locales, *Vivre Ensemble* (Paris: Documentation Française, 1976), pp. 137–39, discusses the pros and cons of this accumulation (in French called *cumul*).

[9] See Léo Hamon, "Members of the French Parliament," *International Social Science Journal* 13, no. 4 (1961): 547 ff. In my opinion the author attributes too great an importance to the role of parties in the nomination of candidates. For a different picture from that provided by Hamon, see Oliver H. Woshinski, *The French Deputy* (Lexington: Lexington Books, 1973), pp. 51 ff. The "typical" Socialist deputy which he presents all but scorns his party and declares that he owes it nothing, least of all his election.

TABLE V. *The First Political Activities of Deputies in the National Assembly Elected in 1968 (in percentages)*

	Parties*				
First Political Activity	Com-munists	Social-ists	Radicals	Gaullists	Inde-pendent Repub-licans
Joining a party	78	67	0	37	19
Elected to office in local government	3	7	70	21	33
Member of the resistance	3	3	10	15	7
Member of a trade union or other interest group	11	23	0	4	7
Personal staff of a Cabinet minister	0	0	10	7	6
Other activities	3	0	10	16	22

* For a description of the parties here listed, see Chapter VIII.

Source: Reprinted and adapted by permission from Roland Cayrol, Jean-Luc Parodi, and Colette Ysmal, *Le Député Français* (Paris: Presses de la Fondation nationale des sciences politiques, 1973), p. 108.

public, was still higher than after the war in 1946. The average age of the deputies elected to the National Assemblies since 1968 has varied between fifty and fifty-two, with little difference between the various parties. The average age of the deputies elected to parliament for the first time in 1981 was only 43.9 years.

Political longevity, however, is of greater significance than chronological age. To acquire substantial influence it is not sufficient to be elected a deputy; it is necessary to remain one. Between 1877 and 1932, the classical era of the French representative system, two-fifths of all deputies were reelected for four-year terms between three and ten times. Three percent of the deputies were in at least seven legislatures and typically kept their seats for about a third of a century.[10] The core of

[10] See Mattei Dogan, "Political Ascent in a Class Society: French Deputies, 1870–1958," in *Political Decision-makers,* ed. Dwaine Marvick (New York: The Free Press, 1961), pp. 57–90 and the same author's "Le Personnel politique et la personnalité charismatique," *Revue française de sociologie* 6, no. 3 (1965): 305–24.

these long-time members were the *ministrables,* the group of slightly over 100 deputies who time and again returned to posts in the numerous governments that succeeded each other. They seldom changed constituencies, but rather frequently changed party labels. Especially in times of crisis, the longevity which prevailed reinforced the voters' distrust for the political class as a self-perpetuating clique. The French version of "throw the rascals out" (*Sortez les Sortants!*) was thus heard at least at each change of regime, and frequently between.

In the Fifth Republic the turnover of deputies has become heavy at times. In 1958, 406 incumbents (out of a total of 537) were not reelected; not all of them, it is true, had stood for reelection. Such a hecatomb of politicians had not occurred since the beginning of the Third Republic. In the elections of 1962 half of the deputies who won a seat were not incumbents. Nonetheless, the recruitment pattern was but little modified. Only slightly over one-fourth of the nonincumbents were truly new to elective office. The others had belonged to parliament in the past, or, most frequently, had held posts in local government. In the elections of 1968 the number of freshmen deputies rose to 139 because of the heavy influx of Gaullists. In 1973 it stood at 151 or just short of one-third of the total. In the landslide elections of 1981 the 182 freshmen made up more than one-third of the assembly and replaced a number of deputies who had served in parliament for a long time.

Women are still vastly underrepresented in parliaments. In the National Assembly elected in 1978 there were 18 women deputies, 2.4 percent of the total. After the 1981 elections their number rose to 26, most of them on either the socialist or the communist benches. There are only 4 women among the 305 members of the Senate.

The social origin of members of parliament has changed significantly since the establishment of the Third Republic in 1871. Then the nobility and the upper bourgeoisie had furnished respectively 34 and 36 percent of the deputies; in the first elections after the First World War, only 10 percent and 30 percent of the deputies could be assigned to these social categories. The middle and the small bourgeoisie were now represented by 35 percent and 15 percent respectively of the deputies.[11] Compared with that of the British House of Commons, the membership of the lower house of the French parliament has been of more modest social origin. From about 1879 on, the representatives of the middle bourgeoisie dominated parliament and Cabinets but later began to be edged out of this dominant role by men of yet lower middle-class origin. Since then, an amalgam of these two groups has become dominant, furnishing before the First World War about one-third of the deputies, during the interwar period one-half, and in the Fourth Republic about 70 percent. The number of deputies with working-class backgrounds has always been smaller than in the House of Commons and other European parliaments, partly because the syndicalist tradition of the French labor movement frowned upon the assumption of parliamentary seats by trade union leaders.

The professional background of today's deputies and the changes that have taken place since the war are illustrated in Table VI. Some of the fluctuations are due to the waxing and waning strength of the parties at a given election; others express more general trends to be observed also in the parliaments of other democracies.[12] The steady decline in numbers of those described as farmers (*agriculteurs*) is of course in part the consequence of the general decline of the farming population. But their designation is altogether misleading, since it includes not only farmers, but also the owners of large estates — and often absentee owners at that. The steadily diminish-

11 See Georges Dupeux, *La Société française 1789–1960* (Paris: Colin, 1964), p. 188; Gordon Wright, *France in Modern Times* (Chicago: Rand McNally, 1960), pp. 356 ff.; and the excellent analysis in Pierre Birnbaum, *Les Sommets de l'État: Essais sur l'élite du pouvoir en France* (Paris: Seuil, 1977).

12 For more detailed information on the background of the deputies of all parties and an excellent analysis of developments between 1945 and 1978, see Daniel Gaxie, "Les logiques du recrutement politique," *RFSP* 30, no. 1 (February 1980): pp. 5–45. Also useful is Cayrol, Parodi, and Ysmal, *Le Député français*, pp. 45–59. There are annoying discrepancies in the published data on the occupational background of deputies. See, e.g., the semi-official tabulation in Jean Bourdon, *Les Assemblées parlementaires sous la Ve République* (Paris: Documentation Française, 1978), pp. 211–12, which varies from the table given on page 158 in the text. The general trends are nonetheless unmistakable.

TABLE VI. Professional Origins of French Deputies (in percentages)

	Workers	White-collar workers	Engineers	Farmers	Teachers	Professors	Journalists	Doctors	Lawyers	Liberal professions	High civil servants	Middle-range civil servants	Middle management	Shopkeepers and craftsmen	Industrialists and managers	Others
1945–58 (Fourth Republic)	11.9	6.3	4.8	12.0	5.9	8.9	5.7	5.8	12.7	—	3.7	2.7	3.8	5.7	6.1	1.4
1958	1.5	2.6	6.0	11.0	2.1	7.7	4.9	12.0	15.9	—	7.9	2.6	7.0	4.7	10.7	0.5
1962	5.1	3.6	4.3	9.0	3.6	6.2	4.0	12.0	11.1	—	8.8	4.5	9.0	5.3	9.2	0.8
1967	4.3	4.9	3.2	8.8	5.9	8.6	3.8	6.3	9.6	3.2	6.1	5.1	10.2	5.7	4.5	3.8
1968	2.4	1.6	3.2	7.4	1.6	6.5	3.7	14.3	10.0	4.9	7.1	6.5	5.3	6.3	10.0	7.1
1973	4.8	3.3	3.5	5.2	3.5	10.1	2.9	12.0	8.0	7.6	11.4	2.9	5.0	2.8	11.4	4.4
1978	2.4	1.6	2.4	3.5	4.9	14.8	4.1	7.3	5.5	6.3	16.9	3.0	5.3	2.4	7.5	7.5
1981	3.1	1.6	3.7	2.2	4.5	28.3	3.2	5.5	5.1	4.7	21.8	1.2	3.0	1.2	4.3	2.4
1978 Total Labor Force	37.7	19.2	?	9.3	2.5	1.1	1.7				1.4	10.2		6.7	3.9	6.2

Sources: For the period 1945–1973 — Pierre Birnbaum, *Les Sommets de l'État* (Paris: Seuil, 1977), p. 71. For parliaments elected in 1978 and 1981 — *Le Monde*. Dossiers et Documents, *Les Élections législatives de Juin 1981* (June 1981), p. 84. For total labor force — Daniel Gaxie, "Les logiques du recrutement politique," *RFSP* 30, no. 1 (February 1980): 25. Used by permission.

158

ing share of blue- and white-collar workers is at least in part to be explained by the "professionalization" of parliamentary personnel: working-class candidates do not possess the skills required in a modern parliament, however diminished its powers. It is significant that the massive entry of new deputies after the socialist victory of 1981 has not reversed this trend. On the other hand, quite a few of the socialist and especially of the communist deputies, while no longer workers or employees at the time of their election, come from working-class families or have once been workers themselves.

The steady decline in the number of lawyers among the deputies started after the war and has been all but constant since then. Before the Second World War, the legal profession supplied one-fourth of all French deputies, many of them prominent, so that lawyers actually accounted for more than one-third of the Cabinet posts. There were some brilliant members of the Paris bar among them. But the vast majority were local notables, trained in law and experienced in local administration. Frequently not less competent than the heads of administrative bureaus, these lawyers imposed their style on the regime and formed the backbone of a parliament which considered the exercise of the tightest possible control over the Cabinet and the bureaucracy to be its foremost mission. Today lawyers continue to be fairly prominent in elective positions at the local level. But their interest in seeking national office has flagged, as has the inclination of parties to select them as candidates. They have been replaced by other professional groups.

Prior to the 1981 election there had been a relatively large and increasing number of businessmen, engineers, and industrial managers among the deputies. But their role in parliament has been minor compared, for instance, with that of medical doctors. The teaching profession is the strongest single group in the National Assembly elected in 1981: teachers and professors make up almost one-third of total membership. Secondary school teachers, designated in French statistics as professors, are particularly numerous among the socialist deputies: almost 60 percent of the socialist group in parliament are or have been members of the teaching profession.

The number of "intellectuals" (in a broad sense) — teachers, professors, journalists, and other liberal professions — has always been higher in the French than in other parliaments. In 1927 an account of the political regime spoke of the "Republic of the Professors." [13] The highly revered *École Normale Supérieure* in Paris, training ground for many university professors, especially in the humanities and in the social sciences, functioned for many generations as a "political seminar." Many parliamentary leaders, predominantly those of the Left, discovered and sharpened their political ambitions while they were students at the school. Undoubtedly, the ideological style characteristic of political life must in part be ascribed to the high proportion of intellectuals in the political class.

> In France, at least, it was the intellectuals who were most impassioned in political debates in the Assembly under the Fourth Republic as under the Third. They were often the most intransigent ideologues. . . . they were apt to pose problems abstractly, with more or less sincerity, and often to expound them with ability. But this aptitude meant that they often proposed unrealistic solutions; and that they fixed upon subtleties and neglected essentials, thus uselessly complicating and prolonging parliamentary debates by inventing false problems and disagreeing among themselves.[14]

Moreover, the participation of intellectuals in French political life has never been restricted to parliament. Perhaps one should call Voltaire the first French "intellectual in politics." In the nineteenth century such traditions continued. In the short-lived Second Republic, a poet (Lamartine) and a scientist (Raspail) played prominent political roles. Subsequently, Victor Hugo and Émile Zola participated actively in politics. More recently, a number of outstanding writers (Gide, Barrès, Malraux, Sartre, Aron, and Mauriac) have let their voices be heard in the political marketplace both on the Right and on

---

13 Albert Thibaudet, *La République des professeurs* (Paris: Grasset, 1927).

14 Dogan in *Political Decision-makers*, Marvick, p. 67.

the Left. De Gaulle was considered by many, not incorrectly, as an "intellectual in uniform."

The large influx of members of the teaching profession into the parliament elected in 1981 does not signal a return to the "Republic of the Professors." In the present republic parliament no longer plays the predominant role it held in the 1920s. And inside parliament the rising influence of the high bureaucracy is an indication that power and prestige have shifted.[15] The number of deputies with civil service status is unusually high, since most of the teachers in public schools and universities are also civil servants and because a few deputies belong to the middle ranks of the administration. All told, 56 percent of the members of the National Assembly have been on the public payroll before they were elected. But politically more significant is the fact that in 1981, 107 deputies, or 21.8 percent of the total, came from the upper ranks of the bureaucracy and more than one-half of these from the administrative elite corps, whose importance in the political system will be discussed below. As Table VI shows, the number of top civil servants in the assembly has risen constantly, another development which the Left landslide of 1981 has not interrupted.

The political involvement of many of the younger bureaucrats is emulating the participation of their elders in the resistance movement during the war. Even more important than their number is the political weight which these deputy-bureaucrats are carrying in parliament. They sit on all major parliamentary committees and frequently serve as their chairmen. They are the rapporteurs of important bills and participate in parliamentary debates on questions on which they have expert knowledge. Their style mixes technical expertise with a certain intellectual flair, quite typical of the top-flight administrator in France.

15 The central problem of the relationship between politics and administration is discussed in all of its intricacies and with a wealth of documentation in the symposium, *Administration et Politique sous la Cinquième République,* eds. F. de Baecque and J.-L. Quermonne (Paris: PFNSP, 1981). For the data that follow in the text, see Francis de Baecque, L'Interpénétration des personnels administratifs et politiques," ibid., pp. 19–60.

Some of the civil servants that stand for election to parliament have previously held positions in the political executive, either as members of the ministerial staffs (for the political role of the latter, see Chapter IX) or as junior ministers. In parliament they expect to be counted among the *ministrables* and hope for a post in the Cabinet, their position enhanced by the fact that they have established themselves in a constituency.

Further evidence of the political engagement of members of the high bureaucracy is their presence in the top leadership of the political parties. Ranking administrators are represented in fairly large numbers on the executive boards of all parties, with the exception of the communists. The higher one goes in the party hierarchies, the more numerous are the civil servants one encounters. This rather recent development shows clearly how solid the links between the "political class" and the high bureaucracy have become.

There is controversy about whether this development has resulted in the politicization of the civil service or in the bureaucratization of politics.[16] To answer the question, if it can be answered at all, it will first be necessary to discuss the role of the bureaucracy in the political system and in society.

THE BUREAUCRATS

France was one of the pioneers of bureaucracy in Europe. When the French kings needed money they did not turn to parliament as royalty did in England, but sold offices. They kept absolutism intact at the price of increasing enormously the number of civil service jobs all through the sixteenth and seventeenth centuries.[17] In the middle of the nineteenth century Tocqueville remarked that "since 1789 the administrative system has always stood firm among the debacles of political

[16] This question is raised and discussed by Jean-Louis Quermonne, "Politisation de l'Administration ou Fonctionnarisation de la Politique," ibid., pp. 329–60. For a comparative perspective, see Joel D. Aberbach, Robert D. Putnam, Bert A. Rockman, *Bureaucrats and Politicians in Western Democracies* (Cambridge: Harvard University Press, 1981).

[17] Zeldin, *France: 1848–1945*, p. 113. His entire chapter "Bureaucrats" provides excellent historical background.

systems." [18] He personally had known top administrators who had entered the ranks of the bureaucracy before the storming of the Bastille and who retired at the end of an uninterrupted career long after the Bourbons had been restored to power. Since Tocqueville wrote, it has become axiomatic that the vagaries of the actors on the political stage have been balanced and thereby rendered largely innocuous by a stable bureaucracy. It is quite true that some of the anarchic and demagogic tendencies of the political system could be indulged in only behind the protective shield of a seemingly regular pattern of administrative behavior. But the latter never did neatly balance the former so that a satisfactory equilibrium could be established. Indeed, since they relied on each other, there was symbiosis as much as opposition between the two systems.

In the judgment of a recent French observer, in many ways a latter-day Tocqueville, "the bureaucratic system of organization of French public administration is certainly one of the most entrenched of such closed systems of social action that has existed in the modern world." [19] This came about not only because an administration, burdened as it was with tasks which it shares in other representative regimes with the political leadership, sought strength in isolation. An intense dislike for all outsiders of whatever social origin had been a characteristic of the civil service under the Old Regime. Later, both the elected representatives — the "political class" — and the bureaucrats waxed intolerant of individuals and associations who wished to take independent action, removed from the aegis of either administration or parliament. The decision makers' aversion to the interference of "outsiders" was deepened by the citizens ingrained and learned incapacity for cooperation and participation. Hence there was in the end congruence between French society and its administrative style. Such congruence goes far to explain the singular success of French bureaucracy in the political system, as well as its shortcomings. A comparison of the pattern of French adminis-

[18] Alexis de Tocqueville, *The Old Régime and the French Revolution* (New York: Doubleday Anchor Books, 1955), p. 202.

[19] Michel Crozier, *The Bureaucratic Phenomenon* (Chicago: The University of Chicago Press, 1964), p. 308.

tration and of its success with that of other countries not only highlights a difference in techniques, in recruitment, and in style. It permits comparing different political cultures on an all-important level.[20]

There are between 3,000 and 10,000 high civil servants in France whose functions correspond by and large to those of the former administrative class of the British civil service. Among the high civil servants about 300 to 500 can be singled out as active and often daily participants in the process of political decision making. In French they are sometimes called the *grands fonctionnaires,* while their next-ranking colleagues are merely high (*hauts*) administrators. (Under the monarchy, the *grands,* the highest noblemen, defied the king on many occasions.)

The selection of even the highest (as well as of the lowest) civil servants takes place by rigorous competitive entrance examinations, in which elaborate rites guard against all favoritism, and give the appearance of upholding the passion for equality. When after the Second World War Michel Debré, the first prime minister of the Fifth Republic, established another grande école, the *École Nationale d'Administration* (ENA), he pursued the same goal as Napoleon I when he founded the *École Polytechnique*: both wanted to open the civil service to "talent," whatever its economic standing or family background. In 1945, the demands for infusing the political and administrative elites with new blood had been particularly strident. It seemed opportune to break the de facto monopoly which the *École Libre des Sciences Politiques* had held over the preparation for entrance examinations to the top positions. The students of that school, founded in 1871, in the aftermath of another floundering political regime, came almost entirely from among the uppermost Parisian bourgeoisie, with an admixture of aristocratic elements. This led to a recruitment for the top level of the bureaucracy which was vastly different from that of the American civil service. By

---

[20] F. Ridley and J. Blondel, *Public Administration in France* (New York: Barnes and Noble, 1969) is implicitly comparative. Invaluable for many of the problems discussed here is Ezra N. Suleiman, *Politics, Power, and Bureaucracy* (Princeton: Princeton University Press, 1974).

and large it can be said that even today in the United States the bureaucracy, both federal and state, represents a cross section of society and is therefore likely to reflect its values. This never has been the case in France. The knowledge and mentality required to pass the various *concours* that gave access to the top administrative positions narrowed the field of successful candidates so drastically that the children of senior civil servants had many advantages. This led to a situation in which the ranking bureaucracy formed something approaching a hereditary class. Even today at least one-sixth of each graduating class of the École Polytechnique, training the ranking state engineers and called respectfully the X, are the sons and grandsons of that school's alumni.

In order to democratize recruitment without abandoning the customary high standards of performance, the new school of administration was to open its training facilities not only to all qualified students, but in equal number to those already serving in the less exalted echelons of the civil service. By their admission to the school they could prepare for advancement to the apex of the bureaucratic pyramid.

Since its establishment the ENA has admitted annually one out of ten applicants and graduated about 100 students each year after a two-year course (since 1972, 10 to 15 percent of the graduates have been women). As an instrument of social promotion, the school has proven a disappointment. As Table II shows, the background of students who graduated between 1970 and 1975 was still overwhelmingly upper class and far more so than that of university students. Prior to a reform of 1971, specifically designed to enlarge the social and geographic bases for recruitment, 95 percent of the admitted candidates had prepared for the entrance examination at the Paris School of Political Science, which enrolls again more upper-middle class students than it did in the immediate postwar years. Since the reform about one-half of the students come from families outside Paris, but many among these "provincials" still find it advisable to prepare at Paris for admission to the ENA.

That the number of successful candidates from inside the civil service has declined, also defeats original intentions. Too few of these candidates, who usually come from modest families, appear qualified. Since the reform of 1971 the number of graduates from this group is on the increase, and the reform has therefore been called a success. But the majority of successful candidates are still recruited among students.[21] The foremost reason for a selectivity that favors upper-class candidates is the nature of the entrance examinations. Like most other academic tests in France, and especially the *concours* opening the grandes écoles, they continue to put a high premium on skills, style, and attitudes that are acquired within the bourgeois family — traditional knowledge, elegance of exposition, and familiarity with and adjustment to the dominant humanistic culture — rather than on original thinking and on "raw" native ability.[22] Once admitted, the performance of many students at the school still varies according to their social status: the higher their class background, the better their grades and therefore their first assignments in the administrative hierarchy. By 1968 some 68 percent of those who, since the founding of the school, had graduated at the top of their class and were therefore free to choose the most prestigious positions in the administration were the children of high civil servants or came from families with a professional or managerial background (a group which in the active population amounts to 9.5 percent). A slow increase in the number of candidates from the middle and lower middle classes is the only transformation that has taken place over almost three decades. But candidates from working-class and from farming families are still rarely successful.[23]

---

21 On the reform and its results see Jean-Luc Bodiguel, "Nouveaux concours, nouveaux 'Enarques'?" *La Revue Administrative* 31, no. 186 (November–December 1978): 610–17. The data on the social composition of the student body given in his article betray an even more unfavorable picture of the ENA's "democratization" than those in Table II.

22 The upper-class oriented characteristics of these examinations are well described and criticized by François Bloch-Lainé, himself an upper-class, high civil servant, in *Profession: Fonctionnaire* (Paris: Seuil, 1976), pp. 45–47.

23 See Jean-Luc Bodiguel, *Les Anciens Élèves de L'ENA* (Paris: PFNSP, 1978), pp. 196; and, in general on the question of the social origin of the top administrators, Alain Darbel and Dominique Schnapper, *Le Système administratif*, vol. II (Paris: Mouton, 1972), p. 104.

The education and training that future high civil servants receive both before and after their admission to the ENA is in many ways different from that of prewar times. If many of them acquire law degrees or political science diplomas before their admission to the ENA, these are fields of study that have themselves been reformed substantially. At the ENA itself more attention is now paid to macroeconomics rather than to narrow fiscal and accounting studies. The passion for system-building based on abstractions has subsided. The discourse between instructors and trainees and among the trainees themselves is pragmatic and deliberately unideological. A modified case method and an attempt to provide an integrated social science knowledge are characteristics of the instruction. While the training shies away from providing much "administrative science," it includes a good deal of administrative practice. The so-called *stages,* periods of in-service training at various administrations in different parts of the country but also at industrial firms, have become more important than lectures and seminars. Uncertainties and discussions about an appropriate curriculum have not abated. In answer to a question on whether the ENA made sense at all, one of the most experienced and widely respected ranking civil servants replied: "Little sense. It brings people together and ranks them. But it doesn't do much to instruct them." [24]

Criticism of the school has come from outside and inside the bureaucracy. The graduates of the ENA, filling the top ranks of the administrative hierarchy, are reproached for lacking sensitivity for human relations, for their ineptitude in contacts with the outside, and for their exclusive commitment to efficiency to the neglect of other values. As late as 1973, a former student and now a ranking administrator confided:

> There is one thing which one does not learn at the School and that's humility. . . . The graduates of the E.N.A. are supposed

[24] Bloch-Lainé, *Fonctionnaire,* p. 236. The author was chairman of a committee appointed to propose reforms of the ENA. See also his pertinent observations in "Réflexions sur l'avenir de l'E.N.A.," *Preuves* (Iᵉ Trimestre, 1970): 113–20.

to be at the service of the people. But all too frequently they act as if they had the monopoly of wisdom while they are in fact cut off from public opinion. The E.N.A. is simply a school of arrogance.[25]

Yet it is quite obvious that the school only reflects a mentality and methods produced by an administrative system whose very centralization bars its operators from contact with life. The deficiencies for which the ENA is frequently impugned can hardly be corrected by mere changes in the school's curriculum, but would require thorough reforms of administrative and educational structures. Because the socialist-led government understands this and not merely because so many ENA graduates are filling top-level posts in its Cabinet and on ministerial staffs, it is likely that the "School of Bureaucrats" will survive unscathed.

Another expectation of the reformers of 1945 has also come to naught: the common training in the ENA has not unified the long compartmentalized civil service. Since the bureaucratic apparatus has remained essentially unchanged, the *grands corps,* the administrative super-elite, are as strong as they were at a time when candidates for these coveted positions prepared individually for exacting entrance examinations that were different for each corps. In practice this amounted to an unabashed cooptation by the senior members of each corps. Now the competition between the students at the ENA to graduate at the top of their class is quite ferocious, for their ranking determines their range of choice among the elite corps whose influence, prestige, and snobbery have remained unbroken for more than a century and a half. The most prestigious corps are, as they have always been, those of the Inspectorate of Finance, of the Council of State, and of the Court of Accounts; the diplomatic and the prefectoral

[25] For this and similar statements and a rebuttal by Pierre Racine, director of the ENA until 1975, see *Contrepoint,* no. 11 (1973): 193–98. For one of the sharpest criticisms of the school, see Jacques Mandrin (the pseudonym for three graduates of the ENA, all of a socialist bent and all of them in important positions since 1981), *L'Enarchie ou les mandarins de la société bourgeoise* (Paris: Table Ronde de Combat, 1967).

corps rank somewhat lower.[26] Other prestigious corps recruit their members among the graduates of the *X* or other grandes écoles. The most brilliant of these state engineers (who can be compared to the United States Army Corps of Engineers) occupy high executive positions in the nationalized enterprises. The corps continue, probably with greater effectiveness than the ENA, the socialization and the training of their younger members.

At present about three-fourths of the approximately 7,000 civil servants in the grands corps come from the highest and predominantly Parisian elite strata in society to which most of their families have belonged for several generations. To their inherited social status is added the prestige which they acquire through their professional status. It has been noted that in a country in which the number of regular church-goers has fallen to 13 percent of the male population (see Chapter III), half of the members of the elite corps attend church every Sunday.[27] They enjoy privileges not granted to others (and not easily granted to many civil servants in any country): they are free to voice publicly their opinion on a wide range of public affairs. Their writings have often been sharply critical of the government they serve; it has always been known that quite a few of them had socialist sympathies or were actually members of the Socialist Party.

What differentiates the members of the grands corps from other ranking administrators are their general competence and mobility. Considered a reservoir for talent of all sorts and held in high repute for a traditional impartiality, they serve not only the administrations to which they are formally attached but are sent on a virtually unlimited number of exacting assignments. At any one time about one-third of the members of the Council of State (which is nominally an administrative

---

[26] For a succinct description of the five grands corps, see Quermonne, *Le Gouvernement,* pp. 486–95. See also, Jean-Claude Thoenig, "La Stratification," in *Où va l'Administration Française,* eds. Michel Crozier et al. (Paris: Éditions d'Organisation, 1974).

[27] See Catherine Grémion, *Profession: décideurs. Pouvoir des Hauts Fonctionnaires et réforme de l'État* (Paris: Gauthier-Villiers, 1979), p. 400, a valuable sociological analysis of the high bureaucracy.

tribunal) and two-thirds of the inspectors of finance might be on detached service or on special missions. They also occupy top positions — the coveted places of *directeur* — in the important ministries. They are in charge of the numerous interministerial committees entrusted with laying the groundwork for the preparation of important decisions. Though they do not always have direct control over decision making, they consider themselves, and with much justification, the "intellectuals" in the administrative machinery. They usually rise much faster in the bureaucratic hierarchy than their fellow graduates who did not "make" the top elite corps.

If the members of all of the grands corps are a somewhat self-conscious caste within the larger group of the high civil servants, the different corps are also divided among themselves. Every corps is both a fortress and a prison for its members, providing an informal network that is sometimes ironically referred to as a mafia. Its rivalries and controversies with other corps stem from a different perspective on what needs to be done. Here decisions are fought over in a passionate and often almost chauvinistic style. This kind of particularism tends to interfere with overall effectiveness and adds instability to the system. It sometimes deprives the country of one of the possible advantages of centralization, namely the coherence of policy making.[28]

Yet in many situations, and especially in times of crisis, the grands corps, together with certain other top civil servants, have provided the personalities that are capable of imposing necessary reforms. Whereas in other countries the administration ordinarily only reacts to innovating impulses originating elsewhere, the French administrative elite can and has in fact become the agent of change for the entire system. But their acquired ways of problem solving and the resistance to change of the bureaucratic system of which they are part even if they

[28] For a discussion of the merits and demerits of the "administrative super-elite," see the chapter which Suleiman devotes to this question in *Politics, Power, and Bureaucracy*, pp. 239–81, and the same author's *Elites in French Society: The Politics of Survival* (Princeton: Princeton University Press, 1978), which is based mostly on interviews with members of what the author calls the "state elites."

are its critics, will regularly "turn reformers into authoritarian, charismatic personalities acting intuitively rather than rationally." [29] An often-heard criticism that the ENA-rques (as the graduates of the ENA are usually referred to) are narrow specialists appears to be quite inappropriate. With some exceptions, neither their training nor their preference have given them specialized skills. They rather think of themselves as generalists, or as "polyvalent managers." Some of them admit quite readily that this encourages a tendency to engage in a superficial "muddling through." [30]

The ethos of the top-ranking bureaucrats has long included the strong conviction that they are the principal if not the sole defenders of the public interest. (The considerations which follow here apply not only to the small "super-elite" of the grands corps but to many high civil servants.) One aspect of their ethos is the absence of corruption. There are hardly any scandals involving the financial integrity of a high civil servant. But, on the other hand, he might easily believe that he alone is virtuous. Until he himself chooses to run for elective office, he resents parliamentary institutions and their traditional personnel as disintegrating forces because, under the assault of special interest and of particularism, they are apt to dismantle the reform proposals hatched in the administrative bureaus.

A close and astute observer of the administrative scene in France, himself a member of one of the elite corps, has distinguished two role conceptions which prevailed among civil servants in the 1950s and 1960s. "For one group among the highest civil servants, the state is the carrier of progress, for the other an important arbiter, but in the eyes of both the

[29] Michel Crozier, *The Stalled Society* (New York: The Viking Press, 1973), p. 90. Crozier's earlier optimism about the positive role of the grand corps, as expressed in his *Bureaucratic Phenomenon*, pp. 297, 309, has been muted rather considerably in his more recent reflections. Very critical also is Alain Peyrefitte, *The Trouble with France* (New York: Knopf, 1981), esp. in Parts III and IV of his vociferous indictment of the French administrative system.

[30] See Suleiman, *Elites*, for an entire chapter (pp. 158–92) entitled "Non-specialization and organisational dexterity."

state is authoritarian and paternal and free from all political ferment." [31]

In the 1970s, and at least in part as a consequence of the explosions of 1968, attitudes changed and many high civil servants admittedly lost faith in the classical bureaucratic model. Many of the benefits they expected to derive from modern management techniques did not really improve planning and output. Technocratic arrogance made room for more moderate views as to what the state can and should do.[32] Undoubtedly some of the rather brilliant achievements of industries in the private sector of the economy impressed the civil servants to the point of persuading them to abandon their assumed role as the preceptors of the nation.

The great problems which the national collectivity had and continues to face (the Algerian problem and decolonization; European integration; foreign and defense policies; desirable priorities in economic and social policies; decentralization and regionalism) have divided the bureaucracy as they have other elites. Before long, seemingly technical conflicts have turned into political disagreements, themselves the result of polarizations concerning fundamentals or personalities. The greater pragmatism that prevails generally has led many civil servants to take a less exalted view of their role as infallible arbiters. They have not abandoned the concept of a general interest whose defense legitimizes the representative role of the civil service. But the concept has lost its metaphysical vagueness. The bureaucracy has been brought around to admit that there is no wall between the public and the private, no clear dividing line between politics and administration, and that

[31] Bernard Gournay, "Higher Civil Servants in France," translated in *European Politics, A Reader,* eds. Mattei Dogan and Richard Rose (Boston: Little, Brown, 1971), pp. 510–12. The entire article, published first in 1964, deserves close study. A well-informed updating of Gournay's insights is to be found in Catherine Grémion, *Profession: décideurs* (Paris: Gauthier-Villiers, 1979).

[32] Typical is a special issue on administrative problems of the respected magazine *Esprit* 38, no. 1 (1970) where (in 200 pages!) a variety of writers, among them highly placed administrators and judges, discuss the crisis of the system.

virtue and vice are not as neatly distributed as they once assumed.[33]

The mobility of the French high civil servant is not confined to moves inside the state bureaucracy but extends to his availability for employment in the private sector. The so-called *pantouflage* — one puts on the "soft slippers" of jobs outside the civil service — has always been a rather common practice in France; other countries have followed the example more recently but on a more modest scale. For the first decade after the war the graduates of the ENA scorned pantouflage as a betrayal of their ideal of public service. The students of the École Polytechnique and of other engineering schools never had such scruples. They graduate from their respective schools as state engineers, but after a few years, between 30 and 50 percent of them are employed by industry. The departure of former military officers for private employment might be even more frequent. By now the pantouflage of ENA graduates has also taken on considerable proportions. Not surprisingly, those who, upon graduation, had not been admitted to the elite corps and whose ambitions had been frustrated, leave public service more frequently than the corps members. But the number of the highly qualified finance inspectors who have assumed leading positions in banking is also very high. Since many of these banks were nationalized in 1945–1946, the former bureaucrats remain on the public payroll even though they are no longer line civil servants. The same is true of the graduates of the engineering schools, who are put in charge of nationalized industries. It is estimated that between 20 and 25 percent of ranking civil servants are presently employed outside of the administrative hierarchy. Forty-three percent of the presidents of the 100 most important business firms have once been in public service, and 12 percent of these belong to the two most prestigious corps, the Council of State and the Inspectorate of Finance.[34]

---

[33] See the important discussion on changes in the bureaucratic mentality by Jacques Chevallier, "Un Nouveau Sens de l'État et du Service Public," in *Administration et Politique,* de Baecque and Quermonne, pp. 163–204.

[34] Here again the data are uncertain. Where more precise figures are given, they are usually based on such somewhat dubious sources as the

What is more important than numbers is the significance of pantouflage for the fusion of elites.[35] Public service and large-scale business (and business associations as well) are manned by a group which is by no means totally homogeneous, but which shares social origin, training, and, often, style of operation. As we have seen, the same personnel have now also entered parliament in large numbers and occupy prominent positions in the political executive, which they might leave later for private employment.

Fusion there is, but this does not mean that a conspiracy of a powerful "technocracy" manipulates French society and its democratic institutions at will. Existing political controls are still effective enough to prevent this, and political impulses have not died out. Both will be discussed in the chapters that follow.

THE JUDGES

All French judges are without exception civil servants. One of the first reforms of the Fifth Republic was to revamp the country's judicial structure (see Figure III). The reform was generally hailed as rational and progressive. It was followed by a reorganization of recruitment and training of judges. Now the principal, though not the only, avenue to a judicial position is graduation from a national center of judicial studies in Bordeaux, renamed in 1970 *École Nationale de la Magistrature* (ENM). Its students are admitted after successful studies in any of the existing law schools and upon passing an exact-

---

Who's Who in France and on personal interviews. Whether, in view of what has been said about the training and the outlook of the high civil servants, they are the most appropriate managers in an expanding economy is a question which cannot be discussed here. But see John H. McArthur and Bruce R. Scott, *Industrial Planning in France* (Cambridge: Harvard University Press, 1969).

35 The literature on pantouflage is now extensive. Existing findings are summarized and evaluated critically in two books by Pierre Birnbaum, *Les Sommets*, pp. 139–50, and *La Classe dirigeante française* (Paris: PUF, 1978), pp. 63–90. For some additional data, see Bernard Brizay, *Le Patronat* (Paris: Seuil, 1975), pp. 288–89, and Suleiman, *Elites*, pp. 226–50 and *passim*.

FIGURE III. *The Judicial System of the French Republic*

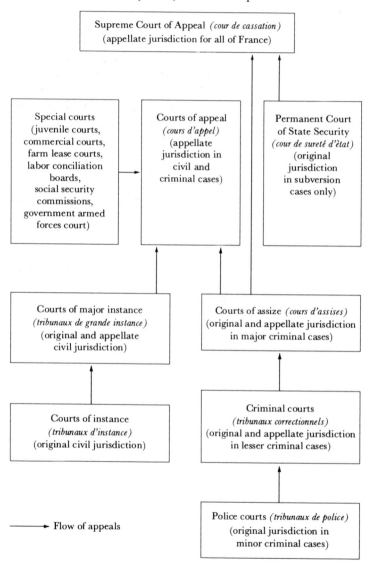

Source: From *The Judicial Process: An Introductory Analysis of the Courts of the United States, England, and France*. 3rd ed., by Henry J. Abraham. Copyright © 1962, 1968, 1975 by Oxford University Press, Inc. Reprinted by permission.

ing entrance examination. The school is admittedly patterned somewhat after the ENA, but preparing, as it does, for a specific activity, the ENM has more of the characteristics of a professional school than the ENA. But while the ENA, for all the criticism that has been voiced against it, has always remained attractive for the ambitious, the School for Judges has been shaken periodically by crises. Especially since the events of 1968, the young men and women at the school have questioned not only some of the assumptions that underlie their training and its style, but also the traditional role of the French judiciary. The discontent of the future judges, which has sometimes been voiced openly, has not been to the government's liking, and at times the ministry was accused of limiting unduly the number of candidates and of preferring to fill vacancies by the lateral entrance permitted by law.[36] The latter opens judicial posts on either a permanent or a temporary basis to persons, usually older, with legal training and experience outside of the school, such as former lawyers, civil servants, etc.

Over the last ten years the number of judges has increased by about 35 percent, but it is still lower than before the First World War and equals about that of a century and a half ago. For a population of 52 million France has now about 5,400 judges; one-fourth of them are serving as public prosecutors. (West Germany, with a population only 8 million larger, has almost four times as many judges.) In spite of a steadily increasing case load,[37] the annual budget of the Ministry of Justice, out of which all judicial personnel is paid, has been below 1 percent of the national budget for thirty years, a reflection on the relatively low prestige of the judiciary.

[36] See the detailed article by Pierre Martaguet, "Comment devient-on magistrat?" *Pouvoirs* 16 (1981): 107–18.

[37] In a 1979 press conference the Minister of Justice stated that within the preceding six years the criminal case load had increased by 44 percent, the number of civil cases before the Supreme Court by 55 percent (*Le Monde*, December 15, 1979). For a general discussion of the "judicial system in crisis," see Robert Boure and Patrick Mignard, *La Crise de l'institution judiciaire* (Paris: C. Bourgois, 1977).

Generalizations about the social and geographical origin of the judiciary are difficult: there are differences not only for different age groups, but also between the graduates of the ENM and those who either became judges prior to the establishment of the school or who entered the profession from the outside. The latter two groups come from solid, upper middle-class families, many of them with a long judicial tradition. Unlike the members of the high bureaucracy, most of these judges do not hail from the Parisian bourgeoisie, but from urban centers in the provinces, mostly south of the Loire River and often from regions of mediocre economic development. The picture changes for judges under forty who make up one-third of the present judiciary, most of whom are graduates of the ENM. While a majority of them also come from professional families, one-third are now of lower middle-class or working-class origin. The outstanding new development is the feminization of the judiciary: presently 21.4 percent of all judges are women, and for the age group under thirty-four, the percentage is as high as 43.8.[38]

In a civil-law country such as France, judges are no longer expected to be automatons who reach their decisions merely by quoting from the appropriate statutes. In all developed societies the range of new problems leading to litigation is enormous. While judicial style in civil law and common law systems may still differ, nowhere can judges keep out of the controversies of the times.[39] They cannot help playing a political role. "Judges are not 'sold to the bourgeoisie,'" a critical judge has stated, "they are part and parcel of it." [40]

[38] For these and other very complete data on the present judicial personnel, see Jean-Luc Bodiguel, "Qui sont les magistrats français? Esquisse d'une sociologie," *Pouvoirs* 16 (1981): 31–42, and Syndicat de la magistrature, *Justice sous influence* (Paris: Maspero, 1981), pp. 187–88.

[39] On this problem, see Henri Mendras, "Une figure de la France," in *La Sagesse et le désordre: France 1980,* ed. Henri Mendras (Paris: Gallimard, 1980), p. 59. He concludes that at present the judicial process in France comes to resemble more and more common law practices. Along the same lines, see Henry W. Ehrmann, *Comparative Legal Cultures* (Englewood Cliffs: Prentice-Hall, 1976), *passim*.

[40] Casamayor, *Les Juges* (Paris: Seuil, 1959), p. 143, and the same author's, "Justice et politique," *La Nef* 27, no. 39 (1970): 35 ff. The entire issue of *La Nef* is devoted to a serious discussion of the judiciary and the

Because of the many new demands made upon the judges, judicial independence is more important than ever. The constitution of 1958 makes the President of the Republic its guarantor (Art. 64). Since entry into the profession, as into all civil service positions, is by examination, there is little if any favoritism prevalent in the selection process, except that once again the cultural advantages of their upbringing will favor the young bourgeois. However, political considerations may have an impact on the judicial career when promotions, the more or less rapid advancement of judges to higher and more important posts, are decided on. A long uphill struggle has been waged in France, and elsewhere, to wrest discretion from the executive, which has an irresistible tendency to reward loyalty and conformism when possibilities for judicial advancement open up.

In the Fifth Republic the situation has deteriorated rather than improved. An announcement made by de Gaulle in a press conference of 1964 had a chilling effect: judicial power, he declared, was just as all other powers, part of the "indivisible authority of the state" and entrusted "in its entirety to the President of the Republic by the people who have elected him." The institutional link between the Head of State and the judicial system is the Superior Council of the Judiciary, presided over by the President and composed, in addition to the President and the Minister of Justice, of nine members, all appointed by the President. Representatives of parliament who had been members of a similar body in the Fourth Republic were eliminated: the five judges on the Council are no longer elected by their peers as they had been previously. The Council has the sole authority to nominate the judges of the Supreme Court (*Cour de Cassation*) and the Chief Justices of the Courts of Appeal. The nomination, thereby also the promotion, of all other judges is in the hands of the Minister of Justice, which means that the powers of the execu-

---

problems of judicial reform. For interesting details on the relationship between political authority and the judiciary see Georges Lavau, "Le Juge et le pouvoir politique," in *La Justice,* ed. Louis Trotabas (Paris: PUF, 1961), pp. 59 ff.

tive are practically unlimited. In the words of a moderate judges' association, the government has promoted to high positions judges whose "lack of seniority is compensated by nothing except merits that have no relation to the way in which they have attended to their professional duties." [41]

Judges cannot be removed without disciplinary proceedings, but they can be moved to out-of-the-way places and under certain conditions against their will. A system of periodic ratings by their superiors promotes, at least where judges are desirous of advancement, conformism and caution rather than originality and daring. In all European systems the control which the Minister of Justice exercises over the public prosecutors is quite open and direct. But since in France the prosecutors share background and training with the judges, and since both are part of the same "corps," there often exists what has been called an osmosis between the prosecutors and the judges on the bench.[42]

Irritation with the heavy hand of the executive was the foremost reason why, in the wake of 1968, judges formed their own trade union. At one time the *Syndicat de la Magistrature* claimed to count more than one-fourth of all judges among its members. It has defended judicial independence and has publicized alleged miscarriages in the administration of justice.[43] Of late, its influence and membership have receded because of its outright partisan stand and of its close identification with

---

[41] *Le Monde,* June 12, 1969.

[42] See Jack Hayward, *The One and Indivisible French Republic* (London: Weidenfeld & Nicolson, 1973), p. 128; and, more comprehensively on the problems of political interference with the judicial process, François Sarda, "L'Intervention du pouvoir dans les instances judiciaires," *Pouvoirs* 16 (1981): 69–78. (The author is a highly respected member of the Paris bar.)

[43] For an excellent short history of the judges' union by one of its founders, now somewhat critical of its later development, see Pierre Lyon-Caen, "L'Experiénce du Syndicat de la Magistrature: Temoignage," *Pouvoirs* 16 (1981): 15–68. For the rather abundant publications by the union, see, among others, Syndicat de la Magistrature, *Au Nom du Peuple Français* (Paris: Stock, 1974), and *Justice sous Influence* (Paris: Maspéro, 1981). It also issues a journal, *Justice.* For an address by the president of the competing and older judges' association, see André Braunschweig, "La Magistrature et le Syndicalisme," in Académie des Sciences Morales et Politiques, *Communications* (October 4, 1976).

the labor movement. But it was joined by the older and more sedate judges' association in lobbying and trying to mobilize public opinion against a bill introduced by Giscard's Minister of Justice, which, in the interest of law and order, circumscribed more narrowly the powers of the judiciary in criminal proceedings. The socialist government promised to abrogate the law; but during its first year in office rising criminality has deterred it from submitting the reform to parliament. What the Prime Minister called the "long awaited" reform of the Superior Council of the Judiciary has also been promised for the near future. Whether this can be done without a constitutional amendment remains questionable.

CHAPTER VII

Interests: Secured and Frustrated

ORIGINS AND FORMS OF
INTEREST REPRESENTATION

In every polity there exist means to bring the demands and desires prevalent in the society to the attention of the decision makers.[1] In France, as elsewhere, this function is served by a variety of structures. As in all modern states, the associational interest or pressure groups which specialize in expressing values and interests through a more or less permanent organization occupy the foreground of the political stage. But other structures have by no means lost all importance. What have been called nonassociational groups, distinguished families, local or regional notables, prominent religious leaders, and especially the modern business firms or "industrial empires," exercise in France an influence which, although it is intermittent, often outweighs that of trade associations, trade unions, or other groups. Some of the most important firms have direct and satisfactory access to the centers of decision making and

[1] See Gabriel Almond and G. Bingham Powell, Jr., *Comparative Politics: Systems, Process, and Policy* (Boston: Little, Brown, 1978), pp. 169 ff. The discussion that follows adopts the framework established by these authors in Chapter VII of their book. It also owes much to a more recent contribution to the comparative study of interest groups, *Organizing Interests in Western Europe: Pluralism, Corporatism, and the Transformation of Politics*, ed. Suzanne D. Berger (Cambridge: Cambridge University Press, 1981).

consider the cumbersome associational groups as an unnecessary concession to democracy. The moral, and sometimes political, influence of church leaders is exercised quite regularly outside the channels of the numerous organizations animated and controlled by the Catholic hierarchy. In rural regions, the mayors and other local officials derive only part of their influence from the associations to which they might belong.

Interests are also generated and articulated within governmental structures themselves. In France, the bureaucracy, both civil and military, does not simply react to pressures from the outside; its cleavages and the frequent absence of political directives have made it quite frequently into an autonomous force of interest representation; they operate as institutional interest groups.

For a realistic appraisal of the role of groups in the policy process one must investigate the actual and relative influence of the various organized and unorganized interests, the effectiveness of alliances, and the impact of countervailing forces, both organizational and ideological.[2] Interest articulation by associational and nonassociational groups takes place at the boundary line between society and the political system. It is, therefore, deeply embedded in the political culture of the country. In modern society "there is no longer," Suzanne Berger has stated, "any conception of a stable division of labor among parties, interest groups, and government, but rather specification of the circumstances under which various configurations emerge."[3]

Discussions about the legitimacy of group activities not only reflect constitutional and philosophical traditions. They are mostly determined by past experiences. Frequently, and not without reason, organized interests in France are held responsible for the fact that a society with egalitarian traditions has so often reproduced and aggravated existing inequalities. In

---

[2] See Jean Meynaud, *Nouvelles Études sur les groupes de pression en France* (Paris: Armand Colin, 1962), pp. 384 ff. An indispensable work for the student of French interest groups. For the situation during the first years of the Fifth Republic, see the same author's "Les Groupes de pression sous la Ve République," *RFSP* 12, no. 3 (1962): 672–97.

[3] Suzanne Berger, "Introduction," in *Organizing Interests,* Berger, p. 10.

other countries too the defense of the status quo might be the dominant concern of interest groups. But in the stalemated society that France has been for so long, such a position has had a special significance for retarding economic, social, and political development. Moreover, the ideological fragmentation of political life has determined the way in which demands are formulated and interest groups are organized. Once formed, the groups have done much to harden ideological divisions.

". . . If the general will is to be able to express itself, it is essential that there should be no partial society within the State and that each citizen should think only his own thoughts." This categorical condemnation by Rousseau of all intermediate groups has occupied an important place in French political theory and has been a factor in shaping legislation for more than a century. The individualism it expresses was shared by most of the philosophers of the French Enlightenment and fed on the observation of oppressive guild practices under the Old Regime. This attitude triumphed in the legislative enactments of the Revolution, especially the famous Le Chapelier law which outlawed all associations. More than a century later a fiery republican leader such as Gambetta would still utter words of warning against associations, "which confiscate the individual, suppress and absorb him." [4] The Chapelier law was rescinded only in 1901, and even then with some reservations. However, the legal obstacles were frequently ignored; many categories of Frenchmen did not wait for the change in legislation to form groups and to constitute in fact the "partial societies" condemned by Rousseau.[5] But the necessity of achieving this by subterfuge was nevertheless bound to shape group practice and to spread doubts about the legitimacy of group activities.

Until a few years ago, "pressure groups" *(groupes de pression)* and "lobbies" were political scare words, partly because

[4] See Theodore Zeldin, *France 1848–1945*, vol. 1 (Oxford: Clarendon Press, 1973), pp. 616 ff.

[5] See Georges Lavau, "Political Pressures by Interest Groups in France," in *Interest Groups on Four Continents*, ed. Henry W. Ehrmann (Pittsburgh: Pittsburgh University Press, 1958, 1964), p. 60.

public attention was focused on the showy activities of disreputable or unpopular groups. The first "modern" lobby in France, made up of many kinds of organizations and manipulating both parliament and bureaucracy almost at will, was the colonial lobby. Formed at the turn of the century, it was responsible for many of the colonial ventures of the Third Republic, and prolonged the costly wars of the Fourth. Other well-known lobbies were those of the munitions makers, the "merchants of death," and those of the interests which spread disease and vice by liquor or prostitution.

In reality, there has never been anything particularly scandalous about the defense of organized interests in France, nor has the pressure been truly irresistible. Indeed, the structure and the organizational means of most associational interest groups are less solid than in many other countries, mostly because Frenchmen do not expect much from collective efforts. Lingering uncertainties about the legitimacy of group activities may be one of the reasons why even today, by comparison with interest groups in other countries, business, labor, and agriculture in France appear less attuned to the intensive use of propaganda and of public relations. With some significant exceptions, few interest groups will use the information media for broad-gauge appeals. Organized business, for instance, has shunned for a long time all endeavors to create a public image of the community it represents. This was due partly to the traditional secretiveness of the French businessman, partly to the conviction that, since France has become a business civilization only of late, the accomplishments of business and of its associations would hardly be appreciated by the public. "What is good does not make a noise, and what makes a noise is not good"; this utterance by a French businessman characterizes the distrust of public relations not only by businessmen but also by some of their organizations.[6]

Actual membership in almost all groups, organized to defend

---

[6] See Jean-Noel Jeanneney, *L'Argent caché: Milieu d'affaires et pouvoir politique dans la France du XXᵉ siècle* (Paris: Fayard, 1981), p. 13, and, generally on the past public relations efforts of the business community, Henry W. Ehrmann, *Organized Business in France* (Princeton: Princeton University Press, 1957), pp. 207–17.

the interests of a specific economic or social sector, amounts to only a fraction of potential membership. There never has been a steady, if slow, progression. Many of the important groups have known a mass influx of new members at dramatic moments of the country's social or political history, such as at the time of the Popular Front victories, the post-Liberation era, or during and immediately after the events of 1968. But as soon as conditions become normal, "normal" individualism reasserts itself and leaves many associations with too small a membership to justify their claims of representativeness. The treasuries of groups are often so depleted that they are unable to employ a competent staff. The modern pressure group official is a fairly recent phenomenon to be found only in certain sectors of the group system, such as business associations.

Given the ideological style of the country's political culture, it is not astonishing that there is a luxuriant growth of groups devoted solely to the promotion of causes, broad or narrow. Some of them, such as the League for the Rights of Men, are centuries old. The vigorous associations which, since the beginning of the Third Republic, have been aligned on the issue of public versus parochial education are still able to mobilize mass support. Other groups spring up and disappear in major or minor crisis situations. At times their impact on public opinion has been considerable; their emotional appeal is well suited for many audiences. Since many of them demand only a temporary commitment, they rarely need the permanent and qualified staff which only few French interest groups can assemble.

A symbolic act or a fortuitous event might become the catalyst for the gathering of a spontaneous movement which is then channeled into a more structured organization. The Women's Liberation Movement was born in 1970 when a group of women deposited a wreath with the inscription: "To the unknown Wife of the Soldier" on the long-honored tomb of the Unknown Soldier in Paris.[7] This imaginative act was enough to bring forth a number of women's movements of different

[7] On the origins of the women's liberation movement, see Margaret Maruani, "Domination et révolte des femmes au travail," in *La Sagesse et le désordre: France 1980,* ed. Henry Mendras (Paris: Gallimard, 1980), pp. 107–10.

ideological allegiances; it also led to the formation of articulate groups on both sides of the controversies surrounding new legislation on abortion and divorce. Inside the trade-union movement special committees started (belatedly) to concern themselves with the rights of women at work.

The events which were to engulf the entire country in the spring of 1968 originated in a confrontation between the university administration of an unattractive suburban campus and students who protested against inappropriate facilities and antiquated methods of examination. For years the official student association had lacked leadership and authority over its constituents. But a small activist and vocal minority found in strife a unity they had never known before. Within a few weeks a revolt against the entire educational system swept most of the universities. The manning of barricades and bitter street fighting was to follow: the dominant ideology of the rebels was a mixture of anarchism and existentialism. When the workers discovered that under pressure the government was willing to promise major reforms, their long-accumulated resentment broke into the open. But the strikes, in which between 6 and 7.5 million workers participated, were also a spontaneous outburst. The trade unions had not foreseen them and did little to organize or even encourage them. The spark of an angry campus debate had ignited another of the dramatic confrontations which have marked French social history.[8]

In all complex modern societies the interests and values of the citizens are represented by such a large variety of groups that group activities might be at odds with each other. Strategies will vary and so will the amount of loyalty exacted by

[8] The literature on the May events is enormous. In English the following accounts are the most interesting: Stanley Hoffmann, *Decline or Renewal? France since the 1930s* (New York: The Viking Press, 1974), pp. 145–84; and Bernard Brown, *Protest in Paris: Anatomy of a Revolt* (Morristown: General Learning Press, 1974). For an interesting comparison between the May events and the "Hot Autumn" in Italy, see Michele Savati, "May 1968 and the Hot Autumn of 1969: the responses of two ruling classes," in *Organizing Interests,* Berger, pp. 331–66. For a good bibliography of the literature on the May events, see Laurence Wylie, Franklin D. Chu, and Mary Terrell, *France: The Events of May–June 1968, a Critical Bibliography* (Pittsburgh: Council of European Studies, 1973).

the groups. In France cross-pressures are more evident than elsewhere. In a country which remains one of small farms and small firms (see Chapter II) and where class stratification is perceived as acute, socioeconomic interests are necessarily highly fragmented. Ideological divisions are superimposed on this fragmentation. Many of the same groups which in other systems defend the interests of labor, of farmers, of veterans, of school children, of consumers, etc., are divided in France according to ideological preferences, even if the latter have little or no relevance for the issues involved. This results in additional splits and thereby inefficiency of the groups: their representativeness becomes questionable when they face competition from organizations that claim to speak for the same clientele.

The defense of agricultural interests has a long record of internal strife. All through the Third Republic competing organizations fought for influence and subsidies: one conservative and church-oriented, the other free-thinking and with easy access to the Ministry of Agriculture after that Ministry had come under the all but permanent control of the Radical-Socialists. The Vichy regime experimented with an integration of rural interests into the state bureaucracy. This corporatist arrangement never succeeded in solving basic conflicts about the future course of French agriculture; moreover, it was compromised by a Nazi-prone ideology.

After the Second World War, it seemed for a moment that the time had come to form a large confederation grouping all rural interests. But before long, subsidiary groups reasserted their autonomy, and the peak association lost all importance. Some of the earlier political differences have been overcome. But the diversity of interests, the individualism, and occasionally the sectarianism of their constituents explain the existence of close to 500 rural defense organizations on the national level alone.

The most prominent rural defense organization, the *Fédération Nationale des Syndicats d'Exploitants Agricoles* (FNSEA), has become the government's instrument for modernizing French agriculture. In the early 1960s rural reform legislation provided for the "collaboration of the professional agricultural organizations." From the outset this collaboration (*concertation* is the official term for systematic contacts between the authorities and the organized interests) was offered only to the FNSEA. Its rejuvenated leadership was attuned to the governmental objectives of nationalizing agricultural production and rural organization (see Chapter II). The strong and at times violent opposition by the farmers to the policies of the French government and of the Common Market authorities led to severe tensions within the FNSEA and to the emergence of rival groups.[9] The strongest of these is the *Mouvement de Défense des Exploitants Familiaux* (MODEF), which capitalizes on the grievances of the smallest family farms. It is openly inspired by the Communist party and pursues a fairly demagogic line of anticapitalism and simultaneous defense of property owners, bitterly opposing the exodus from the countryside, and most Common Market policies.

During the 1970s the position of the FNSEA as a quasi-official union seems to have become unassailable.[10] The government gave representatives of the organization a prominent place on the numerous agencies and committees which reallocate land and distribute funds for rural reorganization. The instruction of farmers and of their families in modern methods of farming and the training of activists for leadership positions which are to enable them to become valid interlocutors for the state are some of the activities that have been turned over to the staff of the FNSEA. While it remains legally an interest group based

[9] For more details, especially on rural strife in 1961, see Gordon Wright, *Rural Revolution in France: The Peasantry in the Twentieth Century* (Stanford: Stanford University Press, 1964), pp. 167 ff.

[10] For the earlier history of the FNSEA and the Young Farmers' Organization, see Yves Tavernier, *Le Syndicalisme paysan, F.N.S.E.A., C.N.J.A.* (Paris: Colin, 1969), and for a model regional study, Suzanne Berger, *Peasants against Politics: Rural Organization in Brittany, 1911–1967* (Cambridge: Harvard University Press, 1972). For later developments I have drawn much information from John T. S. Keeler, "The Corporatist Dynamic of Agricultural Modernization in the Fifth Republic," in *The Fifth Republic at Twenty*, eds. William Andrews and Stanley Hoffmann (Albany: State University of New York Press, 1981), pp. 271–92, and the same author's "Corporatism and Official Union Hegemony: The Case of French Agricultural Syndicalism," in *Organizing Interests*, Berger, pp. 185–208. Both articles are indispensable for a full understanding.

on voluntary membership, the organization lives largely on public funds. In most fields the government recognizes the Federation, which claims a following of 700,000 farmers, as the sole representative of farming interests. The long-time leader of the FNSEA, once a radical reformer, became a minister in the last cabinet of the Giscard administration. Rival organizations are not outlawed. But they complain about subtle, and often not so subtle, pressures, especially in regions in which they represent a serious threat to the FNSEA's hegemony.

The democratic legitimacy of the methods used by the government may be dubious, and they have been denounced as another form of corporatism ("just as during Vichy," it has been said) under a democratic cloak. In its defense it has been maintained that the cooperation between the state and an interest group has helped along the difficult process of modernization and has humanized policies which "faceless bureaucrats" might have made more cruel. Outbreaks of violence, where they have occurred, have been controlled without too much force.

The new socialist Minister of Agriculture was a member of the European parliament in Strasbourg, where she became familiar with the complaints of the French farmers. President Mitterrand promised that the socialist government would fight "hand in hand" with the rural interest organizations for (ever higher) prices in the European Community. Nonetheless the FNSEA all but insulted the new Minister of Agriculture when it discovered that the socialist government was not as willing as its predecessors had been to grant it quasi-monopoly status. In the name of "pluralism" the Minister paid more attention to competing interest groups, especially those defending the smaller farms, and in the name of equality the government announced that although subsidies would flow as amply as before they would no longer go to farmers whose income exceeded an upper limit. The FNSEA's answer to such changes in policy was an expression of sympathy for if not connivance with the sometimes violent manifestations of farmers in various regions.

In no other field had the government collaborated as closely with an interest group as in agriculture. But the marginal farmers were not alone in defending themselves against the threat

190 Interests: Secured and Frustrated

which modernity poses to traditional structures. Those who speak in the name of shopkeepers, artisans, and small industries are insured of a hearing in a country in which the cult of the small is not extinct. But their clientele is not easy to organize, since it is given to atomism, rather than to discipline. Hence these interests seek effectiveness through mass movements rather than through groups with a well-defined program and a long-term strategy. During the crisis-ridden last years of the Fourth Republic, the Union for the Defense of Shopkeepers and Artisans, launched by Pierre Poujade, mobilized the small businessmen threatened by the consequences of modernization and rationalization. Eager as they were to resist authority, if need be by violence, they felt insufficiently protected by the existing interest groups, even though the latter were prepared to shield the marginal units in the economy. For a time Poujade succeeded in transforming the revolt of the injured interests into a political movement which won 2.5 million votes in the 1956 election, but then disappeared when the country had to face graver problems, such as the Algerian war and the transition from the Fourth to the Fifth Republic.[11] For a time regular interest organizations took over the defense of the small. But in 1969 when shopkeepers and artisans felt the threat from large modern commerce, a new organization known as the CID-UNATI sprang up under the leadership of a small-town café owner, Gerard Nicoud. Learning from the experience of Poujadism and especially from the success students and peasants had obtained by taking their protests to the streets, the movement engaged in mass rallies, pitched battles with the police, and the kidnapping of tax collectors. Quite cleverly it avoided identification with any of the existing parties but cultivated the emotional anarchism of its followers.[12] How the governments of Pompidou and the Giscard administrations modified their economic policies in order not to antagonize a mass of voters they needed for maintaining a majority in parliament has been discussed above (Chapter II).

[11] See Stanley Hoffmann, *Le Mouvement Poujade* (Paris: Colin, 1956).
[12] See Suzanne Berger, "Regime and Interest Representation: The French Traditional Middle Classes," in *Organizing Interests*, Berger, pp. 83–102.

Not only interest-oriented mass movements but also established French interest groups occasionally exhibit a radicalism which has become rare in countries of similar development and is more generally found in an early industrial era. They want to demonstrate their militancy when the plurality of ideologically divided organizations forces each of them to compete for the same clientele. Organizations suffering from membership fluctuations try to mobilize potential members and marginal groups by inflated demands and by boldness of action. For groups that lack the means of using the information media, such tactics also become a way to put their case before the public at large.

In such a setting, even the defense of purely economic, social, or cultural interests takes on a political color. In order to intensify their political effectiveness, interest groups and parties, both too weak to act singly, organize alliances which may be more or less temporary but are frequently combative. French history of the last decades is rich in episodes where a merger of lobbies and political movements has shaken the system. Their emphasis has usually been on protest rather than on demands for constructive action. Honored traditions facilitate the transition from protest movements to militant organizations inclined to transcend the limits of legality.

The dramatic events of the great Revolution, the recurrent significance of street fighting and barricades in the upheavals of the nineteenth century, and other romantically embellished reminiscences have made violence "into a sort of second nature of the French political temperament." [13] For the labor movement the myth of the revolutionary strike, propagated by Georges Sorel, an intellectual without any trade union connections, seemed at one time the only means of mobilizing workers for some kind of participation. Taking one's grievances to the street also betrays a pervasive distrust in the satisfactory processing of demands by the political system. In addition, the use of violence is an attempt to obtain by blackmail what one despairs of obtaining by moderate and concrete demands. Because

---

[13] René Rémond, *La Vie politique en France*, vol. I (Paris: Armand Colin, 1965), p. 378.

of the relative frailty of organization in many fields, Martin Luther King's "Riots are the language of the unheard" describes some aspects of the French situation.[14]

INDUSTRIAL RELATIONS

Industrial relations form an important subsystem in the political systems of all developed countries. By their very nature industrial relations are conflictual. Democratic societies leave much autonomy for managing the conflicts arising in the subsystem to the parties involved. How the groups, principally management and labor, proceed, whether and for which reasons group autonomy might be limited and replaced by government fiat, depend to a large extent on the characteristics of the groups. Both trade unions and employers' associations share with other French interest groups such traits as an unreliable membership and a high ideological commitment. Their history and outlook, their self-image and organizational structure determine, together with the existing legal framework, the nature of industrial relations.

The French labor movement has never looked upon itself as an interest group "like the others," nor has it been regarded as such by outsiders.[15] Whatever their political or philosophical persuasion, all of the major labor confederations want to rebuild society and polity on new foundations. Their pervasive anticapitalism feeds on many sources (forcefully expressed in the preamble of their respective bylaws): on Marxist concepts of the class struggle, on Christian or personalist indignation about the iniquities of the existing system, and even on Proud-

[14] This parallel is drawn by Charles Tilly, "The Changing Place of Collective Violence," in *Essays in Theory and History*, ed. Melvin Richter (Cambridge: Harvard University Press, 1970), p. 164. The entire essay provides an excellent background for understanding the place of violence in nineteenth- and twentieth-century France.

[15] For the history of the French trade union movement, see Henry W. Ehrmann, *French Labor from Popular Front to Liberation* (New York: Oxford University Press, 1947), and Val Lorwin, *The French Labor Movement* (Cambridge: Harvard University Press, 1954). For a more recent and complete account, see Jean-Daniel Reynaud, *Les Syndicats en France* (Paris: Seuil, 1975). On political aspects of trade union developments since 1958, see George Ross, "Gaullism and Organized Labor: Two Decades of Failure," in *Fifth Republic*, Andrews and Hoffmann, pp. 330–47.

hon's anarchism which harbors distrust if not defiance of all authority. A propensity for direct action, another legacy of the nineteenth century, leads not infrequently to clashes with competing groups. Historical experiences have driven French labor, unlike other European trade unions, to shun organizational ties with political parties. The present union leadership may consider hostility toward parties as an antiquated prejudice; nonetheless opinion surveys reveal that the most active union members have not overcome a basic diffidence toward parties and toward their parliamentary activities.

Unlike American labor, other European labor movements also have aspired to combine demands for the material betterment of their constituents with the fight for broader ideals of emancipation. But the heavy ideological baggage of French labor has encumbered normal trade union activities. Not infrequently, ideological commitment appears to serve as a compensation for weakness of organization and for the ensuing ineffectiveness of a divided labor movement.

From its beginning, the labor movement has suffered from particularly extreme membership fluctuations. Only since the early 1970s a certain stabilization seems to have occurred so that now membership at least keeps pace with the increase in the labor force.[16] But estimates vary and the unions' claims are questionable. Moreover, all generalizations are difficult: in private industry trade-union membership varies between 5 and 25 percent; among civil servants and in certain nationalized industries 40 to 60 percent of the work force might be unionized. Estimates that about 23 or 24 percent of all eligible wage earners are union members appear high to some observers,[17] but such a rate of unionization is still far lower than that in other countries of Western Europe (Sweden–85, West Germany–42,

[16] For these and other data that follow in the text, see the interesting if opinionated article by Martin A. Schain, "The Dynamics of Labor Policy in France: Industrial Relations and the French Trade Union Movement," and Jean-Daniel Reynaud (commenting on the preceding article), "Déviation ou autre modèle?" *Tocqueville Review* II, no. 1 (Winter 1980): 77–115.

[17] The latter figure seems to be confirmed by a fairly recent public opinion poll; see SOFRES, *L'Opinion Française en 1977* (Paris: PFNSP, 1978), p. 173.

Holland–40 percent). In all countries unionization is most difficult in small firms. In a country such as France where 46 percent of the labor force are employed in firms with fewer than fifty workers, the weakness of labor unions is in part a consequence of the size of the firms. Neither the closed shop nor other practices making union membership near-compulsory exist in France.

The largest and oldest of the labor confederations, the *Confédération Générale du Travail* (CGT) still attracts the largest number of French wage earners and especially of industrial workers in both the private and the public sector of the economy. By its own, probably exaggerated claims, it has more than 2 million members. Since the war the CGT has been identified closely with the Communist party: its two most prominent leaders belong to the Politburo of the party, half of the members of its executive are also prominent party members, the others have always hewed closely to the party line. Yet by tradition and by its relative effectiveness as the largest labor organization, the CGT counts among its members many non-Communists. When in the mid-seventies the Communist party adopted a new, and less dogmatic policy, the CGT obtained more freedom of action. A certain distance between the union movement and the party promised to yield attractive dividends for both. But when, at the approach of the elections of 1978 and 1981, the Communist Party returned to dogmatism and once more declared war on the Socialist Party (for details, see Chapter VIII), the CGT followed suit, though not without meeting opposition in the confederation and in some important unions.

The second strongest labor organization is the *Confédération Française et Démocratique du Travail* (CFDT) with an estimated membership of about 700,000. In many ways the CFDT is the most original and the most interesting of all labor movements in Western Europe.[18] An offshoot of a Catholic

[18] See the informative book by two of its leaders, Edmond Maire and Jacques Julliard, *La CFDT d'aujourd'hui* (Paris: Seuil, 1975). For the tortuous policies of the two major labor confederations during the years of the Giscard presidency, see George Ross, "French Labor and Economic Change," in *France in the Troubled World Economy*, eds. Stephen S. Cohen and Peter A. Gourevitch (London: Butterworths, 1982), pp. 151–79.

trade union movement, it now accepts many of the anticapitalist tenets of Marxism but rejects the Soviet model in favor of workers' self-management (*autogestion*) somewhat along lines of the Yugoslav experiences. The political sympathies of its members are divided but now belong mostly to the Socialist Party.

Another labor confederation, *Force Ouvrière,* was formed at the beginning of the Cold War in 1948 in protest against the Communist domination of the CGT. It adheres to a moderate reformism but has never acquired great strength among industrial workers; nor has the remnant of the Catholic workers' confederation which remains pledged to the tenets of social Catholicism.

Elections of labor representatives to labor courts and other similar bodies afford a better basis for estimating the relative strength of the various union movements than the unions' own claims. It appears that in 1980 the CGT accounted for about 40 percent of total union strength, the CFDT for 22 to 23, the Force Ouvrière for 16, and the Catholic confederation for 6 percent.[19]

As to management since the end of the war, French business has been able to keep trade associations and employers' organizations, large and modern as well as small and traditional firms within one rather imposing and exceptionally well-staffed confederation, the *Conseil National du Patronat Français* (CNPF). Not that divergent interests, differing economic concepts, and indeed conflicting ideologies have not clashed: they have frequently prevented the organization from acting forcefully and at times hampered its representativeness in negotiations with government or trade unions. After the events of 1968 new by-laws have strengthened the hand of a largely renewed national leadership.

The various employers' associations affiliated with the CNPF are served by a staff of at least 7,000. Financing appears to be ample but is provided almost exclusively by big business. The

---

[19] For these figures, see Georges Lavau, *À quoi sert le parti communiste français?* (Paris: Fayard, 1981), pp. 135–36, and Le Monde, *Bilan Économique et social 1980* (Paris: Dossiers et Documents du Monde, 1981), p. 59.

owners of small firms feel that they are better defended by the mass movements described earlier than by the streamlined modern lobby which the CNPF has become.[20] The CNPF enters the field of industrial relations by providing useful documentation to its affiliates and by signing, mostly at the request of the government, some general agreements with one or several of the labor confederations. The agreements treat important questions such as the training and retraining of the work force, conditions of retirement, and the like. But they are usually considered as recommendations rather than as binding obligations.

How do the features of the organizations of labor and management affect industrial relations at the places of work? Behind apparent similarities there are considerable differences between the situation in France and in other countries.[21] Extensive labor legislation narrows, from the outset, the area for agreements among the partners. Collective bargaining agreements exist in all major industries, but their actual importance is generally limited. They do not include what is at the core of collective bargaining elsewhere: actual wage rates and other benefits. Remuneration is usually based on the minimum wage rate, which moves with the price index or is fixed by the government when it appears politically advisable. Lengthy negotiations at the industry level — and more often at the plant level — rather concern the classification of jobs in relation to the minimum; they deal in great detail with working conditions, with firing and hiring, with grievance procedures and workers' representation on a variety of committees, prescribed by legislation. Before 1968 there were no union locals; manage-

[20] There is no comprehensive up-to-date discussion of French business organizations, since Ehrmann, *Organized Business in France*, is now dated. But see Jacques Lautman and Annie Jacob, "Rôles du syndicalisme patronal et évolution économique," in *Tendances et volontés de la société française*, ed. Jean-Daniel Reynaud (Paris: SEDEIS, 1966), pp. 268–84; and Bernard Brizay, *Le Patronat, histoire, structure, strategie du C.N.P.F.* (Paris: Seuil, 1975).

[21] The most thoughtful work on these problems is Gérard Adam and Jean-Daniel Reynaud, *Conflits du Travail et Changement Social* (Paris: PUF, 1978). Excellently informed also, Janice McCormick, "Gaullism and Collective Bargaining: The Effect of the Fifth Republic on French Industrial Relations," in *Fifth Republic*, Andrews and Hoffmann, pp. 348–66.

ment did not tolerate union activities in the plant. Now locals exist in the larger firms and may participate in bargaining negotiations, which a close observer has described as "local guerillas." [22]

For a few short years, at the start of the Pompidou administration, the government made strenuous efforts to encourage the spread of contractual agreements in all branches of the economy.[23] But here *concertation* miscarried; the government was neither inclined nor able to conclude with labor and management the kind of corporate arrangements which it established with the agricultural interest groups.

During the last years of the Giscard administration, the employers' resistance to collective bargaining stiffened: all union interference was resented; industrial relations became once more strictly adversarial. It is true that neither the unions nor the employers' associations ever feel obliged to induce their membership to abide by agreements that have been reached. Whether contracts are broken or upheld depends in many cases on the respective strength of the parties in a given situation.

For the labor unions the situation is complicated by what is euphemistically called "union pluralism" — i.e., the presence of unions belonging to different confederations in the same plant. Even during periods when the confederations might have agreed to act together, animosities at the plant level did not subside and opened to the employers opportunities for maneuvering.[24]

It is obvious that, given these conditions, the state must intervene frequently to prevent protracted labor conflicts or simply the breakdown of negotiations. The departmental prefects, the courts, and state-appointed mediators are called upon to settle disputes. The Minister of Labor can extend any collective

22 Adam and Reynaud, *Conflits,* p. 206.

23 At the center of these efforts was Jacques Delors, who had been active in the CFDT trade unions. Disappointed in the policies of the Pompidou administration, he joined the Socialist Party and occupies the important post of Minister of Finance in the socialist government.

24 On arising conflicts, see W. Rand Smith, "Paradoxes of Plural Unionism in France — CGT and CFDT," *West European Politics* IV, no. 1 (January 1981): 38–53.

agreement by decree to all firms in a given branch, including those who had not participated in the negotiations.

An additional impact of the state on labor relations derives from its role as an employer of many thousands of workers without civil service status in the public sector. Strikes in public enterprises are often particularly bitter, yet collective bargaining is generally more successful, and the pattern set in such firms as the Renault works or the large banks is sometimes followed by private concerns. The transfer of a large labor force from the private to the public sector as a consequence of the nationalizations of 1981 will necessarily enlarge the role of the state in collective bargaining.

The number of working days lost through strikes is higher than in Germany or Sweden, but considerably lower (when one excludes the extraordinary situation of the spring of 1968) than in Italy, Great Britain, and the United States. Here again statistics do not reveal existing differences.[25] Elsewhere, and especially in the United States, the hardest and often the most protracted strikes occur in preparation for new or renewed bargaining negotiations. In such cases strikes are indeed often the continuation of collective bargaining by other means. Because of the weakness of the trade unions this is seldom the case in France. Here strikes frequently break out spontaneously and may be caused by particular grievances or by tensions between management and labor, either of long standing or arising suddenly. Of late, strikes have protested against the closing of an enterprise. Usually strikes are short; the unions, conflict-oriented though they may be, do not have the financial means to support their striking members over a long period of time. They also might not have been consulted by the strikers beforehand.

In about one-fourth of all strikes the workers occupy the struck plant. The courts might declare the occupation in violation of the law, but forceful evacuations are rarely sought. Occupation of a plant makes even a small-scale strike into an

---

[25] On the problems of strikes, see the excellent discussion by Edward Shorter and Charles Tilly, *Strikes in France, 1830–1968* (London: Cambridge University Press, 1974), esp. the conclusions, pp. 335–50.

act of defiance. The national strikes, usually of limited duration, which the trade union confederations or major unions call from time to time, have a similar intent: they usually wish to mobilize public opinion against governmental policy; their success will depend on the political situation.[26] They are usually attempted when industrial relations have become particularly unrewarding for labor.

When the Popular Front government under the leadership of the socialist Léon Blum took office in 1936, it was greeted by a wave of mass strikes. In 1981 the elections were followed by months without any industrial strife. With prominent communists occupying ministerial posts (in 1936 the communists had refused to join the government), the CGT expressed satisfaction with major aspects of governmental policy even though it pledged its membership to vigilance should there be any backsliding on the way to economic and social reform. Yet within the CGT internal tensions have increased. The disastrous defeat of the Communist Party at the polls (see Chapter VIII) has strengthened the arguments of those who have long criticized the relationship between the union movement and a political party as being too close. Some long-time union officials, communists, and noncommunists have resigned their posts. Union activists and members of CGT unions have defied orders issued by the leadership not to participate in demonstrations protesting martial law in Poland. The national convention of the CGT to be held in the summer of 1982, will have to face problems of internal cohesion and discipline.

The affinity between the Socialist Party and the CFDT had opened to officials of that labor confederation a number of important posts on the staff of socialist ministers. The new head of the Planning Office had been active in the CFDT and so had, at an earlier time, the new Minister of Finance. Nonetheless the leadership of the CFDT is anxious to reject any implication that their union movement identifies with governmental policies. It affirms that its freedom of action is not im-

---

[26] Sixty-two percent of respondents in a poll stated that they view trade unions with favor, 21 percent that they mistrust them, and 17 percent gave no answer. The respective figures for sympathies for political parties were 49, 29, and 22 percent. See SOFRES, *L'Opinion . . . 1977*, p. 174.

paired and has actually criticized some of the new nationalizations for following bureaucratic models instead of establishing procedures of self-management.

It was to be expected that the foremost employers' organizations, the CNPF as well as the associations of small and medium-sized firms, would show little sympathy for the socialist government and its announced reforms. During the debate on the forthcoming nationalizations (see Chapter II) the hostility between advocates and opponents became extreme. The CNPF elected a new president, replacing a pressure group official with a businessman, presumably a candidate better suited to defend the interests of the organization's constituents. But if for a time open warfare was feared, the employers' Council soon took a more moderate stance. Its spokesmen have declared that there was much that was worthwhile in the government's plans for a rejuvenation of the French economy. They have made it clear that they were willing to play their normal role as an important interest group all the more as, at least for a time, the climate of industrial relations had vastly improved.

ACCESS AND IMPACT

Interest groups are active in all the arenas from which authoritative decisions can be influenced: in the electoral process and in parliament, through contacts with the political executive and with members of the bureaucracy. The setting of parliamentary and local elections has encouraged strenuous group activity during every campaign. The smallness of the constituencies, the personalized relationship between representatives and electorate, and, at least until recently, the flabbiness of party organization and discipline have at all times driven the groups to appeal directly to the candidate. Before the election, groups rather than individual voters put their demands to him. He was requested to pledge, often "on the dotted line," to defend the groups' concerns. His answers to such requests, whether positive or negative, were published in the newsletter which the group circulated among its membership. A candidate who in the first ballot had to face several competitors and could at best be elected by only a small margin of votes felt inclined to submit to such pressures. Even if he were not to honor his promises once he was elected, the din of organized groups during the campaign often deafened the candidate's political ears and prevented him from discussing larger issues. In this respect, however, the groups did little more than reinforce the traditional style of atomistic representation.

The role which groups played in financing election campaigns (and thereby in the selection of candidates) was admittedly important but also obscure, except for some widely publicized "scandals." [27] Candidates who obtained a stipulated minimum percentage of the total vote of their constituency were and continue to be reimbursed by the government for certain specific campaign expenses. There is, however, no provision for the high costs of modern campaigning; control of total expenditures has always been lax and could easily be circumvented. In the absence of well-filled party treasuries, many candidates simply had to rely on group support, which was likely to limit their freedom of action more than the mere signing of pledges.

In the Fifth Republic the scenario has not changed essentially. During national and local election campaigns, groups still appeal to the candidates, and the candidates show deference or independence according to their temperament and lights. It almost goes without saying that in the first ballot of presidential elections special interest groups, such as the environmentalists, European federalists, etc., come out in favor of the candidates whom they have put in the field. In the second ballot of the elections of 1981 both the CGT and the CFDT called for the election of the socialist candidate, as did other interest groups identified with the Left. But because of divided opinions in their own ranks, groups remain usually on the reserve at least for the first and sometimes also for the second ballot of presidential elections.

In preceding regimes organized interests found parliament the most convenient channel for access to political power. When he wanted to inaugurate a policy of free trade, Napoleon III felt compelled to divest the elected representatives of all influence in the setting of tariffs, since parliament was all too inclined to give in to the protectionist wishes of busi-

[27] For details on some of them, see Ehrmann, *Organized Business in France,* pp. 219 ff.

ness. In the Third and Fourth Republics the highly specialized and powerful committees of both houses of parliament
often became little more than institutional façades for pressure
groups.[28] Open committee hearings, as they take place in Congress, were unknown. Instead, "study groups" brought deputies
and group representatives together behind closed doors but
in the very halls of the National Assembly. Quite frequently,
groups were able to substitute bills of their own design for
those submitted by the government. There have also been episodes when at the moment of important votes lobbyists filled
the galleries of parliament in order to remind the people's
representatives of the obligations they had incurred.

All this added to the climate of confusion and irresponsibility. As in the United States, there was no clear boundary line
between the function of interest groups and that of parties. It
seems, however, that more often than not the actual impact of
the penetration by the groups into the parliamentary arena
was more apparent than real. Many of the bills and amendments which deputies moved on behalf of the lobbies lost out
because of the general inefficiency of parliamentary proceedings. Although the absence of a valid party system increased
the leverage of the groups in the election campaigns, the situation was to some extent reversed in parliament. Since parties
did not provide a shield behind which the deputies could trans-
act business on behalf of groups, the identification of individual representatives as spokesmen for special interests was generally easy to make and soon became detrimental to their effectiveness. Some carefully concerted but discrediting lobbying by
powerful groups resulted occasionally in resounding defeats for
the causes defended by organized interests; the ratification by
parliament of the Schuman Plan for the European coal and
steel industries over strenuous opposition by the business lobby
is one example which had important consequences for the
future of Europe.[29]

---

[28] See Philip M. Williams, *Crisis and Compromise: Politics in the Fourth
Republic* (Garden City: Doubleday, 1966), pp. 374–77.

[29] For details on the defeat of the opponents of the Schuman Plan, see
Henry W. Ehrmann, "The French Trade Associations and the Ratification
of the Schuman Plan," *World Politics* 6 (1954): 453 ff.

It is true that interest groups gained considerable leverage by the myth they had created about themselves in the minds of deputies and senators. Pressures from organized groups were believed to be irresistible. Not to oppose them was considered a legacy of political wisdom handed down, lazily as it were, from generation to generation.

General de Gaulle and his closest collaborators, such as Michel Debré, frequently lumped interest groups and political parties together in the category of "intermediaries" from which the state would not tolerate interference. The foremost reason for reforming and "rationalizing" parliament was the desire to reduce the role of parliament in the making and unmaking of governments. By the same token many of the new rules, established by constitution and legislation (for details, see Chapter X), altered the role of organized interests in the policy-forming process. This did not mean that the groups lost all leverage in the chambers of parliament. The best organized interest groups, which have definite views about the legislation which the government submits to parliament, continue to furnish ample documentation to the members of both houses. A number of important statutes have been modified in line with the wishes of the groups after the government did not find it opportune to oppose the proposed amendments. As we have seen, groups defending marginal interests which feel threatened by industrialization and modernization are still able to obtain favorable rulings. Elective representatives are even more vulnerable than the executive when they can be reproached for not having protected the small, whose votes count heavily in every election.[30]

It is nonetheless true that the transfer of power from parliament to the executive has had important consequences for the tactics of most interest groups. It lessened the status of those groups which in the past had concentrated their activities on parliament and on individual representatives. To be effective, all groups must now use the channels which the best

[30] For concrete cases in which group influence has asserted itself in the parliaments of the Fifth Republic, see Pierre Avril, "Le Parlement législateur," *RFSP* XXI, no. 1 (February 1981): 27 ff.

equipped among them have long found most rewarding, channels which give them access to the political executive and the administration. Here, as in most modern democracies, both institutionalized procedures and the network of personal relations remain important.

Because of the large powers which the Fifth Republic has bestowed upon the President, his staff is a preferred target for all groups weighty enough to be heard at that level. The ministerial *cabinets*, the circles of personal collaborators of every French minister, have always been an important channel for group influence. Since the cabinets have become ever larger and more influential, qualified groups seek and generally find access to their members and through them to the ministers, unless the latter have been reached directly. (For a discussion of the respective role of the presidential and ministerial staffs, see Chapter IX.)

The indispensable collaboration between organized private interests and the state is institutionalized in advisory committees, attached to most if not all administrations. They are composed mainly of group representatives who have thereby acquired the right to be consulted on administrative decisions affecting their constituents. Some of these committees have functioned since the Revolution, but their growth has been made particularly luxuriant through legislation enacted since the two World Wars. On the national level alone, there exist now no less than 500 "councils," 1,200 "committees," and 3,000 "commissions," all bringing together group representatives and members of the bureaucracy, even though they are not all equally active. At present the Ministry of Finance alone "consults" with more than 130 committees of various kinds. Contrary to what has occasionally been promised, few of the advisory boards have been abolished in the Fifth Republic, and many more have been added. There is also a spectacular growth of institutionalized and informal consultation on the level of the 96 departments, of the big and rapidly modernizing cities and of the new regions. If this form of group participation in decision making is widely practiced in all modern democracies, it seems nowhere quite as developed as in France, where the total number of advisory boards is now estimated at about

15,000.[31] At the apex of these advisory institutions which provide official representation to organized interest stands the National Economic and Social Council provided for in the constitution. (For its functions and malfunctions, see Chapter X.)

Frequently the advisory bodies are simply additional channels of influence, and often, from the perspective of the groups, not the most important ones. It is controversial whether the consultation which takes place here leads to a democratization and humanization of administrative procedures or instead to an undesirable fragmentation of authority. Much seems to depend on the way in which bureaucrats use these instruments of what in France is called "administrative pluralism." When the civil servants merely take into account the opinions and the documentation presented to them before they reach an autonomous decision, the effect is beneficial. But many times the authoritative decision is made entirely on the basis of the group's suggestions, so that in effect administrative functions are parceled out to socioeconomic forces. Often administrators no longer dare to make decisions unless the groups are willing to assume responsibility for them. The courage of the administrator, just as that of the elected representative, is a more effective check on group pressures than the ostentatious style of a regime. A student of British pressure groups has distinguished in his discussion of the official contacts of groups between consultation and negotiation.[32] In France there exists no clear dividing line between the two.

The routine contacts between group representatives and the bureaucracy offer to organized interests the most numerous and most valuable points of access. There is nothing scandalous about such contacts. From the perspective of the bureaucracy, interest groups are audience, advisors, and clients,

[31] For a study affording interesting comparisons with an analogous development in the Federal Republic of Germany, see Claus Offe, "The Attribution of Public Status to Interest Groups: Observation on the German Case," in *Organizing Interests*, Berger, pp. 123–58.

[32] See Harry Eckstein, *British Pressure Group Politics: The Case of the British Medical Association* (Stanford: Stanford University Press, 1960), pp. 22 ff.

foremost participants in the process of bargaining over governmental policy, and instrumentalities for the enforcement of its rulings. From the perspective of pressure politics, the administrative bureaus are a decisive center of power.

Since administrative decision making in France is widely dispersed in spite of its formal centralization, interest groups must intervene in a great number of bureaus and agencies, even when concerned with just one decision. To be effective, a group must play on an extensive keyboard in order to touch all the points where its interests or values are affected. No generalizations are possible as to whether in these daily encounters the public interest emerges unscathed or whether the groups "colonize" parts of the administrative machinery to such an extent that organs of state are transformed into institutionalized pressure groups. Both extremes as well as a great many intermediate situations obtain.[33] The so-called vertical agencies, which like the clientele administration or the regulatory agencies in the United States are concerned with a single if sometimes composite interest, are most easily permeated by the views defended by the groups. But when bureaus or entire agencies identify themselves closely with the interests they are called upon to control, the divisions within the bureacracy (described in Chapter VI) are deepened further. Whenever it becomes necessary to overcome them, a yet more intense centralization of the decision making process is initiated.

It is quite natural that some interests have easier access to governmental bureaus than others. An affinity of views between group representatives and public administrators might be based on common outlook, common social origin, or education. The official of an important trade association who has already sorted out the raw demands of his constituents and submits them in rational fashion easily gets a more sympathetic hearing in the bureaus than an organization that seeks to defend atomistic interests by mobilizing latent resentment.

---

[33] For details, see H. W. Ehrmann, "French Bureaucracy and Organized Interests," *Administrative Science Quarterly* 5, no. 4 (1961): 534–55.

Since it is now far more advantageous to impress two well-placed administrators than twenty deputies, the weight of the best organized interests, equipped with qualified staff and useful documentation, has undoubtedly increased. This also holds true of nonassociational interests defended by business firms or some prominent families.

The most complete study of the contacts between the French administration and interest groups reports that high civil servants seek to distinguish between "professional organizations," which they consider "serious" or "dynamic" enough to listen to, and "interest groups," which should be kept at a distance.[34] But the recorded reactions of the bureaucrats the author has interviewed are cautious rationalizations rather than realistic appraisals of the weight of the groups in administrative decision making.

An official committee instituted in the early days of the Fifth Republic to investigate obstacles to economic development concluded:

> Under present conditions, characterized by vertical and watertight compartmentalization of administrators, a great number of civil servants . . . have become accustomed to regard in good faith the defense of the interests which they are called upon to control a natural and essential aspect of their function, an aspect which for them tends to eclipse or to falsify their vision of the general interest.[35]

In the years that have elapsed since this report was published, much has changed in the French economy and society, but the stubborn problems raised in the report have remained.[36] Of

---

[34] Ezra N. Suleiman, *Politics, Power, and Bureaucracy in France: The Administrative Elite* (Princeton: Princeton University Press, 1974), pp. 323–51.

[35] *Rapport sur les obstacles à l'expansion économique* (Paris: Imprimerie Nationale, 1960), p. 24.

[36] In the report on the state of the economy submitted to the Prime Minister after the elections of 1981 (see Chapter II), the earlier account quoted here was specifically mentioned as being still valid. "This shows," the new report concluded, "that we are dealing here with an old vice."

course, they are not peculiar to France, but arise in every pluralist democracy when special interest groups compete with the state, the presumed guarantor of the public interest, for the control of policy making.[37]

---

[37] Samuel Beer described the prevailing situation as "quasi-corporatism"; see his "Group Representation in Great Britain and the United States," *Annals of the American Academy of Political and Social Sciences* 319 (1958): 136. For fuller statements on the relationship between pluralism and corporatism, see Suzanne Berger, "Introduction," and Phillippe C. Schmitter, "Interest Intermediation and Regime Governability in Contemporary Western Europe and North America," in *Organizing Interests,* Berger, pp. 20–22 and 285–327.

CHAPTER VIII

Political Parties

THE TRADITIONAL PARTY SYSTEM

"The character and number of the political parties seeking
to represent the various groups in a country are perhaps the
chief determinants of how far the government acts through a
stable system of interchanges between the key solidarity groups
and the political elite." [1] There is general agreement that until
quite recently French political parties have regularly prevented
the functioning of such a stable system. Except for short periods they were "equally unable to make commitments in the
name of their voters or to obtain legitimacy through transforming the voters' opinions and attitudes into impulses converted
into governmental action." [2]

There are, however, divergent explanations of such inability.
Should one conclude with General de Gaulle that the parties
are merely a mirror of the perpetual French "political effervescence" and an expression of a "Gallic propensity towards divisions and quarrels"? Is it the number of parties or their characteristics that are most to blame? Has the socioeconomic
structure of the country caused both the plurality and the char-

[1] Seymour M. Lipset, "Party Systems and the Representation of Social
Groups," *European Journal of Sociology* 1, no. 1 (1960): 53.
[2] Otto Kirchheimer, "The Transformation of the Western European
Party Systems," in *Political Parties and Political Developments,* eds. Joseph
La Palombara and Myron Weiner (Princeton: Princeton University Press,
1966), p. 180.

acteristics of the parties? Or is the party chaos more apparent than real, hiding as it were behind objectionable forms a basically stable division in the body politic? [3]

Some of the most knowledgeable analysts of election data have been struck by a chronic and seemingly unalterable division of Frenchmen into two camps, two large political "families," each motivated by a different political mood or temperament. Whether one wishes to identify these camps with the "Right" and the "Left" or christen them the "party of order" and the "party of movement" [4] is of less importance than the fact that if one views elections from this perspective, political alignments have remained surprisingly stable over long periods of history.

The party distribution in the first election held under general manhood suffrage (1849) shows that the proportions of votes going to the Right and to the Left were about the same as in the last elections of the Third Republic (1936) which led the Popular Front to victory. The conservative forces that backed General MacMahon in 1877 came from the same regions that supported the authoritarian-minded Poincaré in 1928. In 1962, the opposition to General de Gaulle was strongest where for more than a century republican traditions had had a solid foundation; and the alignments in the presidential elections of 1974 mirrored once more the same divisions, before soon thereafter inroads of the Left into former conservative strongholds began to change the traditional distribution of votes. An electoral system such as that of the Third and the Fifth Republics has apparently favored this simplification of political alignments. In the majority of constituencies the run-

[3] The possible influence of the electoral system has been discussed in Chapter IV.

[4] The classical study of the party system in the Third Republic, François Goguel, *La Politique des partis sous la IIIe République,* 2 vols. (Paris: Seuil, 1946), tries to reduce party orientations to "order" and "movement." The same author's *Géographie des élections françaises sous la Troisième et la Quatrième République* (Paris: Colin, 1970) offers ample historical documentation and cartography. Hervé le Bras and Emmanuel Todd, *L'Invention de la France: Atlas anthropologique et politique* (Paris: Livre de Poche, 1981), pp. 32–35, stated once more, shortly before the 1981 elections, that "since the beginning of the Third Republic, the political map of France has not changed."

off elections have resulted in the confrontation of two candidates, each representing roughly one of the two camps.

A simple and stable division could have resulted in a pattern of two parties, or coalition of parties, alternating in power and opposition and hence giving valid expression to the voters' options. However, to discover simplicity and stability one must view French "political effervescence" from a distance sufficiently great that the tensions and varieties between and within social groups and categories, between and within the coalitions and parties, disappear from sight. Yet these tensions and their organizational expressions in fact shape political reality. "France contains two fundamental temperaments — that of the left and that of the right," Jacques Fauvet has stated quite correctly. But he had to add that she also contains "three principal tendencies, if one adds the center; six spiritual families; ten parties, large or small, traversed by multiple currents; fourteen parliamentary groups without much discipline; and forty million opinions." [5]

French parties, like parties everywhere, exist to fulfill a variety of functions. Most important among them are: the sifting of interests and demands and their transformation into policy; the mobilization of the citizenry for political participation and the integration of the citizenry into the system; the recruitment and selection of political leaders for executive and other posts; and the control of such leadership, especially the control of the government. Finally, parties are "alliances in conflicts over policies and value commitments within the larger body politic." [6] Not all of these functions will be served equally well by all parties or at all times. What must be explained is why

[5] Quoted here from Gordon Wright, *France in Modern Times* (Chicago: Rand McNally, 1960), p. 423. For an excellent historical overview of the divisions in both major camps, see Theodore Zeldin, *France 1848–1945*, vol. 1 (Oxford: Clarendon Press, 1973), pp. 381 ff.

[6] Seymour M. Lipset and Stein Rokkan, "Cleavage Structures, Party Systems, and Voter Alignments: An Introduction," in *Party Systems and Voter Alignments: Cross-National Perspectives*, eds. Seymour M. Lipset and Stein Rokkan (New York: The Free Press, 1967), p. 5. For some thoughtful and important comments on the relationship between party alignments and factional strife within the dominant classes, see Daniel Gaxie, "Les logiques du recrutement politique," *RFSP* 30, no. 1 (February 1980), esp. pp. 40–45.

French parties have done so badly, over long periods, on almost all counts.

Except for the Socialists and Communists, French party organizations have remained most of the time as skeletal as were parties in many countries at the time of their nineteenth-century beginnings. They developed in a largely preindustrial and preurban environment, catering at first to upper-middle class and later to middle-class elements. During the Second Empire, a semi-dictatorial regime hampered the development of all political associations. With the advent of the Third Republic, their foremost, and frequently only, function consisted in providing the organizational framework for the selection and election of candidates for political office on the local, departmental, and national levels. This accounts for the great, and at times enormous, regional differences, not just between political groupings bearing the same name but also between what the Right (or the Left) stands for in different parts of the country. This is only one of the traits which the French and the American parties have in common.

The slow and irregular industrialization of the country hampered the formation of a disciplined working-class party which would have challenged the bourgeois parties to overhaul their own structure, as was the case in Imperial Germany, in Great Britain, and in Belgium. The electoral system and a powerful upper house of parliament with a heavy overrepresentation of the rural population kept the workers in a position of electoral inferiority.[7] Before 1914, the Socialist party was at best an incipient mass party, weakened not only by doctrinal dissensions in its midst, but by the workers' distrust of all institutions of the bourgeois state. Their distrust extended to the Socialist representatives in parliament, most of them of middle-class origin. When after the First World War the Communists were able to mount a well-organized party, the split of the working-class vote between two mutually hostile camps attenuated the threat from the Left. Hence the traditional parties could afford to preserve the loose structure they had previously adopted.

[7] See Otto Kirchheimer, "Private Man and Society," *Political Science Quarterly* 81, no. 1 (1966): 178 ff.

Current typologies of political parties distinguish between organizations that gradually emerge from groupings inside the legislature and those that are created outside the parliament among the voting population. The first category is usually identified with what has been called the cadre or brokerage party, pragmatic and patronage-oriented and little concerned with program. By contrast one will frequently find in the second group mass-based parties, which may be ideological, doctrinaire, programmatic, or at least issue-oriented.[8] Those French parties which have represented the majority of the electorate throughout long periods belong clearly to the first category, the internally created cadre parties. Their major weight is to be found in their parliamentary representation; all truly important party activities occur inside the legislature. Political organization at the local and constituency level aims mainly at ensuring the election or reelection of members belonging to various legislative blocks or factions in parliament. Until recently none of these parties could boast of anything like the constituency structure of a large British or Continental party, a structure which is, of course, also unknown in the United States.

An internally created party is almost always less disciplined and ideologically less coherent than one that has emerged outside the legislature. Its organizational and hence its financial structure will usually be rudimentary; the very notion of membership in the party remains indeterminate, sometimes to the point of being meaningless. The elected representatives have usually been far more of an asset to the party than the party to them.

During the election campaign the candidates can expect little financial support from the party. Between elections, those representing the party are not amenable to any formal party directives coming from outside parliament. Even within a parliamentary group or faction the formal institution of a whip is

8 See Maurice Duverger, *Political Parties* (New York: John Wiley, 1955), especially pp. xxiii–xxxvii. For a recent discussion of Duverger's criteria, see the comparative discussion by Harry Eckstein, "Parties, Political," in *International Encyclopedia of the Social Sciences*, vol. 11 (New York: Macmillan and The Free Press), pp. 436–53.

unknown. Whether the moral authority of a particular parliamentary party chairman is able to overcome the centrifugal trends of divided interests and loyalties depends on the circumstances. In most cases representatives vote, on important as well as on unimportant matters, solely in accordance with the commands of "career, conscience, and constituency." [9]

One of the most decisive reasons for the survival of this form of representation and of party organization has been the voters' preference for it. An electorate which distrusts authority and wishes to be represented at the seats of power only in order to be protected against an always suspected arbitrariness of government was also suspicious of parties organized for reformatory political action.

An egalitarian radicalism that believes in "the people" and its basic soundness but distrusts the solidarity claimed by any organization in the name of collective interests will not easily propound party discipline. The strength of such radical traditions in France, and that of populism in the United States, is undoubtedly one of the major reasons for party weakness in both France and the United States. In the case of France it is of particular significance that the two prevalent political orientations, the representative and the bonapartist (see Chapter I), have for all their mutual antagonism one thing in common: their aversion to well-established and strongly organized parties.

Consequently, party membership, except during short and dramatic situations, has always been low. Organizational weakness and its underlying causes will easily result in a multipolar party system. But the primary cause of such division has been past conflicts over interests and values, many of them but dimly remembered except for the resentments they caused and which have persisted. Historical traditions have determined whether constituencies are regularly on the right or the left of the political spectrum. Different property laws under the monarchy, clerical or secular administration during the Old Régime, differences in agricultural crops or in the speed of industrializa-

[9] See Philip M. Williams, *Crisis and Compromise: Politics in the Fourth Republic* (Garden City: Doubleday, 1966), pp. 348 ff. This work remains an indispensable source for party history during the Fourth Republic.

tion, religious affiliation — all these have shaped political alignments which frequently have perpetuated themselves long after the original causes have disappeared.[10]

Historical references provide justification not only for the major division between Right and Left, but also for the equally important divisions within the two camps. On the right one can still distinguish, among others, traditionalists (not all of them monarchist), "Orléanists," i.e., conservatives with a credo of laissez-faire, and bonapartists.[11] On the left, there were the Jacobins and the Socialists before the Russian Revolution added the Communists. In many cases actual party names have long become meaningless because they too can, in general, be explained only by historical circumstances, especially by the secessions which gave rise to ever new factions.

Every party that operates from a limited base faces a variety of competitors seeking to draw strength from the same clientele. If such parties were to spell out the differences that separate them from their competitors, in realistic and pragmatic terms, the contest would frequently appear merely as one between interest groups or between personalities. In order to avoid such a demonstration and still score over their competitors, parties will define even the most narrow political issues in lofty ideological and often esoteric terms. This is a general phenomenon in multipolar party systems. ". . . The more the number of parties increases, the more their identification becomes a problem; and the remedy to which each party has recourse in order to be perceived as distinct is a punctilious ideological and principled rigidity." [12] It is only seemingly paradoxical that many parties had the characteristics of an interest group and yet indulged in ideological language. Since many French interest groups also conduct their propaganda in

[10] On the historical roots of party cleavages, see Mattei Dogan, "Political Cleavage and Social Stratification in France and Italy," in *Party Systems and Voter Alignments,* Lipset and Rokkan, esp. pp. 182 ff. The entire article provides valuable and comparative data on the social composition of the French parties.

[11] See René Rémond, *The Right Wing in France: From 1815 to de Gaulle* (Philadelphia: University of Pennsylvania Press, 1968). He entitles the "prologue" to his work: "One or Several Rights?"

[12] Giovanni Sartori, "European Political Parties: The Case of Polarized Pluralism," in *Political Parties,* La Palombara and Weiner, p. 159.

ideological terms, the style of parties and groups was frequently identical. But after the elections and in the ensuing bargaining between parties, much of the ideological baggage was discarded. The gap between high-sounding principles and the need for pragmatically based coalitions became painfully obvious. It made ideologies appear as subterfuges and convinced the voters that electoral contests were manifestations of sheer irresponsibility.

The inconveniences of the French multiparty system were compounded by the constitutional arrangements and parliamentary practices of the Third and Fourth Republics. To survive and to govern effectively, a government needed more than just the absence of a majority willing to overthrow it; it needed a positive majority in favor of the government's policy and its legislative proposals. This, however, was difficult to obtain where majorities consisted not of disciplined parties or of parliamentary groups kept in line by an effective whip but to a large extent of ephemeral coalitions. Their cohesion or disruption depended on whatever problem was under consideration. As different problems came up, governments toppled or were condemned to immobility.

Neither Right nor Left was able to govern by itself for any length of time because it would invariably lose its narrow majority. As a normal consequence of the existing party system, a centrist coalition has been in control of the government most of the time, no matter what the outcome of the preceding elections may have been. According to some calculations, during the period from 1789 to the advent of the Fifth Republic, France was ruled by centrist governments for all but thirty years or for more than 80 percent of this period. In a two- or three-party system, it is quite normal that the major parties move toward the political center in order to gain stability and cohesion. But where extreme party plurality prevails, the Center is a "morass" instead of a cohesive political force.[13] It can-

---

[13] The problem of the Center as a "morass" has been analyzed at length by Maurice Duverger, and published in an abridged English translation as "The Eternal Morass: French Centrism," in *European Politics, A Reader,* eds. Mattei Dogan and Richard Rose (Boston: Little, Brown, 1971), pp. 237–46.

not pursue even moderate policies for long without losing necessary support, for there are no clear lines of division between government and opposition. Moreover, the policies of the Center threw substantial sectors of public opinion into permanent opposition, which strengthened the centrifugal strains on the system.

Temporarily successful flash parties or surge movements were not unknown during various periods of the Third Republic but occurred with greater regularity in the Fourth.[14] They were reactions against the immobility induced by a party system that was simultaneously too stable and too weak. They mobilized, if only for a short time, dissatisfied voters, drawing millions of them from the established groupings and a far smaller proportion from those who had abstained in the preceding elections. Typically, all these movements saw the need for a better structured and more active constituency organization and demanded a disciplined vote from their parliamentary representatives. But they all failed to bring this about, whereupon their forces dispersed usually as fast as they had assembled.

During the last eight years of the Fourth Republic none of the parties eligible for a centrist coalition could claim more than about 15 percent of the vote, and many of these parties were plagued by internal dissensions.[15]

In a heterogeneous society such as France, living through a period of intense internal and external pressures, multiple opinions and attitudes were bound to prevail. As before the war, the political parties did little to integrate and simplify them; instead they rigidified and crystallized existing antagonisms. As a result, the preferences expressed by the voters were

[14] On surge movements, see Duncan MacRae, Jr., *Parliament, Parties and Society in France, 1946–1959* (New York: St. Martin's Press, 1967), pp. 268 ff., and the interesting table on p. 233. This is a useful book for party history during the period treated.

[15] For a comprehensive analysis of the relationship between social class and political parties in the Fourth Republic, see the amply documented study by Maurice Duverger et al., *Partis politiques et classes sociales en France* (Paris: Colin, 1955). For party preferences of different social categories, see also the tables in MacRae, *Parliament, Parties and Society*, pp. 257 ff.

ignored or falsified. Instead of functioning as structures con-
veying political power to the executive and enabling the opposition to develop alternative propositions of policy and personnel, the numerous parties lost political leverage to the point
of impotence. Hence, the party system was not resilient enough
to solve the crisis that arose in 1958 over the war in Algeria,
the decolonization of sub-Saharan Africa, and the country's
entry into the Common Market.

The new republic created a new political framework which
had a major, if gradual and mostly unforeseen, impact on all
parties and on their relationship to each other. Many of the
old patterns shine through the new developments. Yet the latter have shaped the functioning of the political system to such,
and again largely unforeseen, extent that in order to explain
the transformation of the French polity since 1958, the characteristics of present-day parties, singly and as coalition partners,
must now be discussed.[16]

PRESENT-DAY PARTIES: THE GOVERNING LEFT

The Socialist Party. In comparison with the solid social-
democratic parties in other European countries, the French
Socialist Party lacked muscle almost since its beginnings in
1905. The party was a fusion of several strands of French socialism of which Marxism was only one and the least original.[17]
Throughout the party's history, unending intraparty discussions reflected conflicting concepts of doctrine, strategy, and
tactics. If the resulting intraparty "pluralism" was the pride of
the party, it did not make for political effectiveness. (The initials SFIO, by which it was known for more than sixty years,
express an idealistic commitment to the cause of international
solidarity; they stand for *Section Française de l'Internationale
Ouvrière.*)

[16] How fluid the party situation has remained throughout the Fifth Republic might be gauged from the fact that in the four editions of this book
(1968, 1971, 1976, 1982) the section that follows had to be rewritten completely each time. Can one expect that the present version will be "de-
finitive"?

[17] See the chapter on "Socialism" in Zeldin, *France 1848–1945,* vol. I,
pp. 725–87.

The slow and uneven industrialization, paired with a reluctance to organize, had clogged the development of labor unions. Their weakness and their syndicalist creed, averse to collaboration with political parties, deprived the SFIO of that base of working-class strength which has come to other social-democratic parties from their affiliation with a valid trade union movement.

Unlike British Labour, the SFIO also failed to absorb the middle-class Radicals (for an explanation of the term, see below), the equivalent of the Liberals in England. Here a French version of doctrinaire Marxism prevented the fusion with the neighbor to the right. For many years the wide gap between a constantly reaffirmed Marxist ideology and a political practice which was frequently at odds with professed ideals created additional problems for the SFIO. The party was never strong enough to assume control of the government by itself. Only in 1936 did the Socialists enter an unstable coalition cabinet, under the leadership of the widely respected Léon Blum. The short-lived and precarious existence of his government is now remembered as a negative experience rather than an inspiration.[18] To avoid the pitfalls of the Popular Front of the 1930s is a constant concern of the socialist government of the 1980s. Socialist participation in some of the inefficient cabinets of the Fourth Republic proved politically disastrous and divisive; the party's membership and electoral following dwindled steadily. From a share of 23 percent of the votes in the first postwar elections, the Socialist vote plummeted to 8 percent in the elections of 1968 (see Table VII). When in the presidential election of 1969 the socialists put their own candidate, the mayor of Marseilles, into the field, in the first ballot he obtained a miserable score of 5 percent. It was estimated that about one-sixth of the working class still voted the Socialist ticket and that about one-fifth of its dues-paying members were workers. Most of the

---

[18] Joel Colton, *Léon Blum, Humanist in Politics* (New York: Knopf, 1966), gives a good account of the development of the SFIO during the long leadership of Blum. For the post–World War II period, see also Henry W. Ehrmann, "The Decline of the Socialist Party, in *Modern France: Problems of the Third and Fourth Republics,* ed. Edward M. Earle (Princeton: Princeton University Press, 1951), pp. 181–99.

TABLE VII. First Ballot of French Parliamentary Elections in the Fifth Republic and Seats Won in the National Assembly in Both Ballots* (Voting in Metropolitan France)

Party	1958		1962		1967		1968		1973		1978		1981	
	% of votes cast	seats in parliament	% of votes cast	seats in parliament	% of votes cast	seats in parliament	% of votes cast	seats in parliament	% of votes cast	seats in parliament	% of votes cast	seats in parliament	% of votes cast	seats in parliament
Registered voters (in millions)	27.24		27.53		28.3		28.3		29.9		34.4		35.54	
Percentage of abstentions	22.9		31.3		19.1		19.9		18.7		16.6		29.13	
Communists (PC)	19.1	10	21.8	41	22.5	73	20.0	34	21.2	73	20.5	86	16.2	44
Socialists (PS)	15.5	47	12.5	66	19.0	121	16.5	41	18.9	89	22.6	107	37.6	267
Left-Radicals	—	33	—	—				8	1.5	12	2.1	10		14
Radicals	7.3		7.8	39							—		—	—
Center outside government majority			9.6		12.6	41	10.3	33	12.4	31				
MRP	22.1	118	9.1	55										
UDF (RI and other center in government majority)	11.6	64	4.4	36	37.7	42	43.65	61	10.6	77	21.4	119	19.2	63
Gaullists	17.6	212	32.0	233		200		293	23.9	184	22.5	155	20.8	87

* Unaffiliated deputies and splinter groups are not included; hence the number of deputies listed here does not add up to the total number of seats in the National Assembly. For some elections data given by various sources vary. In part this is due to different classifications and sometimes to shifts in affiliation.

working-class following of the SFIO was concentrated in a few regions of traditional strength, but the party had some strongholds elsewhere. It had a large following among the winegrowers of the South, fervent devotees of republican ideals, of anticlericalism, and of producers' cooperatives. The proportion of civil servants, especially of teachers, and of other people living on fixed income has at all times been far higher in the ranks and among the voters of the SFIO than in the population at large. This made for a deliberate but not particularly dynamic following, especially since the young were no longer attracted by the party.

Once Gaullism was firmly in the saddle, it became clear that the party was reduced to a permanent and increasingly impotent opposition, unless the Left should defeat the ruling majority in electoral battle. Allies were needed for this purpose, and given the disorganization of the Center (see below), they could be found only on the party's left. But the old leadership of the SFIO refused any closer relationship with the communists. After several false starts which courted disaster, the old SFIO dissolved, forced the resignation of its discredited leadership, and a new Socialist party (PS) saw the light in the summer of 1969.[19]

The party's early success in acquiring a new image, in attracting new members, and in reversing its electoral decline came almost as a surprise. Incipient public disenchantment with the Pompidou presidency and the assumption of the Socialist leadership by François Mitterrand at the party congress of 1971 combined to bring about this reversal in the party's fortunes; ten years later it led to the victory at the polls.

Born into a solidly bourgeois and Catholic provincial family, François Mitterrand had been a student of literature before the war; later he became a lawyer by profession and a politician by vocation. He had participated in the resistance movement after an escape from a German prison camp. Before he ever

[19] On these developments see Christiane Hurtig, *De la S.F.I.O. au nouveau parti socialiste* (Paris: Colin, 1970); Harvey G. Simmons, *French Socialists in Search of a Role, 1956–1967* (Ithaca: Cornell University Press, 1970); and Frank L. Wilson, *The French Democratic Left: Towards a Modern Party System* (Stanford: Stanford University Press, 1971).

joined the Socialist Party Mitterrand had been in public life for twenty-seven years. In the Fourth Republic he had been a deputy for many years, the mayor of a small town in the center of France, and a sometimes controversial minister in eleven short-lived Cabinets. He never belonged to any of the established parties but moved in and out of small and shapeless parliamentary groups, just left of center. In 1958 he had been one of the few non-Communists who had voted in parliament against the Gaullist constitution. Years later in an impassioned book he had denounced the concentration of powers in the hands of the President of the Republic as utterly unrepublican.[20] In the presidential elections of 1965, when he ran against de Gaulle (see Chapter IV), he had proven his ability as a vote-getter.

After he had imposed his leadership in the PS his most notable achievement was that of holding together a party which was rent by internal tensions while it was steadily rising in public favor. Mitterrand's own socialist creed, recent though it was, appeared quite appropriate to provide a needed compromise between the feuding ideologies within the party. He described himself as being committed neither to classical marxism, which he rejected as dogmatic and impractical, nor to a social-democratic reformism which, to him, had become too comfortable within the value system of bourgeois society. His humanist socialism is in the tradition of earlier socialist leaders such as Jean Jaurès and Léon Blum, but bears the distinct traits of his own strong personality. As a writer he is as talented as the earlier socialist leaders from whom he takes his inspiration. His anticapitalism is often strident, yet concern for justice clearly outweighs an interest in economic blueprints for a socialist future. Nonetheless, the new party program of 1972 spelled out in detail the party's commitment to a socialist society.[21]

---

[20] See François Mitterrand, *Le Coup d'État Permanent* (Paris: Plon, 1964). For the best biography of Mitterrand so far, see Franz-Olivier Giesbert, *François Mitterrand ou la tentation de l'histoire* (Paris: Seuil, 1977).

[21] For a succinct history of the new PS during its early years, see Frank L. Wilson, "The French Left in the Fifth Republic," in *The Fifth Republic at Twenty*, eds. William Andrews and Stanley Hoffmann (Albany:

Since the PS, unlike the Communist Party, shuns orthodoxy, different lines of thought and different views on strategy have always found expression within the party, sometimes to the point of near-anarchy. The Marxism of the party's left-wing, represented by the CERES (Socialist Studies and Research Center), draws on the Guesdist traditions within French socialism, but is also quite close to the teachings of the Italian communist Gramsci and to the New Left.[22] In spite of the pronounced elitism of its intellectual leadership, the group had won, at least at one time, the sympathies of about one-fourth of the party's activists. At the party's opposite end are those who feel lukewarm about proposals for further nationalizations. To them it appears more important to overcome stifling bureaucratization in both the private and the public sector of the economy, and they wish to see this done by comprehensive decentralization and by economic reforms introducing *autogestion* (self-management). The concept of self-management draws some of its inspiration from Yugoslav attempts to steer a course between the Soviet system and capitalism. Enterprises large and small, owned and managed by business and labor, would compete in a loosely planned economy. Advocates of this solution, which has been developed in considerable detail, are to be found not only in the PS but also in the unions belonging to the CFDT and in the leadership of a number of associations. Michel Rocard, today the Minister of Planning, is most closely identified with such views. He had joined the new PS even later than Mitterrand. But due to his youth, his

---

State University of New York Press, 1981), pp. 180–88. The most interesting books in French on Socialist party developments are Jean-François Bizot, *Au Parti des Socialistes. Plongée Libre dans les courants d'un Grand Parti* (Paris: Grasset, 1975), and, a more scholarly approach, Hughes Portelli, *Le socialisme français tel qu'il est* (Paris: PUF, 1980). For the text of the party program, see *Changer la vie: programme de gouvernement du parti socialiste* (Paris: Flammarion, 1972). The program was amended shortly before the 1981 election as *Projet Socialiste: Pour la France des Années 80*. The radicalism of this document embarrassed Mitterrand during his campaign, and he tried to distance himself from it.

22 For a statement of the CERES position, see Jean-Pierre Chevènement, the group's leader, today the Minister of Research and Technology, *Les socialistes, les communistes et les autres* (Paris: Aubier, 1977).

style, and the seeming novelty of his ideas addressing the general problems of French society, Rocard at times outranked Mitterrand in popularity with the electorate.[23]

Standing between these two wings of the party, other groups represent less determined views. At each of the annual party conventions disagreements came to the surface, intraparty alliances were formed and dissolved. Mitterrand's position as party leader and as the party's presidential candidate often seemed threatened. But in the end he always succeeded in winning the support of a majority, although not always the same majority.[24] In the socialist Cabinet of 1981 all of the once-feuding factions of the PS were represented — a measure of Mitterrand's effectiveness as a party leader.

The internal difficulties of the PS were not all due to program; the party's strategy was at least as controversial. Mitterrand had set the party on the course of seeking the greatest possible rapprochement with the communists (PC) so as to present to the electorate a plausible alternative to the government and to its policies. But since the public distrusted the communists' ultimate goals, the alternative was suspect to a majority of voters as long as the PC continued to be stronger and better organized than its partner. Mitterrand acknowledged this when he let it be known that the PS was out to establish an equilibrium between the two parties and that he counted on winning for his party millions of voters that had previously voted for the communists. Such frankness might have been one of the reasons why the PC broke the fragile unity that had been created in 1972 behind a Common Program (see below). But it

[23] For an interesting political biography of Rocard, written at the time of his greatest ascendancy, see Hervé Hamon and Patrick Rotman, *L'Effet Rocard* (Paris: Stock, 1980). For a critical but fair discussion of the debate on *autogestion*, see Jean-Pierre Cot (today an Under Secretary in the Foreign Office), "Autogestion and Modernity in France," in *Eurocommunism and Eurosocialism: The Left Confronts Modernity*, ed. Bernard Brown (New York: Cyrco Press, 1979), pp. 67–103. More positive are the remarks by François Bloch-Lainé, *Profession: Fonctionnaire* (Paris: Seuil, 1976), pp. 172–73.

[24] At one point Mitterrand is reported to have said "The P.S. is not a party. It is a political radiation [*rayonnement*] around myself." See Roland Cayrol, "Les avenirs du parti socialiste," *Projet,* no. 94 (1975): 439–49, a well-informed study.

promoted the very goals that it announced: the growing organizational and electoral strength of the PS.

The membership of the PS doubled during the first four years after its resurrection. It was reported to have reached close to 200,000 between the elections of 1978 and 1981. New record figures are reported since then, but have not been verified. There were even more new recruits than these figures indicate, since thousands of old members had left the party, dissatisfied over the new policy of leftist unity. But it is not only in size that the party has changed. Catholics of progressive leanings, workers, professionals, and intellectuals had been left politically homeless when the party they had helped to found after the war, the MRP, had been crushed by the impact of Gaullism. Many of them have joined the Socialist Party and have frequently become committed activists, usually without embracing Marxism. They might be members of both the PS and the CFDT, the labor confederation. Among the young whom the PS has attracted in far greater numbers than previously, there are many who had been awakened politically by the events of 1968. Disappointed by the outcome of that short-lived revolt, they believe to have found in the PS an outlet for political activity.

In terms of social origin the new membership comes predominantly from the salaried middle classes, the professions, the civil service, and especially from the teaching profession. Workers are represented in the PS even more sparsely than they were in the old SFIO, and this is particularly true for the party leadership. It is estimated that workers now furnish 35 percent of the socialist electorate; there are only 15 percent of them among the dues-paying members, 5 percent among the party activists, the *militants,* yet fewer among the delegates to the national conventions and only 2 percent on the top executive. The picture is reversed for upper-class professional people: they account for only 9 percent of the party's electoral following, make up 15 percent of its members, and 80 percent of the leadership.

The party career of many now in the upper ranks of the hierarchy did not follow the pattern that is usual in the European social-democratic parties, which reward long and faithful service in the party organization with a slow ascent to higher positions. A party such as the PS, which had never been in power, needed to attract managerial and intellectual talent so as to prove that it could shoulder national responsibilities. In preparation for a victory at the polls, the party's executive assembled such talent in a number of expert committees; graduates of the ENA (see Chapter VI) moved quickly into leadership positions. Increasingly party discussions were dominated by intellectuals, which made the party even less attractive for workers. Yet according to party claims, socialist sections now exist in about 500 factories or offices, a form of political activity which previously only the communists had practiced successfully.[25]

Both local and national elections testified to the Socialist party's rising popularity. Even during the years of the party's decline, it had continued to hold strong positions in local government, outranking not only the ruling Gaullists but also the Communists. Such strength was due to experienced personnel and honored traditions. In one city in the Southwest the office of the mayor has been controlled for seventy-five years by a total of three(!) Socialists. The patronage connected with positions in local government provided at least some consolation at a time when the party's national status was severely reduced.

Socialist victories in municipal and cantonal elections were the first signal that voters' sympathies were shifting from Right to Left. By 1979 the number of Socialist mayors of cities with over 30,000 population had doubled: out of 221 cities in that category, the Socialists are now controlling 81 (since an additional 72 such cities have communist mayors, the Left now administers 70 percent of them). Even more significant was the Socialist success in cities over 100,000 population: 13 of them (out of a total of 49) now have Socialist mayors. In addition, there are thousands of Socialist mayors in the smaller communities and an estimated 60,000 municipal councillors. The strong position which the PS also holds in departmental and regional councils will become of particular significance when

---

[25] For an account of this aspect, see Roland Cayrol, "Le Parti socialiste à l'entreprise," *RFSP* 28, 2 (April 1978), pp. 296–312.

the proposed reform legislation shifts responsibilities previously held by the prefects to these councils (see Chapter IX).

In 1981 the PS and its leader reaped the benefits of their long and patient efforts. The reasons for and the extent of their success will be discussed, together with the electoral record of the other parties, in the last section of this chapter.

Dissensions within a party such as the PS have not ceased and were voiced quite openly during the first party congress held after the victory at the polls. Not only party activists but also some of the newly elected members of parliament asked for a speeding up of the announced reforms and for more energy in countering what was described as the "sabotage" by the opposition parties. But the power which the party now holds over government and state is a strong tie binding heterogeneous factions and encouraging unity for common goals.

In the National Assembly elected in 1981 fourteen so-called Left Radicals are part of the socialist group. As often in French party history the label is misleading: these deputies stand politically "right" of the Socialist Party since they are a split-off of the former Radical Party, that once-powerful centrist party of past Republics. Among the Radicals who are now allied with the Socialists there are a number of outstanding politicians, but their following is strictly personal. In the first ballot of the presidential elections of 1981 the party's leader had made the poor showing that was generally expected: 2.2 percent of votes cast. For having urged his followers to vote for Mitterrand in the runoff election, he was rewarded with the Ministry of Environment in the Socialist Cabinet.

The Communists. In all democratic countries the Communists are a "party not like the others." For many decades their reliance on directives from Moscow was not equaled by whatever loose international ties other parties might have established. Because of the singular importance of France to the international position of the Soviet Union, the French PC was ordered time and again, and at most dramatic moments, to alter its course abruptly, but always according to the demands of Russian foreign policy. Except for a short interlude after the war, the PC has been excluded since its beginning from any participation in the national government. Yet a party which between 1945 and 1981 has had an electoral following of between 19 and 28 percent of the voters at all parliamentary elections and which is represented by more than 20,000 city and town councillors and by almost 800 mayors administering municipalities with about 5 million people (more than 10 percent of the total population) is also and simultaneously "a party like the others." Its very existence constantly has impinged, nationally as well as locally, on the rules of the political game and thereby on the system itself.

The PC has always been at least as disciplined and centralized as communist parties elsewhere and as no other French party has ever been for any length of time. In the troubled aftermath of the First World War, the French communists succeeded in doing what almost none of the other European communist movements had been able to bring about: the winning over of a substantial majority of the membership of the Socialist Party and of its valuable assets, such as the daily *L'Humanité*.[26] However, by the time of the economic depression of the thirties, what was left of the party was not much more than a bureaucratic apparatus and, around it, devoted *militants*. After the changed tactics of Stalinist Russia made the formation of the French Popular Front possible, the party membership increased massively, and, when after the Liberation a heroic resistance record had blotted out the bitter memories of the Hitler-Stalin Pact,[27] the party claimed to have reached a membership of close to a million. In 1946 its electorate stood at almost 5.5 million. Surrounding the party were numerous, large front-organizations and the communist-dominated trade unions affiliated with the CGT.

[26] For the early history of the PC, see Robert Wohl, *French Communism in the Making* (Stanford: Stanford University Press, 1966).

[27] Fairly typical is the description of attitudes in a Brittany town of moderate political leanings: "During the war years the Communist Party was not regarded as the vanguard of a menacing proletariat, the fomenter of revolutionary disturbances, or the gravedigger of the old republican order, but as the vitalizer of the nation's energies against the occupier, the, leader of the struggle for freedom. . . ." Edgar Morin, *Plodémet: Report from a French Village* (New York: Random House, 1970), p. 172.

What has changed, what has remained stubbornly the same about the party since the end of the war? [28]

Until 1981 the communist electorate has been more faithful than that of other parties. If it too has grown and shrunk with popular feelings about the policies of the Fifth Republic, this is additional evidence that in some respects the party has become an opposition party "like the others." [29] The party has always had an important following in the industrial regions of the North (except in those working-class districts where Catholicism has remained strong) and in the "red belt" encircling Paris and Marseilles. In some rural regions its support has changed with economic developments. But nationally its continuing strength among workers of all categories remained outstanding. (For details on the social composition of the Communist electorate in 1978 and 1981, see Table IX.)

Why the electoral support for the PC has remained so strong and varied over such a long period of time has been discussed widely. Georges Lavau has characterized the party as "tribunitial" in its appeal,[30] likening it to that Roman magistrate

[28] There is no longer a dearth of scholarly (as distinguished from merely polemic) studies of the PC. The most recent and most profound study of the PC past and present is that by Georges Lavau, *À quoi sert le parti communiste français?* (Paris: Fayard, 1981, written before the 1981 elections). The most complete American study (with a rich bibliography) is by Ronald Tiersky, *French Communism, 1920–1972* (New York: Columbia University Press, 1974). The author has updated his findings in two articles, "The French Communist Party and Detente," *Journal of International Affairs* 28, no. 2 (1974): 188–205, and "French Communism in 1976," *Problems of Communism* 25, no. 1 (1976). The English edition of a book by one of the outstanding French experts on communism is Annie Kriegel, *The French Communists: Profile of a People* (Chicago: The University of Chicago Press, 1972). Well documented and rich in original analyses, even if now somewhat dated, is Fondation Nationale des Sciences Politiques (various authors), *Le Communisme en France* (Paris: Colin, 1969).

[29] For details see Table VII. Only the number of votes cast for the PC on the first ballot is an indicator of popular sympathies; under the prevailing electoral system, the number of Communist deputies in parliament depends entirely on whatever arrangements the parties of the Left have made for the second ballot.

[30] See Lavau, *Parti communiste*, pp. 342 ff. The author defends his characterization of the PC which he had proposed earlier with convincing arguments. Among the critics of the term had been the interesting article by Thomas Greene, "The Electorate of the Non-Ruling Communist Parties," *Studies in Comparative Communism* 4 (1971): 86–103.

whose specific function it was to protect the individual plebeian citizen by vetoing arbitrary action by patrician officials. Neither the Roman tribune nor the PC had any power to initiate policies or reforms. The PC does not even have the vetoing power which was granted the tribune after plebeian revolts in the Roman republic. Yet by voicing the citizens' wrath, the PC seeks to mobilize the social plebeians in present-day France and to give them a feeling of strength and confidence.

Against such an argument the point has been made that in fact the PC does not attract the poorest of the workers and peasants but a somewhat higher income group among both. If the economic interpretation were correct the voting strength of the party should have been sapped with the spreading of prosperity and rising real wages. Actually a vote for the PC is an expression of protest which mixes indignation about injustice and mismanagement with more or less vague beliefs in a better society. At least emotionally, a fairly large share of the Communist vote corresponds to the protest which millions of underprivileged citizens of the United States manifest by never casting a vote.

It is entirely in line with the assumed role of a defender of the underdog that the PC claims to have the monopoly of fighting whatever injustices are to be found in society. And since present-day society is a class society, the party insists that its own core must be the working class. In the late 1960s 60 percent of the membership were, according to party sources, manual workers; 18 percent white-collar employees; and 9 percent intellectuals. Such a composition gave to the PC more of a working-class character than any other French political organization at any time. Because of the widespread working-class consciousness, the *ouvriérisme* (discussed in Chapter III), its very composition assured the party working-class sympathies. As a matter of fact the party leadership is more heavily entrenched and bureaucratic than that of almost any other communist party outside of the Soviet Union. When Maurice Thorez died in 1964 he had been the party's secretary-general for thirty-four years! The present incumbent of that office, Georges Marchais, was a favorite of Thorez and is not held in high esteem in many party circles. But both these leaders, their collaborators, as well as the party's representatives in parliament, have all worn the badge of honor of proletarian origin.

Shortly after the events of 1968 the party opened its gates wider than before to young intellectuals, technicians, and professionals; the share of women members was increased from 25 to 30 percent. Wishing to appeal to a wider audience, the party no longer wanted to appear as monolithic as before.[31] Such an opening coincided with a new strategy suggested to the party by both international and domestic developments.

Polycentrism in Eastern and Eurocommunism in Western Europe, the Sino-Soviet split, detente between the super-powers, and at home the decline of the Gaullist élan presumably helped set the PC on its new course. A new party program dropped all reference to the dictatorship of the proletariat and instead developed an opposition platform within the existing institutional framework.[32] In France the time for socialism would come only, the party literature asserted, once a majority of Frenchmen were in favor of it. Until then the party would devote its best efforts to help fight the abuses of monopoly capitalism and of personal power, flagrant in the Fifth Republic. Since that fight could not be won by the Communists alone, they welcomed all allies willing to join, and in the first place the Socialists with whom the PC in early 1972 signed the Common Program.

The Common Program was for a time considered a milestone in the history of the French Left.[33] Instead of merely offering

[31] For this development see two interesting accounts: André Laurens and Thierry Pfister, *Les nouveaux communistes* (Paris: Stock, 1973); and André Harris and Alain de Sedouy, *Voyage à l'intérieur du parti communiste* (Paris: Seuil, 1974).

[32] Published as *Changer de cap: programme pour un gouvernement démocratique d'union populaire* (Paris: Éditions Sociales, 1971). Of even greater programmatic interest was the widely distributed book by the party's secretary general, Georges Marchais, *Le Défi démocratique* (Paris: Grasset, 1973).

[33] Its official name is: *Programme commun de gouvernement: parti socialiste, parti communiste, mouvement des radicaux de gauche* (Paris: Flammarion, 1973). For a more detailed history of the Common Program, see *Eurocommunism,* Brown, pp. 43 ff. For a criticism of the program and an account of the breakdown of Left unity, see Mark Kesselman, "The French Left and the Transformation of French Society: Sysiphus Revisited," in *Fifth Republic,* Andrews and Hoffmann, pp. 192–202.

some basic propositions for an electoral alliance, such as the opposition parties had concluded on several previous occasions, or an outline of a political action program as the Popular Front Program of 1936 had been, it spelled out in detail governmental policies for the five years of a normal parliamentary session. In almost every field the two main partners made substantial concessions to the other's point of view in order to arrive at common objectives; they did so because at the time of signing they were both convinced that there was no other way to turn out the majority that had ruled the country since 1958.

There is no need to discuss this lengthy document (almost 100 pages), since its signatories would admit that it had lost its significance as a program for a government of the Left even before such a government came to power in 1981. After years of incessant polemics between the partners, the break between them occurred ostensibly when, in the fall of 1977, the leadership of the PC wanted to modify the Common Program by lengthening the list of firms to be nationalized. The socialists refused to do this for reasons of their own, but also because it had become evident that the PC wished to dissolve the partnership. The foremost reason was the new popularity of the PS in which the PC saw a threat to its own status. The "better balance" between the two parties, which Mitterrand had described as desirable when he steered his party into the alliance, was turning into a new imbalance, all the less tolerable for the PC as their competitors now seemed to attract some working-class sympathies.

When the PC took refuge in an intransigence which led to the break with the PS, the legislative elections of 1978 were approaching. On the basis of opinion polls and observations, it was widely assumed that the Left would win these elections and that as a consequence the Socialists would form a government in which the Communists would have to play the role of a junior partner — at that time an unacceptable perspective for the party. After the conservatives had once more won the elections, the PC did not resume cordial relations with the PS but tried to turn the party back to the policies it had practiced during the years of its isolation in a political subculture — or a ghetto, as some have termed it.

For all communist parties outside the Soviet orbit, but especially for the French PC, attitudes towards the Soviet Union have always been a barometer registering changes in the party line. During the lifetime of Thorez the party had never entered honestly upon the process of destalinization. The party's approval of the Soviet intervention in Hungary had cost it dearly in popular esteem. It had therefore criticized rather sharply the Russian suppression of the Czechoslovak spring in 1968. For some years thereafter the communist press "regretted" the abridging of intellectual freedom in the Soviet Union, admitted and deplored the existence of labor camps and moved altogether on the line developed by other Eurocommunist parties. But after the alliance with the French socialists had been dissolved, the reversal of attitudes towards the Soviet Union was prompt. Criticism of what had previously been called the "inadequacies" of the Soviet system was first muted and then abandoned. The invasion of Afghanistan was applauded without any reservation.[34]

The party has never claimed to have abandoned the Leninist principle of "democratic centralism." This meant that once policies were set from above, they were binding, and factions such as exist in the PS were not tolerated. Each time the party line changed, the party bureaucracy sought to enforce it not only within the PC itself but also within the so-called mass organizations for youth, women, sports, etc., all controlled by the party. The most significant of these controls, the one exercised over the largest trade union confederation, the CGT, has been discussed earlier[35] (see Chapter VI). But in the late 1970s it became doubtful whether the party still had the means requisite for its ambitions.

Estimates of the party's membership varied greatly even before the electoral defeats of 1981. In 1977 the party claimed

[34] For a brilliant discussion of the party's attitude towards the Soviet Union, see Lavau, *Parti communiste*, pp. 356–414. At one time the PC published a book which assembled moderately critical opinions about Soviet Union developments. See A. Adler, F. Cohen, M. Decaillot, C. Frioux, L. Robel, *L'URSS et nous* (Paris: Éditions Sociales, 1978). The book was hardly published when the party withdrew it from distribution.
[35] For more details, see Lavau, *Parti communiste,* pp. 120–31, 427.

611,000 members, most of them relatively recent. Even at that time outside observers maintained that this figure must be discounted by about one-half, if not more. According to official party figures, at least 100,000 were party militants, the activists whose work was directed by about 2,000 "permanents" or full-time party bureaucrats.[36] The lowest party unit remains the 20,000 party cells, of which less than one-fourth operate in factories.

Even if one takes these impressive figures at face value, they conceal the fact that many party members and even some of the militants have ceased all active participation and that attendance at meetings has become sparse.[37] Presumably the members of factory cells, such as they exist at the Renault works, come together only perfunctorily. An acute internal crisis set in after the Left lost the elections of 1978. The defeat was attributed by many party members to the anti-socialist stance of the PC. A number of articles written by the few outstanding intellectuals who still belonged to the party described in detail and deplored what the writers characterized as the fundamental errors of party line and organization.[38] As long as the criticism came from intellectuals, the party leadership hoped to isolate it as it had done in the past. But it spread to party cells in working-class districts. A respected party leader who represented the "red belt" in the Paris City Council not only joined the critics but started organizing the forces of opposition within the party.[39]

Amidst considerable confusion the party decided to field

[36] See Wilson, "The French Left," in *Fifth Republic,* Andrews and Hoffmann, pp. 172–80, and the sources indicated by him.

[37] For a report on lagging party activities in Grenoble, believed to be typical of many local organizations, see Jacques Derville and Maurice Croisat, "La Socialisation des militants communistes," *RFSP* 29, no. 4–5 (August–October 1979): pp. 760 ff. For an extensive account of local party activities during a slightly earlier period, see Denis Lacorne, *Les Notables rouges: La Construction municipale de l'Union de la gauche* (Paris: PFNSP, 1980).

[38] All reprinted in pamphlet form: see Louis Althusser (one of the outstanding marxist philosophers of our time), *Ce quïi ne peut plus durer — dans le parti communiste* (Paris: Maspero, 1978); E. Balibar, G. Labica, J. P. Lefebvre, *Ouvrons la fenêtre, camarades* (Paris: Maspero, 1979); and Jean-Michel Devesa, *Un parti peut en cacher un autre* (Paris: Maspero, 1979).

[39] See H. Fiszbin, *Les Bouches s'ouvrent* (Paris: Grasset, 1980).

Georges Marchais as its own candidate in the presidential elections of 1981, while seven years earlier the party had supported Mitterrand in both ballots. At the beginning of his campaign the communist candidate attacked his socialist competitor with more severity than the conservative candidates. He also predicted incautiously that he would win 21 percent of the vote and that the enrollment of 1 million party members was the next goal to attain. The actual score of the communist candidate was the lowest ever obtained by the PC since 1936: 15.3 percent of the votes (12.2 percent of the registered voters), a loss of one-fourth of the communist electorate. In the first ballot of the legislative elections that followed, the communist vote was still only a meager 16.2 percent of the total vote (as compared with 20.6 in the elections of 1978 and 21.4 percent in those of 1973). The number of communist deputies in the National Assembly was cut almost in half: forty-four instead of eighty-six.

After their defeat at the polls the communists chose to accept what they had tried to avoid earlier: four ministerial posts of rather secondary importance in the Socialist Cabinet. In a fairly comprehensive agreement, PS and PC pledged collaboration in bringing about the "changes which the country expects," but implicitly or explicitly the communists had to abandon former positions on important questions of domestic and foreign policy.[40]

The leadership of the PC tried to restore discipline in the party by expelling some prominent critics. This, however, did not prevent discontent with the party's past and present course from spreading to the rank and file in many parts of the country; there were numerous resignations from leadership positions at the lower party echelons. Nonetheless the annual party congress in February 1982 confirmed the discredited Georges Marchais and most of the national leadership in their positions. From the rostrum of the congress achievements of the Soviet Union and of its Eastern European allies were described

---

[40] *Le Monde*, June 24, 1981. For an evaluation of the intraparty crisis and reflections on the future course of the PC, see Georges Lavau, "Le recul du P.C.F.: péripétie ou déclin historique?" *Le Débat*, no. 16 (November 1981): 77–83 and Alain Duhamel, "La crise du parti communiste français," *Le Monde*, December 28, 1981.

as "globally positive" and the military regime of Poland was praised. Past mistakes of the party line were touched upon lightly; the commitment to communist participation in the socialist government was described as correct policy. But coupled with such a resolve were attacks against the social policy of the government, especially the latter's willingness to encourage a lowering of wages where a reduction of the weekly working hours had been agreed to.

Quite obviously the PC is confident that it needs only patience to weather its present misfortunes, which are not the first it has endured.

THE RIGHT

The Gaullists. The UNR, as the Gaullist party was then known,[41] thrown hastily together after General de Gaulle's return to power in 1958, is the one true novelty in French party politics. When, only weeks after its birth, it won over 20 percent of the vote and, more surprisingly, almost 40 percent of the seats in the first parliament of the new republic, it benefited largely from the floating vote which in the past had swelled, but never for long, other surge movements. The plethora of seats in the National Assembly, with which the party found itself blessed after the second ballot, resulted from a bandwagon effect which the electoral system chosen by General de Gaulle had been expected to prevent.

During the ensuing years the UNR was first of all, it has been said correctly, a team of Cabinet ministers, then a committee in charge of designating candidates for elections to parliament, and lastly, but only lastly, a party.[42] Such priorities were entirely in line with the views of de Gaulle, who had little

[41] The Gaullist party has changed names and initials quite often. What had been at its founding the *Union pour la Nouvelle République* (UNR) became in 1968 the *Union des Démocrates pour la République* (UDR), and in 1976 the *Rassemblement pour la République* (RPR).

[42] See the outstanding expert on the Gaullist movement, Jean Charlot, *L'U.N.R., étude du pouvoir au sein d'un parti politique* (Paris: Colin, 1967), p. 23. All of Charlot's writings are indispensable for an understanding of the UDR. See also his *The Gaullist Phenomenon: The Gaullist Movement in the Fifth Republic* (New York: Praeger, 1971); and studies published by the Institut Français d'Opinion Publique, edited by him: *Les Français et de Gaulle* (Paris: Plon, 1971); and *Quand la Gauche peut gagner . . .* (Paris: Éditions Moreau, 1973).

use for any party including his own. Like the first Bonaparte he was wont to admonish his compatriots, of whatever political camp, to be "good Frenchmen with him." De Gaulle's distaste for all political parties had been nurtured by his one and only experience as a party leader. In 1947 he had founded the RPF, the Rally of the French People, as an opposition movement in the Fourth Republic. In spite of its name, the "Rally" had become a party "like the others," made up in part of authoritarian right-wingers and in part of the careerists typical of traditional French conservatism. De Gaulle had little use for either and dissolved the party after a few years' trying.

Until his election for a second term as President of the Fifth Republic in 1965, General de Gaulle had been successful in discouraging all attempts to develop the UNR into the structured and disciplined conservative party which France has never known. During the first years of the regime the upper echelons of the party hierarchy constituted almost without exception a "peer group," the "barons" of Gaullism, as they would later be called. All of its members had belonged directly, or indirectly through a single intermediary, to General de Gaulle's entourage during the days of the Free French movement in London and Algiers, or during the post-Liberation period. Since those troubled times had attracted men of widely different background to General de Gaulle, the ties that bound them to each other consisted mostly of their personal loyalty to the leader.

De Gaulle's second prime minister, Georges Pompidou, had never run for political office and was not himself a member of the UNR. But as chief of the government majority he saw the need for a better organized party if future elections were to be won and an orderly succession of the charismatic leader was to ensure a Gaullism *sans* de Gaulle. New bylaws gave muscle to the party organization at all levels and promised to involve the membership in a modicum of decision making. From a membership of not more than 24,000 in 1959 the party rose presumably to between 150,000 and 200,000 in 1972.[43]

---

[43] Like all other membership figures in France, these are subject to doubt. In 1968 an inquiry reported that in the city of Grenoble, a center of fairly intensive political activity, the UNR had "virtually no members." See the important, if now slightly dated study by Suzanne Berger et al.,

In reality the role of the party's membership and of its activists, whether paid or voluntary, remained generally limited to assisting in propaganda efforts at election time. If the UNR was to speak "with one voice," policy making had to be restricted to the top leadership, for divergences were likely to exist between leaders and followers. There was a difference in social origin: the leadership was drawn from various elite groups, especially after the importance of personal relationship with de Gaulle had diminished. Party members and activists were frequently of lower-middle-class origin; they distrusted the "technocrats in Paris" of whom an increasing number occupied leading positions in government and in their own party.[44]

There had been no need for a party program or even platform as long as de Gaulle was the leader. To him, thoughts he had first expressed as a young officer had remained the lodestar: "There exists no absolute truth, either in politics or strategy. There are only the circumstances." [45] What the circumstances demanded, the leadership would decide, and when the leader's mantle fell on shoulders other than de Gaulle's the identification of governmental policy and the party's objectives simply continued.

Its constituency organization and the voting discipline of its elected representatives distinguished the UNR from the classi-

---

"The Problem of Reform in France: The Political Ideas of Local Elites," *Political Science Quarterly* 84, no. 3 (1969): 450. For a later period two richly documented studies about party life on the local and departmental level compare the UDR with parties of the Left in the same districts: Kesselman, "Recruitment of Rival Party Activists"; and Jacques Lagrove and Guy Lord, "Trois Fédérations de partis politiques, esquisse de typologie," *RFSP* 24, no. 3 (1974): 559–95.

[44] On these differences see Kesselman, "Recruitment of Party Activists," pp. 21 ff.; Gilles Martinet, *Le Système Pompidou* (Paris: Seuil, 1973), pp. 81 ff.; and Charles Debbasch, *La France de Pompidou* (Paris: Presses Universitaires, 1974), pp. 79–85, in a chapter characteristically titled: "Gaullism, a Broth with Several Ingredients."

[45] Charles de Gaulle, *War Memoirs, III: The Salvation* (New York: Simon and Schuster, 1960), p. 136. For the most insightful comments on de Gaulle's thinking and the relationship between his thought and action see three excellent essays by Stanley Hoffmann, now reprinted in *Decline or Renewal? France since the 1930s* (New York: The Viking Press, 1974), pp. 185–280.

cal parties of notables, long characteristic of the French Right. Its lack of a program and of an input to policy formation by the membership made it different also from the democratic mass parties as other European countries have known them.

For the first ten years of Gaullist rule the UDR-UNR increased its share of the total vote in each parliamentary election (see Table VII) until in the first ballot of the landslide elections of 1968 the Gaullists and their allies gained an electoral following of over 10 million, 46 percent of the votes cast and 36 percent of the registered voters; Gaullist deputies by themselves held a majority of seats in the National Assembly, in every respect a record never obtained under a republican regime in France. If the more "normal" elections of 1973 brought a reflux, they did not deprive the UDR of its status as the dominant party of the Fifth Republic. Yet only one year later in the first ballot of the presidential elections to elect Pompidou's successor, the party's official candidate, Jacques Chaban-Delmas, mustered not more than 14.6 percent of the vote.

The campaign waged by Chaban-Delmas brought the contradictions of the Gaullist regime and of its dominant party into the open. At the outset of the campaign the voters who had declared their intention to vote for Chaban also voiced opinions which corresponded in every respect to the announced or assumed objectives of his competitor Giscard. When Chaban pledged far-reaching reforms and attacked the former minister of finance as the candidate of an outmoded conservative Right, millions of the UDR's former voters found this reason enough to vote for Giscard. They thereby adjusted their choice of a candidate to their true convictions. Their party could but follow its voters' lead and make Giscard its candidate in the runoff elections.[46] During the first six months of Giscard's presidency the Gaullist party, after their candidate's smashing defeat in the primaries, was in shambles: "it had no leader, no

[46] For an analysis of Giscard as "the best, the only representative of conservatism," see Jean Ranger, "Élections présidentielles: logique d'une évolution," *Politique d'aujourd'hui* (May–July 1974): 2–13. For similar comments written at the time of the elections, see François Mitterrand, *La Paille et le grain* (Paris: Flammarion, 1975), p. 287.

strategy, no policy, and it questioned its own future." [47] Had the UDR been permitted to disintegrate after its electoral debacle, the new president would have had to face the difficulties inherent in a presidential regime in which the government cannot survive without the support of a majority in parliament. The backbone of the majority in the National Assembly elected in 1973 was still the UDR. To save the president constitutional embarrassment and to rescue the party from itself, fell to the prime minister of the new administration, Jacques Chirac.

Chirac's career had been meteoric. After his graduation from the ENA he did not spend much time in the high administrative post to which he was nominated, but became a staff member of Georges Pompidou, then Prime Minister under de Gaulle, and soon his confidant. He entered parliament as a Gaullist deputy from a poor rural district and was nominated to a post in the Cabinet. The events of 1968 found him an Under-Secretary in the Ministry of Labor, mediating successfully between the unions and management. At the time of Pompidou's death, he occupied the important post of Minister of Interior (which in France means the Minister of Police), an excellent vantage point for his intraparty intrigues that insured the victory of Giscard over Chirac's fellow-Gaullist. At age forty-two he became the first Prime Minister in the Giscard administration.[48]

Not content with the role of the majority leader, a role which all previous prime ministers had assumed, Chirac imposed himself as the secretary general of the UDR. Within weeks after he had assumed the post, the entire organization was completely overhauled; the secretary general was given broad powers over the party's executives in each of the ninety-six departments, and he proceeded to purge more than two-thirds of them. The old barons moved into the background,

[47] Jean Charlot, "The Majority," in *The French National Assembly Elections of 1978,* ed. Howard Penniman (Washington, D.C.: American Enterprise Institute, 1980), p. 79.

[48] For many, partly friendly, partly hostile but all interesting comments on Chirac, see "Regards sur Chirac par ses Amis, ses Ennemis . . . et les Autres," *Regards sur . . .* no. 2 (February 1977).

and the new party leader persuaded the deputies that the party's salvation and their own reelection demanded once more the unconditional support of the government and of the president. Presumably morale of the party activists was lifted and the party began to recruit new members.

Chirac resigned as Prime Minister after a little over two years under conditions which were contrary to previous constitutional conventions (see Chapter IX). Rather than being politely dismissed by the president, as were some of his predecessors, Chirac left his post because, as he put it, he was not given sufficient power to govern.[49] The event was widely understood as putting Chirac in line as a presidential candidate.

Soon afterwards Chirac transformed the UDR into the Rally for the Republic, its acronym RPR designed to evoke memories of de Gaulle's own Rally, the RPF. In the mayorality election in Paris the new-old party was able to insure Chirac's election against a candidate supported by Giscard. In early 1978, only a year after its founding, the party claimed to have enrolled over 600,000 members, presumably outranking the PC not only by its membership but also by the solidity of its nationwide organization. The leadership was thoroughly renewed: 40 to 50 percent of the party's Central Committee and Political Council had never belonged previously to any Gaullist organization. They were largely hand-picked by the Rally's president, Chirac. Only in parliament the replacement of Gaullist incumbents by newcomers was not entirely successful.[50]

If the RPR has become, like the earlier Gaullist parties, a solidly organized mass party, able to call for impressive meetings in many parts of the country, its appeal is significantly

[49] For the constitutional significance of the episode, see Jean-Claude Colliard, "L'Équilibre des institutions est modifié," *Regards sur Chirac,* no. 2 (February 1977): 4–5. Politically interesting also is the account in Jacques Chapsal, *La Vie politique sous la Ve Republique* (Paris: PUF, 1981), pp. 566–68.
[50] See Jean Charlot, in *The French Elections of 1978,* pp. 91–93; William R. Schonfeld, "The RPR: From a Rassemblement to a Gaullist Movement," in *Fifth Republic,* Andrews and Hoffmann, pp. 99–107, and, with many details on the organization of the RPR, Kay Lawson, "The Impact of Party Reform on Party Systems," *Comparative Politics* 13, no. 4 (July 1981): 401–19.

different from that of its predecessors. UNR and UDR had furnished the model for what had been described as a novel form of political organization: the catchall party. "National societal goals," the author who coined the term has written, "transcending group interests offer the best sales prospect for a party intent on establishing or enlarging an appeal previously limited to specific sections of the population." [51]

De Gaulle, as other leaders of such parties, had appealed to a broad coalition of groups and classes which often had different reasons to become "Gaullists" at different times. The UNR's electoral inroads into a left-wing labor vote had disturbed traditional alignments, though usually not for long. The "essence of Gaullism," it has been said, "was the judicious use of confusion and ambiguity, the presentation of many faces to many people, all the while continuing in a particular direction." [52]

The RPR and its leader invoke Gaullism as their inspiration, but from their appeal all "confusion and ambiguity" have disappeared. The party's propaganda is as stridently anti-socialist as it is anti-communist. As Prime Minister, Chirac had been dragging his feet on tax and social reforms. As party leader and presidential candidate in 1981, he did not show any of the earlier concerns of Gaullism for the modernization of economy and society. The RPF moved unequivocally within the traditions of the political Right, even though its pattern of organization was different.[53] Chirac's campaign for the presidency was clearly addressed to those who feared change. It developed many of the themes which the Poujadists and similar mass movements had brought forward (see Chapter VII). Op-

[51] See Otto Kirchheimer, "The Transformation of the Western European Party Systems," in *Political Parties and Political Development,* eds. Joseph La Palombara and Myron Weiner (Princeton: Princeton University Press, 1963), p. 186.

[52] Peter A. Gourevitch, "Gaullism Abandoned or the Cost of Success," in *Fifth Republic,* Andrews and Hoffmann, p. 114. See also the entire article for what follows in the text.

[53] See René Rémond (the outstanding student of the French Right), "Jacques Chirac est-il à Droite?" in *Regards sur Chirac,* p. 41. For the mentality of RPR voters, it appears significant that far fewer of them declare their willingness to resist actively the establishment of a one-party state than the average (39 as against 51 percent). See SOFRES, *L'Opinion Française en 1977* (Paris: PFNSP, 1978), p. 226.

position to big government, to budget deficits, and to bureaucracy were the main topics of a colorful campaign carried to big audiences. (Some French newspapers spoke about Chirac's "para-Reaganism"!)

Chirac's record in the first ballot of the presidential elections was as disappointing for the RPR as the vote for Marchais had been for the PC: a mere 18 percent of the votes cast. In the parliamentary elections the RPR gathered 20.8 percent of the vote, down from 22.5 percent in 1978 and 23.9 percent in 1973. The number of Gaullist deputies had shrunk from 184 seats in the National Assembly of 1973 to 87 seats in 1981.

The Union for French Democracy. As early as 1971–1972 Giscard d'Estaing and his closest collaborator, Michel Poniatowski, had launched their programmatic slogan: "France wants to be governed from the Center." We have seen that France had in fact been so governed during much of the Third and Fourth Republics. To prevent the Center's exclusion from power in the Gaullist republic had been Giscard's foremost concern.

Born in 1926, scion of prominent families which have for a long time combined careers in business and banking with service to the state in either parliament or administration, Valéry Giscard d'Estaing graduated near the top of his class from both the X and the ENA. He joined as a matter of course the Inspectorate of Finance, to which his father, his grandfather, and one of his uncles had belonged before him. Elected deputy during the last years of the Fourth Republic to a parliamentary seat held previously by another grandfather, who had long been prominent in conservative politics, he was constantly reelected to the National Assembly and simultaneously to positions in local government. At the age of thirty-two he moved into his first Cabinet post in the first government of the Fifth Republic. Three years later he became minister of finance, a post which he held, with only one interlude, under both de Gaulle and Pompidou until his own election to the presidency.[54]

54 For biographical details, see Jean-Claude Colliard, *Les Républicains Indépendants: Valéry Giscard d'Estaing* (Paris: Presses Universitaires, 1971),

By origin and nature Giscard's party, the Independent Republicans, has been the typical party, or rather nonparty, of French conservatism. It came into existence in 1962, when Giscard and a few other conservative deputies found it inopportune to heed the injunction of their party to leave the government and to join the opposition because of de Gaulle's strictures against European unity and his unconstitutional referendum. From that time on the group provided a small complement of the majority in parliament and furnished some ministers to each of the governments that succeeded each other.

As for most groups of this kind, the voting discipline of its deputies has been mediocre at all times. Not to be cut off from the majority and yet to develop a distinct image called for constant maneuvering. After de Gaulle had dismissed Giscard from his Cabinet post as Minister of Finance and he had become chairman of the important Finance Committee in the National Assembly, Giscard was able to speak out more freely: in 1968 he criticized police brutality, the following year he recommended the "no" vote in de Gaulle's last and unsuccessful referendum. When Pompidou invited him to assume once more the Ministry of Finance post, he did so not only because the parliamentary support of the Independents was welcome to the majority, but also because experiences had shown that it was advantageous to bind Giscard to the governmental team rather than cast him in the role of an outside critic.

Although the mass media provided continuously high personal visibility to its leader, as a political organization his party remained fragile. At the approach of the 1967 elections a loose federal structure tied together the party's sympathizers in the provinces, many of them local notables of conservative leaning. The party's publications steered, like its strategy, carefully away from any doctrinal pronouncements and they

---

esp. pp. 51 ff. The French *Who's Who* lists a total of five Giscard d'Estaings. It also reveals that the former president, all three of his sisters, and his brother are married to members of the high nobility (the nobility of the Giscard d'Estaings is of recent date).

did not develop a well-defined program. In the judgment of public opinion the Independents had shed the image of an exclusively "rightist" party better than the Gaullists: only 43 percent so classified it (as against 63 percent for the UDR), whereas 21 percent regarded the Independents as "of the Center." [55]

Giscard's election to the presidency in 1974 seemed to offer an opportunity to turn the Independents into a strong presidential party. Gaullists were eliminated from many important positions in government and Cabinet; the Gaullist party appeared to be in shambles (see above); the time had come to organize "the Center." The party was to be, according to its leader, Michel Poniatowski, "a true popular union, the first party of France," solidly established in every constituency. Compared to such boasts, the results were mediocre: a frequent turnover in leadership, disappointing mass meetings, almost deliberately vacuous public pronouncements. Whatever strength the party had derived from its representatives in parliament, many of whom moved in and out of Cabinet posts, and from local leaders who occupied fairly important posts in municipal and departmental councils. Renamed the Republican Party (PR), it has never become a party of militants like the Gaullists, Socialists, and Communists, but remains a party of notables.[56]

With the approach of the parliamentary elections of 1978 a better organization seemed necessary not only because of the threat from the Left, but also because the RPR under Chirac has given Gaullism a new elan. Since it appeared hopeless to balance the forces within the majority by emulating Chirac's organizational effort, the way chosen was the one which parties of the Right and Center have always found opportune: an alliance between all groups and personalities who do not be-

---

[55] *Sondages*, 36, nos. 1, 2 (1974): 29.

[56] For a thorough analysis of the PR, see Jean-Claude Colliard, "Le parti giscardien," *Pouvoirs* 9 (1979): 115–30. Equally interesting is a chapter in Pierre Birnbaum, *Les Sommets de l'État* (Paris: Seuil, 1977), pp. 172–83. The meaninglessness of the party's policy pronouncements is described (under an ironic title) by Françoise Giroud (one-time Cabinet minister under Giscard), "La Pratique giscardienne de la politique ou l'art de l'anesthésie," *Pouvoirs* 9 (1979): 105–14.

long to any of the major parties, however heterogeneous and unrepresentative of major political currents these groups might be.

The Union for French Democracy (UDF) was formed only shortly before the election after laborious and for the outsider altogether bewildering negotiations.[57] The name of the new federation invoked deliberately the title of a book by Giscard d'Estaing in which the President had outlined his ideas of a modern pluralist democracy.[58] The affiliates of the UDF were presumably willing to identify with the book's leitmotif. In fact, the UDF is an amalgamate of personalities of a varied, and in the past often antagonistic background: there are here remnants of a Catholic party, the MRP, and the once militant anti-Catholic radicals, former Socialists who have balked their party's alliance with the Communists, and extreme rightists who had frowned on Giscard's collaboration with the Gaullists. The ideological battles of the past had in fact become meaningless, but neither in 1978 nor since then have the parties which formed the UDF found it opportune to abandon their own weak organizational structures. To do so would diminish the chances of their leaders to be reelected to parliament. According to one writer, centrism had become a "myth" since all it wanted was "the distribution of political office to be made on a different basis." [59]

In the parliamentary elections of 1978 and 1981 the parties combined in the UDF have not lagged much behind the Gaullist party in popular votes, but their parliamentary representation has declined steadily (see Table VII and Figure IV). In the first ballot of the presidential elections of 1981 Giscard,

[57] For a detailed description of these negotiations and a political history of the various Center parties, see Charlot, "The Majority," in *Elections 1978,* esp. pp. 78 ff., and William Safran, "Centrism in the Fifth Republic: An Attitude in Search of an Instrument," in *Fifth Republic,* Andrews and Hoffmann, pp. 123–45.

[58] Translated into English as Valéry Giscard d'Estaing, *French Democracy* (Garden City: Doubleday, 1977). The author had held high hopes for the political usefulness of his book. His critics described it as a noble dream rather than as a program of concrete reforms.

[59] See Gilles Martinet, *Le système Pompidou* (Paris: Seuil, 1973), pp. 160–61.

running on the UDF ticket, obtained 4 percent fewer votes than seven years earlier, a bad omen for the final ballot. With the defeat of Giscard in the presidential elections, the UDF, in its new role as an opposition party, might have to find a new leadership. In the fall of 1981 a number of forward-looking Gaullist and centrist deputies declared that the clash of personalities in their midst must cease and that the opposition should meet the challenge of the socialist government by developing an effective political strategy.[60]

Quite typical of the disarray on the Right are the numerous conservative and conservative-liberal clubs and debating societies that have sprung up since the election. Their announced goals are often at cross-purposes, but their activities are not dissimilar to those of the clubs which came into existence on the Left after de Gaulle's rise to power in 1958. They are far less dynamic than the RPR, which continues as a strong and militant party under Chirac's leadership.

MAJORITY AND OPPOSITION:
STABLE AND SHIFTING ALIGNMENTS

The Socialist candidate conducted — and won — the elections of 1981 with the promise of a "quiet revolution" (*la révolution tranquille*). What were the shifts in the electorate, and the reasons for such shifts, that have ended twenty-three years of rule by a conservative majority?

In all democratic elections voters' (and also nonvoters') motivations are so intricate that it is impossible to analyze them with any degree of certainty. That also means that mutations, where they occur, can never be explained fully. Modern polling techniques and statistical manipulations of the survey data enable us to understand better than in the past voters' motivations and to determine with somewhat greater accuracy the nature of the support which the parties receive or can expect. But it must not be forgotten — and this applies to much of what follows in the text — that the only unassailable data are those based on the geographical distribution of votes; all others are never free of subjective evaluations by the respon-

60 *Le Monde,* October 7, 1981.

dents in a survey sample and are often based on arbitrary categories. They are "extrapolations, sometimes exact, sometimes plausible, but not more." [61]

Geographical distribution of votes is best illustrated by electoral maps. Where the latter are comparable over time, they clarify both stability and change, most clearly so where a bipolarization of politics prevails. As we have seen France, a country that has always lived with, and sometimes suffered from, a multi-party system, has nevertheless been divided at almost all times into two camps, or two large political "families" (see p. 210).

The dean of French election analysis has pointed to the striking parallels between the electoral map of the 1974 election and that of the referendum on a draft constitution in 1946 (see Maps 2 and 3).[62] Then as in 1974 the frequently dispersed forces of the Left and the Right found their unity in order to oppose each other, as they have not done in quite the same way during the intervening years. In 1946 only Communists and Socialists had recommended the "yes" vote on a constitutional draft; all other political organizations warned against it because it might ensure the permanent rule of the Left. Twenty-eight years later Giscard became the preferred candidate of all who wished to bar the road to the presidency to the candidate of the United Left. Except for a few significant exceptions which can all be explained by special circumstances, the division between "white" and "red" Departments, those whose electorate voted "no" and for Giscard, or "yes" and for Mitterrand remained all but unchanged.[63]

Seven years later a major change occurred (see Map 4 and Table III). In 1974 Giscard had won by only 1.3 percentage points (13.1 million votes as against the 12.7 million votes cast for his opponent), Mitterrand won in 1981 by 4.5 percent and

[61] Chapsal, *La Vie politique,* p. 524.

[62] See Nicolas Denis (François Goguel), "Du 5 mai 1946 au 19 mai 1974," *RFSP* 24, no. 5 (1974): 893–910. For a detailed analysis of the election results of 1974, see Alain Lancelot, "Élections: la relève et le sursis," *Projet* no. 88 (1974): 941–58.

[63] Space permitting, one could show similarities to earlier crisis elections such as those in 1936 and 1849!

obtained 1.32 million more votes than Giscard. The map illustrating the results of the presidential elections shows that the Right lost many of the departments and regions on which it had had a traditional hold, based mostly on religious allegiance. Maps showing the distribution of votes in the ensuing parliamentary elections reveal the same trends: the strongest gains of the noncommunist Left (and correspondingly the heaviest losses of the Right) occur in traditionally conservative areas in both the West and the East of the country.[64] By contrast, the Left merely held onto its former bastions of strength and actually lost votes in about twenty departments. Gains which the conservative parties made here and there (together with the losses they suffered in their former fiefs) diminished the political division of the country. Even at a time of defeat for one side, both sides are now spread more evenly throughout the country in terms of the popular vote, a phenomenon parallel to recent party developments in the United States.

Table VIII shows that religious attitudes still have an impact on the vote: an even lower percentage of regular church-goers voted for Mitterrand in 1981 than in 1974. But such figures must be understood against the fact that the number of voters in this category is small and had declined further during the seven years between the two elections (see Chapter III).

The geographical distribution of the vote in a rapidly modernizing country shows that traditional ties have loosened; the ascendancy of the Left has in fact been promoted by economic and social transformations. The urbanization, the growth of the salaried middle classes (technicians, middle management, etc.) and of the tertiary sector of the economy, the massive entry of women into the labor market — all these developments tore at the groups which had provided strength to the Right: farmers, small businessmen, the traditional bourgeoisie, and the nonemployed housewives.

[64] For these maps, see Alain Lancelot, "L'Alternance sur l'Air de la Vie en Rose," *Projet,* no. 158 (September 1981): 930. See this excellent article (pp. 915–39) also for much of what follows in the text. Le Bras and Todd, *Invention,* p. 333, wrote about the "conquest of the West by the P.S." well before the 1981 elections.

Map 2.   *French Right and Left: Little change in 28 years*

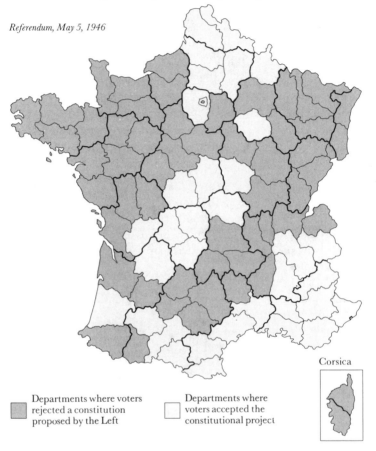

Referendum, May 5, 1946

Corsica

Departments where voters
rejected a constitution
proposed by the Left

Departments where
voters accepted the
constitutional project

Source: Adapted from *RFSP* 24, no. 5, p. 905, with permission from Presses
de la Fondation nationales des sciences politiques.

MAP 3. *French Right and Left: Little change in 28 years*

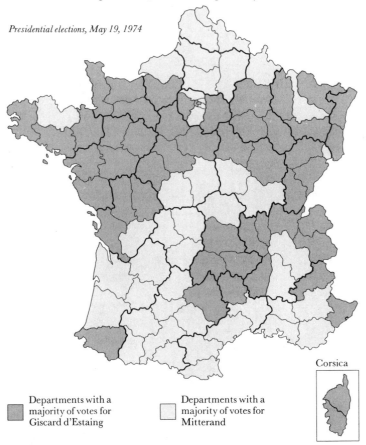

Presidential elections, May 19, 1974

Corsica

Departments with a
majority of votes for
Giscard d'Estaing

Departments with a
majority of votes for
Mitterand

Source: Adapted from *RFSP* 24, no. 5, p. 905, with permission from Presses
de la Fondation nationales des sciences politiques.

Map 4.   *French Right and Left: Change in 1981*

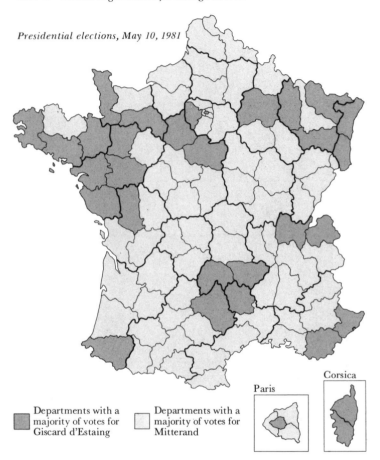

Presidential elections, May 10, 1981

Paris

Corsica

■ Departments with a
majority of votes for
Giscard d'Estaing

□ Departments with a
majority of votes for
Mitterand

TABLE VIII. *Sociological Analysis of the Electorate in the 1974 and 1981 Presidential Elections (in percentages)*

	1974		1981	
	Mitterrand	*Giscard*	*Mitterrand*	*Giscard*
Total	49	51	52	48
Sex				
Men	53	47	56	44
Women	46	54	49	51
Age				
18–24	—	—	63	37
25–34	59 *	41 *	63	37
35–49	49	51	51	49
50–64	46	54	47	53
65 and over	40	60	40	60
Profession of head of household				
Farmers and agricultural workers	31	69	33	67
Shopkeepers and craftsmen	36	64	40	60
Executives, industrialists, professionals, and businessmen	34	66	38	62
White-collar employees	51	49	58	42
Workers	68	32	67	33
Nonemployed	44	56	45	55
Education				
Elementary	51	49	51	49
Secondary	43	57	50	50
Technical or commercial	49	51	58	42
Higher education	49	51	50	50
Religion				
Regular church-goer	23	77	20	80
Occasional church-goer	49	51	40	60
Never goes to church	74	26	61	39
Without any religion	86	14	88	12
Vote in the second ballot of the 1974 Presidential election				
Mitterrand			95	5
Giscard			18	82
Vote in the first ballot of the 1978 legislative election				
Communist (PC)			95	5
Socialist (PS)			90	10
UDF			13	87
RPR			16	84

* These figures refer to the vote of the 21–34 age group.

Sources: 1978 — *France at the Polls: The Presidential Election of 1974,* ed. Howard Penniman (Washington, D.C.: American Enterprise Institute for Policy Research, 1975). 1981 — SOFRES, *Poll, May 1981.* Used by permission.

Another determining factor in the victory of the Left was the vote of the young (eighteen- to twenty-four-year-olds make up 13 percent of the electorate; eighteen- to thirty-four-year olds, 35 percent). Table VIII shows that in the presidential elections of 1981 the two younger age groups voted two to one for Mitterrand. (The eighteen- to twenty-one-year-olds were given the right to vote under Giscard, who must have felt treated with ingratitude.) In the parliamentary elections 45 percent of the two youngest age groups combined voted the Socialist ticket (see Table IX). It can be assumed that these results are to be explained by a combination of economic and cultural motivations: the young feel threatened by unemployment; what has been described (see Chapter III) as a general decline of authoritarian traits in social life seems to have deprived the conservative parties as well as the communists of their attractiveness.

What about the women's vote? As late as 1962 it had been farther to the right than that of men by 13 percentage points. De Gaulle would not have been reelected to the presidency in 1965 had it not been for the vote of the *Françaises*. At the time of the 1978 elections the gap between the party orientation of men and women had narrowed considerably, but polling figures gave somewhat erratic results.[65] There is a rather striking difference in the electoral behavior of women in the presidential as compared with the parliamentary elections: in the latter their party alignment, whether Right or Left, differs but little from that of men, but in both 1974 and in 1981 they favored Giscard over Mitterrand by 7 percentage points. To judge from these figures, the personal charisma of the candidates might have been a factor in the women's electoral choice.

In addition to the long-range societal developments which we have described, realignments and rifts within the two camps, the Left and the Right, influenced the electoral outcome. The steady rise of the PS during the years preceding

[65] See Monica Charlot, "Women in Politics in France," in *Elections of 1978*, Penniman, pp. 171–91 and esp. p. 177; Janine Mossuz-Lavau and Mariette Sineau, *Les Femmes françaises en 1978: Insertion sociale, Insertion politique* (Paris: Centre de Documentation Sciences Humaines, Microfiche, 1980), p. xxiv.

Table IX. *Sociological Analysis of the Electorate in the First Ballot of the 1978 and 1981 Parliamentary Elections (in percentages)*

	Communist Party		Socialist Party and Left Radicals		Environ-mentalists and others		UDF		RPR		Various Majority and Right	
	1978	1981	1978	1981	1978	1981	1978	1981	1978	1981	1978	1981
Total Electorate	21	16	25	38	3	1	21	19	22	21	5	3
Sex												
Men	24	17	25	39	3	1	19	20	20	20	6	1
Women	19	15	25	38	3	2	22	18	24	22	5	4
Age												
18–24	28	18	25	44	4	2	17	14	15	17	2	3
25–34	26	17	24	46	6	3	18	16	17	15	4	1
35–49	19	17	25	37	3	1	20	18	24	23	6	2
50–64	20	18	24	42	3	1	22	19	23	16	7	3
65 and over	15	10	25	27	—	—	27	27	28	30	5	5
Occupation of Head of Family												
Farmers and agricultural workers	9	6	17	32	6	—	33	28	31	32	3	—
Shopkeepers and craftsmen	14	10	23	35	5	—	25	19	26	31	7	5
Executives, industrialists, professionals, and businessmen	9	7	15	38	4	3	27	19	30	28	10	3
Middle management, technicians, and white-collar workers	18	16	29	45	5	2	14	18	20	14	8	3
Workers	36	24	27	44	2	1	16	15	14	14	1	1
Inactive, retired	17	16	26	29	1	—	25	23	26	26	5	5

Sources: 1978 — *The French National Assembly Elections of 1978*, ed. Howard Penniman (Washington, D.C.: American Enterprise Institute for Policy Research, 1980). 1981 — © *Le Nouvel Observateur*, July 4–10, 1981, p. 42. Used by permission.

the elections of 1981 has been noted. In 1978 the Socialists had pulled ahead of the PC for the first time in a national election. In 1981 the relative strength of the two parties was almost exactly the reverse of what it had been twenty-five years earlier. In 1956, 25.6 percent of the votes cast went to the PC, 15 percent to the PS. In 1981 the vote for Marchais was a mere 15.3 percent and that for Mitterrand 25.8. In the parliamentary elections the difference between the competitors, who three years earlier had been separated by just 4 percent, had risen to 22 percentage points. In absolute numbers 1.8 million voters had turned away from the PC ("voted with their feet," as Lenin once called the disaster of the non-Bolshevik parties in Soviet Russia); most, though not all, of the former communist voters turned to the PS. The party's losses were nationwide, even if they were more dramatic in such electoral districts as the "red belt" around the capital. The shift of the working-class votes to the PS (44 percent as against 24 percent for the PC) was particularly grievous for a party that considers itself to be *the* party of the working class (that about 30 percent of the workers regularly vote conservative is a phenomenon that corresponds to "working-class Toryism" in Great Britain).

What caused the communist debacle? The most plausible explanation is not without merit: the voters who wanted to turn out the conservative government found it more useful to vote for Mitterrand (*voter utile,* as it was called), since the Communist candidate did not have a chance of being elected to the presidency. Yet in previous elections, both presidential and parliamentary, the PC had always been successful in urging its followers to use the first ballot as a sort of primary for a show of communist strength. This tactic no longer worked because the internal crisis of the party, its bewildering zigzag course and above all the vociferous antisocialist campaign had alienated voters who for long years had voted for the PC as the "last best hope." Why the party failed to attract the young has already been discussed.

The decline in communist strength harmed the cause of the Right. After the first presidential ballot it was no longer plausible to describe a Leftist victory as a triumph for Bolshevism. Chirac's campaign had only aggravated the long-standing conflict between the two wings of the governing majority, the RPR and the UDF. Because of his (erroneous) assumption that the country wished to be "governed from the Center," Giscard disliked political bipolarization. Even after his efforts at "destabilizing" the Socialists and their Radical allies by winning the moderates among them over to his side had failed, he still dismissed Chirac's suggestions for a solid fighting front against the entire Left. Personality feuds turned into ever-aggravated political conflicts. The few "Gaullist" ministers who had stayed on as Cabinet ministers took their distance from Chirac and the RPR. Since the votes of the RPR deputies were needed by the government to survive in parliament, the party's increasingly independent course was tolerated. But it also became increasingly difficult for the coalition partners to develop a common policy. Governmental paralysis developed in the midst of rising unemployment and recession. In his campaign for the presidency Chirac would bitterly criticize the government which his party had supported for so many years.

What might have sealed Giscard's defeat was the voters' behavior in the final and decisive ballot. The communists asked the voters who had remained faithful to them in the primaries to vote for Mitterrand and, if the polls are to be trusted, 92 percent of the communist voters did so. Chirac had asked his voters, in a language lacking conviction, to vote for Giscard, and not more than 73 percent did so; 16 percent (possibly as many as 800,000) voted for Mitterrand; the others abstained. Mitterrand drew some additional strength from the environmentalists and more from the votes of those who had abstained in the first ballot but now returned to cast a ballot for the candidate who could no longer be described as the "prisoner of the communists." [66]

[66] On the question of voting behavior in the runoff elections, see Jean Charlot, "Le Double enchaînement de la victoire et la défaite," *Revue Politique et Parlementaire*, no. 892 (June 1981): 15 ff., and the interesting if controversial article by François Goguel, "Sur les succès électoraux de la gauche en 1981," *Le Monde*, November 10 and 11, 1981. In view of recent developments, an earlier article by the same author on the phenomenon

The Socialist landslide in the parliamentary elections of the following month (raising the Socialist and Left-Radical contingent of deputies from 117 to 284 seats, of which a few were lost in by-elections after the invalidation of results in some districts) furnished further evidence that the voters, and not necessarily only those who have a definite commitment to the socialist Left, have accepted the bipolarization which has developed under the constitutional system of the Fifth Republic. A comparison of the popular vote in Table VII and the data in Figure IV shows the discrepancy between voting strength and parliamentary representation: the electoral system favors the dominant party (or coalition of parties) to the detriment of the minority. Under a system of proportional representation the Socialists would have won one hundred seats less. What has worked to the advantage of the old coalition was now benefitting the PS.

The (for France) relatively high rate of abstention in both ballots of the parliamentary election (29.6 and 25.4 percent respectively) is difficult to explain. Those who abstained might have been conservative voters, temporarily disgruntled with the past record of their parties but possibly willing to return to the fold, if the Left were to lose popularity. In some districts in which the communist candidate had won the primaries, socialist voters seemed to have abstained in the runoff elections.[67]

For the informed observer the political earthquake of 1981 should not have come as a complete surprise. The "faults" in the majority's cohesion and in its electoral support were well known, as were the expanding sympathies for the PS. Nonetheless, the alternation in power of contending political forces, an essential feature of representative government, had been

---

of bipolarization remains of interest. See his "Bipolarization ou renovation du centrisme?" *RFSP* 17, no. 5 (October 1967): 198 ff. For the continuing controversy on the reasons for the conservative defeat see the note "Le rejet et l'adhésion," *Le Monde,* February 20, 1982.

[67] Anne Chaussebourg, "Abstentions et transfers de voix les 14 et 21 juin 1981," *Le Monde,* July 5–6, 1981, concludes that on balance abstentions and vote transfers in the parliamentary elections (as distinguished from the vote for the president) had not been detrimental to either side.

FIGURE IV. *Political Representation in the National Assemblies (after the elections of 1978 and 1981)*

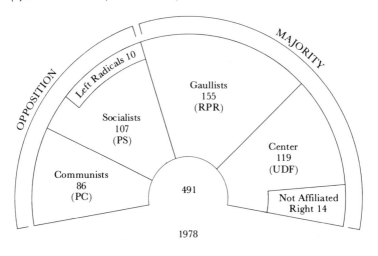

OPPOSITION

Left Radicals 10

Socialists
107
(PS)

Communists
86
(PC)

Gaullists
155
(RPR)

MAJORITY

Center
119
(UDF)

Not Affiliated
Right 14

491

1978

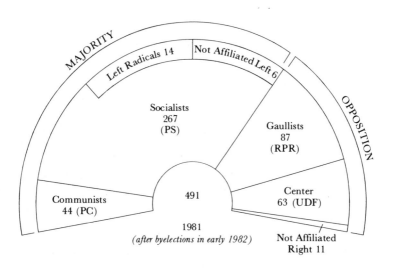

MAJORITY

Left Radicals 14

Not Affiliated Left 6

Socialists
267
(PS)

Communists
44 (PC)

Gaullists
87
(RPR)

OPPOSITION

Center
63 (UDF)

491

Not Affiliated
Right 11

1981
(after byelections in early 1982)

The numbers indicate both the deputies who are "members" of their group and those listed as "affiliated."

long delayed. The unbroken domination of government and state by a coalition of parties and by a political elite united by the same ideology, if occasionally given to quarrels about details, had often been denounced. After de Gaulle's resignation the Fifth Republic had been able to move from rule by a charismatic leader to routinized government. But before the test of the orderly transition of power from the majority to the opposition had been met, it remained uncertain whether the constitution would allow for such a transfer without a major institutional crisis.[68]

Whether this was intended or not, the constitution had awarded a high premium to the incumbent president (or to a successor sharing his convictions) and to the majority in power. It was generally assumed that the system, combining as it does the parliamentary and the presidential model, would function badly, if and when the president and the parliamentary majority were at odds. Since parliamentary and presidential elections are not slated to take place at the same time, candidates for office in either election could always conjure a major crisis if the electorate were to decide on a changed political course. It was known that if the opposition had won in 1973, President Pompidou would have relinquished his office rather than appoint a Socialist prime minister. During his campaign in 1974 Giscard frequently put forward the argument that if he were elected he would be able to start governing the next day, whereas his opponent would face a parliamentary majority hostile to his announced policy. When it seemed almost certain that the elections of 1978 would send a Left majority to parliament, Giscard declared that he would not resign his post and fulfill his duties under the constitution, but described the conflicts that would necessarily emerge and for which the voters would have to bear the responsibility. This, however, not only made *every* election into a plebiscite; it also burdened the electorate at each election with the responsibility for an institutional crisis. Even voters desiring a change in government and policy were likely to shun such a responsibility.

[68] See comments on these questions in Jean-Louis Quermonne, *Le Gouvernement de la France sous la Ve République* (Paris: Dalloz, 1980), pp. 445 ff., under the significant heading: "La permanence du dextrisme" (the permanence of right-wingism).

In 1981 the Socialist candidate faced the problem squarely and declared that if elected he would indeed dissolve parliament in which the parties that had elected him were in the minority. In order to insure effective rather than divided government, he would seek the confirmation of the electorate's desire for change through parliamentary elections. Discontent with the record of the Giscard administration and unhappiness with the perspective of having to endure a fourteen-year president (none of his predecessors had been in office for two full terms) induced the voters to take the risk they had been warned against for many years. In the presidential elections the voters had shown that they preferred bipolarity to divided coalitions. When they gave to the newly-elected president the parliamentary majority he needed to govern effectively, they were acting once more according to the logic of the existing institutional arrangements.

Even those who are unhappy about the course events have taken are bound to admit that the legitimacy of both the institutions and of the party system have been confirmed by the *alternance*, the alternation of power, long dreaded and long desired. "French democracy is more adult than one has thought," concluded one of its students.[69]

69 Lancelot, "L'Alternance," p. 915; in a similar vein, Jean-Louis Quermonne, "L'Alternance au pouvoir et la continuité des institutions," *Le Monde*, May 10–11, 1981.

CHAPTER IX

Policy Processes I

THE PRESIDENT OF THE REPUBLIC:
CENTER OF POWER

When General de Gaulle returned to power in 1958, it was generally expected that the presidency of the republic would be invested with a novel significance in the policy processes of the new republic. De Gaulle's Bayeux speech in 1946,[1] his subsequent writings, and the Gaullist propaganda in the following years constantly emphasized the need for a widely visible chief of state. He was to be placed "above the parties" and empowered to represent effectively the unity rather than the diversity of the national community. In conforming to this concept and departing from earlier republican traditions, the text of the new constitution puts the office of the president first among the organs of government, immediately after the tribute to the principle of popular sovereignty, as if to symbolize what originally was, in fact, the essence of the Fifth

---

[1] This speech by de Gaulle is indispensable for an understanding of his own constitutional thinking and that of his principal advisors. For an English translation see William G. Andrews, ed., *European Political Institutions* (Princeton: Van Nostrand, 1966), pp. 40–43. For an interesting exposition of General de Gaulle's constitutional ideas, drawing on previously inaccessible materials, see Jean-Louis Debré (the son of the former prime minister), *Les Idées constitutionnelles du Général de Gaulle* (Paris: Librairie Générale de Droit et de Jurisprudence, 1974).

Republic: the alliance between the *homme providentiel* and the people.[2]

There is, however, a fundamental difference between the role which the constitution and those who had drafted it assigned to the presidency and the actual significance which the office has taken on in the process of decision making. Its development presents a fascinating example of how within a short time a conjunction of circumstances and of personality can thoroughly transform constitutional institutions and their underlying ideas. (Ironically enough, but not at all accidentally, the constitution of the Third Republic underwent very early a similar and thorough transformation. But then politics traveled in the opposite direction, namely toward parliamentary omnipotence.)

The constitution had left the determination of policies to the prime minister and his government (articles 20–23), and the role of the president was to be that of the guardian of the constitution, "who by his arbitration" was to "ensure the regular functioning of the public authorities" (article 5). In a brilliant exegesis of the constitutional text he had authored in large part, Michel Debré explained that it was the proper function of the arbiter to do little else than to appeal to another power, be it parliament, the Constitutional Council, or the people. The president's right to dissolve parliament (article 12) would permit nothing more than "a short dialogue" between the chief of state and the nation. An electoral college, composed of local notables, should designate the president, for "the President who is elected by universal suffrage is a political leader bound by the daily work of government and command." [3] In Debré's design this was not to be the

2 See Philip M. Williams and Martin Harrison, *De Gaulle's Republic* (London: Longmans, Green, 1960), p. 214.

3 For a translation of Debré's address, see Andrews, *Political Institutions*, pp. 43–55. Very interesting is a comparison of this address and M. Debré's speech given twenty years later and reflecting on his own experiences and "afterthoughts"; see Michel Debré, "The Constitution of 1958, Its Raison d'être and how it evolved," in *The Fifth Republic at Twenty*, eds. William Andrews and Stanley Hoffmann (Albany: State University of New York Press, 1981), pp. 11–24, 497–512. For historical antecedents to Debré's

domain of the French president, who should assume the executive powers of a constitutional dictator only in times of grave trouble (article 16).

That things have turned out so differently is partly due to the fact that the heavily ideological concept of an arbiter serving the cause of national integration "beyond politics" is even more unrealistic today than in the nineteenth century when it was developed as an underpinning for the constitutional monarchies of France and England. Neither the tensions generated by the Algerian war nor, in spite of some appearances, the personality of General de Gaulle permitted him to remain solely that republican monarch whom Debré described as the "keystone of a parliamentary regime."

Even before and again upon assuming presidential office, General de Gaulle introduced a new term to describe the task that awaited him. By claiming that he was not only chief of state but also "France's *guide*," he undertook to play the role which Jean-Jacques Rousseau, in his *Social Contract,* assigned to him who will formulate for the people what the general will truly is. Such a function foreshadowed a permanent rather than the "brief" dialogue between the chief of state and the people which Debré had foreseen for certain specified situations. In this dialogue, moreover, the guide would be able to make fullest use of modern communications media.

A chain of events led to the gradual absorption of most decision making by the chief of state. The president himself became aware of the fact that the inefficiency of problem solving in the sectors to which he paid no attention endangered decision making in domains which were of importance to him. Because he was operating in a highly centralized system, the chief of state was compelled, not only by choice but also by necessity, to hold a close rein on all matters.

When the referendum of 1962 laid the foundations for a popular election of the president, such a modification of the text and the spirit of the four-year-old constitution not only

---

constitutional thinking, see Nicholas Wahl, "The French Constitution of 1958: The Initial Draft and Its Origins," *American Political Science Review* 53, no. 2 (1959): 358–82.

acknowledged the changes which "the circumstances" had brought about. It also endowed the presidency with the legitimacy of a direct popular vote which, it was hoped, would accrue to the office when it was occupied by a less charismatic personality than General de Gaulle.

In 1964 de Gaulle explained in starkly realistic terms the nature of his office and its significance for the policy process.[4] To be sure, he still was prepared to play the role of the supreme arbiter whenever this was necessary. But, he continued, power "emanates directly from the people, which implies that the head of state, elected by the nation, is the source and holder of this power." He insisted, "that the individual authority of the State is entrusted completely to the President by the people who elected him, that there is no other authority — either ministerial, civilian, military, or judicial — which is not entrusted or maintained by him." As to the government, he described it as merely "sitting around him for the determination and application of policy and directing the administration." This amounted to a clear definition of the "republican monarchy" under which France has lived (and continues to live) since 1958.

During the same press conference, General de Gaulle rejected, as Michel Debré had done before him but for different reasons, an American-type presidential system as unsuitable for France. In fact, the differences in the policy process in the two countries remain very great even after de Gaulle's successors in the presidential office have in some respects altered the style of the first incumbent. The rather limited constitutional checks and balances that exist are not those of the classical presidential system. By holding the threat of dissolution over parliament (article 12) and by having at his disposal a number of other disciplinary devices which he can employ in conjunction with the government, the president is able to interfere directly with parliamentary organization and activities. By dissolving parliament he can, like the British prime minister, bring forth new elections at any time which he judges opportune to obtain popular approval for his pol-

[4] For an English translation of de Gaulle's statement, see Andrews, *Political Institutions,* pp. 56–60.

icies and thereby can create at will a plebiscitarian situation in his favor. He can invoke the jurisdiction of the Constitutional Council (articles 56–63) when in his opinion parliament has transgressed its constitutional limitations.[5] (For the new role which a constitutional amendment of 1974 has attributed to the Constitutional Council and a general discussion of the council's functions, see Chapter X.) In situations where the Constitutional Council cannot be or has not been appealed to, de Gaulle claimed that as guardian of the constitution he could sanction political practice by authoritative interpretation.[6]

In case of grave threat "to the institutions of the Republic" (and in a number of other situations broadly and vaguely described), article 16 gives the president wider powers than even the Weimar constitution of Germany provided in its article 48 which served as a convenient cloak for legalizing the Nazi revolution. According to the constitution the French president may be indicted for high treason by a majority vote in the two houses of parliament and then tried by a High Court of Justice (article 68). Since as soon as a state of emergency is declared parliament meets automatically and cannot be dissolved, a president who abuses his rights under article 16 could be brought to trial. But historical experience indicates that in a situation of dramatic tension he who holds power and controls the means of communication will be in the likeliest position to forestall an indictment by open ballot in parliament.

[5] For a comprehensive (semi-official) account of the constitutional and administrative role of the president, see Jean Massot, *La Présidence de la République en France* (Paris: La Documentation Française, 1977). A more critical but also richly documented account is given by Jean-Louis Quermonne, *Le Gouvernement de la France sous la Vᵉ République* (Paris: Dalloz, 1981), pp. 158–200. The best comprehensive analysis of presidential powers in English is Ezra N. Suleiman, "Presidential Government in France," in *Presidents and Prime Ministers,* eds. Richard Rose and Ezra Suleiman (Washington, D.C.: American Enterprise Institute, 1980), pp. 94–138.

[6] The most incisive and richly documented analysis of constitutional law and constitutional practice during the first decade of the Fifth Republic is to be found in Jean Gicquel, *Essai sur la pratique de la Vᵉ République* (Paris: Librairie Générale de Droit et de Jurisprudence, 1968). More vivid because based on the testimony of close collaborators of de Gaulle, Bernard Tricot et al., *De Gaulle et le Service de l'État* (Paris: Plon, 1977).

No other judicial controls limit the exercise of emergency powers as is the case in the United States.[7] Although the French president must consult with other organs of government before and during an emergency, he is under no constitutional obligation to heed the advice that might be tendered him.

General de Gaulle had called the provisions of article 16 "the supreme guarantee of *la patrie* and of the state." Yet he used the emergency powers only once, in 1961, at a moment when the rebellion of the generals in Algiers clearly justified such use.[8] The mutiny collapsed after a few days, not because a constitutional provision provided residual powers but because de Gaulle's authority was unimpaired and hence left the rebels isolated and impotent. So far this has been the only situation in which the emergency powers of the constitution of 1958 have been invoked.

When during the presidency of General de Gaulle fears were expressed that such a plenitude of powers might become a danger to the democratic process, especially under a successor without the temperamental inhibitions of the first incumbent, the defenders of the regime replied that the system was the very incarnation of democracy. Their arguments drew on the traditions of that plebiscitarian democracy which in France has frequently claimed preeminence over the model of a representative system (see Chapter I). According to their views, the dualism of a parliament and executive checking on each other was crowned by what Frenchmen in the tradition of Rousseau like to call the monism of popular sovereignty. Its supreme manifestation is the popular election of the chief of state. His authority is at all times subject to the commands of universal suffrage. Although the president is neither responsible to parliament nor subject to checks or controls by

[7] See, e.g., the well-known decision rendered during President Truman's administration: *Youngstown Sheet & Tube Co. et al.* v. *Sawyer,* 343 U.S. 579.

[8] Excellent on that episode is Martin Harrison, "The French Experiment of Exceptional Powers: 1961," *Journal of Politics* 25, no. 2 (1963): 139–58. For relevant laws and regulations, see *L'Article 16 de la Constitution de 1958* (Paris: La Documentation Française, 1973).

any other constitutional organ, he is nevertheless responsible to the sovereign people and to them alone. Presidential elections and referenda become expressions of the general will and legitimize the concentration of power in one hand. It was in accordance with such a concept of his rule that General de Gaulle relinquished power after failing to win majority approval for his referendum in 1969.[9]

Georges Pompidou, the second incumbent of the presidency, had been General de Gaulle's prime minister for more than six years. His successor, Valéry Giscard d'Estaing, had held the all-important post of minister of finance under de Gaulle and Pompidou for a total of nine years. Both had therefore ample opportunity to observe at close range the working of the constitutional system as it had emerged during the first years of the new republic. Upon assuming office both made it clear, by their explicit statements and by their practice as well, that they fully accepted the constitutional arrangements which they had inherited. Pompidou described them as a "half-way point between a strictly presidential and a strictly parliamentary system," resting on a balance at times "difficult, but allowing for firmness and durability as well as flexibility." At another time Pompidou explicitly praised what he then called the "bastard" characteristics of the constitutional arrangement. As "supreme head of the Executive" the president was, in Pompidou's interpretation, "providing the fundamental drives, defining the essential directions and ensuring and controlling the proper functioning of the government." All there remained for Giscard to say in the first press conference of his regime was a confirmation of the "presidentialist interpretation of our institutions within the framework of existing legislation." [10]

[9] For the most comprehensive statement of the Rousseauan justification of General de Gaulle's exercise of power, see René Capitant, "L'Aménagement du pouvoir exécutif et la question du chef de l'État," in *Encyclopédie Française X* (Paris: Sté. Nouvelle, 1964), pp. 142–62. Understandably enough the same author considered de Gaulle's resignation in 1969 a necessity.

[10] For Pompidou's views, see his press conferences of July 10, 1969, and of July 2, 1970, published in translation by the Ambassade de France, Service de Presse et d'Information. For Giscard's exegesis of the constitution, see *Le Monde,* July 17, 1974, and several texts reprinted in Quermonne, *Gouvernement,* pp. 662–69.

The nearly identical views of the three past incumbents are not matched by a similar agreement among citizens judging the performance of the three presidents. Asked whether they believed that General de Gaulle had been the "president of all Frenchmen" or merely the "president of those who had voted for him," 60 percent of the respondents in a 1977 poll agreed with the first, 26 percent with the second suggestion. For Giscard, opinions were all but reversed: 30 percent rated him the president of all; in the eyes of 60 percent he represented only his own electorate. For Pompidou opinions divided 51 to 41.[11]

The agreement of three presidents on the prerogatives of the office, and especially on its relationship to other organs of government, has helped greatly the institutionalization of the presidency. (For an organizational chart, see Figure V.) When the outlines of the constitution became known in 1958, it was predicted that the two-headed executive (president and prime minister) would almost necessarily lead to conflict situations. None of this has come to pass: three presidents, for all their differences in outlook and style, and each of the prime ministers that have served under them left no doubt that the executive had only one head, namely the president. In order to "control the proper functioning of government" he must, according to this conception, nominate and dismiss the prime minister and the other Cabinet members as well. As we have seen (in Chapter VIII), Jacques Chirac met the threat of being dismissed as Prime Minister by tendering a resignation which had not (yet) been asked for. If this episode had political consequences for the cohesion of the majority, it turned out that the gesture had little constitutional significance.

Within a commonly accepted institutional framework men of different temperaments and working habits have exercised presidential powers in different ways. That one should not expect him to act like de Gaulle was a frequent remark of Pompidou's, though he himself never lacked energy and resoluteness. Existing differences affected the relationship between

---

[11] See SOFRES, *L'Opinion Française en 1977* (Paris: PFNSP, 1978), p. 107. It might be true that eight years after de Gaulle had abandoned the presidency, his role was idealized by the public.

FIGURE V.   *Relationship Between French Public Authorities on the National Level*

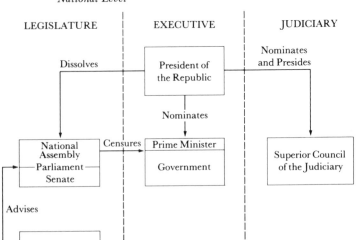

LEGISLATURE | EXECUTIVE | JUDICIARY

Dissolves — President of the Republic — Nominates and Presides

Nominates

National Assembly — Censures — Prime Minister

Parliament — Government

Senate

Superior Council of the Judiciary

Advises

Economic and Social Council

Source: Reprinted with permission from Henry W. Ehrmann, "Politics in France," in Gabriel A. Almond and G. Bingham Powell, Jr., *Comparative Politics Today: A World View*, 2nd ed. (Boston: Little, Brown and Company, 1980), p. 216. Copyright © 1980 by Henry W. Ehrmann.

a president and the public as well as that between him and his "government," the Cabinet. Here the parliamentary streak of the French system requires a special bond unknown in a purely presidential system such as ours. Since it is the prime minister's foremost function to secure for presidential policies the approval of a parliamentary majority, the necessarily close contacts between the two men have often colored the handling of presidential powers. Among the seven prime ministers whom the three presidents have nominated (and dismissed when they were so inclined), there were men with considerable political experience, former collaborators of the president without a political past, high civil servants, and a professor of economics. Such variety in background alone made for contrasts in the relationship, and these contrasts have been the subject of frequent controversies about the characteristics of "presidentialism." With historical distance one will probably conclude that in all essentials de Gaulle's successors have left the institution of the presidency "the way they found it," as Giscard specifically promised he would.

If in the last years of Giscard's presidency a more willful assertion of power was generally noted, this was only partly due to the incumbent's personality.[12] More important was the fact that because of the rift within the majority, the prime minister's control of parliament was weakened, and the president tried to compensate for this imbalance with a more forthright style. Towards the end of the Giscard regime, Michel Debré, father of the constitution, who was soon to oppose Giscard in the presidential election of 1981, remarked that whatever political objections he had to the government's policy, he had none to the way in which constitutional powers were exercised.[13]

François Mitterrand had long been known as an ardent critic of a constitution he had characterized as authoritarian and irresponsible, indeed as a "permanent coup d'état." In a remarkable parliamentary debate with Pompidou, who at the time was de Gaulle's Prime Minister, he had thundered that the country should either adopt an "honest and authentic" presidential regime or else return to the parliamentary form of government.[14]

---

[12] See, on these points, Jacques Cadart et al., "Le Régime a-t-il changé depuis 1974," *Pouvoirs* 9 (1979): 71–84, and Pierre Avril et al., "Monarchie Républicaine, Présidence Impériale ou simple Ostentation du Pouvoir?" *Revue Politique et Parlementaire* 83, no. 891 (March–April 1981): 3–95. Particularly interesting for the president–prime minister relationship because based on statements by advisors on both sides is Suleiman, in *Presidents and Prime Ministers*, Rose and Suleiman, esp. pp. 106–12.

[13] Debré in *Fifth Republic*, Andrews and Hoffmann, p. 21. In an earlier article, the same author had regretted what he regarded as the declining power of the prime minister's position; see "Présidentialisme et Régime d'Assemblée," *Le Monde*, June 6, 1975. While it is true that originally Debré may have had in mind a different division of functions between president and prime minister, he did not insist on the latter's prerogatives while serving under General de Gaulle. He, more than any other prime minister, acted against his own previous convictions (in the Algerian question) whenever the president asked for it.

[14] For the essential passages of the interesting parliamentary debate of 1964, see Quermonne, *Gouvernement*, pp. 636–42.

But Mitterrand as well as the entire Left shifted positions when over the years it became clear that the electorate was quite satisfied with the existing institutions and above all with a strong, popularly elected presidency. During the campaign of 1981 no institutional criticism whatsoever was voiced; the socialist candidate merely insisted that parliament should exercise the rights which the constitution (!) had given it. For Mitterrand the president was now the "voice of France," the interpreter of the "general will." [15] The institutional controversy had ceased.

After his election Mitterrand declared that he would use the powers of the presidency in their fullness "neither more nor less." He proceeded immediately, as his predecessors had done, to nominate the prime minister and saw to it that his choices for members of the Cabinet prevailed. The important post of the speaker of the newly elected National Assembly was filled according to his wishes.

It is generally assumed that by temperament Mitterrand will be at least as forceful a president as those who have preceded him. That he is also the leader of the dominant party in parliament insures the smooth working of the constitution he once maligned.

Since the early days of the de Gaulle administration, the office of the chief of state has been organized so as to make possible the processes by which policy is not only initiated and elaborated but frequently also executed. In terms of function, the staff at the Élysée Palace, the French White House, composed of a general secretariate and the presidential cabinet, has become somewhat similar to the Executive Office of the American president, yet much smaller — a total of about forty persons. But when comparing the White House and the Elysée it must not be forgotten that in France many

---

[15] For the evolution of the thinking of the left about the institutions of the Fifth Republic, see Olivier Duhamel, *La Gauche et la Ve République* (Paris: PUF, 1980). In a televised discussion in 1978, Debré stated that there were no longer essential differences between his own and Mitterrand's interpretation of the constitution; see Michel Debré and François Mitterrand, "L'Exercice du pouvoir," *Pouvoirs* 9 (1979): 89–94. For Mitterrand's statement after the election, see *Le Monde,* July 1, 1981.

executive functions are assigned to the Office of the prime minister (see below).

Civil servants predominated on the staffs of the first three presidents (90 percent under de Gaulle and Giscard, 73 percent under Pompidou); among them a majority belonged to the bureaucratic elite corps; many were trained at the ENA. This has changed under Mitterrand: only 40 percent of his collaborators have a civil service background; only 25 percent are "enarques." Instead there are professors, judges, union leaders, engineers, writers, and even, in an important position, a businessman. Most, but not all, are members of the Socialist Party, while party affiliation was of little significance under Mitterrand's predecessors. The presence of friends and long-time associates on the staff makes the present president's entourage somewhat more similar to that of the White House. In addition, the Secretary General of the Socialist Party, Lionel Jospin, who has no official function, sees the president almost daily and must therefore be counted among his close political collaborators. Altogether relations between the staff and the president and between the staff and the outside are described as far more informal than previously and lacking the monarchical style Mitterrand's predecessor indulged in — to his own detriment.[16]

It is, however, likely that the functions of the staff remain about the same as in the past. A careful study of the Elysée under the preceding administrations concluded that this professional, highly qualified group has almost none of the characteristics of an independent and intriguing "mafia" pursuing its own policy ends.[17] Their initiatives are controlled much more closely by the president than seems to be the case in the White House. Their advice is valuable, but taken only where it confirms presidential intentions.

As the president's eyes and ears his staff members are in-

[16] See Marcelle Padovani, "Comment fonctionne l'équipe Mitterrand," *Nouvel Observateur*, July 25, 1981.

[17] Samy Cohen, *Les Conseillers du Président de Charles de Gaulle à Valéry Giscard d'Estaing* (Paris: PUF, 1980), and the same author's "Le Secrétariat Général de la Présidence de la République," in *Administration et Politique sous la Cinquième République*, eds. F. de Baecque and J. L. Quermonne (Paris: PFNSP, 1980), pp. 104–27.

dispensable for the exercise of presidential powers. They are in constant contact not only with the prime minister's collaborators, but also with individual ministries. There exists a functional distribution of tasks: many members of the Elysée staff are assigned to specific fields and the ministries concerned. Most important for the continuous contacts is the effectiveness of a network of influence based on mutual respect and long-term acquaintance between the ranking civil servants on the staff of the president and of ministers and reaching into the ministries themselves. Through these contacts the president can initiate, impede, interfere, and assure himself that presidential policies are followed.

Of at least equal importance are institutionalized relations between the president, the Cabinet, and the bureaucracy. The regular meetings of the Cabinet are playing a minor role in actual decision making (see below). But already under de Gaulle the so-called *conseils restreints* had become the focus of policy making within the executive. Their meetings take place at the Elysée; they are always chaired by the president, attended by the prime minister, by the ministers involved in the question being discussed, and usually by a number of high civil servants. Some of these councils have a permanent status, such as the Superior Council of Defense (comparable to the National Security Council in the United States), an Economic Planning Council, a Foreign Affairs Council, etc. Others are *ad hoc,* convened whenever a need for consultation on policies and for the preparation of decisions arises. The number of existing councils and the frequency of their meetings indicate the degree of presidential interest in decision making.[18]

THE GOVERNMENT: RULE MAKING
AND APPLICATION

In a system that prides itself on being a halfway house between a parliamentary and a presidential system, the position of the

[18] For a complete discussion of the activities of the various interministerial councils and committees, see Jean-Luc Bodiguel, "Conseils restreints, comités interministériels et réunions interministérielles," in *Administration et Politique,* Baecque and Quermonne, pp. 139–62. In English there is interesting material in Suleiman, "Presidential Government in France," in *Presidents,* Rose and Suleiman.

prime minister and of the Cabinet is bound to be ambivalent. The way in which the constitution (see Articles 20 and 21) describes the functions of the government and of the prime minister are of little help for understanding reality, because political developments have played havoc with constitutional provisions. One can argue that since all powers proceed from the president of the republic, the government headed by the prime minister has become essentially an organ of execution. And indeed in many respects the position which the government occupies resembles far more that of the Cabinet in a presidential regime such as the United States, than that of a government in a parliamentary system such as Great Britain and the earlier French republics.

But it is also obvious that a president, however impressive his prerogatives, cannot effectively govern a modern country and direct a complicated administrative machinery with the small staff at his disposal. To secure parliamentary approval (and the needed funds) for executive policies remains the prime minister's constitutional function. But because of the party discipline which has prevailed since 1962, that task is no longer as arduous as it was previously. The major preoccupation of the prime minister is broader: he must see to it that all policy initiatives of whatever origin are brought before the proper forum (parliament, Council of Ministers, a particular administration, etc.) and that they are given the form which is suitable to turn them into applicable rules. The prime minister and his government, not the president, command the staff capable of implementing policy.[19]

Extensive rule making by the executive prevails in most modern political systems. The French constitution of 1958 sanctioned and extended existing practices by drastically narrowing the prerogatives of parliament (for details, see Chapter X). The powers which parliament lost accrued to the government. In many fields the executive is able to implement policies by legally enforceable rulings without recourse to any elected body.[20]

[19] For a complete (again semi-official) account of the Prime Minister's office, see Jean Massot, *Le Chef du Gouvernement en France* (Paris: La Documentation Française, 1979).

[20] For a succinct treatment of the complicated terminology of rule mak-

Probably the most important of the offices through which the prime minister acts is the General Secretariate of the Government; it was established shortly before the war, but its functions and personnel have been enlarged considerably since then. (Since 1946 there have been only five General Secretaries — with one exception, all members of the Council of State. These five men have served two republics, six presidents, and about three dozen prime ministers — undoubtedly a sign of institutional stability!) About fifty high civil servants manning the Secretariate assume the functions of transmission-belts between the prime minister, the Cabinet, the president of the republic and the two houses of parliament. The Secretariate prepares the agenda and establishes the minutes of *all* official meetings. It processes the flow of policy papers and directs decisions into the proper channels for their publication in the *Journal Officiel,* the French version of the *Congressional Record.* Simultaneously chief of staff, guide, and memory of the top political executives, the General Secretary also supervises administratively the large and varied services attached to the prime minister's office, a total staff of more than 3,000.[21]

The prime minister's personal staff, his *cabinet* (to be distinguished from the Cabinet which is the government as a whole), is given predominantly to political coordination. Since it is similar in structure and composition to the *cabinets* of the single ministers, it will be discussed below.

Decision making at the Cabinet level takes place through another complicated layer of groups designated as (interministerial) committees to distinguish them from the councils (the *conseils restreints*) which include the president of the re-

---

ing in present-day France, see F. Ridley and J. Blondel, *Public Administration in France* (New York: Barnes and Noble, 1969), pp. 22 ff., and Francis Hamon, *Les Articles 34, 37 et 38 de la Constitution de 1958* (Paris: La Documentation Française, 1973). Also useful is William Andrews, "The Collective Political Executive under the Gaullists," in *The Fifth Republic,* Andrews and Hoffmann, pp. 25–56.

[21] See Marceau Long (who served as Secretary General under Giscard and who has agreed to continue in this capacity under Mitterrand), "Le secrétaire général du gouvernement," in *Études offertes à Pierre Kayser* (Aix-en-Provence: Presses Universitaires d-Aix-Marseille, 1979) Tome II, pp. 156–175.

public. The committees are chaired by the prime minister. Who will participate depends again on the problems under consideration: here too the ministers are frequently accompanied by top-ranking civil servants or by members of their own staff — an intriguing network but one that cannot be described here.

Since most decisions are reached in smaller gremiums, the weekly meetings of the Council of Ministers, in which all members of the government participate, merely endorse what has been decided beforehand. At these meetings, always chaired by the president, no votes are taken; consensus is assumed. Nonetheless, for the development of long-term policies, or when the onrush of unforeseen events at home or abroad suggests discussion, Cabinet meetings still offer opportunities for deliberation and controversy.[22] General de Gaulle had described these meetings: "Everybody can voice his viewpoint; I listen to what is being said in order to take it into account should the occasion arise." (Napoleon had been briefer: "I listen to everybody, but my head is my only advisor.") Under four presidents the atmosphere at Cabinet meetings may have changed considerably; but their largely advisory function has not.

The size of the Cabinets and their members' backgrounds have often been an indication of the role the president wished to assign to the government. French Cabinets have always been large by American but not by British standards, since the British, like the French, recognize a hierarchy of ministerial posts unknown in the United States. There exists in both Britain and France a number of more or less independent ministries which in the American system are headed by under-secretaries or assistant secretaries. The organization chart of Pierre Mauroy's government (see Figure VI) illustrates fairly typical features

[22] An excellent description of the sense and nonsense of council meetings by a participant-observer is given by Robert Buron, *Le plus beau des métiers* (Paris: Plon, 1963), pp. 218 ff. Interesting on the job of being a minister under General de Gaulle is Bernard Chénot, *Être Ministre* (Paris: Plon, 1967). More critical, but probably also more realistic, are discussions by Edgard Pisani, *Le Général indivis* (Paris: Albin Michel, 1974), pp. 127 ff., and, for the Giscard administration, Françoise Giroud, *La Comédie du Pouvoir* (Paris: Fayard, 1977), pp. 25–36.

FIGURE VI. *Organization Chart of Pierre Mauroy's Government (1981)*

Prime Minister

Ministers of State

Interior and Decentralization   Planification and Regional Management
Foreign Trade   Research and Technology
Transportation

Minister

National Solidarity

Ministers Attached to the Office of the Prime Minister

Women's Rights   Civil Service and Administrative Reforms
Relations with Parliament

Ministers and Attached Ministers

Minister of Justice, Keeper of the Seal	Agriculture
External Relations (Foreign Affairs)	Industry
Attached to the Office of the Minister of	Commerce and Crafts
External Relations, in charge of	Culture
European Affairs	Labor
Attached to the Office of the Minister of	Health
External Relations, in charge of	Leisure Time
Cooperation and Development	Urbanism and Housing
(Third World)	Environment
Defense	Sea
Economy and Finance	Communications
National Education	PTT (Mail, Telephone, and Telegraph)
Attached to the Office of the Minister of	Veterans
Industry, in charge of Energy	Consumer Interests
	Professional Training

Under-Secretaries Attached to the Office of the Prime Minister

In charge of extending the public sector
In charge of repatriated citizens (from Algeria and Former Colonies)

Under-Secretaries Attached to the Office of a Minister

Attached to the Office of the Minister of the Interior and Decentralization, in charge of
   departments and territories outside of Europe
Attached to the Office of the Minister of National Solidarity, in charge of the family
Attached to the Office of the Minister of National Solidarity, in charge of the elderly
Attached to the Office of the Minister of National Solidarity, in charge of immigrants
Attached to the Office of the Minister of Defense
Attached to the Office of the Minister of Agriculture
Attached to the Office of the Minister of Leisure Time, in charge of tourism

Source: *Le Monde,* Dossiers et Documents. *Les Élections législatives de Juin 1981,* p. 137. Used by permission.

of Cabinet organization. The first Cabinet of the Fifth Republic under Prime Minister Debré counted only twenty ministers and six under-secretaries; the latter belong to the Cabinet but do not always participate in the weekly meetings of the Council of Ministers. The Socialist government of 1981 is so far the largest, with thirty-five ministers and nine under-secretaries, but Jacques Chirac's government also had a total of forty-three members.[23]

Changes in the backgrounds of Cabinet members are more significant than changes in size. The seven prime ministers who preceded Pierre Mauroy had all occupied high public office prior to their nomination. Only two had ever been members of parliament before becoming prime ministers, but all of them sought and won a seat in the National Assembly afterwards. In the first Cabinet of the Fifth Republic almost 40 percent of the ministers had never run for elective office of any kind and were selected for their expertise; most of them were ranking civil servants. This practice, which reflected de Gaulle's and Debré's inclination to make the affairs of state less "political," was gradually abandoned during the years of the Pompidou administration because its results had been disappointing. It first became apparent to the ranking bureaucrats in their own ministries that a minister with no support outside the civil service did not have enough political weight in the councils of government, especially in negotiations with the Ministry of Finance and the staff of the Élysée. This led many of the civil servants to ignore directives coming from one of their former colleagues, whose nomination to a Cabinet post they might have resented, although they were accustomed to accommodating a politician who had his own power base.[24] In turn such rebuffs

[23] For a discussion of Cabinet personnel see Pascal Antoni *Les Ministres de la Ve République* (Paris: PUF, 1976).

[24] See Charles Debbasch, *L'Administration au pouvoir: fonctionnaires et politique sous la Ve République* (Paris: Calmann-Levy, 1969), p. 57, and the rather emphatic statements by high civil servants, related in Ezra N. Suleiman, *Politics, Power, and Bureaucracy in France: The Administrative Elite* (Princeton: Princeton University Press, 1974), p. 231. For complete statistical data on the composition of Cabinets in the Fifth (also as compared with the Fourth) Republic, see Francis de Baecque, "L'Interpénétration des personnels administratifs et politiques," in *Administration et Politique,* Baecque and Quermonne, pp. 23–32.

made some of the ministers understand what advantages for their own effectiveness and authority they could derive from a political mandate.

Abandoned for several years, the practice of nominating "nonpolitical" experts, usually high civil servants, to important posts, such as the Ministries of Finance and of Foreign Affairs, was resumed during the Giscard presidency. This change occurred because the president wanted to reserve these domains for himself (as some American presidents have done when selecting a Secretary of State). In that case an experienced administrator was all that was needed for the post.

But other Cabinet posts too were held by ministers with a civil service background. A number of them, often recent graduates of the ENA, had entered the Cabinet after first seeking elective office, either local or national, or after service on the personal staff of a minister. Hence the members of the government during the last years of the Giscard administration were quite typical of that fusion of administrative and political personnel discussed above (Chapter VI).[25] Given the social background of these politician-bureaucrats, the fusion lent the regime a distinctive "upper-class" image which was widely resented.

The government which came into office after the landslide victory of 1981 was in many ways quite different from its predecessors not only because of its political orientation.[26] All of its forty-four members (our discussion includes the under-secretaries and does not distinguish between the various ministerial ranks) have participated in party politics and usually held important offices in their respective parties. Thirty-seven are Socialists, four Communists, and three belong to small groups of moderate leftist leanings. Twenty-nine have been members of

25 See Pierre Birnbaum, *Les Sommets de l'État* (Paris: Seuil, 1977), esp. pp. 152–66; and, with strong warnings as to what this fusion means for the quality of both the administrative and the political processes, François Bloch-Lainé, *Profession: Fonctionnaire* (Paris: Seuil, 1976), pp. 231–33.

26 For biographical details on the members of the new government, see Press and Information Service of the French Embassy, *Biographical Sketches: Second Cabinet of Pierre Mauroy,* and, more extensively, *Les Élections Législatives de Juin 1981* (Paris: Dossiers et Documents de Monde, 1981), pp. 26–31, 137–39.

one of the two houses of parliament, usually for many years, and have served on important parliamentary committees. There are now only seven members of the administrative *Grand Corps* in the government, and most of these have been engaged in politics for a long time, such as the two most outspoken leaders of the right and the left wing of the Socialist Party, Michel Rocard and Jean-Pierre Chevènement. Among the other former civil servants in the government, several have been members of the teaching profession. The only two ministers with a working-class background are communists. One of them, Charles Fiterman, Minister of Transportation (the running of the nationalized railroad system is one of his responsibilities), is the second-in-command in the hierarchy of the PC; he had fully participated in the anti-socialist campaign of pre-election days. There are six women in the Cabinet. The average age of all cabinet members is 50.5 years.

Not surprisingly (see Chapters IV and VI), most of the new ministers have been or continue to be local government officials; at least fourteen of them are mayors. The two most important posts in the Cabinet are held by mayors of two major cities: Pierre Mauroy, the Prime Minister, a teacher by profession and thereby the first prime minister in the Fifth Republic who did not hold an exalted post in the bureaucracy or university, has been mayor of Lille (population 200,000) for many years; and Gaston Deferre, Minister of Interior and of Decentralization, has been mayor of Marseilles (population 800,000) since 1953. The Minister of Justice, Robert Badinter, is an outstanding member of the Paris bar, long known for his passionate campaign against the death penalty. The Minister of National Solidarity, Nicole Questiaux, a member of the Council of State, had reached, long before her nomination to a Cabinet post, one of the highest administrative positions ever occupied by a woman.

In many ways the first Socialist Cabinet resembles other European cabinets more closely than previous cabinets of the Fifth Republic. As is the case in Great Britain and in most of the democracies of the continent, many of the new ministers have shared a political rather than a professional career and have known each other for a long time. What they are lacking is familiarity with national political office, since their party has not borne governmental responsibilities for more than twenty years.

A traditional institution of governmental practice that has continued into the Fifth Republic will be of help to these ministers. Each French minister has long surrounded himself with a group of personal collaborators, his *cabinet*. The members of his cabinet have always fulfilled functions with which in other countries the top civil servants in each ministry are entrusted. In the past, the frequent changes of government justified an institution which gave to the minister some leverage with a bureaucracy always suspected of seeking to sabotage policy directives which it knew to be ephemeral.

But although under the present regime the life span of ministerial office has been lengthened, the ministerial cabinets have proven as indispensable as before — some ministers have found ways of enlarging their cabinets considerably beyond the legal limit of ten members. The most complete and up-to-date study of the subject concluded that, depending on the minister and the ministry, most cabinets vary from ten to thirty members.[27] The particularities of French bureaucratic organization and the obstacles it puts in the way of innovation explain much of this phenomenon. Insufficient communication between different strata within the same agency leaves the holder of power so isolated that he is unable to overcome inflexible habits and to make a break in routine even when changes in the environment make such a breakthrough necessary. Here the members of the ministerial cabinet are called upon to overcome an isolation that might otherwise condemn a minister to impotence.

[27] The chapters devoted by Suleiman in *Politics, Power, and Bureaucracy* to the cabinets (pp. 181–238) are excellent; they also review the earlier literature. For a more succinct but able discussion of the cabinets, especially in their relations with the bureau chiefs in the ministries, see Jeanne Siwek-Pouidesseau, *Le Personnel de direction des ministères* (Paris: Colin, 1969). For recent discussions of the cabinets of the prime minister, see Aline Coutrot, "Les membres des cabinets du Premier Ministre et du président de la République, 1959–1974," and Marie-Christine Kessler, "Le Cabinet du Premier ministre et le Secrétariat du gouvernement," *Administration et Politique*, Baecque and Quermonne, pp. 61–103. For a vivid account of cabinet activities in the Mauroy government, see "La machine gouvernementale en fin de rodage," *Le Monde*, February 10 and 11, 1982.

At the ministerial level, the cabinets form a link between politics and administration and between administration and the outer environment; the latter comprising other administrations and organized or potential interests, including those in the minister's own constituency. Before the war, and for a short time at the beginnings of both the Fourth and Fifth Republics, ministers frequently appointed their own political friends, journalists, and other "experts in communication," to cabinet positions. But gradually, for the sake of greater effectiveness, an increasing number of high civil servants have entered the cabinets and dominate them, to the extent that before 1981 more than 90 percent of the members of the various cabinets were civil servants. Members of the *grands corps* were predominant among them, which means that they are usually graduates of the ENA or of the *X*, if not of both (see Chapter VI). In a period of sustained modernization the skills and working methods of the elite corps were in great demand. Although all of the *grands corps* were represented, the ubiquitous Inspectorate of Finance and the prefectorial corps were particularly sought after for the most important positions in the cabinets.

When the members of a ministerial cabinet interact with the line officials in their ministry, or when they coordinate activities between ministries, they deal with officials who often share their training and also their social background. As one would expect, these officials, especially the powerful *directeurs,* the division heads in each administration, view the cabinets with mixed feelings, but are on the whole resigned to the functioning of an institution whose longevity seems to indicate a functional necessity.[28] Yet such acceptance in no way precludes the effective if surreptitious resistance by many civil servants to the suggestions coming from their minister's cabinets.

Remarkably enough, many of the civil servants who assume the role of political adjuncts of their minister change not only their style, but also their mentality. They become impatient

[28] Cf. their answers to a questionnaire in Suleiman, *Politics, Power, and Bureaucracy,* pp. 222 ff.

with the routine they encounter and scrutinize the proposals that come from the administrative bureaus for their possible political effect, presumably always "fighting" for their minister. Especially those, and their number is fairly numerous, who have made careers in several cabinets of either the same or different ministries develop a political sensitivity which the line officials, once their fellow students at the ENA, claim to shun. This suggests that an assigned role is a more forceful determinant of administrative behavior than background and training.

Over the last years the cabinets have become a means of faster promotion to more rewarding jobs in the administration or a training ground for political office, including that of junior ministers. It has been said with some justification that in both the Fourth and Fifth Republics the most promising students were considering their training at the ENA as a preparation for high political posts, including that of prime minister, rather than for an administrative career.[29]

If the institutionalization of the cabinets has resulted from specific difficulties for effective decision making, it did not resolve these difficulties and may rather aggravate them. The practice of giving increasing importance to the activities of the cabinets splits an already divided administration even more. The line officials have insufficient contacts with their ministers; they were specifically instructed to have none with members of parliament. Only the members of the ministerial cabinets had direct contacts with the center of decision making: the presidency and the president's own Cabinet. In this way the ministerial cabinets shared in the charismatic power of the presidency, which resulted in yet more centralization.[30]

Because of its lack of experience and the possible hostility of the bureaucracy, the Socialist administration has to rely even more than others on the support which a ministerial cabinet

[29] For statistical as well as sociological data on graduates of the ENA who have served in ministerial cabinets and have sought a political career, see Jean-Luc Bodiguel, *Les Anciens élèves de l'ENA* (Paris: PFNSP, 1978), pp. 181 ff.

[30] See the brilliant development on this point in Michel Crozier et al., eds., *Où va l'administration française?* (Paris: Éditions d'Organisation, 1974), pp. 200–01.

can provide. Three hundred and sixty serve as members of a ministerial cabinet in Mauroy's government as against 234 in the preceding government. With a staff of over fifty the Prime Minister's cabinet is the largest of all. As before, the cabinets include civil servants, who are expected to assist their minister when his or her political initiatives bog down in bureaucratic routine or worse. These civil servants, among them a good number of "enarques," must of course share the political orientation of the ministers they serve. Here French traditions of tolerance have been of help. Even during the long stretch of conservative governments, a fairly large number of socialists, and occasionally even a communist, were serving in the upper ranks of the bureaucracy. They have now moved to the staffs of the cabinets.

Nonetheless, the composition of the cabinets has changed. The percentage of civil servants is somewhat lower than previously, and their places are taken, as during the earlier republics, by journalists, party and union officials, lawyers, numerous members of the teaching profession, and other professionals. Mitterrand knew well that it would not serve the interests of his government if one were to interfere with the institution of the cabinets. But he did suggest, with a great deal of restraint, that in spite of his admiration for the *grands corps,* he wished to see the door to important positions opened wider than before for deserving men and women who might not have gone through that narrow pathway to high status, the administrative *concours* (see Chapters III and VI).[31]

THE CIVIL SERVICE:
MOTOR OR INSTRUMENTALITY?

Because of its frank emphasis on the prestige and the procedures of the administrative state, and because of its dislike for "party politics," it was expected that the Gaullist regime would greatly increase the weight of the bureaucracy in the policy process. What has come about is, in fact, a seemingly contradictory but internally quite consistent development. On

---

[31] See his remarks in his first press conference, *Le Monde,* September 26, 1981.

the one hand, the executive has subjected the bureaucracy to more stringent political controls, but, on the other, the domain open to decision making by the technicians in the civil service has been enlarged considerably.[32]

In most administrative quarters, the lessening of controls and of interference by members of parliament was generally welcomed as a boon to administrative efficiency. Nationalized enterprise and the entire public sector of the economy have been freed almost completely from parliamentary supervision. The taste of the regime for secrecy and its preference for carefully channeled information correspond well to the working methods of the French bureaucracy. And although a change of ministers has been a fairly frequent occurrence, the civil service has on the whole welcomed the greatly increased governmental stability. Even more fundamentally, the resurrection of a viable "state" was greeted by civil servants who had suffered from its decline under the Fourth Republic. In the words of one of the most distinguished career ambassadors: "How unbearable and often painful it is to serve in an important post the ghost of a state, a regime which has not faith in itself, a country which lets itself slide downhill into decadence." [33] The restoration of governmental authority impressed even those who were politically indifferent or hostile to Gaullism. It remains doubtful, however, whether the new republic has been truly successful in its efforts to impose political directives on a vast bureaucracy. The previously described activities of the ministerial cabinets would be unnecessary if the ministers were able to move the bureaucracy in a direction desired by them. This is generally not the case, and even unduly large personal staffs have not remedied the situation; moreover, as we have seen, their intervention had to be paid for by more centralization.

[32] This proposition was first put forward by Georges Vedel in his contribution to a roundtable concerned with "Technocracy and the Role of Experts in Government," organized by the Fifth World Congress of the *International Political Science Association* and held in Paris in 1961. Since then his thesis has been widely accepted as essentially correct. See also Victor Silvera, "Réflexions sur la stabilité gouvernementale et l'action administrative depuis 1958," *La Revue Administrative* 17 (1964): 545–55.

[33] Léon Noël, quoted here from a book review by François Goguel, *RFSP* 24, no. 2 (1974): 367.

An outstanding Gaullist, Albin Chalandon, who has been in charge of important ministries, has spoken out sharply against the bureaucracy: "Every civil servant considers himself the owner of his post. The head of a business can give orders. A minister is obliged to convince his own directors. This leads to an administrative totalitarianism, in the face of which public power is struck by impotence." And Pompidou himself complained in an address to members of one of the bureaucracy's elite corps, about the "administrative labyrinths." [34] In a speech celebrating the twentieth anniversary of the Fifth Republic, Giscard d'Estaing warned against the threat which might arise for democratic institutions from a "technocratic regime." "Political power," he said, "based on the vote of the electorate should not be occulted and subordinated by the technocracy, by its obscure language and by its decisions which are far removed from the people and their roots." [35] The warning voiced by men in power, with more anxiety than precision, gave expression to a widely felt concern about an omnipotent bureaucracy.

According to official estimates the number of people on public payrolls has about doubled during the last twenty-five years. Without counting those employed in nationalized enterprises, some statistics classify about 3.4 million, about 16 percent of the total labor force, as being employed either by the national or local governments.[36] But these figures are not only uncertain, they are also not meaningful for an assessment of the problems of bureaucracy, since they include hundreds of thousands of teachers and postal employees.

There is no doubt that in a country rich in bureaucratic traditions, the Gaullist constitution was bound to give further impulse to administrative growth. Since the rule-making power of the government was explicitly extended in 1958, top-ranking

---

[34] Both quoted here from Suleiman, *Politics, Power, and Bureaucracy,* pp. 31 ff.

[35] The speech is reprinted in Quermonne, *Gouvernement,* p. 669. Giscard proposed decentralization as a remedy. On this problem, see the concluding section of this chapter.

[36] See Jean-François Kessler, *Sociologie des fonctionnaires* (Paris: PUF, 1980), pp. 8–9. Other much lower figures published by the official Institute of Statistics arrive at only 1.8 million classified as "state agents." But classifications are unclear.

bureaucrats have prepared important policy decisions in every detail without consulting parliament or other elective bodies. Some of the measures for which the technicians in the government bureaus assumed de facto responsibility and about which there was little or no discussion in parliament, were the currency reform of 1958 and the host of economic measures accompanying it; the stabilization plan of 1961 with its far-reaching consequences; the thorough reforms of the court and of the social security systems. The complete revamping of the administrative structure of the Paris region, affecting more than 9 million people and far more important than the changes introduced by Baron Haussman during the days of Napoleon III, was briefly debated in parliament, but in all essentials shaped by governmental bureaus.

The integration of the French economy into the structures of the European Common Market and into its trade practices was the exclusive work of government bureaus. Parliamentary discussions of the seven modernization plans were perfunctory, if they took place at all. But excluding parliament from these and many similarly important matters also meant most of the time the absence of any meaningful public discussion. How democratically responsible can an administration remain under such conditions? Have the problems been compounded by the fact that the same governmental majority has remained in power for so long and that there was little input into decision making by the opposition? Was the regime tending towards a spoils system quite alien to French traditions of a merit system and of bureaucratic neutrality?

The easy transition between posts in the bureaucracy, the ministerial cabinets, the political executive, and possibly in parliament had destroyed functional separations as they existed previously. Proven political allegiance seemed to rank at least as high as competence. During the last years of the Pompidou administration the amalgamation between Gaullism and the administration had become so extensive that one spoke about a "UDR-State" (UDR being at that time the acronym for the Gaullist party). One of the reasons for Giscard's election in 1974 was the hope that this amalgamation would be undone.

But, as we have seen, the functional fusion did not cease,

even though Gaullist influence and party identification receded. A long-time observer and former member of the high
bureaucracy has described the situation that prevailed in the
administrative bureaus during the Giscard years as a "politiza-
tion in the vacuum." [37] There was little specific political pressure and certainly no crusading spirit emanating from the top.
But even highly placed officials preferred caution to decisive-
ness and routine to innovation, since they had to wait for decisions from the Elysée Palace (or the Prime Minister's office), not
only where broad policy directives were involved but also concerning minute details. Such a mentality was passed on to
lower echelons and resulted easily in inefficiency, if not paralysis.

It is of course impossible to generalize on attitudes and practices prevalent in a vast administration. Yet it became increasingly clear to many that if the "administrative labyrinths"
about which Pompidou had spoken functioned badly, this was
also due to a congenital weakness of the political system itself:
the centralization of decision making in the President's office
encouraged and reproduced the almost spontaneous centralization that took place amidst a fragmented bureaucracy.[38] Every
administration is rule-bound, but in France the rules are so
dense and appear so rigid that in practice they are swamped by
exceptions. Yet since exceptions can only be granted by senior
officials, the constant transfer of responsibilities to the highest
administrative echelons is intensified. The traditional administrative way of problem solving, or rather of solution-defer-
ment, leads to that "stalled society" in which development is
impeded by a blocking of decision making. A British observer
has described situations that resemble an administrative "Alice
in Wonderland," and the foremost French student of the administrative process has reached similar conclusions.[39] The

[37] François Bloch-Lainé, "Une politisation par le vide," *Promotions* (the
ENA alumni magazine) 100 (1977): 9 ff.

[38] Excellent on the relationship between "presidentialism" and administrative centralization is Ezra M. Suleiman's "Administrative Reform and
the Problem of Decentralization in the Fifth Republic," in *Fifth Republic,*
Andrews and Hoffmann, pp. 79–90.

[39] The literature on the misdeeds of administrative centralization is vast
and interesting. Mostly anecdotal but based on multiple experiences is
Alain Peyrefitte's *The Trouble with France* (New York: Knopf, 1981).

blocks in the way of effective decision making can be blasted away only by a frankly political determination originating outside the bureaucracy. This was done by General de Gaulle when he opted for Algerian independence and set the country on the course of decolonization. But there have been few such examples since.

During the presidential campaign of 1974 Mitterrand had proposed a thoroughgoing reform and partial dismantling of the Ministry of Finance, likened by some to a "medieval fortress," by others to an "octopus." Its control of all financial operations, large and small, is extraordinarily cumbersome and throttles initiative. Although the ministry is generally known from the geographical location of its Parisian headquarters as the *Rue de Rivoli,* its agents are practically the masters of all administrations in the capital as well as in the provinces.[40] Neither during his 1981 campaign nor after his election to the presidency did Mitterrand repeat such proposals. He has entrusted the Ministry of Finance in all its "fullness" to an able economist, Jacques Delors, a man with varied experience and, in the past, critical of overcentralization.[41]

A "Ministry of Civil Service and of Administrative Reforms" is headed by a communist, Anicet le Pors, who for long years has combined membership in the party with a position in the upper ranks of the administration. As yet he has not announced far-reaching reform plans. But the Prime Minister let it be known that a number of civil servants in politically sensitive posts who had participated prominently in decision making under the preceding governments would be given other assignments without losing their civil service status. In the early days of the Fifth Republic about 400 posts had been designated

More analytical is Michel Crozier et al., *Où va l'administration française* (Paris: Editions d'Organisation, 1974); and Michel Crozier's last chapter of *The Stalled Society* (New York: The Viking Press, 1973), pp. 155–77. Much material is also found in Vincent Wright, "Politics and Administration under the French Fifth Republic," *Political Studies* 22 (1974): 44–65.

[40] An excellent description of the ministry's operation is provided by Jack Hayward, *The One and Indivisible French Republic* (London: Weidenfeld & Nicolson, 1973), pp. 158–67.

[41] For Delors's beliefs, see Échange et Projets, *La Démocratie à la portée de la Main* (Paris: Michel, 1977).

as to be filled by special governmental appointment. Though fewer in number, they are the equivalent of presidential appointments in the United States. Most of the civil servants who held these positions were moved during the first months after the elections. But, as in the field of telecommunications, the president of the republic and the prime minister have been careful to explain that no political "witch hunt" was intended: they know that at a time of substantial administrative changes it is important not to impair the good will of an experienced bureaucracy.

DECENTRALIZATION: HOW AND WHEN?

Without waiting for the parliamentary elections, the new government let it be known that it considered a comprehensive program of decentralization a matter of top priority. To find the French Left among the advocates of decentralization is a fairly recent phenomenon.[42] True enough, the first generation of French revolutionaries, the Girondins, had celebrated decentralized government and had some dreams of federalism. But the war against the reactionary armies of Europe and counterrevolutionary uprisings in the provinces forced the Jacobins into a strictly centralized rule. Progress and republicanism were to be defended from the capital. In the nineteenth century one strand of French socialism and especially of syndicalism, the forerunner of the modern trade-union movement, drew its inspiration from Pierre-Joseph Proudhon, an author critical of all state organization, in favor of decentralization and a curious form of European federalism. Marxism won out over Proudhonism and with it came renewed concern for conquering centralized state power and using it to destroy the enemies of the disinherited — and the Catholic Church. Local government was suspect because it was in the hands of reactionaries, especially in the countryside. After they split from the socialists, the communists adopted Lenin's model of cen-

[42] For the attitudes of the Left towards local government reform, see the excellent chapter in Peter Gourevitch, *Paris and the Provinces: The Politics of Local Government Reform in France* (Berkeley: University of California Press, 1980), pp. 153–66.

tralization as suitable for both party and state organization. Although they were far less hierarchically organized than the communists, the socialists did not pay more attention than their enemy-brothers to restructuring the existing state. Democratization of society was to be effected from above. After the Left had conquered many municipal governments, the socialist and even the communist mayors became working partners of the prefects, the representatives of the central power, just like other local government officials (see Chapter IV). Even after the Gaullist republic had pushed the Left into permanent opposition, prevailing attitudes persisted. "Down to the early sixties, the Jacobin current remained hegemonic among the parties of the left." [43] The first serious endeavors to reform the state apparatus and to shift power away from the center came from the other side of the political spectrum.

When General de Gaulle announced early in 1968 that he wanted to give a new impetus to regional reform, he did so admittedly because he had become convinced that the country's overcentralization was choking policy making. "For centuries," he said, "centralization was necessary in order to enable our country first to achieve and then to maintain its unity. But this is no longer required. On the contrary: now regional activities are needed to give us economic strength." [44] It is true that such insights were not new: Napoleon III had argued similarly, and yet his announced reforms came to nothing. [45] After the events of May–June 1968 de Gaulle decided on making regional reform the core of the referendum that went down to defeat a year later. His successor drew the lesson and submitted a new bill through regular parliamentary procedure. The law enacted in 1972 but implemented only in the fall of 1973 supplemented earlier legislation, and was hailed by a Gaullist minister quite immodestly as it turned out as a "small institutional revolution."

[43] Ibid., p. 158.

[44] See P. Brongniart, *La Région en France* (Paris: Colin, 1971), p. 4 — a useful collection of data and documents on regional reform.

[45] See Theodore Zeldin, *France 1848–1945*, vol. 1 (Oxford: Clarendon Press, 1973), p. 538. Both in the 1860s and in the 1960s the amount of publications concerned with regional reform was staggering.

Conceived as a more rational division of the territory and as a counterweight against excessive centralization, regionalism in France has had a long and honorable tradition.[46] Before and after de Gaulle had spoken, a number of thoughtful proposals tried to describe the conditions for regional organization in a modern France.[47] They outlined, with some variations, two major interconnected reforms in territorial organization: on the one hand the areas should be large and viable enough to be able to develop and live, at least in part, on their own human and financial resources; on the other, the authorities in charge of the newly created regions should become more truly autonomous, less dependent on binding directives from the capital. As a precondition for or as a consequence of these reforms, it would also be necessary to proceed, as France's neighboring countries have done, with a merger of many of the historical pygmy communes and their local government units which had proven so grossly inappropriate to their tasks.

The changes which were introduced by legislation and executive decrees were far less sweeping. The country is presently divided not into the fairly large ten or twelve regions which many economists have recommended, but into twenty-two regions which comprise several departments. (See Map p. xxiv. It may be noted that this map shows only the regions, while maps 1–4 show in outline the 96 departments which even after the reforms enacted by the socialist government will not lose their administrative and political importance.) If one disregards the most and the least populous, i.e., Paris and Corsica, the twenty remaining regions vary in population between 4.7 million

---

[46] See Stanley Hoffmann, "The Areal Division of Powers in the Writings of French Political Thinkers," in *Area and Power, A Theory of Local Government*, ed. Arthur Maas (Glencoe, Ill.: The Free Press, 1959), pp. 113–49, and the fairly complete review of past thinking and efforts, by Lawrence Gladieux, "Regionalism in France," *Public and International Affairs* 5, no. 1 (1967): 135–57.

[47] See Pierre Mendès-France, *A Modern French Republic* (New York: Hill and Wang, 1963) and also, among many, Club Jean Moulin, *Les Citoyens au pouvoir: 12 régions, 2000 communes* and *Quelle réforme? Quelles régions?* (Paris: Seuil, 1968 and 1969); Club Nouvelle Frontière, *Le Dossier du 27 avril* (Paris: Grasset, 1969); and Edgard Pisani, *La Région, pour quoi faire?* (Paris: Calmann-Lévy, 1969).

(Rhône-Alpes) and 0.7 million (Limousin); they also vary considerably in economic development.[48]

A regional reform that set out to combat the sluggishness and developmental imbalance resulting in part from overcentralization had to choose between two methods: decentralization or deconcentration of decision making. Decentralization would have implied that suitable regional bodies, legitimized by elections and disposing of adequate financial means and administrative structure, would have been put in charge of their region's development. The French government chose deconcentration, a hierarchical arrangement by which the organs of the central government located in the regions are supposed to take the initiative for launching development projects without referring the final decision on every detail to Paris.

The linchpin and chief executive of the regional organization was the regional prefect of that department in which the regional capital is situated.[49] Assisted by a special staff of civil servants, his major task was the supervision and coordination of the work of the departmental prefects of his region in all matters concerning development. Cooperating with the field services of the national ministries, operative in each department, the regional prefect sought to ensure the greatest possible rationality in the allocation of public investments, which are provided to a large extent by the national treasury.

In several respects the structure as established in the early 1970s sanctioned fewer changes than the text of the referendum of 1969 had proposed. This is not to suggest that either the earlier proposition had been particularly bold or that its features had caused the rejection of the referendum.[50] The legis-

---

[48] By way of comparison: Paris excepted, five of the German *Laender* have a larger population than the most populous of the French regions.

[49] Hayward, *The One and Indivisible*, pp. 37–47, gives an excellent critical account of the regional setup. Richly documented is William Andrews, "The Politics of Regionalization in France," in *Politics in Europe*, ed. Martin O. Heisler (New York: David McKay, 1974), pp. 293–322.

[50] For a discussion of the reasons for the defeat of the referendum, see Chapter IV. In fact in 1971, 64 percent of respondents in a public opinion poll were in favor of "creating regions with considerable powers" with a mere 12 percent disagreeing. See *La Région* (Paris: La Documentation Française, 1973), p. 76.

lation merely took notice of the fact that the notables in the departments, aided by the prefectoral organization were able to make any setup inoperative which did not respect the traditional equilibrium between local, departmental, and national authorities. As we have seen (Chapter IV), such an equilibrium is inevitably threatened by urbanization and industrialization. The local notables, especially the mayors and departmental councillors of rural France, and their allies, the prefects, were fearful that structures which protected them would be altogether destroyed if effective regional authorities would draw away further power from the departments.[51]

Hence the cautious reform of 1972 did not give to the regions the status of a "territorial collectivity" (which would have likened the regions to the communes and the departments) but only that of a yet less autonomous "public establishment" whose specific functions are granted and can therefore also be changed or eliminated by the state. There was no room in this setup for either a popularly elected executive (such as a United States governor) or for an elected regional parliament, since direct elections would have given to the regional organs a democratic legitimacy and thereby undesired strength. A directly elected regional assembly would also be in direct competition with the traditional departmental councils and would, because of its broader geographical basis, easily outweigh them. Instead, each region was endowed with a regional council and an (advisory) economic and social committee, both of which met annually for short sessions (see Figure II). The councils' members had been elected for other functions in their respective departments: deputies and senators and an equal number of departmental and local officials. The advisory committees brought together representatives of interest groups and associations as appointed by the government. This was a structure that was entirely acceptable to local notables and political representatives; it conformed to the model

[51] With many telling details on this struggle, Pierre Grémion and Jean-Pierre Worms, *Les Institutions régionales et la société locale* (Paris: Copedit, 1968), and for more recent developments, Pierre Grémion, *Le Pouvoir périphérique: Bureaucrates et notables dans le système politique français* (Paris: Seuil, 1976).

which President Pompidou had described as appropriate: "The region," he had stated, "should not be an administrative level which imposes itself on top of those which exist, but instead a union of the existing departments."[52]

As it turned out, the regional organization, while doing little for effective decentralization, sanctioned a compromise between the Pompidou administration and the forces bent on conserving traditional arrangements: rural interests would not interfere with the government's drive for rapid industrialization (see Chapter II), but as a reward they continued to enjoy the protection which the centralized administration had always afforded them. That the Communal Merger Act of 1971, which aimed at consolidating minuscule local government units, was an all-but-complete failure has been discussed earlier (see Chapter IV).

Before he acceded to the presidency Giscard had advocated a strengthening of the regional organization by the direct popular elections of the regional councils. But in 1975 his prime minister, his minister of interior, and finally the president himself declared that the legislation of 1972 would not be amended in any way. Chirac allayed the fears of the local notables and of those they represented by declaring in somewhat extravagant terms that only "dreamers and irresponsibles" could think of popularly elected regional executives and assemblies,[53] one of the proposals contained in the Common Program of the Left.

How far the Left had moved away from its centralist creed

---

[52] *Le Monde*, October 21, 1970. The article by Pierre Gremion, "Réforme régionale et démocratie locale," *Projet*, no. 44 (1970): 427 ff., had correctly foreseen this development. In a subsequent article the author drew an almost entirely negative balance sheet of the attempted reforms; see his "Crispation et déclin du jacobinisme," in *La Sagesse et le désordre: France 1980*, ed. Henri Mendras (Paris: Gallimard, 1980), pp. 329–50. L. J. Sharpe, "French Local Government and Society," in *Local Government in Britain and France: Problems and Prospects*, eds. Jacques Lagroye and Vincent Wright (London: Allen & Unwin, 1979), pp. 88, 95, reaches similar conclusions. An evaluation of the 1972 legislation is also offered by Sidney Tarrow, "Local Constraints on Regional Reform: A Comparison of Italy and France," *Comparative Politics* 7, no. 1 (1974): 34 ff.

[53] In an address before Gaullist deputies, see *Le Monde*, September 27, 1975.

had become evident when the Common Program, signed in 1972, devoted an entire chapter to the problem of administrative decentralization at all levels, municipal, departmental, and regional.[54] Socialists had been converted faster than the communists. The membership of the new PS was less committed to marxist teaching than the old SFIO. The events of 1968 had sensitized many of the younger socialists to the problems of participation and democratic decision making. For all its vagueness, the concept of *autogestion* (discussed in Chapter VII), which many of the "new men" in the PS had accepted, paid much attention to the decentralization of various aspects of public life. Michel Rocard, who had also attracted a following outside the party, had furnished an important contribution to the problem of regionalism.[55] The mayors of large cities, who had become the mainstays of the PS in many regions, had for themselves circumvented the inconveniences of prefectoral tutelage (see Chapter IV). But through their involvement with the problems of surrounding towns and villages, they perceived the inadequacy of existing structures in a modernizing economy. The anticapitalism which the trade unions affiliated with the CFDT had inherited from social catholicism had always been closer to the "federalist" Proudhon than to a centralizing Marx.

Finally, the stirring of nationality groups could not leave opposition parties inactive.[56] In response the PC also abandoned that form of jacobinism which looked on all nationalism as a reactionary plot. The largely folkloric regionalism of the

[54] See *Programme Commun de Gouvernement* (Paris: Flammarion, 1973), pp. 73–76.

[55] See Michel Rocard (now Minister of Planning and Regional Management), *Décoloniser la Province* (Paris: Rencontre Socialiste, 1966); Michel Philipponeau, *La Gauche et les Régions* (Paris: Calmann-Levy, 1967); and Edgard Pisani, *Socialiste de raison* (Paris: Flammarion, 1978), esp. pp. 121–235.

[56] See the article by one of the national secretaries of the Socialist party, Dominique Taddel, "Gauche française et 'nationalitaires,'" *Le Monde,* December 28, 1973. Jean-Paul Sartre's journal *Temps Modernes* had published earlier a special 555-page issue on the "Minorités nationales en France," nos. 325, 326 (1963). Robert Lafont, *La Révolution régionaliste* (Paris: Gallimard, 1967), makes a strong statement in favor of the nationality groups.

past was giving way, at least among political activists, to a sharpened sense of particularity (if not of separateness), especially where linguistic differences are coupled with the economic underdevelopment of a region. This is today the case in Brittany, Corsica, the Basque region in the Southwest, and the Languedoc in the Center South. The clashes between police and rebellious Corsicans have been the most publicized. Yet violence has erupted and acts of sabotage been committed in other centers of regionalist and nationalist agitation to which the government has reacted usually with severity.

An important factor that united the signers of the Common Program behind proposals for regionalization was the recurrent failure of the Right and Center to bring about any effective reforms. In spite of solemn promises and extensive reforms, neither the majority in parliament nor the mildly reform-minded bureaucrats who had given attention to the problem had succeeded in transforming an administrative system which the electorate had come to resent as burdensome and inefficient. An excessive timidity in responding to political pressures had defeated good intentions.[57] An opposition program was apt to draw advantages from such disappointments.

In the campaign for the presidency, Mitterrand and other socialist speakers had good reasons never to mention the Common Program. But whenever they spelled out their commitment to the radical decentralization which the program had advocated, they earned sustained applause.

To make Gaston Deferre, the mayor of Marseilles, a Minister of State in charge of both the Interior and of Decentralization was a symbolic act. The Minister of Interior controls the prefectoral corps which, because of its power of tutelage over local government, has been, ever since its creation by Napoleon, the pivot of administrative centralization. An effective shift of power from center to periphery had to transform the relationship between the representatives of state power, the prefects, and those who represent the electorate on the local, the departmental, and the regional level.

[57] A former Gaullist minister and advisor of Giscard admitted this after the election of 1981 in a voluntary "confession"; see Pierre Sudreau, "La Décentralisation sans malédiction," *Le Monde,* July 10, 1981.

A bill submitted to the newly elected parliament restructured this relationship and outlined thereby bold future reforms which are expected to extend over at least two years. Decisions made by the local government councils of the future — and the regional councils will be elected directly, as the general councils of the departments and the municipal councils are now — no longer need approval by either the departmental or the regional prefects. They will have force of law unless their legality is contested *afterwards*. The councils' chairmen will have executive power over their respective areas, subject only to control by the councils' membership. All of the councils, but particularly the regional councils, will have a prime responsibility in assuming the burden and receiving the benefits of their share in the national economic plan.

The once-upon-a-time prefects will be renamed *commissaires du gouvernement*[58] and will have continuing responsibilities for police and public order. Field offices of various national administrations will continue to assist local government in technical matters. But they will be responsible to those whose needs they serve. Decentralization will take the place of what has been mere deconcentration in the past. "Many Paris bureaus will close doors," Deferre declared hopefully.[59]

The bill, already known as the Deferre Law, was heavily amended in both houses of parliament. (The government's task was not facilitated by special legislation it felt obligated to introduce at the same time in order to pacify Corsican autonomists.) Members of the opposition denounced the reform as opening the gates to anarchy or at least to irresponsibility, and supporters of the government insisted on changes that reintro-

[58] In French the word "commissar" does not necessarily evoke Bolshevik practices, but has a venerable French tradition renewed by General de Gaulle, when he nominated *"commissaires du gouvernement"* at the time of the country's liberation from the Nazis.

[59] See two important declarations by Gaston Deferre in *Les Élections Législatives de Juin 1981* (Paris: Supplément aux Dossiers et Documents du Monde, 1981), pp. 45–46, and *Le Nouvel Observateur*, July 18, 1981, pp. 24–27. For critical statements on the reform by two prefects with long experience in office, see Roger Generbrier, "Mainteneurs de l'État," and Jacques Gandouin, "Coordinateurs et Contrôleurs," *Le Monde*, July 19, 1981.

duced into the reform bill some traditional features. The essentials of the reform were nonetheless saved.[60]

The government and its supporters admit that many problems have to be tackled before the reform becomes operative: the system by which the various councils are to be elected; the respective responsibilities of local, departmental, and regional governments; how to avoid having new levels of authority become new levels of bureaucratic organization. The entire system of local finances must be reorganized; not only an equalization of charges but also effective control of fiscal management must be provided for. New tasks are awaiting a personnel not yet prepared to assume them.

When Deferre and other members of the new administration were asked why they rushed into such a complicated undertaking without more careful preparation and further advice, their answer was predictable: spectacular measures, taken while electoral victory was fresh, should create an irreversible trend towards uprooting century-old habits and administrative routine. Once the legislation had redesigned channels of authority, more detailed provisions could be fitted into the new structures.

Will the reform be able to replace the Napoleonic state by more appropriate structures? Past experiences seem to suggest that anything less than vigor is bound to fail.[61]

[60] Two excellent articles written while the reforms were acted upon by parliament provide historical perspective and prospective thought. See Pierre Grémion, "Régionalisation, régionalisme, municipalisation sous la Ve République," and Bertrand Éveno (an inspector of finance), "Pour démocratiser la décentralisation," *Le Débat*, no. 16 (November 1981): 5–27.

[61] The previous edition of this book concluded this chapter by asking (in 1976): "If the Left came to power, would the end of the Napoleonic State be near?" It might.

CHAPTER X

Policy Processes II

PARLIAMENT: THE NATIONAL ASSEMBLY —
FROM OMNIPOTENCE TO FRUSTRATION

The constitution-makers of 1958 had the announced ambition of endowing France with a "true" parliamentary regime, with "a Parliament," in the words of General de Gaulle, "intended to represent the political will of the nation, to enact laws and to control the executive, *without venturing to overstep its role*."[1] Ever since the establishment of the Third Republic, constitutional and political discussions had centered on the question of the proper role of parliament in the policy process. The prevailing distrust of executive authority had tipped the balance in favor of tight and continuous supervision of the government by both houses of parliament. Techniques to make such supervision effective were developed early and steadily refined over time.[2] In both the Third and the Fourth Republic the power of the government to counteract a

[1] Speech of General de Gaulle of September 4, 1958 (italics supplied), William G. Andrews, ed., *European Political Institutions* (Princeton: Van Nostrand, 1966), p. 42.

[2] Philip M. Williams, *Crisis and Compromise: Politics in the Fourth Republic* (Garden City: Doubleday, 1966), pp. 208 ff., gives the most complete account of parliamentary activities in the Fourth Republic. For the same period, see also Duncan MacRae, Jr., *Parliament, Parties and Society in France, 1946–1958* (New York: St. Martin's Press, 1967), pp. 181 ff. and passim.

vote of censure, i.e., a threat to its own existence, by dissolving parliament and calling for new elections was constitutionally granted. But one early misuse of this right by a military president (General MacMahon in 1877) had been enough to deprive this governmental privilege of its republican respectability and legitimacy. Hence it fell into disuse.

In the French republics the concept of parliamentary "sovereignty" included more than the right to cause the downfall of the government. It also left parliament at all times in complete control of its own proceedings and gave it the choice of topics to be debated. Its committees were entitled to alter the text of bills proposed by the government, even before they were considered by the Assembly. Like congressional committees, and unlike the corresponding bodies in the House of Commons, the standing committees of both houses were highly specialized. The constant watch which parliamentary committees kept over each of the ministries was all the more effective because the chairman of an important committee was often regarded as the most likely successor to the incumbent minister. Such an assumption would hold even where committee chairman and minister belonged to the same party.

Besides its other effects, the political harassment of the government led to the physical and mental exhaustion of its members — this has been described by many politicians of the period in their memoirs, and it perturbed Colonel Charles de Gaulle in his encounters with the leaders of the Third Republic.[3] Yet formal supremacy was not sufficient to give to the parliaments of the Third and Fourth Republics that power which institutions derive from an effective handling of their functions. Having sought to fuse parliamentary and executive functions, a parliament desirous of keeping the executive weak weakened itself in the process. Since there was no longer any clear focus for decision making, the resulting loss of momentum communicated itself to all parts of the policy machinery, to parliament as well as to government.

The way in which parliament discharged its role as law-

---

[3] Charles de Gaulle, *War Memoirs, I: The Call to Honour* (New York: The Viking Press, 1955), pp. 26 ff.

maker illustrates the impotence of seeming omnipotence. In French constitutional doctrines every single law is the expression of the general will — by which the people through their representatives manifest their sovereignty. At least on the level of theoretical considerations, every statute takes on the same symbolic significance which the constitution has in the United States. Since only parliament can enact a law, only another act of parliament can rescind it.[4] But political realities have deprived the legislator of so exalted a place.

When after the First World War and especially during the depression of the thirties a more active role was thrust upon the state, a parliament which lacked stable majorities proved unable to provide the needed legislation. In order to avoid chaos, it periodically abandoned its legislative authority to the government. During the interwar years, eleven governments obtained special powers from parliament to override existing laws and to enact new legislation by so-called decree-laws. "While decree-laws enabled the executive to act where the legislature would not, they encouraged evasion of responsibility by the deputies and of parliamentary control by the administration . . . the authority given was very widely drawn and still more widely interpreted."[5] Because of an unsteady party system, the composition and political orientation of a government never conformed for long with the wishes which the electorate might have expressed in the previous elections. To give but one example: although no new elections had taken place, in 1938 decree-laws annulled important parts of the social legislation which the Popular Front government had enacted two years earlier, and deputies who had turned over an essential part of their functions to an unrepresentative Cabinet lost the respect of their constituents.

The constitution of the Fourth Republic sought to forestall such practices and their political consequences by addressing

[4] For a classical (and remarkable) statement of the role of the law in French constitutional thinking, see R. Carré de Malberg, *La Loi, expression de la volonté générale: étude sur le concept de la loi dans la Constitution de 1875* (Paris: Recueil Sirey, 1931).

[5] Williams, *Crisis*, p. 270; pp. 271 ff. give interesting details on the practice followed in the Fourth Republic.

a stern prohibition to the National Assembly against delegating its legislative authority. But since the reasons for political disorder had not been removed and no disciplined majority emerged in parliament, constitutional provisions were flouted. Using only slightly different techniques than before the war, parliament found ways to surrender its sovereign powers as the law-making authority to the executive. Yet as if to compensate for such weakness, it continuously shortened the life span of succeeding governments.

In line with previously developed Gaullist principles, the Constitution of 1958 strove to put an end to the subordination of the government to parliament. Debré's acknowledged model was the political system of Great Britain where the place of parliament in policy making is as well defined (though by conventions rather than by law) as it is strictly limited. Whether Debré fully understood that such limitations are primarily an outcome of the party discipline which permits the Cabinet to control the majority in the House of Commons, is a moot question.[6] He simply started with the assumption that the French voter could never be expected to send coherent majorities to the National Assembly.

Therefore the constitution and the so-called organic laws, enacted in conjunction with the constitution, fitted strict rules of behavior, something like a steel corset, on each individual deputy and on parliament as a body. This, it was hoped, would ensure what Debré and General de Gaulle have repeatedly described as the needed equilibrium between parliament and the executive.

During the first years of the Fifth Republic the executive engaged parliament in harsh confrontation politics. The text of the constitution and of the parliamentary standing orders were interpreted by the president, the government, and by the Constitutional Council in such a way that the "no trespassing" signs which were erected always warned the parliament, seldom

6 The foremost British expert on French politics concludes that the makers of the 1958 constitution set out to import "mainly from Britain, institutions they understood very imperfectly in detail and not at all in spirit." Philip Williams, *The French Parliament: Politics in the Fifth Republic* (New York: Praeger, 1968), p. 114.

the executive, to stay within its bounds. The government would argue that so painful a process of "reeducation" was necessary to forestall a return to the folkways of the political class. Deputies and senators reacted all the more with pain and anger, as the preceding republics had never been willing to acknowledge that in all modern democracies the role of parliament in the political process has declined. Pressed into new and unfamiliar roles, prevented from overturning the government at will, the members of parliament did not know how to keep the government responsive, a task for which the new institutional setup offered some opportunities. Little by little the politics of confrontation have given way to a modicum of collaboration between executive and legislature. Of course, the emergence of a stable governmental majority in the lower house has facilitated a more relaxed handling of the rules. Over the years the players have come to adapt to their new roles although some of their attitudes and expectations are still contradictory.

The Cabinet, not parliament, is effectively in control of proceedings in both houses and can require priority for bills which it wishes to see adopted quickly. Although previously both the National Assembly and the upper house, the Senate, sat almost permanently, they are now confined to sessions of closely regulated length (amounting to a maximum of six months), so that "the government has time to reflect and to act." [7] It is true that the constitution foresees the possibility of parliament's meeting in special session on a specific agenda at the request of either the prime minister or of the majority of the deputies (article 29). But in 1960 President de Gaulle set a precedent requiring, in spite of the wording of the constitution, at least the tacit assent of the president of the republic to any demand for parliament to meet in special session. In 1979 Giscard did not withhold such an assent, although it was quite apparent that the demand for a special session was submitted by the leader of the Gaullist RPR, Jacques Chirac, in order to embarrass the government.

[7] Speech by Debré before the Council of State, reprinted in Andrews, ed., *European Political Institutions*, p. 46. Other quotations from Debré's statement are taken from the same speech.

It remains the parliament's function to enact laws. But the domain of the "law" is strictly defined (article 34): major areas of modern life such as the regulation of civil liberties, the budget, important treaties, and at least the principles governing state intervention in economic and social life belong to this domain. But everything not specifically listed is subject to rule making by the government. Such a distribution of tasks between the Cabinet and the assemblies is designed to avoid what Debré has described with telling realism as the "double deviation of our political organization: a parliament overwhelmed by bills and rushing in disorder towards a multiplication of detailed speeches, [and] a government treating without parliamentary interference the gravest national problems."

The legislative output of the parliaments in the Fifth Republic has been quite respectable. The average of only ninety-six laws enacted yearly during the first twenty years of the new republic was much lower than between 1946 and 1958, when the annual average had been 241.[8] But the simple counting of laws is not entirely meaningful, since their importance must be weighed. As the new constitution limits the domain of the law to certain vital fields, it is obvious that there are important statutes among the more than 2,000 laws enacted between 1958 and 1979 by both houses. If all but 13 percent originated in bills proposed by the government and if many propositions put forward for consideration by members of parliament failed, this is not an unusual record in Western European parliaments; in postwar Great Britain, for instance, private member bills dwindled to 18 percent of the total legislative output. Under such circumstances the amendments incorporated by either of the two houses into the final text are a better measure of the contribution which parliament furnishes to the legislative output.

In an average session the government moves about 400 amendments to bills under discussion; the parliamentary com-

---

8 On the legislative record of parliament, see John R. Fears, "Parliament in the Fifth Republic," in *The Fifth Republic at Twenty,* eds. William Andrews and Stanley Hoffmann (Albany: State University of New York Press, 1981), pp. 58–64, and Pierre Avril, "Le Parlement législateur," *RFSP* 31, no. 1 (February 1981): 15–31.

mittee principally concerned with the bill and individual deputies move about six times as many. But here too the importance of amendments is more significant than their numbers. About 44 percent of all amendments are adopted, but the "success rate" of amendments moved by the government is about 80 percent, that of a parliamentary committee 60 percent, and that of opposition deputies insignificant. But such a record is not unusual in any parliamentary system with disciplined parties. Since the fathers of the 1958 constitution did not have much confidence in such a discipline, they introduced a novelty unknown in other systems: article 44 empowers the government to force parliament by the so-called blocked vote to accept a bill in its entirety with only the amendments agreed to by the government.[9] During the first twenty years the government has used this "disciplinarian" device in both houses of parliament not less than 246 times. But its use has diminished considerably during later years when deputies and parliamentary committees were more willing than before to abide by the government's initiatives and refrained from moving unacceptable amendments.

Another article of the constitution (article 38) invites parliament to abandon "for a limited time" its legislative function to the government if the government wishes to act as legislator "for the implementation of its program." Once parliament has voted a broad enabling law, the government enacts legislation by way of so-called ordinances. It is sometimes said that the governments of the Fifth Republic have made use of this possibility of "executive law making" a mere thirteen times between 1958 and 1978. But substantial legislation necessary to settle the Algerian war, to prepare for French entry into the Common Market, to enact a reform of the social security system, and to deal with other weighty problems have all been eliminated in this way from consideration by a parliament whose rights are already seriously limited by other constitutional provisions. It is true that during later years article 38 has fallen into disuse, at least for deciding matters of importance.

[9] For an interesting case study of a rather significant bill see Alain Brouillet, *Le Droit d'amendement dans la Constitution de la Vᵉ République* (Paris: PUF, 1973).

The socialist government announced that it would resume the procedure of legislating by ordinance, since it wished to quicken the enactment of its comprehensive reform program. The government had no trouble finding a majority for such a project. But it meant that, contrary to Mitterrand's electoral promises to enlarge the prerogatives of parliament, parliament is once more shoved aside. Need for speed and efficiency has won out, as it did during the years of de Gaulle's rule.

There were nineteen standing committees in the National Assembly of the Fourth Republic, but their number is now reduced to six in each house. With a membership ranging from 60 to 120 representatives, the committees are made intentionally large so as to impede their effectiveness as organs of control and their permeability by interest groups. It is true that by forming subcommittees the deputies have been able to circumvent the new formula and, in this one respect, have all but restored the previous situation.

The new constitution redefined the rights of parliament in financial matters. Article 40 declares out of order all parliamentary initiatives that would result either in a decrease of public revenues (such as tax privileges) or in an increase in expenditure. Here the government has made concessions in the course of time; it has not always been unwilling to yield on this point when deputies of the majority were seeking small sums to please their electorate clientele.[10] In the budget discussions the role of the once very powerful Finance Committee of both houses is reduced, but by no means negligible. Yet should parliament ever fail to accept the budget submitted by the government within the constitutionally allotted time of seventy days, the Cabinet can enact the budget by ordinance — a procedure which so far has not been applied since parliament has hastened its deliberations to meet the prescribed deadline. The chairman of the Finance Committee in the Senate complained as recently as 1973 that pressures on his committee to dispatch the budget were unbearable. According to a one-time Cabinet

---

[10] Jack Hayward, *The One and Indivisible French Republic* (London: Weidenfeld & Nicolson, 1973), pp. 177–78. See ibid., pp. 172 ff. for a good and realistic account of the actual budgetary process.

member and faithful Gaullist, the organization of the budget debates since 1959 "seems to be dominated by a single objective: speed. This horror of losing time consumes the managers of the National Assembly, the *rapporteurs-généraux* and the government." [11]

The pressure of time impedes the effectiveness of parliament also in matters other than the budget. A recent article described parliamentary activities realistically under the title "the race against time." [12] The constitutionally prescribed shortness of the session does not permit an orderly transaction of business by either house. In an average year parliament meets for less than eighty days, far less than other parliaments of Western Europe, to say nothing of Congress. The situation worsened already under Giscard because of the greater number of bills which the government submitted to parliament, especially during the first years of the administration. With the advent of the socialist government and its urge for reform legislation, the situation deteriorated further. It has been suggested that parliamentary sessions be lengthened.[13] This would be altogether more in line with Mitterrand's electoral promises than the use of article 38, which the government now envisages as a means to win time. Special sessions might be added, but (because of article 28 of the constitution) lengthening of the ordinary sessions would require cumbersome constitutional amendments.

It is not surprising that the new constitution spelled out in detail the conditions under which the National Assembly could overthrow a government. Since on the one hand the principle of parliamentary responsibility of the Cabinet was to be maintained, and since on the other there was unanimous agreement that the previous frequency of Cabinet crises was harmful to the policy process, possibilities for a vote of censure were left open but strictly regulated.

[11] Léon Hamon, here quoted from Williams, *The French Parliament*, p. 77.

[12] See Michel Couderc, "La Bataille parlementaire contre le temps," *RFSP* 31, no. 1 (February 1981): 85–120.

[13] "Un calendrier inadapté," *Le Monde*, August 5, 1981.

The rule that a government need resign only when a majority of the National Assembly had voted its downfall was given muscle and stated in more elaborate terms (articles 49, 50). Yet more important: it was made clear that in the event of a motion of censure the president of the republic would make use of his solemnly stated right to dissolve the National Assembly and to call for new elections (article 12). This General de Gaulle did in 1962, the only time that a motion of censure has carried in any of the parliaments of the Fifth Republic. Ever since the elections of that year the government has been able to count on a more or less coherent majority in parliament so that none of the other motions of censure, a total of twenty-two since 1958, carried. When de Gaulle dissolved parliament in the spring of 1968, well before its normal life span of five years had expired, he did not act in response to a parliamentary vote of censure, but in order to capitalize on the confusion which the preceding events had created. The elections turned into a Gaullist landslide. Similarly, Mitterrand's dissolution of parliament in 1981 in the wake of his election to the presidency led to a Socialist landslide. In both situations a dissolution of parliament by the president had a frankly plebiscitarian appeal. In cases of conflict between parliament and government the power of the president, who himself is not subject to parliamentary censure, to disband parliament and to call for new elections at almost any time gives him the means of appealing to a presidential majority in the country, should the parliamentary majority fail his prime minister.[14]

Under the new constitution the vote of censure is the only means by which parliament can effectively criticize the conduct of government. As in the past, parliament can normally obtain information from the government by means of debate, confrontation of the prime minister or of members of his Cabinet, written and oral questions, or formal investigations. However, backed by rulings of the Constitutional Council, the government made it clear that under the new regime the deputies would never have the right to express their appraisal of the

[14] The only limit consists in his inability to dissolve parliament twice within one year (article 2, paragraph iv).

information thus obtained by a vote or a resolution.[15] Such votes, the government explained, would bring back the practices of harassment which had proved so detrimental in the past because they had led to the gradual weakening of most Cabinets. If the National Assembly wished to voice its displeasure with the government, it should gather sufficient votes for a motion of censure. As long as this major weapon was not wielded, no poisoned arrows should be shot in the direction of the benches occupied by Cabinet members.

If the government wishes to put its survival on the line it can do so at any time by asking for a vote of confidence (article 49); and this has indeed been done by various prime ministers eleven times between 1959 and 1981. According to the constitution the vote of confidence can be put to use for yet another and quite objectionable purpose. If the government seeks approval for a bill which the parliament is not inclined to accept, the government can make parliamentary approval a question of confidence (article 49, paragraph iii). Once it has done so, the only way in which the Assembly can reject the bill in question is to vote, within the next twenty-four hours, a motion of censure risking thereby a dissolution of parliament by the president. The subsequent elections would easily have again all the characteristics of a plebiscite pinning the deputies against the president. Since 1958 the government has used this procedure not less than twenty-four times and each time parliament has preferred to give in.

Important bills, such as that establishing France's nuclear striking force, have become laws in this manner. The preceding debate had made it clear that in the National Assembly of 1960 abstentions and negative votes would be numerous enough to defeat the government's intention of launching France on its career as a nuclear power. But since the motion of censure closing the debates was not carried by the required vote of half of the Assembly's total number of deputies, the Speaker could announce that "in consequence the bill for the program re-

[15] For an English translation of some interesting phases of the discussion pertaining to the new standing orders of the National Assembly, see Andrews, *European Political Institutions,* pp. 377–85. The minutes of the entire debate fill 200 pages of the *Journal Officiel.*

lating to certain military equipments [sic] *is considered*
adopted. . . ."

A leading textbook on French government has described this
extreme form of insuring executive control of legislation as
"bordering on the absurd." [16] After having proclaimed (article
3) that national sovereignty shall be exercised by the people
"through their representatives" (or by way of referendum), the
constitution enables the government to create laws, possibly
concerned with vital matters, without a vote, the fiction being
that the silence of the deputies is tantamount to approval. It is
true that, to become law, the text must be approved by the
upper house, but that approval too might be fictitious (see
below).

After 1968 the government refrained for a number of years
from coupling the vote of a law with a vote of confidence. Since
it was able to rally a parliamentary majority behind its legislative program, the government had no need to force the hand of
parliament in this way. The situation changed when after Giscard's election and Chirac's resignation, neither the presidency
nor the Prime Minister's office were held by the Gaullist RPR,
still the largest party in the governmental coalition (see Chapter VIII). Without the votes of the Gaullist deputies the government had no majority in parliament.

When the government submitted to parliament a law authorizing elections to the European parliament in Strasbourg to
take place by direct popular vote in the Common Market countries, the Gaullists refused to approve it because of their fundamental objections to any supernational organization. The government had to put the question of confidence, and since the
RPR found it inopportune to move a vote of censure, the legislation was "considered as adopted" (article 49, iii) without a
vote in the Assembly — not a particularly brave way of initiat-
ing an important policy.

During debates on the budget for 1980 a similar rift within
the majority led to a constitutional conflict which left the
country for a moment without a valid budget. The government

16 See Jean-Louis Quermonne, *Le Gouvernement de la France sous la
Ve République* (Paris: Dalloz, 1980), p. 232.

had tried to meet a Gaullist refusal to approve one part of the budget by invoking the procedures of article 49. This accepted the proposed revenues without a preceding vote on expenses, a procedure which the Constitutional Council (see below) declared null and void. An extraordinary session of parliament had to be called to repair the damage; the entire episode gave evidence of some malfunctioning of budgetary and parliamentary procedures in general.[17]

As regards the parliamentary control of the executive it has become somewhat more effective over the years. The constitution, once more trying to emulate British practices, had stipulated expressly that oral questions and the replies by the government be made a weekly priority item (article 48). In his official comments on the new constitution, Michel Debré had been confident that oral questions "would guarantee to the opposition that its voice be heard." [18]

It was also hoped that the question period would take the place of the "interpellation" by means of which, under previous regimes, the deputies had harassed the government. The vote taken at the end of frequently lengthy debates on such interpellations had been a convenient way of gauging the Cabinet's vanishing support. Hence the new standing order of the National Assembly saw to it that the exchanges between deputies and government arising from a question period could never lead to a vote or a resolution. However, in the eyes of representatives accustomed to embarrassing a government rather than to scrutinizing its actions, such an arrangement deprived the question period of its major interest. Measured by their potential usefulness in as tight lipped a regime as the Fifth Republic, oral questions were for years an unmitigated failure: there was none of the lively give-and-take of the British model; sessions devoted to questions were poorly attended;

---

[17] The antagonism between the government and its "majority" in parliament is described in Jacques Chapsal, *La Vie Politique sous la Ve République* (Paris: PUF, 1982), pp. 631–40. For the conflict over the budget for 1980, see Quermonne, *Le Gouvernement*, pp. 320–23.

[18] On the practice of parliamentary "questions," see the interesting account and the statistics in Patrick Nguyen Huu, "L'Evolution des questions parlementaires depuis 1958," *RFSP* 31, no. 1 (February 1981): 172–90.

the deputies were inclined to clothe their questions in lengthy speeches, just as the members of the government read lengthy answers prepared for them by their staffs; and often ministers would send an assistant to represent them, just as President de Gaulle was known to have prevented senior Cabinet members from appearing before certain parliamentary committees. Both sides had difficulty in believing that a confrontation, instead of precipitating the downfall of a government, could serve the ends of compromise and correction.

In 1970, at a time when earlier tensions started to give way to a new outlook on the role of parliament, the National Assembly made room for a weekly session devoted to a new kind of question period, the *questions d'actualité*, far more like the British (and West German) question period: a dozen or more brief questions were selected beforehand; for a time the competent minister or secretary of state answered them succinctly and indicated remedies for the complaints that had been submitted by the questioner. They reflected a greater eagerness on the part of the deputies to control rather than to attack, and less disposition on the part of the government to hide behind the cloak of official secrecy.[19] But after three years the new practice proved a disappointment. It was found that the government answered a mere 30 percent of the questions put. Embarrassing questions raised by the opposition were eliminated by the speaker under pressure from the majority and probably the government. Because of his resolve to lower the tension between parties and to give more visibility to the opposition, Giscard insisted on a reorganization of the "questions to the government," as they are now called. The reform has indeed resulted in a greater number of such questions (over 300 per session, slightly more than half of them raised by deputies from the opposition benches). Satisfaction derived from the ministers' answers has varied with the political climate. It is certain that in spite of all good intentions, this device has at no time acquired the central importance which it occupies in the British system.

19 The new practice was viewed skeptically by Christian Bidegaray and Claude Emery, "Le Contrôle parlementaire," *Revue du Droit Public et de la Science Politique en France et à l'Étranger* 89, no. 6 (1973): 1733.

The other forms of "oral questions with or without debate" continue to take much of the Assembly's time since they amount to speech making but elicit fewer and fewer answers from the government. "Written questions" and the answers thereto provided by the administration are published in the *Journal Officiel.* They continue to fulfill the function of a gigantic service of free and official legal information. A single issue of the *Journal* may contain more than 100 such questions and answers; many thousands are disposed of in a single year and are invaluable to deputies and to constituents.

The possibility of controlling the executive machinery by ad hoc committees of investigation has always existed in the French republics and has always had meagre results. The committees have rarely been used effectively and have never been able to overcome administrative reluctance to disclose the truth.[20] At present their proceedings are strictly regulated. Committees can at all times exclude press and public from their hearings and do not need to publish their findings. Moreover, the majority is able to determine the membership at will, which makes the committees meaningless to the opposition. All this has meant that only a few matters have been made the subject of investigations; when the opposition suggested that seemingly scandalous situations be investigated, the government was frequently able to prevent the organization of a committee of inquiry. During the first twenty years of the Fifth Republic the National Assembly conducted a total of sixteen investigations by special committee and the Senate another seven, some of them dealing with fairly innocuous issues. But even when investigations were permitted to proceed, they were usually given little publicity and their reports remained largely unknown; so far the only exception has been a report on a scandal involving the public radio and television. Only during the last years of the Giscard administration did investigations become somewhat more thorough and frequent. Characteristically enough many Frenchmen, including the po-

---

[20] For the situation prevailing under the Third Republic, see Henry W. Ehrmann, "The Duty of Disclosure in Parliamentary Investigation: A Comparative Study," *The University of Chicago Law Review* 11, nos. 1, 2 (1943/44): 1–25, 117–53.

litically interested public, found the various Watergate inquiries a strange and somewhat unwarranted spectacle. Since
corruption in politics is assumed to be all-pervasive, parliamentary investigations are deemed wasteful. Such public indifference has permitted the parliamentary majority to make
inquiries ineffective or to prevent them altogether.[21] A constitutional amendment of 1974 has substantially increased possibilities for scrutinizing the legislative initiatives of the parliamentary majority and of the government by making it possible
for sixty deputies or sixty senators to appeal to the Constitutional Council (for a discussion, see below in this chapter).

During General de Gaulle's presidency, parliament was deprived outright of one of its constitutionally granted prerogatives. The constitution of 1958 had stipulated that any constitutional amendment needed the approval of both houses
of parliament: if that approval was voted by a simple majority, the text had to be submitted to a popular referendum; if
the proposed amendment was backed by a three-fifths majority
of both houses meeting together, no referendum was needed
(article 89). In the fall of 1962 de Gaulle knew that there was
no majority, neither simple nor qualified, for his proposal to
change article 6 of the constitution and to introduce the popular election of the president. (See Chapter IV.) He therefore
submitted the referendum directly and without prior parliamentary debate or vote. According to the wording of the constitution, and in the opinion of almost all experts on constitutional law, article 11, which the president invoked to justify
this procedure, was clearly not designed to amend the constitution. But after a majority of the electorate had approved the
text of the amendment, the Constitutional Council rejected an
appeal by the Speaker of the Senate to declare the procedure
unconstitutional. The Council declared that it lacked jurisdiction in cases where the *vox populi* had spoken.[22] If this way

21 The failure of parliamentary investigations as a means of control is
discussed extensively by Bidegaray and Emery, "Le Contrôle," pp. 1634–
1721. See also the comprehensive account of various forms of parliamentary
committees in Maryvonne Bonnard, "Les Commissions spéciales à l'Assemblée nationale, 1959–1979," *RFSP* 31, no. 1 (February 1981): 191–210.

22 For the text of the terse decision by the Constitutional Council, see
Année Politique 1962 (Paris: PUF, 1963), pp. 687 ff.

of altering the constitution were to prevail, the constitution would become extremely, and perhaps dangerously, flexible. All it would take to bring about even the most fundamental of changes would be a president willful and forceful enough to persuade a majority of the electorate of the wisdom of his constitutional proposals.[23]

It is not possible to determine to what extent General de Gaulle's decision to use a referendum once more when he wished to enact additional constitutional changes contributed to the defeat of the referendum in 1969. Whatever the voters' motivation might have been, this misadventure restored to the National Assembly and the Senate their primary responsibility for deciding on as weighty an issue as the constitution. Both Pompidou and Giscard d'Estaing took the initiative for proposing constitutional amendments, but they have sought to obtain the three-fifths majorities in both houses and not even tried to avail themselves of the other method permitted by article 89: to organize a referendum after both houses had approved the text of a constitutional amendment by a simple majority vote. In a speech before the Constitutional Council, Giscard d'Estaing declared that no constitutional amendment was "possible" without a previous vote by both houses of parliament, thereby excluding the direct appeal to the electorate which de Gaulle had chosen twice before.[24]

Since 1962 the only amendment of importance, the broader access to the Constitutional Council, was approved by the required majorities in both houses without a referendum. Other proposals, favored by both Pompidou and Giscard, were discarded because they lacked the needed support in parliament. One was concerned with the length of the presidential mandate

[23] Only the restoration of a full-fledged monarchy seems to be prohibited by article 89 which states that "the Republican form of government shall not be subject to amendment." But there are "republican monarchies" of various kinds. Moreover the procedural provision of article 89 had already been sinned against.

[24] For the text of a speech, quite interesting for Giscard's constitutional thinking, see Quermonne, *Le Gouvernement*, pp. 66, 664–66. At the beginning of his presidency Giscard had thought differently: he stated that he might use the direct appeal to the electorate in order to amend the constitution; see *Le Monde*, July 27, 1974.

(at present seven years and renewable); the other with the so-called incompatibility clause (article 23). According to this much heralded and even more criticized innovation of the constitution, members of the Cabinet must resign their seat in parliament upon assuming ministerial office (a provision also contained in Bismarck's constitution of the German Reich). A rather large number of Gaullists rejected the proposed changes, because they feared that to loosen some of the foundation stones of the constitution would endanger, sooner or later, the entire edifice and could steer the regime in the direction of either a full-fledged presidential or a classical parliamentary system.

Of late a new practice has developed to familiarize members of parliament with the work of the bureaucracy. Deputies have been attached for a limited time to various ministries and administrations. They are expected to voice the concerns of their voters while legislative texts are being prepared. If the experiment succeeds, members of parliament would contribute at least in part to an input frequently reserved all too exclusively to pressure groups. During Giscard's administration these opportunities were offered only to deputies belonging to majority parties. It remains to be seen whether the socialist government will extend them also to members of the opposition.

Under a constitution which intentionally limited the power of parliament and the initiatives of its members, the material conditions of deputies and senators have improved considerably. Their salaries and fringe benefits, very mediocre in the past, were increased so as to make the representatives more independent of outside support and resources. Little by little they have acquired material facilities which were sorely lacking in the past: office space, secretarial services, audiovisual aids, and computerized information. Means of communication with their constituents have been facilitated.[25] All this might still not be the equal of what is provided on Capitol Hill, but French representatives are finally granted the means to exercise their functions in a modern democratic state, even while their constitutional role remains restricted.

[25] See Claude Gibel, "L'Évolution des moyens de travail des parlementaires," *RFSP* 31. no. 1 (February 1981): 211–26.

During the years of the greatest imbalance between the powers of parliament and of the executive, deputies of all political persuasions intensified the energetic defense of constituency interests. Such concerns are easily preponderant in all countries with weak parties. An electoral system with fairly small single-member constituencies and the severe constitutional limitations of their role as lawmakers and as watchdogs of the executive encouraged the most active representatives, young and old, to be the agents of their constituents in the capital.

Even more than previously the deputy was "a lawyer with a monthly salary, an interpreter, an indefatigable broker . . . and also an extremely busy and often the most efficient social worker in his department." [26] Although they were no longer sought out by those interest groups which preferred direct access to the civil service, many deputies found it worthwhile to negotiate in the name and for the sake of local government authorities. In a system where a local savings bank might need an authorization from Paris to finance the paving of a village street, the services of the deputy are highly appreciated. However, an interesting study of mail received and sent by deputies revealed that they are not primarily distributing favors to their constituents but are forever trying to explain to them the complexities of the administrative process and, if possible, to alleviate its rigidities.[27] Deputies themselves frown on an image which presents them mainly as defenders of local and of constituency interests. They regret that their own voters and the public at large are inclined to slight the "national significance" of their elected representatives.[28]

[26] Robert Buron, *Le plus beau des metiers* (Paris: Plon, 1963), pp. 81 ff. The enthusiastic and yet realistic account by the author who has been a long-time deputy and minister under both the Fourth and Fifth Republics, remains extremely valuable.

[27] See Marie-Thérèse Lancelot, "Le courrier d'un parlementaire," *RFSP* 12, no. 2 (1962): 426–32.

[28] See Oliver H. Woshinsky, *The French Deputy* (Lexington: Lexington Books, 1973), and Roland Cayrol, Jean-Luc Parodi, and Colette Ysmal, *Le Député français* (Paris: Colin, 1973); and also two detailed articles by Cayrol, Parodi, and Ysmal, "L'image de la fonction parlementaire chez les députés français," *RFSP* 21, no. 6 (1971): 1173–1206, and "French Deputies and the political system," *Legislative Studies Quarterly* 1 (February 1976): 67–99. Philip E. Converse and Roy Pierce, "Representative Roles and Legis-

According to public opinion polls, voters approve of parliament as an institution and of the role played by their deputies. Year by year the number of those who would like parliament to be given a larger place in public life has risen. Shortly before the parliamentary elections of 1978, 46 percent of the electorate (74 percent of the communist and 66 percent of the socialist voters) wished to see parliament play a larger role than heretofore. Fifty-two percent of the general public thought that parliament, and only 31 percent that the president of the republic, should determine major policy orientations. Eighty-three percent ranked the defense of civil liberties highest among the assignments of their representatives. Sixty-eight percent of the respondents considered politics either a very honorable or at least an honorable calling.[29]

The hostile criticism directed against parliament before 1958 has largely subsided. The fact that the greatest sympathies for parliament are to be found among those on the Left might yet encourage a broadening of parliamentary powers, now that the Left has won.

PARLIAMENT: WHICH UPPER HOUSE?

There were several reasons why the new regime wanted to create a "powerful second chamber." [30] Because they assumed that coherent majorities would never emerge in the "purely political body," as they called the National Assembly, de Gaulle and Debré attributed to the upper chamber an important role in supporting the government. A house whose members were to be elected, as in the past, mostly by the municipal and departmental councillors would mirror "one of the fundamental aspects of French sociology" — namely the continuing

---

lative Behavior in France," *Legislative Studies Quarterly* 4 (November 1979): 525–62, based on findings collected in the late sixties, draw some general conclusions about representation in a comparative perspective.

[29] See SOFRES, *L'Opinion Française en 1977* (Paris: PFNSP, 1978), pp. 226, 238. For a useful and complete discussion of the institution of parliament and its image in public opinion, see Pierre Avril, *Les Français et leur parlement* (Paris: Casterman, 1972).

[30] Debré in his speech before the Council of State, in Andrews, ed., *European Political Institutions*, p. 50.

existence of an inordinate number of small communes. Whenever the National Assembly might yield to perennial temptations to overstep its boundaries, the government hoped to turn
to the Senate for support.

Once more the hope of diminishing the realm of the political proved unrealistic. A thinly disguised lack of confidence in
the representative expression of universal suffrage had to be
paid for quite dearly. Almost from the beginning of the Fifth
Republic the Senate has failed to play its assigned role. And
the more it disappointed unwarranted expectations, the more
drastically it was excluded from any meaningful participation
in the policy process.

The composition of the Senate and the methods of its election have remained essentially unchanged from what they
were at the beginning of the Third Republic, when a republican leader called the upper house, not without scorn, the
"Great Council of the *Communes*." He might as well have
spoken of the *petites communes,* for at all times the small communities have been heavily represented in the electoral college
which designates the senators for a nine-year term of office.
(Like the electoral college choosing the American president,
this body never meets, its members voting, as it were, "at
home.") All countries without a federalist structure are forever
in a quandary as to which units of government or which elements of political life their upper chambers should represent.
In a highly centralized system such as that of France, the
difficulties are multiplied and lead to a continuous ambivalence toward the legitimacy of an indirectly elected assembly.
This explains why every new constitution has determined
anew the powers and functions of the upper houses.[31]

At present the delegates of municipal councils are still the
predominant element among the electors: more than 100,000
of them cast their ballots together with about 3,000 members
of the departmental councils. Because of the lilliputian size of
so many local government units, 41 percent of the delegates of

[31] For a competent symposium on the Senate in three republics, see "Le
Sénat de 1884 à 1970," *Politique,* nos. 45–48 (1969): 3–326. For an up-to-
date study of the present Senate, see Jean Grange, "Attitudes et vicissitudes
du Sénat (1958–1980)," *RFSP* 31, no. 1 (February 1981): 32–81.

the municipal councils represent units with less than 1,500 inhabitants, or 23 percent of the total French population. On the other end of the scale, only 17 percent of the municipal delegates represent the 35 percent of the total population who live in cities of more than 30,000. In the Senate itself, the sparsely populated regions are overrepresented: more than half of the 32 senators represent only 40 percent of the population.[32]

Because of the weight of the country's rural sector, the Senate has long been dubbed by its critics the "Chamber of Agriculture." Quite unavoidably, a body whose political roots are particularly strong in the economically least developed parts of the country tends toward parochial conservatism which is frequently out of touch with the problems of a rapidly modernizing country. Yet, in the past, the Senate has not invariably been found on the right of the political spectrum. Its hostility to social and economic change has been balanced by a forthright defense of traditional republican liberties, and by a stand against the Catholic church and against demagogic appeals to latent antiparliamentary feelings.

In the Fifth Republic, neither the local elections which determine the membership of the electoral college nor the senatorial elections themselves have ever been touched by the Gaullist ground swell characteristic of most past elections to the National Assembly. At a time when the Gaullists held the absolute majority of seats in the National Assembly, their representation in the Senate amounted to not more than 12.7 percent of the total and never rose to more than 13.5 percent. To speak here of a "revenge of the notables" is no exaggeration. These local notables transmit their own and their voters' outlook to senatorial candidates of similar leanings. In turn, numerous senators covet a seat in the upper house mainly because of the advantages they derive from it for the exercise of their functions as mayors or other local government officials. In 1980, 54 percent of the Senators were also mayors (seven among them of cities over 100,000 population) and 57 percent

[32] In the Upper House of a federal system such discrepancies are more functional than in a unitary system such as France, since even small or thinly populated states, "sovereign" as they are, might have a claim to "equal treatment."

members of Departmental Councils (more than one-third of them serving as the Council's president). However, the two categories are overlapping, since many mayors also sit on the Departmental Councils. The average age of Senators is fifty-nine years; 45 percent are older than sixty.

It is not astonishing that in such a body the communists are even more underrepresented than the Gaullists. Prior to the socialist landslidè in the 1981 elections to the National Assembly, the socialists' strength was about equal in both houses. But conservatives and centrists elected under a variety of not-too-meaningful party labels still hold a comfortable majority of Senate seats. As a result, the Senate has withstood the strong trend towards bipolarization so characteristic of the general elections to the lower house and of political life in general.

During the first years of the Fifth Republic the Senate, usually defending traditional positions, has disagreed with the government on many major policy decisions. The conflict over the revision of the constitution in 1962 led to a pitched battle between the upper house and the president of the republic. The Speaker of the Senate used his constitutional position to denounce in the Senate and before the Constitutional Council the violation of the constitution by president and government.

For years afterward, General de Gaulle and his prime minister saw to it that the government was represented at Senate sessions not by the minister with jurisdiction over the questions under discussion, but by a junior member of the Cabinet, usually an undersecretary. This provided a constant irritant to the senators. Their weapon of holding up legislation by either rejecting bills or amending them copiously was blunted by the new constitution which provides that if there is disagreement between the two houses concerning pending legislation, the government can appoint a joint committee (article 45). If the views of the two houses are not reconciled, it is up to the government to decide which will prevail. A weapon originally designed to discipline an unruly lower house could now be turned against the Senate. Like the British House of Lords, "the senatorial opposition could always win the battle, never the war." [33]

---

[33] Williams, *The French Parliament*, p. 110.

Some legislation of great importance, such as the atomic striking force, the organization of military tribunals in cases involving high treason, and statutes regulating municipal elections and strikes in public services, was enacted in spite of senatorial dissent. Nonetheless, of the approximately 2,000 laws enacted by parliament between 1959 and 1980, only sixty were passed over the total opposition of the Senate. On all other statutes joint committees arrived at a compromise text.[34] It is generally recognized that many of the technical and legal amendments proposed by an upper house, which is working in a more leisurely fashion, have resulted in improvements. In a typical single year (1978) over 2,600 amendments to bills under discussion were moved on the Senate floor and almost half of them were adopted.

Nevertheless, criticism of the Senate and proposals for its thorough reform have come from many sides, and not from the Gaullists alone. For the Senate did not really provide the balance which advocates of a bicameral system consider desirable; since it was so unrepresentative of a modernizing country that to entrust it with additional powers was likely to lead to deadlock rather than to progress and growth.

It has been argued that the most appropriate solution would be a chamber in which the major economic, social, and cultural interests of the nation would be represented. In his speech at Bayeux, General de Gaulle had favored such an institution. But when in 1958 the time for constitution-making had come, General de Gaulle was prevailed upon to abandon such a scheme, to give to the upper house its traditional form and leave interest representation to another body already in existence.

An Economic and Social Council has functioned, under slightly different names and under a variety of statutes, almost continuously since 1924 in spite of the constitutional vicissitudes of the period. Appointed either by major interest groups or by the government, the members of the council deliberate on all bills which have an impact on economic and social matters and on the modernization plan. The Council also studies

34 For interesting statistics, see Grange, "Attitudes," p. 72.

weighty problems before they have reached the stage of proposed legislation. After extensive debates in plenary sessions and committees, the Council formulates its advice, publishing if need be majority and minority reports. There is general agreement that since its beginnings, but especially since it was reconstituted in 1946, the Council's work has been generally of high quality; its debates have often been more interesting than those in parliament. But it is also general knowledge that neither government nor parliament pay any attention to the Council's labors and advice. Its contribution to the policy process has been negligible if not nil.[35]

The question whether and how to give to the Economic and Social Council more weight in the decision-making process was often discussed earnestly with not always well-informed reference to experiences with similar bodies in other European countries (Holland, the Weimar Republic, etc.). In European constitutional tradition, suggestions that the representatives of organized interests be invested with decision-making powers belong to the arsenal of authoritarian concepts. Corporatist chambers are usually devised as a defiance of the parliament based on universal suffrage. But in France more than elsewhere, anticapitalist syndicalism has frequently been very close to corporatist concepts, and the latter were shared by socially progressive industrialists, usually themselves influenced by the ideas of an earlier social Catholicism. This explains why since 1958 conservatives as well as authentic liberals have backed the idea of transforming the upper house into a forum for interest representation.[36] The arguments advanced by the protagonists of such a body usually ignored the many and weighty reasons that have long been voiced against this solution. More than anything else, the proposals, and the urgency with which they were made, expressed a widespread uncertainty about the

[35] On the functioning of the Economic and Social Council, see J. E. S. Hayward, *Private Interests and Public Policy: The Experience of the French Economic and Social Council* (New York: Barnes and Noble, 1966), pp. 36–50.

[36] See, e.g., the importance which a liberal such as Pierre Mendès-France attributes to the institution in *A Modern French Republic* (New York: Hill and Wang, 1963), pp. 78–81.

place of parliament in the policy process and about the idea of representation in a modern democracy. Quite typically, all sides professed the hope that an upper chamber of this kind would diminish the dominant role of the bureaucracy — a forlorn hope if past experience is a guide.[37]

When after the events of 1968 General de Gaulle decided that the time had come for another "revolution from above," his design included a thorough renovation of the upper house. The new proposal reverted to the suggestions made more than twenty years earlier in the Bayeux speech, modified by the lessons which the recalcitrant notables of the Senate had taught the Gaullist regime. Just under one-half of the new senators were to be interest representatives, chosen by their groups. A majority of the members of the new house would represent, as before, local constituencies. All legislation, including constitutional amendments, would have to be submitted to this hybrid body, which, however, had only advisory powers. It did not need to be overruled; it could not rule.

The project for a new upper house was well suited to conjure the opposition, rational as well as instinctive, of traditionalists and progressives, of conservatives and liberals. It was seen as another attack against parliamentary sovereignty, weakening the defenders of republican liberties at the expense of the executive. The local notables saw their status diminished; the center and left-wing parties considered the bill as an assault against their positions in the municipalities.[38] The defense of the old Senate had assumed a symbolic value which the actual role of the institution in the policy process hardly deserved.

[37] When similar proposals were ventilated in Germany during the First World War, Max Weber expressed the contrary opinion: the position of the bureaucracy would be strengthened whenever it had to settle unavoidable conflicts between parliament and a chamber representing economic and social interests. See his remarkably clearsighted article "Parliament and Government in a Reconstructed Germany: A Contribution to the Political Critique of Officialdom and Party Politics," now reprinted in translation in Guenther Roth and Claus Wittich, eds., *Economy and Society* (New York: Bedminster Press, 1968), p. 1453.

[38] For a discussion of the referendum from the viewpoint of the Senate and its defenders, see Jacques Cadart, "La Crise référendaire," in *Politique*, nos. 45–48 (1969): 261–84.

With the survival of the status quo, the only reform of the upper house that was envisaged was a limited redistribution of Senate seats which could be enacted by ordinary legislation and which would give to the urban population a somewhat more adequate representation. But since one wished to avoid eliminating any seats, one merely added thirty-three new ones, as one had earlier added a dozen seats for the new departments of the Paris region (there will be 316 Senators in 1983). Such a procedure, however, did little to alter the fundamental lack of representativeness of the Senate. The first government of the Giscard administration has applied a constitutional provision which previously had been ignored: article 49 empowers the prime minister to submit to the Senate for its approval a "declaration of general policy." This is now being done at the beginning of each legislative session. Since the Senate can never overthrow a government, the latter can come before the upper house even when there is disagreement between governmental policy and senatorial opinion.

If this procedure had little more than symbolic value, it was just one more proof that the oldest, and also one of the most controversial of republican institutions had weathered another storm just at the time it was celebrating its centennial.

During the last year of the Giscard administration the Senate attempted to tackle once more a comprehensive reform of local government, a matter of special interest to a body in which local government officials predominate. Endless debates leaving the status quo essentially unchanged because of conflicting viewpoints and of cross-pressures did little to enhance the prestige of the upper house. If the Senate has won once more the battle for its legitimacy, it still has to define its identity, its proper role in a modernizing society.

With only 105 seats out of a total of 305 the socialist government has no majority support in the upper house. As the staunch defender of private property the Senate rejected outright the legislation providing for the nationalizations (see Chapter II), whereupon the government treated the upper house in the same way conservative governments had treated it at times: it was ignored and the legislation was passed by the National Assembly in its original form. New laws dismantling some of the "law and order" measures enacted under de Gaulle, Pompidou, and Giscard were supported by the Senate. The latter played a more active role when it had to pass on the comprehensive decentralization statute (see Chapter IX). Instead of resorting to outright opposition the senators, concerned as they are with the future of local government, engaged in careful scrutiny of the new arrangements and improved on what they considered all too hasty improvisations. Here differences between the two houses were ironed out in joint committee and, with some reluctance, the National Assembly accepted a compromise bill.

There is one constitutional situation in which a majority in the upper house cannot be overruled: any constitutional amendment needs the approval of either a simple or a three-fifths majority of senators (article 89). General de Gaulle circumvented this roadblock by introducing the popular suffrage of the presidency through direct referendum (article 11, see above). At least for the time being it appears unlikely that if there were to arise a conflict between their government and the Senate, the Socialists would use a stratagem which they had denounced as utterly unconstitutional in 1962.

CHECKS AND BALANCES

France has no tradition of judicial review. As in other countries with civil law systems and in Great Britain as well, the sovereignty of parliament means that the legislature has the last word and that a law enacted in constitutionally prescribed forms is not subject to further scrutiny. This principle seemed to be infringed upon when the Constitution of 1958 brought forth an institutional novelty, the Constitutional Council (articles 56–62).[39] The Council in certain cases must, and in other cases may upon request, examine legislation and decide whether it conforms to the constitution. A legal provision declared un-

---

[39] The most important book on the Constitutional Council by one of its former members is François Luchaire, *Le Conseil Constitutionnel* (Paris: Éditions Economica, 1980). Also excellent is a special issue of *Pouvoirs*, no. 13 (1980), devoted almost entirely to a discussion of the increasingly important role of the Constitutional Council.

constitutional may not be promulgated. However, this departure from previous doctrine and practice was primarily conceived as a safeguard against any legislative erosion of the constraints which the constitution had placed upon the prerogatives of parliament. For years the Council would ward off parliament when its standing orders or bills would encroach upon the supremacy of the executive, such as on its rights to control parliamentary proceedings and to regulate vast areas of public policy by administrative decrees and ordinances. This did not preclude the Council, in its explorations of the boundary line between executive and parliament, from deciding sometimes against the government. But neither its personnel nor the extent of its jurisdiction qualified the Council as a judicial body.

The presidents of the two houses of parliament each choose three of the Council's members and the president of the republic chooses another three for a (nonrenewable) nine-year term (any living former president of the republic becomes an ex-officio member). This clearly political selection has resulted in the nomination to the Council of a number of ex-ministers and an ex-ambassador; if they were legally trained, hardly any of them was a specialist in constitutional law. The Council's present president, Roger Frey, has no legal education whatsoever but was an early participant in the Gaullist movement and later a high government and party dignitary. Those who nominate the Council's members were until recently, together with the prime minister, the only ones entitled to apply to the Council for constitutional scrutiny, which politicizes proceedings yet further. Until 1974 this meant that the possible appellants were all Gaullists, with the sole and unforeseen exception of the president of the Senate. Some of the most important decisions by the Council were indeed rendered upon an appeal by the president of the Senate; without him the opposition would have had no possibility of having its case heard.

When Debré introduced the new constitution, he had predicted a "moralizing role" for the Constitutional Council. Yet it was soon regarded as "the government's thing." When it declined jurisdiction for passing on the constitutionality of the 1962 referendum, the council did what was probably unavoidable: the United States Supreme Court would have spoken about the nonjusticiability of a political question. Nonetheless, its failure to rule lessened further the Council's prestige.

When, after General de Gaulle's resignation, political tensions had abated, the Council slowly changed its public image by a series of painstaking decisions. The first of these, rendered in 1971, was concerned with a statute that in fact sought to amend the 1901 law on associations. The bill had been introduced by the minister of interior, who since the events of 1968 had been much preoccupied with combatting radical groups and their propaganda. Whereas under the old law a simple registration with the authorities was sufficient to give legal status to any association, the new bill authorized the prefects to refuse registration to any association which in their opinion was likely to engage in illegal activities.

In a terse one-page decision the Council declared unconstitutional the registration provision of the new bill, which had been approved by a large majority in the National Assembly. To require any advance authorization violated, according to the decision, the freedom of association, one of "the fundamental principles recognized by the laws of the Republic and solemnly reaffirmed in the preamble of the Constitution." The invocation of the preamble was to become highly significant for the Council's future decisions.[40] Rather than defining the "fundamental principles," the preamble of the constitution of 1958 had referred to the constitution of 1946 as having "reaffirmed and completed" those principles as well as the Rights of Man. Thereby the Constitutional Council, by a stroke of the judicial pen, transformed the extensive Bill of Rights, which the liberal-minded constitution-makers of the postwar period had formulated, into valid constitutional law. Unaccustomed to the broad legal categories familiar to the American constitutional lawyer, French lawyers have criticized the invoking of

---

[40] For the text of the decision, see *Receuil des décisions du Conseil Constitutionnel 1971* (Paris, 1972), pp. 29 ff. For an extensive legal commentary from a broad historical perspective, see two articles by Jean Rivero, "Décision du Conseil Constitutionnel du 16 juillet 1971," *Dalloz-Sirey Jurisprudence*, October 1971, pp. 537–42; and "Les 'principes fondamentaux reconnus par les lois de la République': une nouvelle catégorie constitutionnelle?" *Receuil Dalloz-Sirey, Chronique* 41 (1972): 265–68.

"general principles" as dangerously vague. But in fact the Council of State (to be discussed later in this chapter) had declared them to be part of the law of the land as early as 1911. However, only the Constitutional Council, not the Council of State, was in a position to annul legislation which infringed upon the recognized principles.

For introducing full-fledged judicial review in defense of civil liberties, the decision has been greeted by some as the French equivalent of *Marbury* v. *Madison*. If the United States Supreme Court waited half a century before it exercised a second time its power to annul national legislation, the Constitutional Council rendered, after a mere two years, two more decisions of lesser importance but also striking down provisions which it adjudged an abridgement of citizens' rights. Yet as long as access to the Constitutional Council was restricted to four officials who might all be close to the government and to the majority in parliament, the Council's review powers could not be relied upon to effectively control the legality of executive and parliamentary enactments. This, however, is the essence of judicial review.

The critics of the present constitutional setup who wish to see it develop into a regular presidential system have always spoken out in favor of a supreme court endowed with enough powers and prestige to act as a check on the other branches of government. Giscard's own party had been among its advocates; but also the Common Program of the Left contained provision for establishing a Constitutional Court for the protection of civil rights. Upon his ascendancy to the presidency, Giscard has made more modest reform proposals in order not to antagonize the Gaullists in parliament whose votes were needed for any constitutional amendment. The bill sent to parliament suggested two new ways for submitting legislation to the Constitutional Council for its scrutiny: (1) when the members of the Council decided that the exercise of their jurisdiction could "ensure a better defense of civil liberties as defined by the constitution" or (2) when a given number of senators and deputies, representing a minority of their colleagues, wished to test the constitutionality of a bill.

In a somewhat confused debate, the National Assembly criticized sharply the first proposal, and the government retreated in order not to split the majority on a constitutional question. But it succeeded in obtaining the needed votes in both houses for the second proposal, so that now "sixty deputies or sixty senators" may also submit cases to the Constitutional Council. This modification of article 61 became thus the first substantial change of the Constitution of 1958, accepted in accordance with the constitutionally prescribed amendment procedures, rather than as the result of an unconstitutional referendum.

The first appeal by members of parliament came to the Constitutional Council shortly afterward, when eighty-one deputies demanded that the new law legalizing abortion under certain conditions be declared unconstitutional. The appellants belonged to the various parties of the governmental majority, which had sponsored the legislation but which, in view of the nature of the bill, had not insisted on voting discipline. For a variety of procedural and substantive reasons, the Council upheld the statute. But the principle of using the jurisdiction of the Council for protecting minority interests had been given its first trial.

During the following five years forty cases were brought before the Council to test the constitutionality of legislation. Most, but not all, of the appellants were deputies or senators belonging to the opposition. In a series of searching decisions the Council has upheld or invalidated, wholly or in part, important laws pertaining to a wide range of problems. In one form or another, most decisions turned on questions of civil rights: police searches of automobiles, employment in private schools, union rights in the shop, equality before the tax laws. Other decisions were concerned with conflicts between national statutes and international law.[41] The prestige of the Constitutional Council has steadily grown. It would be even greater if the selection of its members were less political than it is at present. But there are now some outstanding lawyers and con-

---

[41] For a collection of the most important decisions rendered by the Council between 1958 and 1979 and followed by extensive comments, see Louis Favoreu and Loïc Philip, *Les grandes décisions du conseil constitutionnel,* 2nd ed. (Paris: Sirey, 1979).

stitutional specialists among its members. (In 1981 the average age of Council members was seventy-four years.)

After the elections of 1981 had insured the victory of a socialist majority pledged to major reforms, it was to be expected that the Constitutional Council would play an even more important role than previously. The opposition parties have repeatedly appealed to the Council and requested that much of the new legislation be declared unconstitutional. In most cases the Council rejected the appellants' plea outright or insisted at most on some technical modifications. The most important decision, awaited on all sides with some anxiety, concerned the nationalizations. While insisting on more generous compensations for the shareholders (see Chapter II), the Council upheld the government's right to proceed with the nationalizations. It based its decision not only on the preamble of the constitutions of 1946 and 1958, but also on the Declaration of the Rights of Man which had justified the transfer of private property to public ownership in cases of "public necessity." In a lengthy and carefully worded decision the Constitutional Council agreed with the government that massive unemployment and economic dislocation could be regarded as an instance of public necessity.

The Council was obviously unwilling to play the role which the United States Supreme Court assumed in its fight against the New Deal legislation. Given the traditional French distrust of judicial review and of what is critically called the *gouvernement des juges* the Council found it unwise to attack a major piece of legislation introduced by a government swept into power only recently and by a landslide election. But if in this case the government hastened to introduce the modification the Council had requested, the communists and soon thereafter spokesmen for the socialists also have let it be known that the popular will represented in parliament would not always bow to the rulings of an irresponsible tribunal. Public discussions about the legitimacy of judicial checks on the majority will are not likely to abate if the Council's verdict will be invoked as frequently as it has been during the first months of socialist rule. When, subsequent to the decision on nationalizations, the Council refused to invalidate the comprehensive law on decentralization and regionalization (see Chapter IX), it gave another proof of its self-imposed reserve.

The much older Council of State — in its present form it dates back to 1799 — is a multifunctional institution par excellence and respected for all of its varied activities. The council is consulted by the government on all bills before they are submitted to parliament and on the more important government decrees and regulations before they are enacted; it also may give advice on the interpretation of constitutional texts. It is true that its advice is never binding, but its prestige is so high that its recommendations are seldom ignored.[42]

Of the Council's four sections, the *Section du Contentieux* has the most direct impact on the rights of citizens. A deep-seated distrust of the prerevolutionary judiciary has, since the days of the Revolution, barred the ordinary courts from deciding on claims that might arise from wrongful acts of officials in the exercise of their duties. A court decision in such matters would be regarded as an undue interference of the judiciary in the spheres belonging rightfully to the administration. But this does not leave the citizen altogether helpless.

The judicial section of the Council of State, acting either as a court of appeal or, in more important cases, as the court of first instance, is the apex of a hierarchy of administrative tribunals. By an extensive body of case law, the Council has become "the great protector of the rights of property and of the rights of the individual against the State, the great redresser of wrongs committed by the State." [43] Whenever official acts

[42] The literature on the Council of State is vast. Concise and up-to-date discussions in English are Dorothy Pickles, *Government and Politics of France* 1 (New York: Harper & Row, 1972), pp. 293–99; Hayward, *The One and Indivisible*, pp. 124–27. The leading French study is Marie-Christine Kessler, *Le Conseil d'État* (Paris: Colin, 1968). Most interesting is a recent concise discussion of the juridical and political role of the Council: Francis de Baecque, "Le Conseil d'État, Conseil du Gouvernement," in *Administration et Politique*, Baecque and Quermonne, pp. 129–38. For a comparison of both the Constitutional Council and the Council of State with institutions in other legal systems, see Henry W. Ehrmann, *Comparative Legal Cultures* (Englewood Cliffs: Prentice-Hall, 1976), pp. 128–31.

[43] Joseph Barthélemy, *Le Gouvernement de la France* (Paris: Payot, 1924), p. 199.

are found to be devoid of a legal basis, whether they be those of a Cabinet minister or of a village mayor, the Council will annul them and grant damages to the aggrieved plaintiff. To define legality the Council has steadily broadened its criteria and included in the "general principles of law" equality before the law, freedom of speech and association, the right to natural justice, the right to be heard, the right not to be subjected to retroactive legislation, and other similar privileges.

There are, however, limits to the Council's control and effectiveness. Administrative justice is as slow as it is inexpensive. Once a decision is made, its enforcement is not a foregone conclusion since compliance will frequently depend on the very administration against which the council has found. It has been estimated that about a third of the Council's decisions remain unenforced; among all administrations the powerful Ministry of Finance is described as being particularly adept at circumventing tax decisions.[44] Were it otherwise, it might not have been necessary to experiment, as France has done recently, with the nomination of an ombudsman, the "mediator," seeking redress against administrative transgressions.

Amidst the tensions created by the Algerian war, the Council of State challenged President de Gaulle when, shortly after an attempt on his life, he set up a military court of justice to try future plotters. The Council of State decided that the presidential decree lacked legality because it denied the right of appeal to defendants appearing before the court. For a time de Gaulle considered sanctions against the Council, and the situation resembled President Roosevelt's court fight. But, as in the American argument, a compromise was reached.[45] The Council's prestige as the "great redresser of wrongs" has remained unimpaired.

[44] See Hayward, *The One and Indivisible*, p. 127.
[45] In his *Memoirs of Hope: Renewal and Endeavor* (New York: Simon and Schuster, 1971), p. 317, de Gaulle comments sarcastically on the motives of some Council members who had tried to interfere with his exercise of power. But he then pays tribute to the institution and to its "principles of impartiality which are its raison d'être and have made for its greatness." On the problem of the protection of civil liberties in general, see Jean Rivero, *Les Libertés Publiques* (Paris: PUF, 1973).

A Court of State Security was created in 1963 through ordinary legislative channels. Its judges were specially appointed by the government and were assisted by military officers. The court served as a tribunal for crimes of a political nature. Though not frequently used since the end of the Algerian war, it remained a symbol of repression and was abolished by one of the first legislative actions of the socialist government.

CHAPTER XI

Change in France

LEGITIMACY AND CHANGE

Alexis de Tocqueville recognized in the French of his time the traits which Julius Caesar had drawn some 2,000 years earlier when he described the Gauls as *rerum novarum cupidi,* eager for all things new. Many of the great French novels of the nineteenth century are concerned with social change and illustrate masterfully the conflicts between traditional and modern values. Yet there have been long periods of immobility in the history of modern France when the process of change seemed blocked or unduly slowed. It is true that decades during which nothing really new was tried were interrupted by bold if usually brief experimentation. Such a sequence of events gave rise to doubts as to whether Frenchmen were really eager for change and did not rather dread it as a threat to privilege and tranquillity. During the early years of the Fifth Republic Michel Crozier, whose writings have explained why the bureaucratic and bourgeois system of France has favored the blossoming of a highly individualist culture clinging to its preindustrial ways, denied that Frenchmen dislike change: "What they fear is not change itself, but the risk they may encounter if the stalemate that protects them (and restricts them at the same time) were to disappear." [1]

Mitterrand's campaign for the presidency and his party's

[1] Cf. Michel Crozier, *The Bureaucratic Phenomenon* (Chicago: The University of Chicago Press, 1964), p. 226.

bid for power were an apt response to such concerns. A program of bold reforms promised to transform state and society
in ways that would touch every household. The outside world
reacted to it with some stupefaction. But to the French voters
it was presented as the guarantor of "tranquillity." After more
than twenty-five years of conservative rule the transfer of
powers to a socialist party, long excluded from all national responsibilities, was equally "tranquil": after one night of danc-
ing in the streets there were no further disturbances of public
order in a nation traditionally given to political exuberance,
and frequently, violence.

The popular reactions to the events which took place in the
spring of 1981 were additional evidence that the institutions
which the country had been given in 1958 had acquired legitimacy. Since the revolution of 1789 more than a dozen constitutional texts had to seek a new legitimacy for the order which
they established and for the values they wished to represent.
In one way or another each French constitution became a vic-
tim of French politics, yet this bestowed legitimacy on neither.
As long as General de Gaulle was at the helm of the Fifth Republic, there was uncertainty as to whether its institutions had
won that general and lasting acceptance which is the earmark
of stability and legitimacy. Lessons of the past suggested that
regimes which begin, as did the Gaullist republic, in a near-
revolutionary situation and which center around a charismatic
personality are usually the most transient.[2]

But two orderly transfers of presidential powers (in 1969 and
1974) without a crisis of succession revealed the almost general
acceptance of the new constitutional order and especially of
the popular election of the president.[3] After the elections of
1981 the regime finally met that important test of democratic
legitimacy which consists in the conveyance of power to the
opposition and in the alternating of competing political forces.

Given such a consensus and the heavy agenda of the socialist

[2] See Harry Eckstein, *Division and Cohesion in Democracy: A Study of
Norway* (Princeton: Princeton University Press, 1966), p. 274.

[3] On the legitimacy of the institutions before the elections of 1981, see
the incisive remarks by Jean-Louis Quermonne, *Le Gouvernement de la
France sous la Ve République* (Paris: Dalloz, 1980), pp. vi, 87 ff.

government on other matters, it is unlikely that much attention will be paid to constitutional reforms. During his campaign and in his first press conference Mitterrand has explained what he meant when he spoke about improving the balance between the various branches of government: a shortening of the presidential term of office or, alternately, restriction to one term of seven years; wider use of a strictly legislative referendum; a lessening of executive influence on judicial nominations.

Promises of giving parliament a larger role in the political process did not survive the experiences of a few months in office. Even in a majority-controlled National Assembly, parliamentary procedures proved too cumbersome for moving an extensive program of innovation through regular legislative channels. Hence the input of both houses was limited rather than encouraged. The other constitutional reforms which the president had described as desirable could not be introduced without a constitutional amendment, a cumbersome procedure unless the opposition is willing to cooperate. The only foreseeable constitutional conflict (mentioned in Chapter X) concerns the powers of the Constitutional Council. Should there be frequent and principled conflict between the Council and the government over the constitutionality of further reforms, the parties which support the government might insist on eliminating or transforming an institution which so far has not acquired the same respect which the Supreme Court commands in the United States.

CONSENSUS FOR CHANGE?

A call for change is a common electioneering slogan. During his successful campaign in 1974 Giscard d'Estaing, standard bearer of a conservative electoral clientele, had promised change to combat a morose skepticism and a generalized lack of faith in the future which had become prevalent in the midst of an expanding economy and in spite of rising real incomes. A belief that they lived in an unjust society was still shared by many Frenchmen. Once elected Giscard declared that he would assume personal responsibility for "guiding the change" and thereby live up to the amorphous expectations which opinion polls expressed. At different times he explained quite correctly the difficulties which such a task involved in as complicated a society as modern France. Previous chapters have described why after considerable initial successes initiatives for reform were blocked and why the projects of an uninspiring and directionless conservatism lost credibility.

It is never easy to determine which "mandate" the voters have given to those who represent them; however, the socialist landslide in the parliamentary elections confirming Mitterrand's victory took place after the new government had outlined in broad strokes the nature and the substance of its reform program. One can therefore conclude that at the time of the elections the desire for even drastic change was strong. But the undisturbed "tranquillity," the lack of any participatory élan, also seemed to indicate that the change that is expected is to come from the state. And the critical question always remains: what will be altered in fact, when politics change? [4]

Mitterrand and members of the government never tire of explaining that their bills and projects, varied though they are, all express a coherent strategy: to attack, and wherever possible, to eliminate, the obstacles which in the past have obstructed reform. Nationalizations, decentralization, a new "magna carta" for industrial relations, and other proposals should be regarded as single instances of a more general purpose.

To launch an initial and quite daring assault on administrative centralization recommended itself because the frustrations with the existing system are widespread and shared by many operators of the system in the high bureaucracy. It is also a field in which the gap between repeated promises of reform and achievements had been particularly evident (see Chapter IX). But, as we have seen, the French model of extreme centralization of decision making is not restricted to national and local administration. It is deeply embedded in the political culture and both cause and consequence of a style of authority often found inappropriate to modernity. Will the devolution

---

[4] See Richard Rose, ed., *The Dynamics of Public Policy* (Beverly Hills: Sage Publications, 1976), pp. 23 ff. The discussion that follows may usefully be compared with that by Richard Rose in the concluding chapter ("A Changing England?") of his *Politics in England* (Boston: Little, Brown, 1980), pp. 358–80.

of power, hopefully initiated by the administrative reforms, also take hold in other large organizations, in public and private corporations, the educational system, the cultural life, and in associations?[5] Without it the basis for elite recruitment will remain as narrow as in the past.

For all their professed optimism the new men in power are conscious of the fact that to order decentralization by authoritative command from the top might appear contradictory.[6] Institutional changes will remain fragile (which could induce the reformers to become more authoritarian) as long as they are not backed by a change in mentality. It is quite true that during the last decades value systems have responded to transformations in society and have changed sometimes faster than institutions (see Chapter III). Public opinion polls in the summer and fall of 1981 testified to a large popular support of the planned reforms: the nationalizations were approved by about 50 percent of the respondents and opposed by only 25 percent; regionalization (i.e., administrative decentralization) was approved by 73 and opposed by 7 percent; the proposed wealth tax ranked highest in approval (82 percent); only enthusiasm for a fifth week of paid vacations was equally strong. Another poll, conducted among upper-class respondents, also approved of the wealth tax (59 percent) and of decentralization (70 percent, with 14 percent opposed); even in this group one-third approved of nationalizations. The only reform for which both groups of respondents showed a strong dislike was the proposed abolition of capital punishment.[7] A majority in parliament (joined in this instance by some members of the opposition) passed the unpopular legislation, a close parallel to the situation in Great Britain.

[5] The need for such a devolution in many fields is pointed out with great forcefulness by Christian Stoffaes, *La grande menace industrielle* (Paris: Calmann-Lévy, 1978), pp. 344–45.

[6] On the fragility of all reforms "by decree" see the, perhaps overcritical, comments by Michel Crozier, *Strategies for Change: The Future of French Society* (Cambridge, Mass.: MIT Press, 1982).

[7] For the results of opinion polls see *L'Express*, July 10, 1981; and *Le Point*, Oct. 12–18, 1981. The polls indicate that a rather rapid conversion must have taken place since the elections; about two years earlier only 39 percent of respondents in another poll favored nationalization, 28 percent a tax reform; see Jacques Capdevielle et al., *France de gauche vote à droite* (Paris: PFNSP, 1981), p. 25.

Possibly more significant than a general commitment to reform was the willingness of 56 percent of respondents to accept a loss of real income if that was necessary to reduce unemployment (with 34 percent opposed). For a nation whose citizens have often been described as willing to accept change only if it was not touching their own lives, such an attitude, if generalized, would indicate a changed mentality. Yet a government bill which sought to alleviate the deficit of the unemployment insurance fund by a slight contribution from tenured civil servants had to be withdrawn hastily because of strong opposition by the trade unions and — the Socialist Party.

To reach its ambitious objectives the government needs more than favorable polls and more than a solid majority in parliament. Can it find the broader consensus which it deems necessary in order to turn legislative output into effective change? The political fronts are drawn starkly. Parliamentary debates and speeches at party congresses are passionate and doctrinaire; both sides rejoice in announcing (verbal) class warfare. Compromises of any kind between majority and opposition are neither sought nor possible. The "socialo-communist" majority is fought by the opposition as an undifferentiated block; epithets of "fascism" are launched in both directions. Since the orderly transfer of powers has precluded the "crisis of the regime" which conservative leaders had forecast in the event of a socialist victory, they are now bewailing the "crisis of society" into which the country has been plunged.

Even if political alliances are not in sight, this does not preclude support from organized and unorganized groups in society and from various elites, among them ranking bureaucrats. The attitude of practicing Catholics will, at least in part, be determined by future agreements and legislation on the status of the private schools, a problem which could regain its potential for bitter antagonism. Indirectly its solution will also have an impact on the reform of public education, which must be tackled anew, and will have to overcome past obstacles to a broader accord.

For many reasons the government seeks novel ways of including the young into a new social consensus. Unemployment among the young is rampant. But as a searching and disturbing government report has shown more is needed than merely their integration into the work place. Apathy and alienation sweep many; political radicalization is widespread among others. Under these conditions the rather massive swing of the young voters to the Socialists which contributed to the latter's victory in 1981 could well be turned around. Whether there be a resurgence of militancy (and in which direction such militancy might go) could depend on success or failure of governmental policies.[8]

Before he became Minister of Finance in the socialist government Jacques Delors, then a member of the European Parliament, had insisted that in the modern welfare state there existed no "dichotomy between social and economic policy" and that "the challenge of the future will be to find social consensus."[9] The experiment in which France is engaged has little chance to succeed without the kind of collaboration between capital and labor which the country has seldom known for any length of time. Mitterrand himself has admitted that he considers it his mission to avoid the failures of two socialist leaders who have preceded him and who had not been able to master social conflict: Leon Blum, French Premier in the Third Republic, and the Chilean President Salvatore Allende.

As explained earlier (see Chapter VII) France could never be counted fully among such democracies as the Benelux and Scandinavian countries, Austria, and (to a large extent) West Germany where centralized interest groups interact regularly with the government to produce bargains on the major issues of a modern economy and on social policy. What has been called democratic corporatism, "a consensus-making machine operating within a quasi-public framework"[10] has never worked in France in the field of industrial relations. The de-

---

[8] For an extensive and disquieting report on the state of mind of the young in many regions see Nicolas Beau and Edwy Plenel, "Jeunesses de l'Après-Mai," *Le Monde*, Dec. 9, 10, 12, 1981. The report requested by the government has been published; see Bertrand Schwartz, *L'insertion professionnelle et sociale des jeunes* (Paris: Documentation Française, 1981).

[9] See Organization for Economic Co-operation and Development (OECD), *The Welfare State in Crisis* (Paris: OECD, 1981), p. 67.

[10] See the classifications in an article by Harold Wilenski, "Democratic Corporatism, Consensus and Social Policy," ibid., esp. pp. 189 ff.

scribed weakness of the organizations of labor and capital, their inability to enforce agreements on their memberships, their conflict-orientation, and their diffidence not only toward each other, but also toward the government, have prevented lasting agreements.

Members of the Cabinet who are more attuned than their colleagues to the traditions of European social democratic parties are making strenuous efforts to induce the social partners to accept practices of regular and institutionalized collaboration. So far there is little evidence that the government has been able to overcome the hostility of small and medium-sized business to its general policies. Many of these firms neither hire nor invest. Nor has all of big business accepted the discipline it has always refused to its own professional organizations, when the latter sought to promote collaboration with the state. The government is committed to combat unemployment by a strategy of work sharing: "collectively we shall work more, individually less." But this is not possible without plant- or industry-wide agreements. Not nearly enough of them have been concluded so far. The labor unions, not only those affiliated with the communist-oriented CGT, seldom appear willing to give up a traditional resistance to innovations in the work place or to engage in negotiations conducive to the new social consensus upon which the government banks.

DOMESTIC AND INTERNATIONAL CONSTRAINTS

"How much room for economic maneuver does a middle-size country like France really have?" is the appropriate question raised in an essay that views the Socialist experiments as "major movements in a narrow space." [11]

The transitory two-years plan as well as the preparations for the five-years plan (see Chapter II) indicate that the government is committed to the reflation of the economy. Revitalizing and further modernizing industries in both the public and

[11] See Stephen S. Cohen and Peter A. Gourevitch, "Postscript" in *France in the Troubled World Economy*, eds. Cohen and Gourevitch (London: Butterworth, 1982), pp. 180–89. This essay as well as the entire volume makes a major contribution to the problems discussed in the text.

the private sectors are major concerns. Before the Socialist Party came to power, it had been critical of nuclear energy programs, of the nuclear striking force, and the massive armament exports. New priorities have displaced such reluctance. The building of nuclear submarines and of a new family of missiles has been resumed and so has that of nuclear reactors; the drive to reduce energy dependence has strong public backing which a weak environmentalist movement cannot stem. An armament industry which employs 300,000 workers and exports 40 percent of its products will not be interfered with by a government that seeks to reduce massive unemployment. It is, however, admitted quite generally that a combination of a vigorous policy of armament exports and the emphasis which the French nuclear program places on plutonium is likely to accelerate proliferation.[12]

The announced goal of "reconquering domestic markets" hopes to diminish dependence on imports in other than energy fields, especially in areas where French industry has not kept pace with technological advances and where productivity is lagging. Such efforts appear all the more indispensable as the desired stimulation of the economy will easily increase imports and thereby aggravate the large trade deficit. Should the international economic situation deteriorate further, French exports would encounter additional difficulties and the trade balance would be threatened from yet another side. This would in turn add further to the inflationary pressures which growing budgetary deficits are apt to produce.

At the beginning of 1982, 9 percent of the total labor force was unemployed (over 2 million) which compares with an average of 9.7 percent in the ten Common Market countries. The number of young Frenchmen entering the labor market is estimated to exceed retirements annually by 250,000. The government's resolve to combat unemployment without substantial reduction of take-home pay, to raise minimum wage levels, and to significantly improve social services, especially in the health field, implies a commitment to policies which most Western

---

[12] Stephen S. Cohen, "Informed bewilderment: French economic strategy and the crisis," in *ibid.*, p. 38.

democracies have deemphasized if not abandoned. After vigorous economic growth and its fiscal dividends had subsided, even countries most identified with the policies of the welfare state, such as Sweden, Norway, and Labour Britain, came to recognize that social transfer payments are not immune to fluctuations in the economic growth rate. By its tax reforms and a series of connected proposals the Mitterrand administration demonstrates that it continues to consider social transfers a valid instrument for reducing social inequality. But such measures are limited by the government's simultaneous concern for stimulating investments by drawing on available profits and savings. Altogether it appears impossible to approximate announced goals without a substantial increase in public expenditures and deficit financing.[13] When critical observers warn that France moves in the opposite direction from that chosen by other Western nations, the government points to the singular lack of success which deflationary and monetarist policies have had in Great Britain, the United States, and elsewhere.

Even before the recent nationalizations public control of the financial system was comprehensive enough to enable the government to set investment priorities and to determine lending policies. The recent consolidation of such controls opens additional possibilities of using the credit system not only to implement industrial policies but also to manage public finances with a great amount of freedom. But if there is no Paul Volcker (i.e., a Federal Reserve System) counterbalancing governmental policies from within, the "Volcker factor" is nonetheless paramount: as long as the United States practices a policy of high interest rates, the French government cannot lower its own and as long as the value of the dollar is bolstered by such rates, French oil imports (purchased in dollars) are increasingly burdensome.

Without ignoring any of the difficulties which French economic and social policies will encounter, a report issued in early 1982 by the usually cautious Organization for Economic

[13] One of the socialist civil servants on the staff of the Planning Commissariate asserts nonetheless that the "traditional solution" of financing investments by inflation is "no longer possible"; see Denis Piet, "Une Stratégie du Court-Moyen Terme pour la France," *Tocqueville Review* III, no. 2 (Fall 1981): 421 ff.

Co-operation and Development (OECD) was guardedly optimistic about possible chances for success.[14] The report believes that existing policies stimulating demands and investments will permit a 2.5 percent growth in GNP (the government assumes a 3.3 percent increase which compares with a growth of 0.5 in 1981 and 1.7 in 1980). Neither unemployment, inflation, nor trade deficit would be rolled back substantially, but to keep them at present levels appears possible and would be a salutary reversal of trends that have dominated the country's recent past. It can also be assumed, though the report does not insist on this, that a lessening of inflationary pressures on wholesale and consumer prices on an international scale and the existing oil glut might bolster stabilization. Should such stabilization prevail, the long-term objectives of the government to reduce unemployment and inflation over a longer stretch of time do not appear unrealistic to the OECD.

It is true that its prognostics are tied to a certain number of conditions: demands for wage increases should be kept moderate in exchange for an improvement of working conditions; once productivity increases, employers should refrain from raising prices to make up for the higher unit costs which social policies have caused; clearly announced investment policies should aim at eliminating the uncertainties which have hampered production and employment in private enterprise; the shortening of the work week and the advancement of the retirement age, commended though they are in the report, will have to be worked out with extreme care lest they provoke a new inflationary spiral of wages and prices; carelessness in managing the public debt and in enlarging administrative costs could compromise the undertaking.

If such are the conditions for success, it will depend domestically on practices and on a mentality which, as our discussion has shown, no longer seem out of reach yet are also far from being assured. The report is realistic enough to warn that even if all domestic preconditions were fulfilled, a continuing aggravation of the worldwide economic recession would de-

---

[14] The OECD comprises the twenty-four most industrialized nations and monitors the economic policy of member nations. For a summary of the report discussed in the text see *Le Monde*, February 2, 1982. For an American comment see *The Wall Street Journal*, February 2, 1982.

stroy the chances for recovery in France. In such a case the temptations to engage in protectionist practices might be great, as even under the best of circumstances governmental policies will bear fruit and have an impact on international markets only after several years.

The socialist leadership is publicly committed to the opposite course: a strengthening of the European Community and its free trade area; an intensification of North-South economic exchanges. (The left wing of the Socialist Party has in the past shown some preference for more nationalist economic policies, as have the communists and former Gaullists. For the time being such voices are muted.) To meet the objection that its policies cannot possibly bring about speedy recovery, the government refers to its likely longevity in office not matched elsewhere: a strong executive power in the hands of a president elected for seven years and at least until the next national elections in 1986, a cohesive Socialist majority in parliament.

A break in the present coalition between Socialists and Communists would not deprive the government of majority support. The presence of communist ministers in the Cabinet was (in January 1982) approved by 40 percent of respondents in an opinion poll and opposed by 35 percent. But even many of those who hope that the communists will remain in the Cabinet expect a rupture to occur before the end of the parliamentary term. However, such a rupture is unlikely before the municipal elections in 1983 which will be regarded as a test for public reactions to the first government of the Left in the Fifth Republic. For the time being neither the PC nor the communist-oriented unions are strong enough to capitalize on any discontent that might spread when high expectations are disappointed. But this must not always be the case, nor are these the only dangers which the latest French program for change will have to face.

The outcome is uncertain on many grounds. As long as French politics remains democratic, it will move rather more vigorously than the politics of other communities between the poles of cohesion and of diversity. This makes for its fascination. It also makes any prediction concerning the course of political change a hazardous undertaking.

Suggestions for Further Reading

The footnotes of this book provide a rather complete and updated bibliography of books and articles in English and French. It will prove useful, I hope, to both the undergraduate and the graduate student engaged in specialized research. The reader in search of factual information, either current or historical, will find indispensable the Paris daily *Le Monde* (of which a weekly "Selection" is available outside of France both in French and in English) and *L'Année Politique*, published every spring (Presses Universitaires de France). The journal of the French Political Science Association, *Revue Française de Science Politique*, contains a regular section *"Les Forces Politiques en France"* that is of great value.

The following bibliography lists, quite selectively, some books, all in English, which the reader may find useful when he or she wishes to become familiar with a variety of viewpoints on various periods and aspects of French politics.

Ambler, J. S. *The French Army in Politics, 1945–1962*. Columbus: Ohio State University Press, 1966.

Anderson, Malcolm. *Conservative Politics in France*. London: Allen and Unwin, 1974.

Anderson, Malcolm. *Government in France: An Introduction to the Executive Power*. Oxford: Pergamon Press, 1970.

Andrews, William G., and Hoffmann, Stanley, eds. *The Fifth Republic at Twenty*. Albany: State University of New York Press, 1981.

Ardagh, J. *The New France: A Society in Transition*. Baltimore: Penguin Books, 1973.

Campbell, Peter. *French Electoral Systems and Elections Since 1789*. New York: Praeger, 1958; 2nd edition, 1965.

Charlot, Jean. *The Gaullist Phenomenon: The Gaullist Movement in the Fifth Republic.* London: Allen and Unwin, 1971.

Cohen, Stephen S. *Modern Capitalist Planning: The French Model.* Berkeley: University of California Press, 1977.

Crozier, Michel. *The Stalled Society.* New York: Viking Press, 1973.

Curtius, Ernst R. *The Civilization of France: An Introduction.* New York: Vintage Books, 1962.

Gilpin, Robert. *France in the Age of the Scientific State.* Princeton: Princeton University Press, 1968.

Gourevitch, Peter A. *Paris and the Provinces: The Politics of Local Government Reform in France.* Berkeley: University of California Press, 1980.

Grosser, Alfred. *French Foreign Policy under de Gaulle.* Boston: Little, Brown, 1967.

Hayward, Jack. *The One and Indivisible French Republic.* New York: Norton, 1973.

Hoffmann, Stanley, et al. *In Search of France.* Cambridge: Harvard University Press, 1965.

Hoffmann, Stanley. *Decline or Renewal? France since the 1930s.* New York: The Viking Press, 1974.

Kesselman, Mark. *The Ambiguous Consensus: A Study of Local Government in France.* New York: Knopf, 1967.

Lichtheim, George. *Marxism in Modern France.* New York: Columbia University Press, 1968.

Lorwin, Val. *The French Labor Movement.* Cambridge: Harvard University Press, 1954.

MacRae, Duncan. *Parliament, Parties and Society in France, 1946–1958.* New York: St. Martin's Press, 1967.

Paxton, Robert O. *Vichy France: Old Guard and New Order, 1940–1944.* New York: Knopf, 1972.

Penniman, Howard R., ed. *France at the Polls: The Presidential Election of 1974.* Washington, D.C.: American Enterprise Institute, 1975.

Penniman, Howard R., ed. *The French National Assembly Elections of 1978.* Washington, D.C.: American Enterprise Institute, 1980.

Peyrefitte, Alain. *The Trouble with France.* New York: Knopf, 1981.

Rémond, René. *The Right Wing in France from 1815 to de Gaulle.* Philadelphia: University of Pennsylvania Press, 1969.

Ridley, F., and J. Blondel. *Public Administration in France.* New York: Barnes and Noble, 1964; 2nd edition, 1969.

Siegfried, André. *France: A Study in Nationality.* New Haven: Yale University Press, 1930.

Suleiman, Ezra N. *Politics, Power and Bureaucracy in France: The Administrative Elite.* Princeton: Princeton University Press, 1974.

Suleiman, Ezra N. *Elites in French Society: The Politics of Survival.* Princeton: Princeton University Press, 1978.

Tarrow, Sidney. *Between Center and Periphery: Grassroot Politicians in Italy and France.* New Haven: Yale University Press, 1977.

Thomson, David. *Democracy in France Since 1870.* New York: Oxford University Press, 1964.

Tiersky, Ronald. *French Communism, 1920–1972.* New York: Columbia University Press, 1974.

Vaughan, Michaline; Kolinsky, Martin; and Sheriff, Peta. *Social Change in France.* Oxford: Martin Robertson, 1980.

Williams, Philip M. *Crisis and Compromise: Politics in the Fourth Republic.* New York: Anchor Books, 1964.

Williams, Philip M. *The French Parliament: Politics in the Fifth Republic.* New York: Praeger, 1968.

Wright, Gordon. *France in Modern Times, 1760 to the Present.* Chicago: Rand McNally, 1962.

Wylie, Laurence. *Village in the Vaucluse.* Cambridge: Harvard University Press, 1957.

Zeldin, Theodore. *France, 1848–1945.* Oxford: Clarendon Press, 1973.

Chronology of Events

1870	Franco-Prussian War; surrender of Napoleon III at Sedan; Government of National Defense
1871	*March to May*, Paris Commune
1875	Constitutional laws of the Third Republic
1879–82	Educational reforms terminating clerical control and banning religious instruction from the public schools
1889	Movement in favor of General Boulanger collapses with Boulanger's flight
1890	Charles de Gaulle born in Lille
1892	High-tariff policy inaugurated by J. Méline, minister of agriculture
1894	Captain Dreyfus convicted for treason
1899	Dreyfus pardoned
1905	Law for separation of church and state
1914	*July*, Assassination of the socialist leader Jaurès on the eve of the French mobilization for the First World War
	September, Battle of the Marne
1917	Clemenceau government with extensive wartime powers
1919	*June*, Treaty of Versailles
1923	*January*, Occupation of the Ruhr
1934	Stavisky scandal; Attempted coup d'état by the right-wing leagues
1936	Electoral victory of the Popular Front; Léon Blum prime minister
1937	Fall of the Popular Front government
1938	Munich agreement on the dismemberment of Czechoslovakia
1939	England and France declare war on Germany
1940	*June 18*, General de Gaulle calls from London for continued resistance
	June 22 Pétain government signs the armistice with Germany
	July, Vote in Vichy of constitutional laws establishing the French state
1942	*November*, Allied landings in North Africa; Germans move into unoccupied France
1944	*June*, Allied landings in Normandy
	August, General de Gaulle enters Paris
1945	The Constituent Assembly confirms General de Gaulle as head of the Provisional Government
1946	*January*, Commissariat of the Modernization Plan established; General de Gaulle resigns his office

June, Speech at Bayeux, outlining General de Gaulle's constitutional ideas

October, Constitution of the Fourth Republic approved by referendum

1947   *May,* Dismissal of the Communist ministers from the government

October, A newly formed Gaullist party (RPF) gains 40 percent of the votes in municipal elections

1949   NATO Treaty ratified by France

1951   Law (Barangé) granting state subsidies to parochial schools

Ratification of the treaty creating the European Coal and Steel Community

1954   *May,* Defeat of the French army in Indochina at Dien Bien Phu

June, Mendès-France government invested

July, Geneva accords on armistice in Vietnam

November, Nationalist insurrection in Algeria begins

1955   *February,* Mendès-France government falls because of its North African policy

June, General de Gaulle announces his total retirement from public life

1956   Independence for Morocco and Tunisia; French troops participate in the attack on the Suez Canal

1957   Ratification of the Rome treaties establishing the European Common Market

1958   *May 13,* Insurrection of French settlers in Algiers; formation of a committee of public safety demanding the return to power of General de Gaulle

June 1, General de Gaulle government invested

September, Constitution of the Fifth Republic approved by referendum

December, General de Gaulle elected president of the republic

1959   *September,* General de Gaulle proposes self-determination for Algeria

1960   Gradual independence for French Black Africa accomplished

1962   *March,* Cease-fire agreement for Algeria signed at Evian

July, Independence for Algeria approved by referendum

October, Amendment to the constitution, introducing the popular election of the president, accepted by referendum

1965   General de Gaulle reelected president of the republic

1966   France leaves the North Atlantic Treaty Organization and demands the withdrawal of all foreign troops stationed on her territory

1968   *May,* The "events": student riots and mass strikes

          June, Massive Gaullist victory in parliamentary elections

1969   *April,* Constitutional referendum defeated; General de Gaulle resigns as president

          June, Georges Pompidou elected president of the republic

1970   *November,* Death of General de Gaulle

1972   Socialists, Communists, and Left Radicals sign a Common Program of Government

1974   *April,* Death of Georges Pompidou

          May, Valéry Giscard d'Estaing elected president of the republic

1977   Signatories of Common Program break off further negotiations

1978   Gaullist-Conservative victory in parliamentary elections

1981   *May,* François Mitterrand elected president of the republic

          June, Socialist landslide victory in parliamentary elections; Pierre Mauroy forms government including four Communist ministers

The French Constitution of 1958

(This abridgment includes only those parts which are referred to in the text of this book. A complete version of the constitution may be obtained from the Press and Information Division of the French Embassy, New York.)

PREAMBLE

The French people hereby solemnly proclaim their attachment to the Rights of Man and the principles of national sovereignty as defined by the Declaration of 1789, reaffirmed and completed by the Preamble to the Constitution of 1946.

. . .

TITLE I — ON SOVEREIGNTY

Article 2. France is a Republic, indivisible, secular, democratic and social. It shall ensure the equality of all citizens before the law, without distinction of origin, race or religion. It shall respect all beliefs.

The national emblem is the tricolor flag, blue, white and red.

The national anthem is the "Marseillaise."

The motto of the Republic is "Liberty, Equality, Fraternity."

Its principle is government of the people, by the people and for the people.

Article 3. National sovereignty belongs to the people, which shall exercise it through their representatives and by way of referendum.

No section of the people, nor any individual, may attribute to themselves or himself the exercise thereof.

Suffrage may be direct or indirect under the conditions stipulated by the Constitution. It shall always be universal, equal and secret.

All French citizens of both sexes who are of age and who enjoy civil and political rights may vote under the conditions to be determined by law.

Article 4. Political parties and groups shall play a part in the exercise of the right to vote. They shall be formed freely and shall carry on their activities freely. They must respect the principles of national sovereignty and of democracy.

Title II — The President of the Republic

Article 5. The President of the Republic shall see that the Constitution is respected. He shall ensure, by his arbitration, the regular functioning of the governmental authorities, as well as the continuity of the State.

He shall be the guarantor of national independence, of the integrity of the territory, and of respect for Community agreements and treaties.

Article 6.* The President of the Republic shall be elected for seven years by direct universal suffrage.

The procedures implementing the present article shall be determined by an organic law.

Article 7.* The President of the Republic shall be elected by an absolute majority of the votes cast. If no such majority obtains on the first ballot, a second ballot shall take place on the second Sunday following the first ballot. Then only the two candidates who have received the greatest number of votes on the first ballot, after taking into account, if need be, better placed candidates who have withdrawn, may present themselves.

The Government shall be responsible for organizing the election.

The election of the new President of the Republic shall take place at least twenty days and not more than thirty-five days before the expiration of the powers of the current President.

In the case of vacancy of the Presidential office for any reason whatsoever, or if the President is declared incapable of exercising his functions by the Constitutional Council, the question being referred to the latter by the Government and the decision being taken by an absolute majority of the members of the Council, the functions of the President, with the exception of those listed in Articles 11 and 12, shall be temporarily exercised by the President of the Senate, or, if the latter is in turn incapable, by the Government.

* [Adopted by referendum of October 28, 1962.]

In case of vacancy or when the Constitutional Council declares the President permanently incapable of exercising his functions, the ballot for the election of the new President shall take place, except in case of *force majeure* officially noted by the Constitutional Council, at least twenty days and not more than thirty-five days after the beginning of the vacancy or the declaration of the permanent character of the incapability.

In case of vacancy of the Presidency of the Republic or during the time between the declaration of the incapability of the President of the Republic and the election of his successor, Articles 49, 50 and 89 may not be invoked.

Article 8. The President of the Republic shall appoint the Prime Minister. He shall terminate the functions of the Prime Minister when the latter presents the resignation of the Government.

On the proposal of the Prime Minister, he shall appoint and dismiss the other members of the Government.

Article 9. The President of the Republic shall preside over the Council of Ministers.

Article 10. The President of the Republic shall promulgate the laws within fifteen days following their final adoption and transmission to the Government.

Before the end of this period he may ask Parliament for a reconsideration of the law or of certain of its articles. This reconsideration cannot be refused.

Article 11. The President of the Republic, on the proposal of the Government during Parliamentary sessions, or on joint motion of the two Assemblies, published in the *Journal Officiel,* may submit to a referendum any bill dealing with the organization of the public authorities, entailing approval of a Community agreement, or authorizing the ratification of a treaty that, without being contrary to the Constitution, might affect the functioning of the institutions.

When the referendum decides in favor of the bill, the President of the Republic shall promulgate it within the time limit stipulated in the preceding article.

Article 12. The President of the Republic may, after consultation with the Prime Minister and the Presidents of the Assemblies, declare the dissolution of the National Assembly.

General elections shall take place twenty days at the least and forty days at the most after the dissolution.

The National Assembly shall convene by right on the second Thursday following its election. If this meeting takes place between the periods provided for ordinary sessions, a session shall, by right, be held for a fifteen-day period.

There may be no further dissolution within a year following these elections.

. . .

Article 16. When the institutions of the Republic, the independence of the Nation, the integrity of its territory or the fulfillment of its international commitments are threatened in a grave and immediate manner and when the regular functioning of the constitutional public authorities is interrupted, the President of the Republic shall take the measures required by these circumstances, after official consultation with the Prime Minister, the Presidents of the Assemblies and the Constitutional Council.

He shall inform the nation of these measures by a message.

These measures must be inspired by the desire to ensure to the constitutional public authorities, in the shortest possible time, the means of fulfilling their assigned functions. The Constitutional Council shall be consulted about such measures.

Parliament shall meet by right.

The National Assembly may not be dissolved during the exercise of emergency powers.

. . .

Article 19. The acts of the President of the Republic, other than those provided for under Articles 8 (first paragraph), 11, 12, 16, 18, 54, 56, and 61, shall be countersigned by the Premier and, should circumstances so require, by the appropriate ministers.

TITLE III — THE GOVERNMENT *

Article 20. The Government shall determine and direct the policy of the nation.

It shall have at its disposal the administration and the armed forces.

It shall be responsible to Parliament under the conditions and according to the procedures stipulated in Articles 49 and 50.

Article 21. The Prime Minister shall direct the operation of the Government. He shall be responsible for national defense. He shall

---

* [The Constitution uses the term "government" in the narrow sense of the responsible ministry, the Cabinet.]

ensure the execution of the laws. Subject to the provisions of Article 13, he shall have regulatory powers and shall make appointments to civil and military posts.

• • •

Article 23. Membership in the Government shall be incompatible with the exercise of any Parliamentary mandate, with the holding of any office at the national level in business, professional or labor organizations, and with any public employment or professional activity.

An organic law shall determine the conditions under which the holders of such mandates, functions or employments shall be replaced.

TITLE IV — THE PARLIAMENT

Article 24. The Parliament shall comprise the National Assembly and the Senate.

The deputies to the National Assembly shall be elected by direct suffrage.

The Senate shall be elected by indirect suffrage. It shall ensure the representation of the territorial units of the Republic. Frenchmen living outside France shall be represented in the Senate.

• • •

Article 28. Parliament shall convene by right in two ordinary sessions each year. The first session shall begin on October 2nd and last eighty days.

The second session shall begin on April 2nd and may not last longer than ninety days.

Article 29. Parliament shall convene in extraordinary session at the request of the Prime Minister, or of the majority of the members of the National Assembly, to consider a specific agenda.

When an extraordinary session is held at the request of the members of the National Assembly, the closure decree shall take effect as soon as the Parliament has exhausted the agenda for which it was called, and at the latest twelve days from the date of its meeting.

Only the Prime Minister may ask for a new session before the end of the month following the closure decree.

• • •

TITLE V — RELATIONS BETWEEN PARLIAMENT AND THE GOVERNMENT

Article 34. All laws shall be voted by Parliament.

Laws shall establish the regulations concerning:

— civil rights and the fundamental guarantees granted to the citizens for the exercise of civil liberties; the obligations imposed by national defense upon the persons and property of citizens;

— nationality, status and legal capacity of persons, marriage contracts, inheritance and gifts;

— definitions of crimes and misdemeanors as well as the penalties applicable to them; criminal procedure; amnesty; the creation of new types of jurisdictions and the statute of the judiciary;

— the basis, the rate and the methods of collecting taxes of all types; the currency system.

Laws shall likewise determine the rules concerning:

— the electoral system for the Parliamentary and local assemblies;

— the creation of categories of public corporations;

— the fundamental guarantees granted to civil and military personnel employed by the State;

— the nationalization of enterprises and the transfer of property from the public to the private sector.

Laws shall determine the fundamental principles of:

— the general organization of national defense;

— the free administration of local communities, the extent of their jurisdiction and their resources;

— education;

— property rights, civil and commercial obligations;

— labor law, trade-union law and social security.

Finance laws shall determine the resources and obligations of the State under the conditions and with the reservations to be provided for by an organic law.

Laws pertaining to national planning shall determine the objectives of the economic and social action of the State.

The provisions of the present article may be developed in detail and completed by an organic law.

Article 35. Parliament shall authorize the declaration of war.

Article 36. Martial law shall be decreed in a meeting of the Council of Ministers.

Its prolongation beyond twelve days may be authorized only by Parliament.

Article 37. Matters other than those that fall within the domain of law shall be subject to rule-making.*

.   .   .

Article 38. The Government may, for the implementation of its program, ask Parliament to authorize it, for a limited period, to take by ordinance measures that are normally within the domain of law.

The ordinances shall be enacted in meetings of the Council of Ministers after consultation with the Council of State. They shall come into force upon their publication, but shall become null and void if the bill for their ratification is not submitted to Parliament before the date set by the enabling act.

At the expiration of the time limit referred to in the first paragraph of the present article, the ordinances may be modified only by law in those matters which are within the legislative domain.

Article 39. The Premier and the members of Parliament alike shall have the right to initiate legislation.

Government bills shall be discussed in the Council of Ministers after consultation with the Council of State and shall be filed with the Secretariate of one of the two assemblies. Finance bills shall be submitted first to the National Assembly.

Article 40. Bills and amendments introduced by members of Parliament shall not be considered when their adoption would have as a consequence either a diminution of public revenues, or the creation or increase of public expenditures.

Article 41. If it appears in the course of legislative procedure that a private member bill or an amendment is not within the domain of law or is contrary to a delegation of authority granted by virtue of Article 38, the Government may request that it be ruled out of order.

In case of disagreement between the Government and the President of the assembly concerned, the Constitutional Council, upon the request of either party, shall rule within a time limit of eight days.

.   .   .

Article 44. Members of Parliament and of the Government shall have the right of amendment.

---

* [i.e., by the Cabinet]

After the opening of the debate, the Government may oppose the examination of any amendment which has not previously been submitted to a committee.

If the Government so requests, the assembly concerned shall decide, by a single vote, on all or part of the bill under discussion, retaining only the amendments proposed or accepted by the Government.

Article 45. Every bill is discussed successively in the two assemblies with a view to agreement on identical versions.

When, as a result of disagreement between the two assemblies, a bill has not been passed after two readings in each assembly, or, if the Government has declared the bill urgent, after a single reading by each assembly, the Prime Minister is entitled to have the bill sent to a joint Committee composed of equal numbers from the two assemblies, with the task of finding agreed versions of the provisions in dispute.

The version prepared by the joint committee may be submitted by the Government to the two assemblies for their approval. No amendment may be accepted without the agreement of the Government.

If the joint committee does not produce an agreed version, or if the version agreed is not approved as provided for in the preceding paragraph, the Government may ask the National Assembly, after one more reading by the National Assembly and by the Senate, to decide the matter. In this case, the National Assembly may adopt either the version prepared by the joint committee or the last version passed by itself, modified, if necessary, by one or any of the amendments passed by the Senate.

. . .

Article 47. Parliament shall pass finance bills under conditions to be stipulated by an organic law.

Should the National Assembly fail to reach a decision on first reading within a time limit of forty days after a bill has been introduced, the Government shall refer it to the Senate, which must rule within a time limit of fifteen days. The procedure set forth in Article 45 shall then be followed.

Should Parliament fail to reach a decision within a time limit of seventy days, the provisions of the bill may be put into effect by ordinance.

Should the finance bill establishing the revenues and expenditures of a fiscal year not be filed in time for it to be promulgated before the beginning of that fiscal year, the Government shall immediately request from Parliament the authorization to levy the taxes and shall make available by decree the funds needed to meet the Government commitments already voted.

The time limits provided for in the present article shall be suspended when Parliament is not in session.

The Court of Accounts shall assist Parliament and the Government in supervising the implementation of the finance laws.

Article 48. The discussion of the bills submitted or agreed upon by the Government shall have priority on the agenda of the assemblies in the order determined by the Government.

One meeting each week shall be reserved, by priority, for questions asked by members of Parliament and for answers by the Government.

Article 49. The Prime Minister, after deliberation in the Council of Ministers, may pledge the responsibility of the Government before the National Assembly with regard to the program of the Government, or if it be so decided with regard to a declaration of general policy.

The National Assembly may call into question the responsibility of the Government by the vote of a motion of censure. Such a motion shall be in order only if it is signed by at least one tenth of the members of the National Assembly. The vote may only take place forty-eight hours after the motion has been introduced. Only votes favorable to the motion shall be counted. It shall be considered adopted only if supported by a majority of the members of the Assembly. Should the motion of censure be rejected, its signatories may not introduce another motion in the course of the same session, except in the case provided for in the next paragraph.

The Prime Minister may, after deliberation in the Council of Ministers, pledge the Government's responsibility before the National Assembly on the vote of all or part of a bill or motion. In that case, the text shall be considered as adopted, unless a motion of censure, filed in the succeeding twenty-four hours, is voted under the conditions laid down in the previous paragraph.

The Prime Minister shall be entitled to ask the Senate for the approval of a general policy declaration.

Article 50. When the National Assembly adopts a motion of censure, or rejects the program or a declaration of general policy of the Government, the Prime Minister must submit the resignation of the Government to the President of the Republic.

• • •

Article 55. Treaties or agreements duly ratified or approved shall, upon their publication, have an authority superior to that of laws, subject, for each agreement or treaty, to its application by the other party.

Title VII — The Constitutional Council

Article 56. The Constitutional Council shall consist of nine members, whose term of office shall last nine years and shall not be renewable. One third of the membership of the Constitutional Council shall be renewed every three years. Three of its members shall be appointed by the President of the Republic, three by the President of the National Assembly, three by the President of the Senate.

In addition to the nine members provided for above, former Presidents of the Republic shall be members ex officio for life of the Constitutional Council.

The President shall be appointed by the President of the Republic. He shall have the deciding vote in case of a tie.

. . .

*Article 61.** Organic laws, before their promulgation, and the rules of procedure of the Parliamentary assemblies, before they come into application, must be submitted to the Constitutional Council, which shall decide whether they conform to the Constitution.

To the same end, laws may be submitted to the Constitutional Council, before their promulgation, by the President of the Republic, the Prime Minister, the President of either assembly, *sixty deputies or sixty senators.*

In the cases provided for by the two preceding paragraphs, the Constitutional Council must make its ruling within a time limit of one month. Nevertheless, at the request of the Government, in case of emergency, this period shall be reduced to eight days.

In these same cases, referral to the Constitutional Council shall suspend the time limit for promulgation.

Article 62. A provision declared unconstitutional may not be promulgated or implemented.

The decisions of the Constitutional Council are not subject to appeal. They are binding on public authorities and on all administrative and judicial authorities.

. . .

* [The passages in italics were added by a "Constitutional Law" (Amendment) adopted on October 29, 1974.]

TITLE VIII — ON JUDICIAL AUTHORITY

Article 64. The President of the Republic shall be the guarantor of the independence of the judicial authority.

He shall be assisted by the High Council of the Judiciary.

An organic law shall determine the status of magistrates.

Magistrates may not be removed from office.

Article 65. The High Council of the Judiciary shall be presided over by the President of the Republic. The Minister of Justice shall be its Vice President ex officio. He may preside in place of the President of the Republic.

The High Council shall, in addition, include nine members appointed by the President of the Republic in conformity with the conditions to be determined by an organic law.

The High Council of the Judiciary shall present nominations for judges of the Court of Cassation [Supreme Court] and for First Presidents of Courts of Appeal. It shall give its opinion, under the conditions to be determined by an organic law, on proposals of the Minister of Justice relative to the nominations of the other judges. It shall be consulted on questions of pardon under conditions to be determined by an organic law.

The High Court of the Judiciary shall act as a disciplinary council for judges. In such cases, it shall be presided over by the First President of the Court of Cassation.

Article 66. No one may be arbitrarily detained.

The judicial authority, guardian of individual liberty, shall ensure the respect of this principle under the conditions stipulated by law.

. . .

TITLE X — THE ECONOMIC AND SOCIAL COUNCIL

Article 69. The Economic and Social Council, at the request of the Government, shall give its opinion on such Government bills, ordinances and decrees, as well as on the private members' bills as are submitted to it.

. . .

Article 70. The Economic and Social Council may likewise be consulted by the Government on any problem of an economic or social character of interest to the Republic or to the Community. Any plan, or any program-bill of an economic or social character shall be submitted to it for its advice.

• • •

TITLE XIV — AMENDMENT

Article 89. The initiative for amending the Constitution shall belong both to the President of the Republic on the proposal of the Prime Minister and to the members of Parliament.

The proposed amendment must be passed by the two assemblies in identical terms. The amendment shall become effective after approval by a referendum.

However, the proposed amendment shall not be submitted to a referendum when the President of the Republic decides to submit it to Parliament convened in Congress;* in this case, the proposed amendment shall be approved only if it is accepted by a three-fifths majority of the votes cast. The Bureau of the Congress shall be that of the National Assembly.

No amendment procedure may be initiated or pursued when the integrity of the territory is in jeopardy.

The Republican form of government shall not be subject to amendment.

* [i.e., a joint meeting of both assemblies]

Index

JUL 12 1985

JUL 2 3 1985
DISCHARGED
DISCHARGED

DISCHARGED
DISCHARGED
DISCHARGED

DISCHARGED

DEC 9 1988